Duty of Care in the Human Services

Mishaps, Misdeeds and the Law

The human services exist to support the most vulnerable and marginalised people in our society. Yet media and other reports frequently highlight a disturbing picture of industry failures, malpractice and abuse.

This book addresses the response of legal and quasi-legal bodies to human service failures. It outlines those areas of law which are most likely to be activated by human service shortcomings, and those aspects of direct human service delivery which are most likely to attract legal attention.

Essential reading for those studying or working in human services and social work, this book is designed to alert people to the legal risks arising as a result of inadequate human service delivery.

Rosemary Kennedy is Senior Lecturer in the School of Psychology, Social Work and Social Policy, University of South Australia.

Duty of Care in the Human Services

Mishaps, Misdeeds and the Law

Rosemary Kennedy

University Printing House, Cambridge CB2 8BS, United Kingdom

Cambridge University Press is part of the University of Cambridge.

It furthers the University's mission by disseminating knowledge in the pursuit of education, learning and research at the highest international levels of excellence.

www.cambridge.org
Information on this title: www.cambridge.org/9780521720243

© Rosemary Kennedy 2009

This publication is in copyright. Subject to statutory exception and to the provisions of relevant collective licensing agreements, no reproduction of any part may take place without the written permission of Cambridge University Press.

First published 2009

Edited by Eve Merton

A catalogue record for this publication is available from the British Library

National Library of Australia Cataloguing in Publication data
Kennedy, Rosemary.
Duty of care in the human services : mishaps, misdeeds and the law / Rosemary Kennedy.
9780521720243 (pbk.)
Includes index.
Bibliography.
Human services – Australia – Care.
Human services – Australia – Administration.
Human services – Australia – Law and legislation.
Social services – Australia – Care.
Social services – Australia – Administration.
Social services – Australia – Law and legislation.
344.0320994

ISBN 978-0-521-72024-3 Paperback

Cambridge University Press has no responsibility for the persistence or accuracy of URLs for external or third-party internet websites referred to in this publication, and does not guarantee that any content on such websites is, or will remain, accurate or appropriate.

Reproduction and Communication for educational purposes
The Australian Copyright Act 1968 (the Act) allows a maximum of one chapter or 10% of the pages of this publication, whichever is the greater, to be reproduced and/or communicated by any educational institution for its educational purposes provided that the educational institution (or the body that administers it) has given a remuneration notice to Copyright Agency Limited (CAL) under the Act.

For details of the CAL licence for educational institutions contact:
Copyright Agency Limited
Level 15, 233 Castlereagh Street
Sydney NSW 2000
Telephone: (02) 9394 7600
Facsimile: (02) 9394 7601
Email: info@copyright.com.au

Reproduction and Communication for other purposes
Except as permitted under the Act (for example, a fair dealing for the purposes of study, research, criticism or review) no part of this publication may be reproduced, stored in a retrieval system, communicated or transmitted in any form or by any means without prior written permission. All inquiries should be made to the publisher at the address above.

Cambridge University Press has no responsibility for the persistence or accuracy of URLs for external or third-party internet websites referred to in this publication, and does not guarantee that any content on such websites is, or will remain, accurate or appropriate. Information regarding prices, travel timetables, and other factual information given in this work is correct at the time of first printing but Cambridge University Press does not guarantee the accuracy of such information thereafter.

For Barry and others in the human services whose recognition of an imperfect world motivates them more strongly to deliver services which cast minimal shadow.

Contents

Acknowledgements	*page* ix
Author's note	xi
Foreword	xiii

Part 1: Positioning and mapping the territory of human service mishaps and misdeeds

Chapter 1: The shadow world	3
Chapter 2: Ideals, actors and actions	22

Part 2: Mishaps and misdeeds through a law lens

Chapter 3: Public law of general application	49
Chapter 4: Public law of particular relevance to the human services	68
Chapter 5: Private law and suits	87
Chapter 6: Private law – negligence	104
Chapter 7: Private law – other torts and civil actions	125
Chapter 8: Legal processes, quasi and indirect legal scrutiny	140

Part 3: Mishaps and misdeeds through a human services lens

Chapter 9: Service delivery – screening, assessment and planning	165
Chapter 10: Service delivery – implementation and closure	185
Chapter 11: Information and records management	208
Chapter 12: Relationships, rifts and reactions	234

Part 4: Mishaps and misdeeds through a unified lens

Chapter 13: The consequences lottery   249

Coda   267

Appendix: Finding the law and cases   275

References   278

Index   305

Acknowledgements

A BOOK IS SELDOM the product of a single mind or set of hands, and this one is no exception. It would not have come into existence without the initial commitment of Zoe Hamilton at Cambridge University Press. My colleagues and friends Di Gursansky and Judy Harvey as always shared their extensive knowledge about human service practice, followed the book's progress with interest, and responded to my material and questions with wise counsel. They and others in the School of Social Work and Social Policy at the University of South Australia dealt generously with my perpetual distractedness. My colleague Tania Leiman found many relevant cases and worked valiantly at keeping me alert to legal nuances, while also very capably supporting my teaching. Aphy Hughes willingly and competently made diagrams behave. I value beyond measure their assistance. Needless to say the final responsibility for the content herein and its flaws rests with me.

Author's note

I AM A LONG-STANDING and committed member of the human services, first as a psychologist, then as a public welfare manager, later and currently as a social work and human service educator, researcher and consultant. Along with other human service actors at all levels, I share collective responsibility for the sector's greatnesses, mediocrities and shames. The use of the third person in this book is not intended to distance myself from the mishaps and misdeeds recounted herein. Nor is the focus on negative events any indication of my disenchantment with the human services. Rather it stems from a powerful desire to see the human services become more effective, to stand proud, and from a belief that facing up to demons is one of the first steps in vanquishing them. To the best of my knowledge and ability the law discussed herein was current as at March 2009.

Adelaide
April 2009

Foreword

THE HUMAN SERVICE SECTOR plays a vital but far from public role in contemporary society, dealing as it does with vulnerable and marginalised people with multiple needs in what are often fraught and contested situations. Decisions by human service workers regularly exercise profound effects on people's lives and therefore hold the potential for foreseeably adverse, including counter-therapeutic, consequences. Human service workers wield considerable entitlements and statutory powers, but with such rights and privileges come legal consequences and ethical responsibilities. It is important that workers' decision making be considered, founded in accurate facts, characterised by sound reasoning and approaches, and generated by the least restrictive and intrusive options that are reasonably available, consistent with the safety and wellbeing of vulnerable people. And yet experience over a lengthy period of time, and now an important sequence of legal authorities chronicled by Rosemary Kennedy, has established that the skill levels, knowledge base, methodologies and decision-making processes of human service workers have too often left a great deal to be desired.

In *Duty of Care in the Human Services*, Kennedy explores different parameters and measures of accountability for human service workers. Until now this has been a relatively obscure area, shadowy, as she puts it, and inadequately analysed by lawyers and human service workers and managers alike. It is an important and difficult sphere of law and, more fundamentally, a confronting issue of contemporary public policy. What Kennedy calls the 'dark human service domain' has often remained hidden until it has been exposed (not always fairly) by scandals and inquiries in the aftermath of tragedies. Such exposures occur mostly at the behest of the media and often by way of inquiries by special appointees, coroners, and decision-makers in civil actions in the courts. Sometimes the inquiries are genuinely independent and characterised by suitably broad terms of reference. On other occasions the inquiries are internal, fettered by arbitrary constraints and unlikely to address effectively the real issues that have brought about the unacceptable delivery of services. This has happened in recent years in relation to the

xiii

failures of care to those with mental illnesses, intellectual disabilities and brain injuries, aged people, asylum seekers, children in care and at risk, prisoners, probationers and Indigenous people. No doubt there are others.

The more authentic of the inquiries have tended to reveal systemic deficiencies of troubling duration, scope and incidence. Sometimes, individual workers are shown to have behaved in problematic ways, often because of lack of knowledge and resources, but occasionally because of predatory or malign motivations. The victims are generally those in a disempowered position in our community, for whom legal or political redress may be no more than a theoretical concept, unless the wrongs done to them are championed by others with better access to means of recourse.

This is why the shining of light by Kennedy into the hidden corners of human service delivery is so welcome. Illuminating the shadows and scrutinising the inquiries and the (successful and unsuccessful) legal actions for negligence, misfeasance, non-feasance, breach of contract and breach of fiduciary duties in the aggregate provides an opportunity to identify patterns and trends. It is a valuable contribution.

An important issue raised by Kennedy is the relative dearth of regulation of most human service providers. Those who are registered as psychologists are subject to state and soon national regulatory processes that will address deficits in conduct, performance, health and fitness to practise. However, social workers have not achieved the status of registration, and the limited role of the Australian Association of Social Workers in effectively regulating its diverse profession, highlights the consequences of the absence of formal registration and regulation. The situation is the more concerning in relation to other practitioners, such as carers, psychotherapists, counsellors, youth workers and others with even less professional affiliation and guidance from a professional association and network.

Traditional regulatory approaches used to focus upon dealing with professional reprobates, outliers or those whom Kennedy refers to as the 'bad apples'. It was principally directed toward responding to individual instances of unacceptable professional conduct and although it formally eschewed punishment or retribution as a response, its focus was upon both specific and general deterrence, thereby delineating standards of ethical conduct and endeavouring to establish and maintain public trust in the professions.

However, 'the new regulation' will concentrate upon validating ongoing fitness for practice which is only in part determined by satisfaction of initial entry requirements to the vocation. It will become an aspect of ongoing entitlement to practise for the practitioner to establish involvement in continuing professional education and development, working only within identified parameters of skills, maintenance of health, and positive evaluation by reference to the perspectives of both colleagues and recipients of services. It will emphasise the need for practitioners to sustain satisfactory levels of professional performance and suitable conduct. Most importantly, it will acknowledge the reality that deficits in both performance and conduct arise from a range of different influences, numbered amongst which are toxic systemic factors within which service providers work, including pressures exerted by employers and government, poor physical or mental health, substance abuse, emotional traumas related or external to work and professional burnout and compassion fatigue, to name but a few. An increasingly important aspect of professional regulation is the provision of practical and ethical guidance to practitioners so as to communicate effectively the location and means of dealing with areas of impropriety, such as boundary transgression, conflicts of interest, proper billing, inadequate generation of documentation, failure to adhere to parameters of professional competence, and impoverished approaches to communication and provision of information. A side effect of regulation, experienced latterly in Victoria, for instance, in the context of Chinese medicine, has been the impetus that it gives to self-definition of regulated professions and the encouragement that it provides for professional reflection and ethical discourse. While these might, at first blush, seem to be nebulous and diffuse notions, they can also be said to lie at the heart of what it is to be a professional. Responding to errors, learning from the experiences of 'moral friends' and exposing oneself to accountability in order to improve practice is part and parcel of professionalism and genuinely ethical practice. It is another way of saying that expression of grievances about service provision provides an opportunity for professional growth and skills enhancement.

The trend of professional regulation is to be seen in the recent introduction into New South Wales and New Zealand legislation of provisions that enable partial regulation of unregistered health practitioners. In this way it can be seen that the ambit of regulation is spreading. Why? Out of a recognition that more than the traditional health professions of medicine, dentistry, nursing, pharmacy and psychology have the potential to do harm. It is a declaration by government on behalf of the community that by the institution of formal mechanisms of oversight and professional governance there is the potential for better accountability to service recipients and for needed improvements in the quality of practice. The fact that human service providers, psychologists excepted, are currently not embraced by such regulatory arrangements is increasingly anomalous and concerning, given the need for it so eloquently established in these pages by Kennedy. When she contends that a 'cultural shift is required in human service workplaces, professional bodies and in professional education for lapses to be confronted, atomised and incorporated in future systems and practices', Kennedy is providing an insight into the inevitable and desirable future of the governance of human service professionals.

An integral aspect of Kennedy's approach is to explore the relatively unpopulated space in the human services where mishaps and misdeeds are scrutinised. It has often been observed that law is a blunt instrument for social reform and for engendering improved professional practice. And yet there are five ways at least in which law has long embraced a role of trying to improve standards of professional conduct.

The first, and the least availed of, is the sentencing of professionals found to have engaged in criminal behaviour, such as sexual interference with those in their care who are mentally ill or intellectually disabled. Denunciation of such abuses of power and deterrence of others similarly located in positions of authority who may also be tempted to transgress boundaries and exploit vulnerabilities is at the heart of the sentencing function.

Secondly, an explicit aim of the law of tort has always been not just to place victims so far as possible in the position they would have been in had not tortious behaviour taken place, but also to dissuade those in the position to engage in unacceptable risks to the foreseeable detriment of others. Thereby tort law promotes proper professional conduct that does not cause foreseeable harm to others.

Thirdly, equity through actions for breach of fiduciary relationships seeks to provide redress to those whose vulnerability has been exploited.

Fourthly, at the very heart of the modern coronial function, but also an ancient aspect of 'speaking for the dead', is the prophylactic role of promoting avoidance of avoidable dangerous behaviour and clarifying the public record where unsafe or irresponsible conduct (including by professionals) has led to deaths. This is the public health and safety role of the coroner, which has found clear expression in the *Coroners Act 2006* (NZ) and the *Coroners Act 2008* (Vic).

Finally, regulatory law has promoted the naming, shaming and, where necessary, exclusion of professionals from entitlement to practise when transgressions have been egregious and actually or potentially harmful. Part of the disciplinary role of tribunals and courts has been mentoring in relation to acceptable practice through chastisement, guidance and mandated supervision, further education and auditing. Part of the role has been the drawing of lines in the professional sand where conduct has crossed over into being incompatible with registered status.

It has to be conceded that the increasingly real prospect of both civil litigation and exposure of undesirable practices by coroners has the potential to engender risk-averse behaviours by a range of professionals, human service workers amongst them. A shortsighted and ethically undesirable response is conservative practice that prioritises human service approaches that do not assume protective responsibilities and that focus upon documentation of oversight rather than taking empirically justified decisions to protect. Confronting and working with this risk is an issue for today's courts and those of tomorrow.

The challenge assumed by Kennedy of drawing together, from the vast annals of reported and unreported case law, important precedents of professional conduct within the human service sector that have been the subject of litigation and regulation is demanding but valuable. Not only does it provide guidance as to where the various courts and regulatory bodies have made authoritative decisions and been critical of particular forms of behaviour, it also assists to document trends in public tolerance, or lack of it, in respect of areas of professional behaviour. It also helps human service workers and managers to know better where the law has made important pronouncements in relevant areas from which guidance can be garnered and applied to practice. As Kennedy puts it, 'Law cases provide one of the few windows into human service shortcomings' from which practical lessons can and should be learned to improve practice. Hence the opportunities from documented mishaps and misdeeds.

What is evident from Kennedy's work is that the legal system, responding to increasing levels of community concern about what has taken place in the child protection, penitential, probation, migration detention and disability sectors, to name but some, is increasingly prepared to make a wide range of professionals, human service providers among them, liable for conduct that breaches their duty of care and causes foreseeable harm. In this book Kennedy goes a considerable way toward penetrating and making accessible shadowy areas of silence, sometimes the subject of conspiracies of inaccessibility. However, by her documentation of the increasing role of the law in regulating and imposing accountability on both human service systems and individual practitioners, it is to be hoped that her work will send out important ripples. It has the potential to play a constructive role not just in improving standards of professional practice (sometimes referred to as promoting a conspiracy of professionalism) but in being a catalyst for a conspiracy of virtue whereby human service workers, conscious of their potential not just to do good but also to cause harm, will increasingly engage in reflective and ethically based practice. If this is a consequence of *Duty of Care in the Human Services*, Kennedy will have played a role in setting in train changes that are truly worthwhile for service recipients and providers alike.

> Ian Freckelton SC
> Barrister, Crockett Chambers, Melbourne
> Professor, Law Faculty, Department of Psychological Medicine,
> Department of Forensic Medicine, Monash University
> June 2009

Part 1

Positioning and mapping the territory of human service mishaps and misdeeds

1

The shadow world

HUMAN SERVICE ACTORS face the world with imagined identities built on good intentions and high ideals, while simultaneously casting a deep and sinister shadow. These reflexive human service images are constructed around and promulgated through the aspirational language of professional literature and education, codes of ethics, principles undergirding social policies, organisations' mission statements, standards of practice and individual belief systems. Identities are understandably articulated through lofty rhetoric, stamped with a leitmotif of human rights and social justice. These concepts are both the ostensible rationale for, and drivers of, much human services policy and system, organisation, program and worker activity. The slogan 'duty of care' peppers the lexicon of the human services. Under this honourable banner – but often based on an imperfect understanding of its legal meaning, limitations and implications – the human services march with confidence in the integrity of their endeavours.

The shadow world on the other hand is declaimed through commissions, reviews, enquiries, inquests, court cases, complaints mechanisms, advocacy groups, victims' stories, the media and popular books.[1] It is inhabited by tales of extensive, sustained and repeated neglect, cruelty and maltreatment in institutional and community services. Vulnerable groups

---

[1] For example: Maushart, S. (2003). *Sort of a Place Like Home: Remembering the Moore River Native Settlement.* Freemantle: Freemantle Arts Centre Press. Hill, D. (2007). *The Forgotten Children: Fairbridge Farm School and its Betrayal of Australia's Child Migrants.* Sydney: Random House. Raymond, B. (2007). *The Baby Thief: The Untold Story of Georgia Tan, the Baby Seller who Corrupted Adoption.* Sydney: Random House.

in society – the mentally ill, children, adolescents, aged people, prisoners, Indigenous people, asylum seekers and the disabled – are in this world routinely abused and neglected by service systems, agencies and workers in the realm of the human services. The shadow world has been populated in recent times by media-driven images of a child's body floating in a suitcase, children dead of starvation, mentally ill citizens incarcerated in immigration detention centres and innumerable others, equally shocking, discordant and seemingly inexplicable. These images are etched into the public consciousness.

In relatively recent times, many formal reports of failures of child protection systems and of child care in institutions and the community have emerged (eg Stanley 1999; Layton 2003; Crime and Misconduct Commission 2004; Senate Standing Committee on Community Affairs 2004, 2005; Mudaly and Goddard 2006; Mullighan 2008; Wood 2008; AAP 2008e). British child migrants have been brutalised in state and non-government organisations that are meant to be caring for them (eg Hill 2007). Care by and in immigration systems and facilities has been the subject of damming reviews (eg McMillan 2005; Palmer 2005; Raynor 2005). The treatment of Indigenous children taken into care or left unprotected in the community is a perennial weeping sore in Australian society (eg Wilson 1997; Haebich 2000; Wild and Anderson 2007). The failure of mental health systems and services is a recurring theme (eg Burdekin 1993; Williams and Keating 1999; ABC 2008a). Aged-care facilities and services have come under scrutiny through deaths and injuries in nursing homes and deaths in the community that have gone unnoticed for weeks (eg Glenndenning 1999; ABC 2000; IBN News 2006). Young people in need of a home and quality care have been short-changed (eg Burdekin 1989). Disabled people have been treated inhumanely in care (eg Office of the Health Complaints Commissioner Tasmania 2007; ABC 2008b) or have received less-than-adequate care (eg Carter 2006). Prisoners have been brutalised routinely in prisons (eg Nagle 1979; Grabosky 1989). There is a litany of major failures to care or in care.

This shadow world is also populated by innumerable large and small individual hurts, sour relationships, lost opportunities, discourtesies, indignities and unmet expectations, which are contributed to by routine system, agency and worker action and, commonly, inaction. These private misfortunes are not the stuff of media stories, or investigatory processes, nor are they the focus here, but they contribute nonetheless to the depth and impact of the human service shadow world.

It is not surprising that the human services are attended by shadows – they engage with the most vulnerable and marginalised people. Society's ambivalence about the function, rights and status of the vulnerable and the marginalised has been extensively rehearsed by sociologists. Human service agents are subject to the ebb and flow of changing social norms, political agendas and mixed messages about the deserving and undeserving in society, their rights and responsibilities, and the objectives and standards of assessment and intervention. Human service agents operate in the most contested and fraught arenas of social life, where interests, rights, responsibilities and risks are finely balanced, and human dysfunction is usually present and often extreme. As Webb (2006 p. 3) says of the social services and the whirlpool of contradictory imperatives in which they operate and are shaped – they are 'at the eye of the storm'.

The human services function as the sweepers of society, gathering up and containing human debris. Their social legitimacy, like that of their clients, is doubtful, even more so when a law-and-order agenda prevails. The human services, made up largely of women, are seen as doing dirty and not particularly skilful work (Camilleri 1996). In Stoesz's (2002 p. 23) words, 'social work, much to its detriment, has become associated with providing second-class services to second-class citizens'. Much of the social unease about the human services is played out in its poor, or sad and marginal (Henderson and Franklin 2007) public image, in which it is seen as ineffective at best (Franklin and Parton 1991; Golding 1991; Brawley 1995; McInnes and Lawson-Brown 2007; Mendes 2008).

Society's ambivalence both underpins and is affirmed by the strange paradox of the human services. On the one hand, human service functions involve the management of extremely sensitive and contested negotiations between individuals, groups, communities and society. To be performed competently, these negotiations demand considerable wisdom, knowledge and skill. On the other hand, human service functions are actually undertaken by variably qualified and often inexperienced, relatively low-status people, accessing limited resources, relying on what is widely construed as common knowledge, in an occupationally unregulated sector. This situation is a recipe for disappointment or even disaster, and an infinite number of incipient shadows. However, the paradox also gives rise to examples of extraordinarily committed, courageous and creative human service activities.

Every profession and many areas of human endeavour are advertised as highly principled, while simultaneously sponsoring a dark side – their shadow. Schön's (1991) seminal work detailed the crisis of confidence in all professional groups and arenas since the 1960s. Health systems, the law, religion, politics and sport are examples of professions and fields in which high ideals and positive aspirations coexist with villainy, malfunction and calamity. Nevertheless, there are some particularly jarring inconsistencies and peculiarities about the human service shadow world and the one which creates it.

The human services shadow world is composed of failures that are particularly terrible, recurrent and wide-ranging. Several generations of Indigenous families, whole populations of client groups (eg children in residential institutions), and a great number of other individuals (eg in immigration detention, and mental health and alternative care), have been damaged if not destroyed by systems, agencies and workers with mandates ostensibly anchored in humanitarian principles. Yet, this trail of destruction is completely at odds with the public rhetoric and self representations of the human service 'real' or 'official' world. Although the human services imagine themselves stepping forward into the sun and caring, observers see the looming shadows which attend them. Shadows are more apparent to observers than to those who cast them.

The extent of trauma and the public clamour contrast starkly with the strangely loud silence in the world which casts the shadow. Apart from bouts of Stoesz's notion (2002) of professional victimhood, the mainstream 'official' professional human service practice world behaves as if its shadows, and the accompanying public distrust, do not exist.

The reluctance of any profession or sector to engage in public self-flagellation is unexceptional and the few human service attempts may not have been considered newsworthy. However the public profile and the breadth and depth of tragedy in the human services shadow world is strangely underrepresented in academic and other commentary, which is targeted primarily at an internal audience. There is a significant imbalance between the weight and extent of external material on failures in the human services, and the limited literature that specifically addresses policy, system, organisational and worker shortcomings, and the resultant harm. The professional and scholarly commentary on misadventure and malpractice in the human services is minimal in Australia, and only slightly more extensive overseas. The core curriculums of human service courses, social work included, do not address past and current deficiencies that have injured clients and communities or that have the potential to do so again. In fact Schorr (2000 p. 133), from the United States, has castigated schools of social work for being 'studiously blind to endemic violations of good practice'.

Australian Social Work, published by the Australian Association of Social Workers (AASW), is arguably the major professional journal for the sector, yet it contains few articles that focus on malpractice, or significant human service failure. A search by the author of this book, from 1948, a year after the first version of the journal began, until December 2008, for titles indicating a central concern with legal liability for damage caused, malpractice, negligence, breaches of ethics or standards, or committees of inquiry into human service endeavours, produces a tiny list, most concerning children. Browne's three articles (Gaha 1992) on the Maria Colwell death and the Beckford Inquiry in the UK in the 1970s–1980s are clearly attempts to understand how and why human service systems produced or failed to prevent tragedy. More recently, there has been one article on legal suits (Collingridge 1991), one on breaches of the AASW code of ethics (Murray and Swain 1999), one on the abrogation of practice standards in alternative care (Gilbertson and Barber 2004), one on the Queensland Crime and Misconduct inquiry into the abuse of children in foster care (Lonne and Thomson 2005), one on the risks to children of risk assessment procedures (Gillingham 2006) and one on the role of continuing education in protecting clients from social worker-caused harm (Kent 2006).

This is not to say that other articles in *Australian Social Work* and elsewhere do not attend to substandard or potentially substandard systems and activity, but this tends to be incidental to the main focus of the articles and not of interest in its own right (eg on later access to records for institutionalised children, see Murray et al. 2008, and Healy 2004). For example, the Australian social work law writer Swain is represented in law journals with articles on social work liability and social work failure (eg Swain 1996; 2003). There is some psychology commentary in Australia on how to avoid malpractice suits (eg McBride and Tunnecliffe 2001; O'Brien-Malone and Diamond 2006). Service failures are also sporadically recognised in the childcare literature (eg Kiraly 2002; Penglase 2004). As will be evident throughout this book, there are a number of Australian law commentators, most notably Freckelton (eg 2007a), who have analysed recent high-profile human service cases. Even so, within Australian legal literature there is no compilation of human service cases and commentary.

Internationally, there is a body of scholarly literature in the United States on social work malpractice and legal liability, in which the comprehensive work of Reamer (1992; 1995; 2000; 2001; 2003a; 2003b) predominates. Even so, Reamer (1992 p. 168) notes the denial of and/or inattention to impaired social workers and their activities within the profession in the US, and asserts that: 'members of the profession must be vigilant in their efforts to confront the incompetence, unprofessional conduct, and unethical activities of their colleagues'. Also in the US, Besharov's (1985) *The Vulnerable Social Worker* and Bullis' (1995) *Clinical Social Worker Misconduct* do not take a broad human service perspective, although their material is generalisable. Instead, they incline towards the individual social worker as the target of malpractice and private legal suits. There is also a body of more theoretical and policy-orientated material in the UK, including works that detail human service failure in the context of related questions, such as media images (eg Franklin and Parton 1991), the aetiology of scandals (Butler and Drakeford 2005), and the phenomenon of risk, which is discussed later in this chapter.

There are many interconnected reasons for this apparent silence within. The human service shadow domain is perpetually raw; never amenable to reflection from a safe historical and emotional distance as new tragedies regularly emerge. From within the human services, the shadow world is the product of a few individual 'bad apples', or 'the other' (occupational or professional grouping or organisation, or part of the sector), or the result of a previous approach to intervention, or the product of inadequate resources or bad policies, or all of these things. Of course these views are valid in particular situations, but they are incomplete.

No tradition and few mechanisms exist in the official human services world for dealing with contributions to the shadow world and their legacies. The human services, unlike medicine or aviation (eg Merry and McCall-Smith 2004; Ranson 2006), have minimal or rudimentary acceptance of and processes for responding formally and consistently to errors, adverse events and negative consumer experiences. However, standing committees on child deaths connected to child protection services are becoming more common.

Manthorpe and Stanley (1999 p. 232) commenting on institutional failures in the human services argue that external public enquiry is the prevailing 'tradition' for dealing with bad outcomes and that little relevant research is conducted because it is difficult. Research on system, organisational and individual worker shortcomings does face ethical and legal hurdles, and is not popular with research funding bodies or sponsors. Multiple consecutive enquiries produce large amounts of information about the forms of failure and the damage caused, and keep the shadow world well populated. However, the phenomenon of multiple enquires does not build knowledge about integrated service system structures, arrangements for effective service delivery, helpful intervention methods or supportive policies and procedures. Enquires seldom have a role in the implementation or monitoring of responses to earlier recommendations. Each new enquiry discovers yet again what has been found by earlier investigations. At times of catastrophe, shortcomings of the human services are reviewed from the outside, to show that something is being done, and with a reactive, rather than a prospective, agenda.

The human services are not well endowed with research money and lack a tradition of practice and outcomes research and research-informed practice (Gibbons 2001; Stoesz 2002; Furedi 2004; McDonald 2006). Human service approaches to service delivery, assessment and intervention, are undeveloped or compromised, depending on one's epistemological position. Some social theorists (eg Webb 2006) argue that social work practice has been colonised by technical rationality and has lost touch with its value and ethical base.

Others (eg Gambrill 2006), including the author of this book, take a more empiricist, evidence-based practice stance. We argue that intervention activity is not well-supported by continually emerging data or debates about new techniques, processes and procedures, but is largely ideologically based (eg Gibbons 2001) and haphazard. Bessant's (2004 p. 12) assertion about operationalising human rights aspirations in youth work applies here: 'rights talk often remains rhetorical'.

Perhaps there is a deficit of commonplace technical conversation in the human services, which serves in many other professions to occupy the very wide space between lofty ideals and professional failures. This kind of conversation can assist us to understand and tackle performance deficits. High ideals have a powerful presence in social work literature (the predominant form in the human services); failures are absent and between the extremes are only sporadic conversations about things that are amiss.

Those responsible for human service systems and institutions are generally busy closing ranks in the wake of a recently exposed or unfolding tragedy. In Lonne's (2005) reasonable view, such people seldom take responsibility for shortcomings. Human service organisations are likewise frequently preoccupied with defending, negotiating and regrouping in the face of exposed failures (Senate Standing Committee on Community Affairs 2004). Commentaries from within the organisation, such as Harris' (1998) on the failings of the Church Missionary Society with Indigenous people in Northern Australia, are exceptional.

It appears that human service organisations and managers rarely record and promulgate practice successes (eg Manela and Moxley 2002;

Rotheram-Borus and Duan 2003), so there is even less likelihood that they will declare their failures. They do not have ready access to safe and appropriate forums for engagement in these conversations, nor do they have traditions that promote such engagement (Patti 2003; Kennedy and Kennedy 2008).

At the professional level, the heterogeneity of the human service workforce dilutes professional identity, control and voice. No single professional or occupational group would wish to take responsibility for the litany of past and present wrongs. In Australia, this is a very real dilemma faced by the most recognisable professional group in the sector – social work – and the AASW, its professional association. Gillingham (2007) concludes that the AASW is not a force in social policy debates because of historical, cultural and structural factors, not the least of which is its small membership. Psychology, which might also claim a voice in and for the sector, has traditionally allied itself with health, standing apart from the rough and tumble of human service work, which is perceived to be lower status and professionally diffuse.

The AASW has not been moved to bid for the mantle of leadership of the entire human service arena, although it has recently staked its territorial claims publically in the context of broader concerns about child protection systems (eg see Australian Association of Social Workers 2008; Overington 2008). A so far unsuccessful public interest case for state registration of social workers has been launched by the AASW, which acknowledges that social workers can be harmful (Australian Association of Social Workers 2004). The case for registration recognises possible mental, emotional and financial risks to clients of inappropriate social work activity, and rather gingerly offers limited examples of social workers who have behaved unlawfully. In this, the AASW is caught in a bind. If it pronounces social workers as seriously dangerous it sabotages its own professional image, but minimising the potential for harm weakens its case for registration.

Its registration case is also somewhat disingenuous given that a much larger proportion of the human service workforce is not qualified in social work, yet it services the same clients and poses the same risks as social workers, and works alongside them in the same organisational and service systems. Sections of the workforce also share social work values and approaches (eg Hughes 2008). Other professional associations in the human service arena (eg Australian Institute of Welfare and Community Workers, Australian Counselling Association) lack the membership coverage, resources and legitimacy to even attempt the task of speaking for or representing the human services.

While a great many of the activities of human service agencies and workers are regulated, workers themselves, apart from psychologists, are not. Thus, there are no registration boards and connected disciplinary processes to take a central position in professional life, promulgate worker misdeeds and malpractice, and help to embed and consolidate notions of adequate, inadequate and harmful practice. Registration does not prevent malpractice, as demonstrated by registered professions such as medicine and psychology, but it does raise the profile of malpractice and its consequences within a profession.

At the level of the individual worker, voices may be silent for many reasons. A few people do of course whistleblow in the face of systemic mishaps and misdeeds, but many are muzzled by legislative, contractual and employment-related prohibitions on speaking out. According to Franklin and Parton (1991), there is also a prevailing attitude and strategy, in United Kingdom social work at least, of keeping a low profile in the face of media reporting. It has been argued that well-documented feelings of powerlessness and helplessness in many human service workers (eg Bar-On 1995; Charles and Butler 2004) blind them to their potential for both positive and negative impact.

Galloway's (2005) analysis of Australian welfare workers' constructions of Aboriginal reconciliation is instructive in the context of individual voices – she suggests an individualised rather than a collective approach to social problems. Among her small group of research respondents, workers felt that they should not take responsibility for things past or for matters that they saw as the remit of government. As Lymbery (2004) and others have acknowledged, the distance between the ideal and the real is often appreciated by front-line workers, although they do not generally declare this publically or in any permanent form. There are institutional barriers to contributing actively to knowledge development (Healy 2005) and continuing education forums are not the norm in this arena (Barker and Branson 2000). Moreover changing imperatives within universities and professional exclusivity in social work have contributed to the demise of public intellectuals who speak out on social matters and act as 'the conscience of the nation' (Karger and Stoesz 2003 p. 65).

This book is positioned in that relatively unpopulated space in the human services where mishaps and misdeeds are scrutinised. It is about the role of the law in respect to the mishaps and misdeeds that comprise the shadow world. It holds a mirror before the human services so its actors, while still reaching out to the light, might recognise, confront, better understand and rise to the challenge of the shadow world. In the analysis thus far, there is something of the gothic drama, but the events and tragedies are neither confected nor overstated. It is hoped that an audience naturally reluctant to turn towards the shadows may feel compelled to do so by the telling of the dark tale. There is a risk that some will be repelled, yet there are ample rewards for attending to the shadow world – within it are moral, professional and educational lessons that have the potential to alter future events.

WHY CONSIDER SHADOWS?

Answers to this question range from the proselytising to the pragmatic. If human service activity casts unintentional shadows, the sector is morally, ethically and professionally bound to assume at least some responsibility for acknowledging and explaining them. Individual actors in the human services contribute different amounts to the magnitude and intensity of the shadow world, but all are darkened and bear some collective responsibility. The sector will be haunted by the weight of its shortcomings until human services actors acknowledge them, attempt to elucidate their multiple causes, and incorporate them into the language and aspirations for future service delivery systems, organisations and work practices. Public distrust will not diminish while the current silence continues.

In more transparently confronting their own demons, the human services will be better placed to assume greater control of the mishaps and misdeeds agenda. By doing this, they will they create opportunities for articulating and promulgating the aetiologies of failure more comprehensively, including social, political and organisational causes. A confrontation of this kind is a precedent condition for enhanced service delivery and, potentially, an improved public image.

A focus on mishaps and misdeeds may be justified by the motivation to improve service quality. As Swain (1996 p. 57, quoting Sharwell 1979) has argued, understanding incompetent practice can teach us about competent practice as they are 'two sides of same coin'. Improved practice evolves from research and assertions of the desirable, but equally from systematic scrutiny of adverse events, their origins and characteristics. This argument is not driven by an interest in allocating blame, although blame allocation is sometimes justified and does occur in legal action, but by a view that information about what can go wrong and why may be used constructively.

Swain (2008 p. 195) in discussing the significance of client case files in social work history, articulates a position equally relevant here:

... just as our practice in the present has been shaped by a history that is neither as simple nor unidirectional as we may have imagined, it also leaves a trail into the future, a trail encompassing oppression, and empowerment, abuse and care. We cannot predetermine the nature of that trail, but an awareness of its presence will surely serve to moderate the worst possible abuses.

A cultural shift is required in human service workplaces, professional bodies and professional education so that lapses may be confronted, scrutinised and understood, and incorporated in future systems and practices.

Risk phenomena, mentioned above, needs to be considered briefly here because it permeates the context of the human services, the service systems, the organisational arrangements, polices and procedures and all practices. Risk and failure are inextricably linked, and risk sensitivity in times of uncertainty is a phenomenon that has been articulated and debated extensively by social theorists. In a society that increasingly 'worships safety' (Kemshall 2002 p. 98), the human services are now preoccupied with risk control activity, either in relation to their own accountability or in the prioritising and rationing of services (Parton 2001; Kemshall 2002; Titterton 2005; Webb 2006; Connolly and Ward 2008). In the words of Phillips (2007 p. 144) 'care has been redefined as risk aversion and protection'. Kemshall (2002) argues that risk replaces need in the primary position in service provision, with 'increasingly corrective and compulsory services' (2008 p. 28).

Webb (2006 p. 10) extends Kemshall's analysis and claims that risk and need have been conflated in current human services, as social work has accepted the dominant neoliberal ideology and its 'technologies of care' – prescribing and proscribing need and the organisation of service delivery. In his view, the social services and social work are primarily concerned with imprecise and value laden actuarial strategies to prevent and mitigate risky occurrences. In the words of McLaughlin (2007 p. 1263) in this context (and the context of a drive for registration for social workers in the United Kingdom), social workers 'are simultaneously seen as assessors of risk, at risk and as a risk'.

Anxiety about taking risks can stultify and distort the human services, making them rigid and 'negatively' defensive (Harris 1987 p. 65) rather than responsive, and more inclined to limit client independence and choice. There are many other practical illustrations of this overemphasis on negative risk and its potential for harm in the human services. Gillingham's (2006) overview of risk assessment tools in child protection in Australia demonstrates how risk assessment tools can blinker practitioners from information beyond the parameters of the tool, absolve them from interpretative and discrimination responsibilities, distort decision-making by privileging safety over harm factors, and bias them towards an acceptance of mothers as the primary protective force in children's lives. Fitzgibbon (2007) shows how over-defensive assessments in corrections can result in an increased probability of prisoners returning to custody when essential community treatment is not available to them. Milligan (2006) details the conflict between health and safety risk assessments that primarily serve agency purposes in residential care for children, and the normalisation of child experience, which involves ordinary risk-taking behaviour through play and exploration.

Positive risk is seldom acknowledged in this negative risk paradigm (Harris 1987; Titterton 1999; Carson and Bain 2008), although recently theorists such as Webb (2006) have observed the balance shifting back towards active risk taking as mangers adapt to a competitive, performance-management environment in which entrepreneurship is valued. The consequences of this shift are yet to be seen and detailed – active risk taking also has both negative and positive aspects.

In the context of a risk-obsessed culture, it is apposite to study anxieties that are realised; failures that have not been avoided. Human service mishaps and misdeeds are expected in a risk culture, and happen despite efforts to prevent them. Paradoxically, they may be the product of risk aversion or the overenthusiastic risk taking that is encouraged by a risk-obsessed culture. Returning to McLaughlin's (2007) discussion about social work registration, human service actors may fail in their assessment of risk, in their responses to risks that face them, and by exposing others to risk through their behaviour.

Law is one of the mechanisms increasingly deployed to regulate and control activity in a risk culture. A legal suit is arguably more likely in a risk environment, where there are imperatives to identify and blame those responsible. The fixation with risk is echoed in law, with a similarly robust debate about defensive practice, liability of bodies functioning in socially contested areas, and loci of responsibility for damage caused.

SHADOWS AND THE LAW

The shadow world of the human services may be usefully explored through a law lens. Law is not the only lens, but given the place of law in risk culture, the human services must understand law's response to mishaps and misdeeds. A wide appreciation of the law can assist human service actors in making informed judgements about legal risk, and has the potential to liberate them for conscious engagement in positive risk taking, so essential for good practice. Carson (1996; 1997; 2006; 2008) has consistently argued the position, subscribed to here: risks of success can and must be taken in the human services. Such risks are potentially both legally protective and defensive. In his view, the focus on negative risk and the law has underplayed the legal risks of omissions and inaction, which are professionally dubious. To practitioners who wish to minimise their legal risk, he says: 'they need to organize the law's concepts and procedures to their own ends, and before the harm occurs' (1996 p. 5).

Research in medicine shows that fear of legal action evolves through processes akin to hearsay rather than by informed opinion (Allsop and Mulcahy 1996 p. 175). This is consistent with Titterton's (2005) argument that fear of being sued in the human services derives from a confused understanding among policy makers and senior managers of law and the legal process. Human service actors familiar with the law, its reasoning and its mechanisms for determining standards, can be better informed about deliberately acting so that their planned and managed positive risk taking is professionally and legally justifiable. Strategic practice of this kind, in Parton's words the 'assessment and management of uncertainty' (2001 p. 69) can serve to free actors from a reliance on crude negative risk techniques, which can prescribe practice and disguise ambiguity. A demystification of the real threats posed by the risk of legal action in the human services is required.

Law cases provide one of the few windows into human service shortcomings; they are a source of information about human service actions and resultant damage. In legal cases, human service mishaps and misdeeds are revisited and scrutinised and 'real life' human service stories are made public. Rich seams of human service material are revealed. Although technical aspects of the law in these stories may be challenging to people who are not familiar with the law, the facts of the cases are recognisable to human service consumers. Learning from law cases may also be generalised, but with caution, as law cases are not statistically representative of events.

Even a few human service law cases can have a radiating effect (Allsop and Mulcahy 1996 p. 20) as the law is declared through them – fostering public debate and having an impact on future practice through accurate and imperfect understandings of their significance. In 2009, there are more and more significant human service legal cases that command attention than there were when Collingridge (1991) and Swain (2001) commented on the paucity of Australian cases in this area.

Human service accountability may be measured by a variety of means and from different perspectives, one of which is law (Braye and Preston-Shoot 2001; 2006). Legal scrutiny of human service activity is reactive, retrospective and expensive. It operates in accordance with legal rules and language, which commonly do not accommodate the nuances and complexities of human service intentions and experience. The law is an intermittent accountability mechanism; its activation is unpredictable. Nonetheless, it is the primary means by which society regulates and orders itself, and through which behaviour is commanded, judged and legitimated.

Hall (2006 p. 157), who examines connections between human service events and compensation, and proposes ways that cultures of dependence and power may be better understood and the perpetuation of past wrongs avoided, says: 'Law is properly conceptualised both as a response to wrong-doing and as the prism through which society explains and understands wrongdoing'. Law is the prism or lens through which this book looks.

THE SHADOW WORLD AND THE BOOK

This book straddles several professional domains and invites curiosity beyond traditional knowledge boundaries. It brings together material not formerly compiled and annotated in human service or legal literature, and attempts to interpret it in a way that speaks to both spheres. It is pitched primarily at the informed human service reader, although the legal consumer will also find human service reasoning and positions informative. The book is presented in four parts.

PART 1

The first part, including this chapter, sets out the rationale for the book and its parameters. Chapter 2 describes the human services sector, the justification for choosing it as an arena for attention, and the ideals that characterise it. Three levels of human service activity or 'actors' are posited as contributing to the shadow world: the service system, the organisation and the individual worker. Each of these levels and the potential for malfunction is considered alone or in combination by examining responses by the law and attributions of responsibility for failure. Acts or events that constitute human service failure are investigated and a typology of mishaps and misdeeds is offered as a vehicle for bridging human service and legal conceptions of wrongdoing.

PART 2

In Part 2, mishaps and misdeeds are viewed through a traditional law lens. Various categories of law are briefly summarised and grouped as private or public law areas under which human service cases have arisen or have the potential to arise. Legally mandated Australian authorities that investigate and respond to human service failure are examined, along with legally based disciplinary processes that apply in the human services. The language of law dominates in the conceptual arrangement and selection of material in Part 2, and human services cases are used as illustrations of the different areas of law. Obstacles to legal action are described and emphasised throughout. Part 2 is ambitious in that it traverses the surface of a vast area of law – there is a deliberate attempt to map the territory of legal risk in the human services, but at a level midway between a generic introduction and material for law experts.

There are four significant aspects of the coverage of law throughout the book:

- The material is not a substitute for expert legal commentary in the specific areas of law addressed in this book – a selection of current authoritative books is suggested for further reading on the points raised.
- The focus is Australian, but the human services material has international application and the law is of relevance to all countries with a common law tradition.
- All cases are reviewed with attention to legal principles and an equal focus on the human service story. Cases were selected on the basis of the following principles:
  - An effort has been made to include all significant Australian human service cases in which law has been developed or senior courts commentaries about human service activity.
  - Significant cases from other common law jurisdictions are mentioned if they have been influential in the development of Australian law (even if they have not yet been tested in Australia) or contain human service 'fact situations' (or events) of particular pertinence.
  - Less legally significant, mostly Australian, cases have been included if they illustrate specific human service fact situations involving human services personnel, work, failure or agencies.
  - Some health, education or allied health cases have been included if the facts or the law have applicability to the human services.
- Human rights law would seem to be, but often is not, fundamental to human service activities, particularly those which go amiss, in Australia

POSITIONING AND MAPPING HUMAN SERVICE MISHAPS

and internationally (see 'Human rights law and the human services'). However, human rights cases do not feature largely in the book. Why is this?

Human rights law and the human services

Social work has been described from within as a human rights profession, with a range greater than and beyond the law (Ife 2008). Human rights are critical in most fields of human services practice. In the United Kingdom, human rights law has become increasingly significant with the enactment of the *Human Rights Act 1988* (UK), which incorporates the European Convention on Human Rights into domestic law (Schwehr 2001; Brammer 2003; Brayne and Carr 2003; Williams 2004; Arthur 2006; Dalrymple and Burke 2006; Braye and Preston-Shoot 2006). Moreover the European Court of Human Rights is increasingly challenging human service activities.

Human rights law does not feature largely in Australian law. Australia does not have a constitutionally founded bill of rights or human rights legislation, although the Australian Government has stated its intention to consult on a federal charter of human rights (Lynch 2008). Australia is a signatory to a range of United Nations conventions and treaties – for example, the International Covenant on Civil and Political Rights (ICCPR), the Convention on the Rights of the Child (CRC), and the Convention on the Protection and Promotion of the Rights and Dignity of Persons with Disabilities. This confers moral obligations, but although courts may interpret legislation in terms of international covenants, they are not necessarily given effect in Australian law (Kennedy and Richards 2007).[2] Some covenants are given partial effect in Australian law; for example, the Convention on the Elimination of All Forms of Discrimination against Women is given effect through the *Sex Discrimination Act 1984* (Cth) (Kennedy and Richards 2007). Some protections for human rights exist in explicit and implied constitutional rights arising out of the British tradition; for example, writs for habeas corpus (O'Neill et al. 2004). The human rights 'watchdog' in Australia is the Australian Human Rights Commission (Chapter 8), and there is also reactive protection for some rights under anti-discrimination and related legislation. Some of this more oblique legal attention to human rights will be seen in some of the cases in the book.

---

[2] For example: *Kioa v West* [1985] HCA 81; (1985) 159 CLR 550; *Minister of State for Immigration & Ethnic Affairs v Ah Hin Teoh* [1995] HCA 20; 183 CLR 273.

Some states and territories have or are considering human rights leg-islation. The *Human Rights Act 2004* (ACT) and the *Charter of Human Rights and Responsibilities Act 2006* (Vic) do not permit individuals to enforce their civil and social rights, but they do bind public authorities, and all legislation in the jurisdiction must be compatible with human rights. The legislation in the ACT and Victoria covers civil and political rights and has limited potency, but Freckelton (2006b) argues there is evi-dence, in health cases at least, that it is prompting a cultural shift towards rights thinking in the courts of these two jurisdictions. Other health law commentators (Hunt 2008; McSherry 2008; McSherry and Darvall 2008) also contend that rights to health and to service are increasingly being positioned within a human rights framework in more general legal argu-ment in the courts. The Tasmania Law Reform Institute has recommended the enactment of a charter that includes civil, political, economic, social and cultural rights in Tasmania (Tasmania Law Reform Institute 2007) and the Western Australian government has received a similar recom-mendation (Consultation Committee for a Proposed Human Rights Act 2007).

PART 3

In Part 3, mishaps and misdeeds are scrutinised through a human services lens, such that human service language and concepts govern the choice, organisation and significance of the material. Within each chapter, linkages are made between a human service activity and the law. Human service direct work with clients and practice matters that may raise the possibil-ity of legal action or complaint are emphasised. Reamer (2003b p. 77), commenting on the situation in the United States, provides a partial ratio-nale for this bias – most malpractice suits arise out of direct practice with families, individuals and groups.

Human services intervention is generally accepted as involving several phases of activity – 'the helping process' or 'the planned change process' – which prevail regardless of theoretical orientation, the practice tools or the targets of intervention. Generic approaches to human service intervention (eg Hepworth et al. 2006; Kirst-Ashman and Hull 2006; Miley et al. 2007; Sheafor and Horejsi 2007), case work (eg Gambrill 1983), counselling (eg Corey 2009; Cormier et al. 2009) and case management (eg Rothman and Sager 1998; Holt 2000) (Gursansky et al. 2003; Summers 2009) all use these phases in their conceptualisation of the life cycle of the professional practice relationship.

Although different terminology and emphases may be applied to the phases, and overlap and cyclical operation occurs, the phases are fundamental to the accepted helping process:

1. Intake, screening for service eligibility and assessment of need.
2. Planning and decision making regarding parameters, goals and methods of intervention.
3. Implementation, monitoring, review and reassessment.
4. Winding down and service termination.

Expectations and demands regarding record keeping, and the management of information and interpersonal relationships are superimposed on the helping process. These core phases of activity set the chapter structure for Part 3.

Within each chapter in Part 3, human service failures are addressed through relevant legal cases. Conditions, activities and events particular to the phase of activity that pose legal risk are considered in relation to the legal material in Part 1. Issues of potential human service legal liability (eg failure to detect suicide indicators) and some areas of law (eg criminal, discrimination, occupational health and safety) are relevant across the life of intervention. In Part 3, these issues are included where they can be brought into sharpest relief.

At appropriate places in each chapter, liability considerations arising from the preceding material are discussed. These are intended to promote informed decision making about legal risk at the system, agency and individual worker levels. The liability considerations listed:

- are not definitive of substantive law, nor are they substitutes for legal advice about specific fact situations
- are not risk checklists, but aim to encourage broad reflection about judgements made in appreciation of legal and practice imperatives
- confirm, rather than develop, existing material on quality practice and practice standards in the human services, as good practice and protection from legal action overlap (although they are not synonymous)
- attempt to draw attention to essential positive risk taking in human service work to counterbalance the emphasis on risk minimisation through inaction which is a common by-product of legal action

PART 4

Part 4 of the book contains two chapters that attempt to draw together strands from the other three parts of the book, from a legally informed human service perspective. Chapter 13 explores the important question of what does or does not attract the attention of the law and why. Chapter 14 returns to the matter of ideals, actors and actions, and identifies challenges to human service actors suggested by the acts and outcomes covered in the book.

A FINAL CAUTION

Despite some high profile recent human service cases in Australia, very few adverse human service events ever result in legal action and even fewer get to court. Statistically the risks of a lawsuit are very small indeed. Thus, the cases reviewed in this book represent the tip of the iceberg of mishaps and misdeeds. Any case that comes to court stands for innumerable similar fact situations that do not make it to court, some more damaging and some less so. This point is as significant as the cases that do get to court and contribute to the evolution of the law. Once something is understood of the way in which a legal action begins and evolves, it is impossible to see each legal case as a fact aberration, although its elevation to the courts is just that. Human service readers are invited to look into the mirror that is this book and to anticipate some discomfort.

2 | Ideals, actors and actions

W<small>HO AND WHAT</small> are the human services and what mishaps and misdeeds characterise them? This chapter examines the human services, the actors and the actions that contribute to the shadow world, to set the stage for an approach to the law and legal cases in later chapters. The ideals that, in theory, underpin and guide the operations of the human services are given in overview, including the people and circumstances that contribute to breaches of the ideals and possibly the law, and the law's response. Finally, the range of human service breaches, mishaps and misdeeds is discussed. A typology demonstrating the interface between these actions and the law (introducing legal concepts that are significant in legal liability) is proposed as a mechanism for bridging human service and legal understandings of wrongdoing.

THE ARENA – HUMAN SERVICES AND IDEALS

The term 'human service' (also 'community or social welfare services' or 'social care') suggests a domain in which human needs are serviced. Human needs are many and varied. In the human services there are also a variety of service systems, forms of service delivery, professions and occupational groups, staffing services, service recipients and agencies.

There are multiple definitions of human services (eg Lyons 2001; Zins 2001; Meagher and Healy 2005; Mehr and Kanwischer 2008) with the boundaries expanding or contracting according to the positions of the commentators. Woodside and McClam (2006), taking an inclusive approach that is favoured in this book, suggest that the human services serve social control, social care and rehabilitation functions in society. Despite debates about the parameters of the human services, they generally encompass family, child, youth, aged, income maintenance, disability, crisis, vocational and other rehabilitation, community development, overseas aid, family violence, substance abuse, refugee and resettlement, and accommodation services.

The health and human services spheres overlap in terms of workers, functions and services. For example, Australian Bureau of Statistics 2001 census data indicates that about an equal number of social workers are employed in community service and health sectors (Meagher and Healy 2006). For the purposes of this book, the community health and mental health components of the health sphere are included in the human services. The human services domain also overlaps with the domains of:

- education – student support, counselling, school retention, parenting support and social development services
- arts and recreation – recreational and arts programs designed to reduce social deficit and enhance wellbeing
- justice – juvenile and adult correctional services.

Any field of practice or service in which there is systematised activity to restore or enhance personal, community and social functioning, is included in the definition of human services and prevails in the selection of law and legal cases for the purposes of this book.

The human services thus encompasses a huge variety of jobs, workers with different educational and experiential preparation for the work, carers and volunteers, service providers, service networks, and professional and occupational groups (eg Wearing 1998; McDonald 1999; Kennedy and Harvey 2001; Meagher and Healy 2005, 2006). Psychology, nursing, social work and counselling are four obvious groups of workers in the human services that consistently claim professional status, but psychology and nursing are the only state-licensed professions in the human services in Australia. Social work, counselling and all of the other occupational groups in the human services are not. Psychologists and nurses more commonly report working in health than in human services (Meagher and Healy 2006), of which they make up only a small proportion. Thus, the bulk of the human services workforce is not licensed by the state for occupational title or practice methods. It is this group that is the focus of this book – nurses and nursing cases are not addressed, and cases involving psychologists are used if they are generalisable to the human services and if there is a pertinent point of difference which can be drawn from them.

In the absence of state registration, eligibility for membership of a professional association is significant for individual workers and employers seeking status, identity and predictable training. Only part of the human services workforce has formal social work qualifications that render it eligible for membership of the professional body, the Australian Association of Social Workers (AASW) (O'Connor et al. 2000a). Only a small proportion of all human services jobs require AASW-eligible qualifications – even social work jobs do not necessarily require such qualifications (McDonald 1999; Kennedy and Harvey 2001; Healy 2004). Nevertheless, many people assume that human services workers are or must be social work qualified, even some of those within the human services.

Workers not qualified in psychology or social work constitute the bulk of the human service workforce, but within this group there is a large and growing group of workers with three-year post-schooling qualifications (McDonald and Jones 2000) making them eligible for membership of the Australian Institute of Welfare and Community Workers. This group is akin to the social pedagogy group in the European tradition and the 'human service profession' in the United States (eg Zins 2001; Neukrug 2007).

Within the human service workforce, particularly in the non-profit sector, there is a significant group without post-schooling qualifications (McDonald 1999; McDonald 2000; Meagher and Healy 2006). Figures vary slightly depending on definitions, but it is reported based on Australian Bureau of Statistics 2005 data that 13% of welfare and community workers and 9% of social workers, were without post-schooling qualifications (Australian Job Search n.d., quoting ABS Education and Work Australia 2005; Australian Job Search n.d.). Nearly 90% of the workforce are women and earnings are not generally high (Australian Institute of Health and Welfare 2007). The unpaid workforce made up of carers and volunteers is about twice the size of the paid workforce (Australian Institute of Health and Welfare 2007).

Job titles within this diverse domain are multitudinous, and occupational distinctions and classifications can be obscure (Vaughan 2006). Changes in human service system arrangements and new approaches to service delivery, such as case management and multidisciplinary team work (eg see Wearing 1998; McDonald 1999; Malin 2000; Gursansky et al. 2003; McDonald et al. 2003; Lewis and Bolzan 2007), mean that professional and occupational identities and job functions are in flux. Some jobs are designated by a recognisable professional title (eg social worker, psychologist), some are named by function or approach to service delivery (eg counsellor, case manager, case worker, welfare worker, community worker), some are named according to the target group served (eg family support, youth, domestic violence, child protection worker, custodial officer). Jobs with different titles and eligibility criteria may have similar functions, or similar titles may apply to dissimilar functions, skill and knowledge sets. For the purposes of this book, all of these workers are included under the generic title 'human service worker'. Law and cases which involve human service professions and occupations, particularly unregistered ones, even if they are working outside of the human services, or human service agencies and human service functions and services, are within the scope of this book.

Human service workers are generally employees of government and increasingly non-government organisations (NGOs) (Jones and May 1992; Wearing 1998; McDonald 2000; Gray et al. 2003; Lewis and Bolzan 2007), but there is a growing privately employed group in the areas of job seeking, child care and aged care. Even though an expanding range of human services are delivered by NGOs such as charitable, church based and community agencies, they are mostly funded by government (Lyons 2001; Australian Institute of Health and Welfare 2007). Most NGO human service organisations have a local focus and are managed locally, rather than nationally (Lyons 2001). Although many of these NGO human service organisations offer specialist local services (eg residential care or supported accommodation for particular client groups), most of the large ones and nearly half of the smaller ones offer a range of services in several locations to a range of population groups (Lyons 2001).

In the context of the contemporary human service world it is becoming more common for individual workers to be subcontractors, particularly in services such as home support. A small number of workers, particularly psychologists, counsellors and those offering alternative treatment modalities, work in private practice. Status as a public body or as an employee or contractor is critical in questions of legal liability. The full range of human service agencies is represented in the cases throughout this book – large and well-known church-based organisations, government departments, smaller local agencies and a few private practitioners.

This book examines a miscellany of services, organisations, professions, occupational groups and workers for several reasons. First, it is evident that the human services is an expanding domain, with momentum and coherence, despite professional territorial claims and different historical, occupational, methodological and philosophical traditions (eg Healy 2004, 2005; McDonald 2006, 2007). Some resist, ignore or lament a shared position in the world, particularly those from more aspirational and organised professional groups such as social work and psychology, but the reality is clear from employment patterns and through public image. From outside the human services (and often from within), professional, occupational and functional distinctions are confusing and a hazy perception of the more generic 'helping', 'counselling', 'caring' or 'social work' is common (Kennedy and Harvey 2001; Henderson and Franklin 2007).

The second reason for positing an inclusive human services is that, whether or not job titles and functions are shared, knowledge, technology and values are. In many places throughout this book, the terms 'social work' and 'social workers' are used, because the source uses the terms and is intra-professionally focused. Nevertheless, this material is applicable to and applied across the human services. More importantly human service clients are shared (eg McDonald 2007; Swain, 2008) and it is the clients' experiences of service failures that lead to most complaints and then to significant human services legal cases. It is not the distinction between, status or self-reference of the workers which concern them or the media or others who speak for them, but rather what does or does not happen for them in and across services. While individual workers may well be targeted by clients and or their advocates, the outrage is less likely to be fuelled by the fact that they are a social worker or a youth worker or whatever, than it is by the belief that their service has been deficient in some way. The same analysis is applicable to individual agencies which are the subject of complaint or legal action. It is their alleged service failure which is in question rather than their identity and form, although the latter may compound the claimant's feelings of betrayal when the disjunction between mission and action is so compelling.

Despite their differences, aspirations about interactions with and hopes for clients are generally shared by human service workers and agencies. Ife's (2008 p. 225) plea for 'discourses of unity' in regard to human rights is enlisted here in support of worker coalescence around client and community interests. As McDonald (2007 p. 88) has pointed out in her challenge to social work in the contemporary human service environment: 'exclusivity . . . is itself unhelpful'. The third reason for taking an inclusive approach to the human services is thus about shared ideals.

There is accord in the 'big' aspirations across the human services, which is manifested in codes of ethics, mission statements, charters of user rights, professional literature and public statements about ethics and professional roles and functions. To take the analogy used by Kerridge et al. (2005 pp. 42–4) about the overlapping health domain, they are 'moral friends' or at least 'moral acquaintances'. In professional codes of ethics in the caring professions, Hugman (2005 pp. 143–4) finds consensus in the stated desire to guide behaviour towards right action and a:

... 'principalist' synthesis of respect for persons, beneficence, non-maleficence and justice, with particular detailed references to values such as autonomy, honesty, veracity, fairness, dedication to service and so on.

Thus, there is agreement throughout human service rhetoric that human services endeavours should foster self-determination, share resources equitably, do no harm, promote the wellbeing of others and of society in general, and be characterised by truthfulness and trustworthiness. Such principles are endorsed in the wider society, which expects them to be displayed in practice, particularly when individuals are making judgements about their own human services experiences (or the experiences of those close to them).

Lower-order guides to action in the human services tend to be variably prescriptive, proscriptive, specific and generally directed at individual workers. These include codes of conduct, practice standards and operating procedures, which are sometimes called applied or clinical ethics, and are commonly organisationally sourced. Some of these represent genuine efforts to operationalise the broad principles or ideals of the human services and are underpinned by sympathetic policies, others are examples of what Hugman (2005 p. 148) calls quasi-legal, absolutist procedures – these are divorced from a pluralist value base and designed primarily for risk management purposes (an illustration of the negative risk critique outlined in Chapter 1).

Many guides to action have mixed purposes. Within and across the human services, the relative weightings accorded to rights and risk avoidance agendas wax and wane. There are commonalities with respect to more specific guides, as the effects of the shared principles cascade downwards, and generalisable law underpins common risk-containment characteristics.

This brings us full circle to the law and the argument for considering the human services as a whole. The response of the law to human service failures, psychology registration case law aside, has a common application across the domain. A legal challenge to any one of these individual workers or agencies has resonance and relevance for all actors within the domain.

Do broad human service ideals and guides to action translate into law? If human service activity does not live up to its high ideals, it does not automatically invite the attention of the law. There are disjunctions and conflicts between law and professional ethics, although they interact and common principles and values influence both (eg Freegard 2006; Corey et al. 2007; Kennedy and Richards 2007; Kerridge et al. 2008; Stewart 2008). Much will depend on whether or not values and positive rights are expressed in the legislation that applies to the facts or trends in arguments in the relevant common law. There is extensive commentary about the majority of law, which does not mandate positive rights, is relatively value free and procedural, or which proscribes rights (eg Preston-Shoot et al. 2001; Williams 2004). A contravention of professional principles and values may invite the attention of the law if the law has been broken (eg a crime committed), but not because of the contravention per se.

Guides to action in the human services generally do not have the direct force of law, although there are some exceptions, such as the code of conduct for Australian public servants as detailed in s 13 of the *Public Service Act 1999* (Cth). These more specific guides or procedures often carry indirect legal weight because breaches may invoke a range of disciplinary responses based in law. Many examples of breaches of this kind and their implications are described in this book.

THE ACTORS

How do breaches of ideals, guides to action or the law occur in the human services? What actors or circumstances are involved and how does the law recognise and respond to them? Individual actors are the most familiar culpable targets when something goes wrong, but their actions have both endogenous and exogenous roots that must be factored in to any understanding of mishaps and misdeeds. Three levels of responsibility for mishaps and misdeeds are considered here: the individual, the organisational and the service system. These levels mirror the micro, mezzo and macro levels familiar in the lexicon of the human services for identifying objects of endeavour or the arenas in which practice takes place.

INDIVIDUALS

Responsibility for mishaps and misdeeds in the human services is easily and commonly ascribed to individuals. Psychological explanations are the stock-in-trade for human service intervention. Despite rhetoric to the contrary, responsibility in practice is frequently directed at the individual with the difficulty, rather than the contextual conditions that have stimulated and promoted that difficulty. Explanations made by workers regarding their clients' situations and behaviour may be equally applied to workers who stand ostensibly at the forefront of negative incidents.

The proverbial 'bad apple' – the rogue worker, volunteer or foster parent – is the 'scoundrel' in Golding's (1991 p. 90) memorable list of social work caricatures in public opinion, along with the 'saint', 'simpleton' and 'scapegoat'. A 'bad apple' invokes the image of an individual who actively and deliberately infringes human service ideals, generally in pursuit of their own interests. Such individuals sexually assault children, steal or betray the confidences and trust of vulnerable others, or transgress in other egregious ways – sometimes individual pathology is involved. The role of worker impairment in misconduct is becoming increasingly recognised (eg Reamer 1992; Freckelton 2007). Truth in the bad apple imagery may be particularly vivid because of the disjunction between expressed ideals and the conduct of those who supposedly represent them, and examples are many, although numbers are small – child care and religious personnel who sexually abuse children in their care, sometimes repeatedly (eg Moulden et al. 2007; Terry and Ackerman 2008), senior people in NGO and charitable organisations who defraud the organisations (Gibelman and Gelman 2002, 2004). A great deal of policy, procedural and practice activity in the human services is directed at excluding such bad apples or limiting their opportunities for undesirable conduct.

However, it is not only bad apples that breach codes, guides or the law. All individual decision makers in the human services at some time or other, make mistakes, blunder, fail to see, get things wrong, forget and in multiple ways reveal their human fallibilities. Human service life is replete with mostly minor and some major hurts, indignities, discourtesies, confusions and misunderstandings. Often these are due to temporary inattention or sporadic errors of judgement. Many of them constitute breaches of ideals, but are not unlawful, and some are breaches of both law and ideals. If breaches are deliberate, they may not necessarily be ill intentioned, but may result from choices made between conflicting imperatives, or by necessity in emergency situations. If breaches are inadvertent, they may be the product of limited knowledge, incompetence or impairment. Unintended breaches may not have been reasonably foreseeable or may have been foreseeable, but not realistically preventable – these are accidental in the taxonomy of errors proposed by the medical writers Merry and McCall (2004 p. 29).

Ideals may be passively violated through lack of action, although as inaction has traditionally not been of interest to the law, harm through inaction is less likely to be unlawful than harm through action. Individual motivations and behaviours within prescribed boundaries are very much of interest to the law. The chapters of this book are scattered with stories about individuals who, for some reason or other beyond ill intent, found themselves the subject of legal scrutiny.

Given the size and diversity of the human service workforce, generic conclusions about its quality or levels of competence cannot be made. Common sense, and indirect and anecdotal evidence suggests that bad apples are in the minority, despite the opportunities afforded them in human service environments. The same evidence sources suggest that most workers are hardworking and committed, and sometimes extraordinarily capable. Given that expertise in the human services is ill defined and job eligibility criteria flexible, the sector probably provides a haven for passive or less confident individual actors at all levels of responsibility – avoiding or escaping more demanding entry, accountability and performance expectations. The inexperience of sections of the workforce, particularly in demanding and complex areas, such as child protection, has been noted in many of the investigatory and commission reports mentioned in Chapter 1.

Workers with some formal educational may not have been particularly well served, although as Pope and Bouhoutsos (1986) have shown, lack of education is not a major contributing factor in malpractice. The knowledge base and educational offerings of the human services are fragmented and uneven (Staller and Kirk 1998), easily construed as 'common knowledge' (Abbott and Wallace 1998), derived from an uncertain knowledge base, 'over-organized, under-whelming in . . . expectations, and inferior in product' (Stoesz 2002 p. 21) and relatively easy of admission (Barker and Branson 2000). McDonald (2007) argues persuasively that dissonance and probably confusion is created in students through their education due to a lack of connection with the realities and demands of human service work life. Patti (2003) argues that education does not prepare graduates well for management in the human services. These arguments raise an intriguing question about the legal liability of educational institutions due to claims from graduates who are inadequately prepared for their work, or from employers or clients who have the same view. However, no known human service cases have considered this question in Australia.

Individual responsibility is the prevailing paradigm in law. Legal understandings and responses to unlawful (especially criminal) conduct are very comfortably centred on the individual. Individuals can face legal action by the state. Individuals exercising statutory authority commonly face quasi-legal review processes for decisions that are allegedly either procedurally or substantively unlawful. Very occasionally, individuals may have to contend with a civil suit. Law is a product of society's desire to explain, determine moral culpability and lay blame, and this is carried out most satisfyingly through identifiable individuals. However, people and circumstances that sit behind the mishap or misdeed are shielded. In the words of Merry and McCall (2004 p. 242), 'singling out an individual actor – sometimes one who occupies a relatively junior position within a highly complex organisation – may obscure the real nature of responsibility for an incident'. The law is ill equipped to deal with groups, teams and other combinations of people (eg on teams in health, see Magnusson 2007). An individual whose behaviour breaks the law and is detected, faces prosecution regardless of the contextual factors that may have contributed to their conduct – the individual is at fault, and is charged and sanctioned if found guilty. The individual's team will not be charged, although other individuals in the team might be. Neither will organisational or environmental factors be accorded a central position in law. A limited airing of these factors may occur during legal activity, in sentencing submissions in particular, but in the final analysis the individual accused stands alone.

The centrality of individual responsibility is qualified to some extent by the notion of vicarious liability in law – that is where responsibility for the unlawful behaviour of an individual may be attributed to another who, in turn, had responsibility for and control over that individual. The most common and (for present purposes) pertinent relationship that invokes vicarious responsibility is that of employee and employer. Organisations can be held liable for actions of employees who err while going about their employer's business. Vicarious liability may apply if there is a breach of a particular statute that provides for it. For example, if a worker acts in a discriminatory manner in breach of legislation that makes that behaviour unlawful, their employer may be deemed to have contravened the relevant Act. Vicarious liability may also apply if the behaviour of employees can found a civil suit against the agency. There are statutory limitations on vicarious liability, which are associated with an organisation's reasonable efforts to prevent the offending behaviour and whether or not it occurred in the course of work.

Vicarious liability is the subject of robust policy debates in law and it exercises courts (eg Luntz and Hambly 2006), particularly in cases where new types of relationships are involved. Contractors and contracted service providers, which are increasingly common in the human services, are not comfortably accommodated in traditional understandings of vicarious liability. The following chapters describe cases in which vicarious liability applies, is argued, contested or appealed, and where secondary legal and or disciplinary actions by the employer against the worker are triggered.

Throughout the chapters of this book, individual human service actors appear as targets of legal action. These actors include individual workers, volunteers, carers, managers, government ministers and decision-making bodies. Decision-making bodies are included here because they are single legal entities that produce individualised decisions and are also composed of individual decision makers. Decision-making bodies, such as parole boards, and guardianship and mental health tribunals, are routinely subject to legal appeals against their decisions – sometimes they too are challenged in civil actions. The decisions of government ministers are similarly subject to legal review and challenge.

ORGANISATIONS

The effect of the work environment on individual worker's behaviour is well documented (for errors in medicine, see Merry and McCall-Smith 2004 and for professional crimes, see Smith 2002), and there is extensive human service literature that shows how pressured, poorly managed and difficult work environments can foster or permit deliberately, passively or inadvertently undesirable behaviour in individual workers and compromise their self-efficacy (Besharov 1985; Braye and Preston-Shoot 2001; Mendes 2001; Lymbery and Butler 2004; Lonne and Thomson 2005; McIvor 2006; McDonald and Chenoweth 2009). This material is not elaborated here, other than several points that bear upon the potential for malfunction and the capacity for managing underperformance. Since Hasenfeld's (1983) influential analysis of human service organisations, the vague goals, the morally ambiguous operational contexts, the uncertain and disputed technologies, and the contested and relatively unrefined effectiveness measures have been repeatedly discussed. Recurring themes have emerged, which are discussed below.

Supervisors and managers in the human services are often inexperienced, and agencies frequently lack depth in performance appraisal, practice auditing and misconduct processes. In the non-government sector, unsophisticated management and organisational systems (eg Lymbery and Butler 2004), underdeveloped human resource practices (eg Lyons 2001), and organisational 'fragility' in terms of financial viability, compliance and accreditation processes (Spall and Zetland 2004 p. 291) are commonly observed. In government agencies and in parts of the non-government sector, increased bureaucratisation and regulation, and the diminished role of professional judgement are widespread (eg Abbott and Meerabeau 1998; Clarke 1998; Exworthy and Halford 1999; Lymbery 2004; Webb 2006).

However, Evans and Harris (2004) argue persuasively that the agency of individual workers (for good and bad) is perhaps less constrained than has been claimed. Staff express feelings of being 'trapped in a cycle of mediocrity' (Lipsky 1980 p. 80) where increased resources are consumed by an ever-increasing demand for services, and ever-increasing complexities in client circumstances over-tax their physical, psychological, knowledge and skill resources. High levels of staff stress are apparent (eg Lonne 2003; Charles and Butler 2004; Coffey et al. 2004) as is low morale, high staff turnover, alienated front-line workers estranged from managers, fraught teams (Pemberton et al. 2007), and worker resistance to or avoidance of organisational demands (eg Jones 2001; Webb 2006).

These features are not unique to the human services, but it may be concluded that there are patterns of organisational confusion and toxicity in the sector, which are preconditions for risk adverse and risky practices, and fragmented, misdirected, and indifferently managed and monitored work.

Some environments are intrinsically more risky than others, because they provide particular opportunities and dangers (Carson and Bain 2008). Many human service workplaces are potentially dangerous due to:

- their objectives (eg to restrain and reform)
- their client characteristics (eg drug and or violence profiles)
- their service delivery arrangements (eg grouping involuntary or disaffected people in the same place)
- the personal calamities that underpin their functions (eg family breakdown; child protection).

There is a long sociological tradition of commentary (eg Goffman 1961; Foucault 1967; Jones and Fowles 1984) on the poisonous character of some human service settings. For example, secure mental hospitals are notorious for their capacity for distorting the behaviour and mental processes of both staff and residents. Organisational researchers have observed opportunities and structures in some organisations which foster or at least do not inhibit inappropriate staff behaviour (eg on sexual abuse in the catholic church, see White and Terry 2008). This commentary is paralleled by equally relevant psychological research showing, for example, the power and role of authority in influencing human behaviour towards harmful conduct (eg see Milgram 1965; Haney et al. 1973).

Newer models of service delivery have also been criticised; for example, many community care settings group together and abandon disadvantaged people assessed as low risk (eg Scull 1984; Kemshall 2002). Risk is also endemic in residential and other human service worksites, where clients have very little power compared to staff, opportunities for predation are high and work is carried out in relative isolation (Stanley et al. 1999; Wangmann 2004; Stein 2006; Terry and Ackerman 2008; White and

Terry 2008). Much human service activity is, as Pithouse (1998 p. 6) states, 'unobserved and uncertain'. It is commonly assumed that human services for children and other vulnerable individual attract predators. The legal writer Hall challenges this 'honey pot' assumption and proposes a 'crucible' hypothesis described thus (Hall 2000, 2006 p. 138):

> ...the combination of isolation, power imbalance and hierarchy is con-
> ducive to the development of internal cultures in which abuse becomes
> normalised, creating abusers among susceptible adult staff and vulnerable
> child residents.

In her view, settings in which vulnerability, secrecy and discretion prevail may create predatory behaviour.

Thus, mishaps and or misdeeds can be triggered, shaped, ignored in the making or promoted by organisational settings. There are cases and reports included in this book that have arisen from prisons and children's residential and other human service services, where the negative impact of the service environment is marked and acknowledged. Nonetheless, the environment itself is very unlikely to be the focus of legal action, although it may be profiled in quasi-legal investigations. In general, individuals within a setting may be targeted in actions by the state and the organisation responsible for the setting may be subject to a civil suit.

There are some specific statutory breaches with which managers and or their agencies can be charged, based on their own behaviour and some-times that of their employees if vicarious liability applies. A few examples crop up in the following chapters. However, as will be shown Chapter 3, managers seldom face criminal charges unless they have personally acted with the requisite intent. Organisations, more than workers, face civil suits for injury caused by their operations as it is generally thought that they will have deeper pockets than individuals from which to pay damages. Civil suits in the human services are, however, rare. If managers oversee a work environment that is chronically dysfunctional and injurious, and people in it experience serious harm, a full-scale investigation and exposure of their role may ensue. However, reactions of this kind, as will be seen later, are not automatic. Generally, unless a set of conditions that support scandal are present, managers and organisations can escape attention. Even if a scandal develops, legal charges do not always follow. Supervisors and man-agers do not figure largely in this book, although organisations, including government departments, are quite well represented.

Government departments and authorities warrant special comment. As indicated in Chapter 1, there is a vigorous debate in law about defensive practice and the desirability or otherwise of legal immunity for public authorities who function in socially contested arenas (eg see Feldthusen 1998; Brennan 2003; Wangmann 2004; McIvor 2006; Freckelton 2007a). The need for operational efficiencies, limited resources and the wide responsibilities of public bodies have to be weighed by courts against important individual freedoms and rights. This very difficult balancing act tests them – as McLay (2004 p. 154) says in respect of child protection, Australian courts 'have struggled with creating a coherent theory of government liability in general'. Legal debates that complement the arguments in human service risk analyses are evidenced in a number of cases covered in the following chapters. There is a forceful argument that legal decisions made in favour of private litigants, claiming harm by adverse health and human service events, inhibit and enfeeble future services and practice. This is because the mounting of a defence ties up valuable and scarce public resources, which are then denied to other clients, and often result in retreat to negative risk management policies that fetter discretion.

Besharov (1985) argues the undesirability of successful vicarious liability criminal suits against organisations, because they result in defensive practice and closures of services. McIvor (2006) is similarly of the view that child protection officials must be free of fear of legal action if they are to exercise their decision-making powers in the best interests of all children. Child protection workers will on occasion be too zealous in removing children they perceive to be at risk, or not swift enough in removing children who are at risk. However, legal redress for the individual who has suffered harm as a result of these actions can result in more harm for other and future service users. Faced with the problem of rights of the wronged child or parents, McIvor opts for compensation schemes rather than legal action. Rogers (1994) also writing of child protection in the United Kingdom, recognises the irreconcilability of claims of the harmed individual with those of other and future clients, and argues for parliaments to legislate on this question, rather than leaving it to courts. Similar assertions about the negative effects of complaints processes and disciplinary investigations on service quality have been advanced (on rural health, see Henderson et al. 2005).

However, the exercise of private rights, in particular against the state, is claimed to be a hallmark of a democratic society. This presumes equal access to law, legal assistance and the personal resources necessary to sustain a case, all of which are often absent. Arthur (2006) and others argue that the presumption of defensive practice is a hypothesis unsupported by research data, and that a duty of care and a robust standard for proving breach should reinforce rather than deter good social welfare practice. Whether or not successful legal cases stultify or enhance future practice is determined largely by the extent to which the cases are properly understood by human service decision makers. Without this understanding, human service managers are subject to the rumour mill or may be at the mercy of legal advisors who, if they do not fully comprehend human service responsibilities, may take an overly cautious position. Systematic and regular analysis, and communication about significant human service cases in the human services sector could serve to challenge and improve practice. Whatever the shortcomings of a private suit as a mechanism for compensating for state-caused harm, at present the right to take one exists and, as McLay (2004) observes, it might be the only option for enforcing private rights in some situations. Many of the significant civil cases covered in this book vindicate this position.

Sometimes human service organisations are the direct target of legal interest and sometimes they are vicariously involved. However, even when the organisation is the subject of legal action, the behaviour of individuals within it, especially workers, is always forensically scrutinised.

SERVICE SYSTEMS

Human service systems – policies, education and training programs, networks of agencies, professions and occupations, and service programs – can function in ways that are unsatisfactory and sometimes injurious. There is a wealth of information about child protection (eg Stein 2006), youth support (eg Bessant 2004b; Bessant et al. 2005), mental health (Butler and Drakeford 2005) or disability care (Carter 2006) systems failing or abusing their clients.

Sector-related government policies and inter and intra-organisational policies, procedures and practices do result in eligibility gaps and overlaps, service deficiencies and inadequate protocols for sharing information. This causes problems in managing referrals, monitoring across programs and ensuring seamless and safe service delivery (eg Lymbery and Butler 2004; McDonald and Zetlin 2004; McDonald 2006). Performance measurement and accountability systems in the human services are relatively underdeveloped (eg on child protection, see Tilbury 2006). Nonetheless, as Carson and Bain (2007, 2008) note, the law is not well placed to deal with system deficiencies and malfunctions because it relies on the blameworthy individual. Cases in which a litigant attempts to implicate the state for failing to provide adequate resources or service networks, for particular populations or service systems, are very rare indeed. They are unlikely to get off the ground and unlikely to succeed if they do. One reason for this is the reluctance of courts to encroach on the social policy prerogative of parliaments. In Australia, the absence of human rights law, which entrenches broad social and economic entitlements, is also a factor.

In some circumstances, those nominally responsible for policies and service systems, such as government ministers or the state itself, may be subject to legal challenge, when it is alleged that their actions are unlawful or negligent. Ministers as individual decision makers, ministers as representatives of the state and the state itself are defendants in a range of cases addressed in this book.

ACTS – MISHAPS AND MISDEEDS

What mishaps and misdeeds occur in the human services and how endemic are they? Research is limited in regard to these questions. Mistakes, misconduct and other less-then-ideal practices and events are notoriously difficult to scrutinise in any arena. Even more so in an arena where so much inherently ambiguous business occurs in private with vulnerable populations (who are not likely to complain).

In the human services, such acts may be unnoticed, unadmitted, or may not be recognised as problematical, and will ostensibly leave no traces. They may be a low priority for potential complainants experiencing multiple and overwhelming life difficulties. Social norms change, such that acts that are unacceptable in one era are not in another. Acts that have been occurring for a long time may only emerge into public and professional consciousness in a later time period – a well-documented phenomenon in relation to the abuse of children (Wangmann 2004; Stein 2006).

Research about mishaps and misdeeds in the human services is sparse, often dated, generally focused on the individual wrongdoer and lacking in comparative findings, and predominantly conducted in North America. Research that is available often focuses on only one component of the human services arena – one professional group (eg social work), one field of practice (eg child protection) or one aspect of unsatisfactory conduct (eg sexual misconduct). Legally mandated in-depth enquiries are, by definition, focused on a single adverse event, agency or subgroup of workers. Nonetheless, the data viewed together suggest an outline of the picture.

There is a wide spectrum of adverse events in the human services, ranging from the serious (including death and sexual assault) to the less serious in both commission and effect. A Canadian review of crime (Moulden et al. 2007) reports that 10% of adults who sexually offended against children were employed as child care providers, but larger numbers were caring for children informally. One in six witnesses during the Australian Inquiry into the Separation of Aboriginal and Torres Strait Islander Children from Their Families reported sexual abuse while in human service care (Wilson 1997; Wangmann 2004). However, despite what is known about the extent and opportunities for sexual and other predatory activity in the human services, it is not possible to conclude that this behaviour is actually more prevalent there than elsewhere. Australians Sampford and Blencowe (2002 p. 257) comment in relation to professions in general that 'professional work falls into a normative continuum of which crime is only a small part' and in the absence of data to the contrary, this can be applied to the human service professions. It is also not known if crime is on the increase, as some events attract more public attention now than previously (Hayne 2002) and elicit more definite responses.

It is just as difficult to accurately depict other less dramatic mishaps and misdeeds in the human services, although there are some indirect sources of data. There are data from professional associations relevant to social work, for example, but they are generally North American, dated, limited to members of associations and based on complaint or insurance claims, both notoriously unreliable measures of mishaps and misdeeds because:
- only some adverse events result in complaints or claims
- claims may not concern breaches
- claims may not be investigated because an association's by-laws place them beyond jurisdiction
- claims may be categorised differently by different researchers and bodies
- there can be discrepancies between the number of complaints lodged and the number of complaints finalised.

Comparisons between total numbers of complaints are fraught because numbers reflect the size and coverage of the profession, association or sector. Nevertheless, complaints and claims findings can still be contextually informative.

Besharov's (1985) study of insurance claims arising in relation to the National Association of Social Workers (NASW) in the United States between 1965 and 1985 is frequently cited. He found that there were more claims against individuals than there were against agencies. For claims against individual social workers, sexual impropriety was the most frequent, followed by incorrect treatment. For claims against agencies, improper child placement was at the top of the list, followed by sexual impropriety. Pope and Bouhoutsos (1986) start their major overview of sexual impropriety with an estimate of one in 10 male therapists engaging in sexual intimacies with clients. Berliner (1989) reported on NASW cases alleging individual or agency violations of ethical standards between 1979 and 1985 and found that 25% of sustained complaints were about social worker conduct. Eight per cent of these concerned sexual misconduct, with the majority of these involving private practitioners. Twenty-seven per cent of complaints were about responsibility to colleagues, and 28% were about wider professional responsibility to the profession, organisation and to society. Reamer's (1995) study of NASW insurance claims between 1969 and 1990 placed incorrect treatment at the top of the cause list, followed by sexual impropriety and then breach of confidence. Incorrect treatment that masked the need for or delayed necessary intervention made up a large proportion of the treatment category.

Strom-Gottfried (2003) analysed NASW complaints between 1986 and 1997 and found no evidence that they were on the rise in that period. The majority of complaints were filed by clients, but supervisors and employees also filed against each other. Men were much more commonly targets of complaints and associated with ethics violations, a finding supported by Ellard's (2001) conclusions about sexual infractions among Australian professionals (not including social workers or other human service groups). Strom-Gottfried found fewer complaints about private practitioners than other workers, but when they were accused, there were higher rates of proved violations among them. The most common complaint she found involved sexual activity followed by dual relationships and other boundary violations. Ringstad's (2005) self report survey of NASW members found one-quarter of respondents admitting to committing an assaultive or aggressive act, predominantly psychological, on clients.

In Australia, Murray and Swain (1999) analysed 94 queries from social workers and members of the public between 1992 and 1996 to the ethics committee of the Victorian branch of the AASW. Many of the queries related to confidentiality and privacy. Another large proportion of the queries, presumably from social workers, concerned employment matters (eg quality of supervision, and treatment and rights of clients). More recently in 2004, the AASW itself reported an attempt to analyse the 149 enquires it received in an eight-month period in 2003. The study was hampered by the limitations of the AASW's own data as they did not include a detailed breakdown of the content of the enquiries. It did, however, find that since 1999, nine social workers have been declared ineligible for membership of AASW. Some of the nine resigned before the conclusion of an investigation and some were non-members who are now precluded from future membership.

Information collected by registration boards for professions such as psychology, which operate partially within the human services, also provide data on the issues that result in formal responses. Hammond and Freckelton (2006), for example, reviewed the complaints made to the Psychologists Registration Board of Victoria between 2000 and 2004, and found that the highest number of complaints concerned inadequate standards of practice and inaccurate or biased reports, followed by breaches of confidentiality and dual-role conflicts.

Health and community services complaints authorities in Australia collect relevant information, as do special population bodies (eg children's, guardians). These bodies will be revisited in Chapter 8. Again, the data must be approached cautiously as the mandates of the bodies vary (eg some only cover the health domain) and they collect, investigate and report information differently, depending on their legislative remit. In addition, bodies that cover health and the community services do not routinely separate out complaint information for each sector – when they do, it is apparent that public health services and hospitals dominate the complaint statistics. Nonetheless, such reports are useful indicators about events or actions that prompt citizens to complain about service delivery and about systemic problems in the relevant sectors. Table 2.1 shows the most common complaint categories dealt with by these bodies, as recorded in their most recent annual reports.

Treatment complaints are the most prevalent across the jurisdictions, and include concerns about medication, diagnoses, rough treatment and unskilful or incomplete treatment. The access to services category includes matters such as delay, refusal of service, discharge arrangements and no service. The professional conduct category includes complaints about breaches of standards, worker impairment and or incompetence, illegality and sexual impropriety. The communication category includes worker attitude, wrong or inadequate information, absence of caring, inconsiderate or undignified service and failure to consult. The pattern of data from these bodies is similar to that provided by the Aged Care Complaints Investigation Scheme under the *Aged Care Act 1997* (Cth) for the period 2007–2008 (Elliot 2008) where the most common cause of complaints was personal care (analogous to treatment), the third-most common about communication, the fourth about staff and the fifth about abuse.

Professional or occupational classification is not reported consistently in relation to complaints to these bodies, but it is on record that in the

Table 2.1 *Issues of complaints to health and community services complaints bodies*

Jurisdiction annual report year	Data source	Sector	Most prevalent issue	Second-most prevalent issue	Third-most prevalent issue
ACT 2007–2008	Human Rights Commission	Health[1]	Treatment	Professional conduct	Communication
NSW 2006–2007	Health Care Complaints Commission	Health	Treatment	Professional conduct	Communication
NT 2006–2007	Health and Community Services Complaints Commission	Health and community services	Treatment	Access to services	Communication
Qld 2006–2007	Health Quality and Complaints Commission	Health	Treatment	Access to services	Communication
SA 2006–2007	Health and Community Services Complaints Commissioner	Health and community services	Treatment	Access to services	Communication
Tas 2006–2007	Health Care Complaints Commissioner	Health	Treatment	Access to services	Professional conduct
Vic 2007–2008	Office of the Health Services Commissioner	Health	Treatment	Communication	Access to services
WA 2006–2007	Office of Health Review	Health	Treatment	Access to services	Cost

[1] Disability and children's services data not summarised numerically.

2002 to 2006 period, 2% of the complaints received by the Health Care Complaints Commission in New South Wales concerned unregistered practitioners. Just less than 20% of this small group involved complaints against social workers, and a similar proportion is given for counsellors and therapists (NSW Health 2008). An intriguing inconsistency is evident in the annual report of the Health Care Complaints Commission of New South Wales, which reports on psychologists – although treatment concerns were most prevalent across the total figures (Table 2.1), 60% of complaints about psychologists related to professional conduct and only a small proportion to treatment. Competence was the largest contributor to the professional conduct category, followed by written reports and certificates. There were also a number of complaints about illegal practices and breaches of confidence. The discrepancy between the figures for psychologists and the other professional groups reflects the fact that psychologists are not involved in invasive medical and drug treatments (Health Care Complaints Commission 2007 p. 22).

It is unknown whether this pattern of complaints against psychologists is reflected more widely across the human services, but it is consistent with data about worker conduct in the professional association material previously covered. It may be hypothesised that factors associated with workers and their behaviour in sectors other than health are more significant for service users, because intervention approaches and methods are less tangible.

In Western Australia, more than 80% of disability complaints related to non-government, not-for-profit services (Office of Health Review 2007) – although it is possible that these services provide the bulk of services in that state. Of all disability complaints, the highest number concerned service quality, then communication, followed by service withdrawal, and the majority of complaints, whatever their type, arose in accommodation services. The ACT Human Rights Commission report comments on the complex circumstances and problems experienced by most disability complainants and their fear of speaking out (Human Rights Commission 2008). The South Australian Health and Community Service Complaints Commissioner notes in the 2006–2007 annual report (South Australian Health and Community Service Complaints Commission 2007 p. 5) that only approximately 5% of people speak out about things that go wrong for them in health and community services because they lack information, fear retribution or do not think that their complaint will influence a well-defended service.

What is the relationship between these types of mishaps and misdeeds and the law? How are wrong or injurious deeds categorised in law? Why is

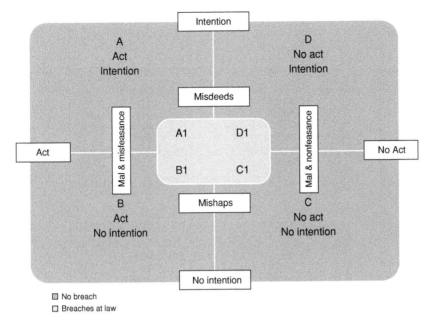

Figure 2.1 Mishaps and misdeeds in context

it that legal action is sometimes possible, but often not. The relationships between three major variables – the act, the intention and the breach – form a framework for approaching these questions:

- The act – the law is tuned for positive acts rather than failures to act, but a failure to act can have dire consequences.
- The intention – did the actor or actors intend to act in the way they did, were they aware of unlawfulness and the risks and consequences of actions, and were the actions avoidable? The mental dimension, or understanding of the elements of the act, is very important in determining culpability in criminal law, and in civil liability actions (although from a different approach) where the foreseeability of the harm is at issue.
- The breach – no matter how offensive or improper or morally questionable the act, it will not invite legal interest unless it is in breach of legislation or can found a common law action.

The interaction of these three variables produces a range of differently characterised situations, each with a complex set of legal implications and related nomenclature. A diagram of the relationships between these variables and the resultant situations is displayed in Figure 2.1.

Figure 2.1 locates the small number of acts that invite legal scrutiny (light grey) within the wider context of all acts (dark grey). The commissions or

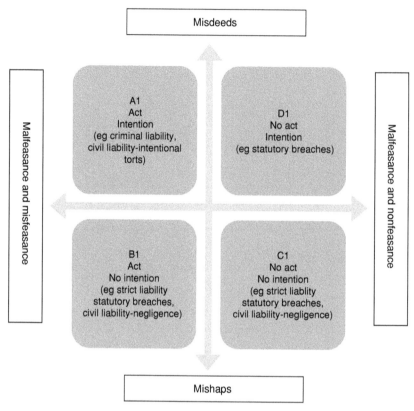

Figure 2.2 Typology of mishaps and misdeeds – breaches at law

omissions which fall within the dark grey areas of quadrants A–D may be ill or otherwise intentioned or unintended, harmful, neutral, helpful, morally or ethically questionable, but none of this matters to the law because they are outside the parameters of a legal breach. Acts that fall within the breach parameters (light grey) are the focus of this book. These are further detailed in Figure 2.2.

In quadrants A1 and B1 in Figure 2.2, acts that constitute violations of sort some have been committed. They are commonly described as misfeasance or malfeasance. Malfeasance (quadrant A1) is the doing of a wrongful or illegal act with awareness of illegality and intention (eg raping or stealing from a client). Misfeasance (quadrant B1) is the doing of a legal act badly or inappropriately, or in a manner that causes damage or loss without awareness or intention of illegality (eg using permitted restraints on a client, but seriously injuring the restrained person). Misfeasance also covers the following examples: wrongful sacking of an employee, removing a child from its parent because of erroneously premised concerns about its safety, wrongful refusal of a benefit due to inaccurate interpretation of a piece of legislation, or actions that result in the dissemination of a critical piece of sensitive personal information. These violations, although intended as actions, do not intend unlawfulness or injury.

Quadrants D1 and C1 in Figure 2.2 depict omissions that are malfeasance if they are unlawful. For example, an individual may misconstrue the degree of discretion permitted them, and intentionally not comply with a statutory reporting requirement (D1). Or, an individual may not report because they are unaware of any law that obliges them to do so (C1). If an omission is potentially lawful, whether it is intentional or not, it is considered to be nonfeasance. For example, an agency might intentionally ignore requests for information from another agency about a client who subsequently harms a third party (D1). Although this omission is not unlawful, it results in harm that may have legal consequences. Or, an agency and its workers may fail to notice that an aged client is not eating and is suffering from malnutrition, and thus fail to act (C1). This omission is not inherently illegal, but it results in harm and may attract legal liability.

Quadrant A1 of Figure 2.2 is relevant to criminal law, other statutory breaches which require a mental element, and intentional torts. The acts therein may also give rise to civil liability. Many of these legal possibilities apply to quadrant D1 as well. Criminal law has traditionally required the performance of acts, but with legislation increasingly including crimes such as criminal negligence, it can be included here. Where special relationships exist (eg fiduciary and contractual ones), knowingly failing to act may constitute a breach of a statute and can also attract the civil law. Strict liability crimes and statutory breaches that do not require a mental element (eg erroneous administrative and employment decisions and negligence claims resulting from damage done by acts without intent) are relevant in quadrant B1. In quadrant C1, breaches of statutes that compel action and strict liability crimes are relevant, as are civil actions such as negligence where failure to act causes damage. Acts or events that fall in any or all of these breach quadrants can also result in quasi-legal investigations, which can result in disciplinary action against the workers involved.

Although misdeeds and mishaps are not words with legal meaning, here they are used in the interests of linking the commentary in this chapter with the material in the chapters that follow. They are also intended to assist human service readers with legal thinking. In Figure 2.2, quadrants

A1 and D1 are here designated as misdeeds because the mental element indicates that the acts are done or not done knowingly, deliberately or recklessly. The omissions and commissions within quadrants B1 and C1 are designated as mishaps because of the absence of intention, although they may be no less injurious.

In this chapter, the arena and the actors of interest have been identified, and a typology of mishaps and misdeeds offered. The following chapters turn to the law and consider in more detail how it operates in relation to human service events that breach ideals or the law.

Part 2
Mishaps and misdeeds through a law lens

3 Public law of general application

RELATIONS BETWEEN LEVELS of government and between government and citizens are regulated by public law. In public law, cases are brought by the state against citizens, or by citizens against the state, when either has not met their public law duties. Although the historical distinction between public and private law is now blurred, as is the distinction between state and private entities, it is still useful for setting the parameters of this chapter. This chapter considers statutory law concerning public order and offences against the state. Human service actors are potentially subject to public law of general application in society.

CRIMINAL LAW

In every jurisdiction in Australia, common law and legislation designate as offences certain commissions, omissions and states, generally accompanied by mental intention (mens rea), or recklessness or criminal negligence.[1] Human service workers (and sometimes agencies) who engage in conduct proscribed by this law (eg dishonesty, causing death, physical violence, sexual contact, drug activity, corruption in public office) may find themselves the subject of charges prosecuted by the state.

Although criminal laws apply generally in society, increasingly they include special provisions for people in positions of trust, such as human service workers. For example, s 49 (5) and (6) of the *Criminal Law Consolidation Act 1935* (SA) make it an offence, and allow for imprisonment for 10 years, for guardians and teachers to have sexual intercourse with

---

[1] On criminal law, for example, see Bronitt, S. and B. McSherry (2005). *Principles of Criminal Law*, 2nd edn. Sydney: Lawbook Co.

a person under 18 years of age, or for anyone to have sexual intercourse knowingly with someone who has an intellectual disability, such that they cannot understand the consequences of sexual intercourse. Sections 51 and 52 of the *Crimes Act 1958* (Vic) cover sexual contact with a person of impaired mental functioning by a medical, or other therapist, or by providers of special programs (ie residential care staff), and consent is no defence. Section 66F(2) of the *Crimes Act 1900* (NSW), like the Victorian legislation, is directed at service providers who have sexual intercourse with people with an intellectual disability.

Some United States jurisdictions have gone further and enacted sexual exploitation statutes that criminalise any sexual contact between psychotherapists, including social workers, and all adult clients (eg Pope and Bouhoutsos 1986; Kagle and Giebelhausen 1994; Bullis 1995; Kane 1995; Sloan et al. 1998; Corey et al. 2007). These sexual exploitation provisions, which are not a feature of Australian law, may be of doubtful use according to McMahon (1997 p. 191), given 'the inefficiency of existing criminal sanctions'. Her assertion in 1997 that there had been no successful prosecutions in Victoria based on s 51 of the *Crimes Act 1958* (Vic) regarding sexual relations between therapists and people with an intellectual disability, still holds. Wilson (2002) refers to the reluctance of prosecutors to pursue such offences, and the irony of a law designed to protect people who by virtue of their mental characteristics may be unconvincing witnesses in criminal courts. However, since 2002 there have been a number of cases in Victoria on s 52 of the Victorian Crimes Act, two of them suggestive of a more robust prosecution position. In *DDP v Barnes* [2007] VSCA 51, a sentence imposed on a residential care worker who pleaded guilty was appealed by the state, albeit unsuccessfully. In *DDP v Scott* [2004] VSC 129 the crown appealed, again unsuccessfully, against the dismissal of charges against a residential worker in the lower court.

In North America, there are also examples of individual social workers who have faced criminal charges when children have died while on their child protection case load. Regehr (2001) outlines two Canadian cases in which criminal negligence charges were laid against social workers, both finally acquitted, for failing to protect children. A number of commentators from the United States (see Besharov 1985; Alexander and Alexander 1995; Pollack and Marsh 2004) have detailed a small but growing number of successful criminal prosecutions in similar circumstances. As far as can be ascertained, there are no such cases in Australia. Child protection legislation in this country does provide workers with some immunity from legal action that may result from their activities in good faith under the Act. For

PUBLIC LAW OF GENERAL APPLICATION | 51

instance, the *Child Protection Act 1999* (Qld) s 22 provides civil, criminal and administrative process immunity for honest notifications under the Act, immunity from claims of breach of professional ethics and standards of professional conduct, and defences to defamation and breach of statutory confidentiality actions.

Although some Australian human service workers have faced special criminal provisions, more have been charged with criminal offences of general application for commissions somehow connected with their work. Sexual offences against clients are one such example as evidenced by the spent conviction appeal case of *R v Tognini and Maguire* [2000] WASCA 31, where the second defendant, a senior staff member of a Salvation Army rehabilitation centre, was charged under s 323 of the *Criminal Code* (WA) which carries a penalty of five years and found guilty of indecently assaulting an adult female resident. He had been released conditionally, but in the cited case, the spent conviction order was put aside. That conviction, as will be seen, has implications for future employment in the human services.

The case of *Dalton v Department for Families and Communities* [2006] SAWCT 31 reveals a different set of circumstances invoking the criminal law. In this case, the social worker manager was pursuing a claim for psychological injury caused by work. The injury claim was stalled over a dispute about production of documents related to suspicious work financial transactions approved by the social work manager amounting to $1.3 million. An affidavit from the police tendered in that case attested that criminal charges under the *Criminal Law Consolidation Act 1935* (SA) would be laid against the social worker in respect of those transactions.

The question of criminal liability of human services organisations, as opposed to individual workers, is more complicated. Traditionally, 'the organisation' has confounded criminal law because criminal liability has been predicated on natural persons, guilty minds and the prospect of imprisonment. It becomes complex when an abstract entity and multiple people (and minds) are involved, particularly as they are often far removed from the event that invokes the criminal law. However, increasingly corporations are being prosecuted rather than individuals within them (eg Fisse and Braithwaite 1988) and provisions for corporations are being made in Acts that specify offences. The *Corporations Act 2001* (Cth) details some offences that involve the application of the Commonwealth *Criminal Code Act (1995)*. The potential for corporate criminal liability is expanding as regulatory law of this kind develops, particularly liability in relation to deaths or serious injury in workplaces, environmental damage and financial collapse.

52 | MISHAPS AND MISDEEDS THROUGH A LAW LENS

An organisation may be held directly liable if the person acting, most likely a senior manager or director, is the corporation for legal purposes. For example, s 258 of the *Children and Young Persons (Care and Protection) Act 1998* (NSW) states that where corporations contravene the Act, the directors will be liable unless they can show that they exercised due diligence, did not know of the contravention or could not influence the corporation against the contravention. Front-line staff may represent a company under the wording of some legislation. For example, ss 26 and 27 of the *Children's Services Act 1996* (Vic) require staff and proprietors of a children's service to ensure that reasonable precautions are taken to protect children from hazards that might cause harm or injury, and that adequate supervision is supplied at all times. Intention is not indicated in the wording of the legislation and proprietors are named. In 2003, a three-year-old child got out of an ABC childcare centre in Melbourne and was later found wandering in the street by neighbours. ABC Developmental Learning Centres Pty Ltd, not the staff concerned, was prosecuted under the sections of the Act and was found guilty of inadequate supervision. The company appealed in *ABC Developmental Learning Centres Pty Ltd v Wallace* [2006] VSC 171, claiming that the staff were responsible for the criminal actions as there was no evidence of systemic breakdown. The company's appeal failed and the magistrate's view that the company was responsible for the criminal failure of its staff was upheld.

There has long been provision for corporate offences for directing unprofessional conduct. This is now of interest in health as service delivery is increasingly corporatised (eg Wilson 2002). There is also now an emerging acceptance in law that a corporation can commit sexual offences, either as a secondary party or as a primary party, through, for example, causing the act to be committed (Lanham et al. 2006). As the international research of Gibelman and Gelman (2004) on non-government agencies shows, there is firm evidence that human service organisations have been involved in embezzlement, fraud, theft and other financially related criminal activity, and that individual workers, trustees and directors have faced criminal charges as a consequence.

An organisation might be held directly or vicariously liable for the criminal acts of employees, if the employees were acting within the scope of their work, with authority, with the requisite state of mind, and if the relevant legislation intended the application of vicarious liability (Bronitt and McSherry 2005). Corporations can be liable directly under provisions of the *Criminal Code Act 1995* (Cth) for the criminal acts of employees if the corporate culture was such that criminal acts or non-compliance

PUBLIC LAW OF GENERAL APPLICATION

with relevant provisions was tolerated, condoned and permitted (Bronitt and McSherry 2005). However, this is only relevant to federal offences. In Australia, some jurisdictions (eg ACT) have taken a cue from the *Criminal Code Act 1995* and enacted industrial manslaughter legislation that provides for imprisonment. In other jurisdictions (eg SA), occupational health and safety legislation has been strengthened to allow for strict liability (ie no guilty mind necessary) criminal prosecutions, heavy fines and even imprisonment of employers for deaths at work (Hall and Johnstone 2005; Sarre and Richards 2005).

It is unlikely that employing organisations could be found directly or vicariously liable in the sorts of criminal cases outlined earlier against individual workers – the activities in those cases were not furthering the employer organisations' objectives, did not result in deaths and were not authorised, directed or committed by directors of the organisations concerned. However, the emerging appreciation in the criminal law of organisational culpability – for unhealthy corporate culture that nurtures and condones wrong behaviour – raises tantalising possibilities about the criminal culpability of human service organisations. So many of the major human services scandals have emerged in workplace cultures that involved the complicity or involvement of senior staff, or at best their denial that they knew of other staff members' activities. There are parallels between a culture that sustains the conditions, and is thus criminally liable, for worker deaths or environmental damage, and one that 're-abuse(s)' (Gillingham 2006 p. 86) or engages in 'sanctioned abuse' (Stein 2006 p. 16) of vulnerable children and young people. However, there are many obstacles to immediate legal expansion here. The presence of guilty or recklessly indifferent minds is difficult to establish in this context and social policy considerations will continue to deter legislation to make welfare organisations strictly liable for the criminal acts of employees.

An agency may face accreditation and funding difficulties as a result of worker actions. Company directors may also face personal industrial action if their workers commit crimes, as evidenced by a director of nursing in a retirement village being sacked as a result of staff assaults on residents (AAP 2008c). The agency may well face a civil action built on its vicarious liability for the criminal behaviour of its workers or its own criminal negligence, but the action will take place under different law – often much of it in private. All that said, individual human service workers facing criminal actions are very exposed and isolated. It is the behaviour of the worker that is scrutinised in a public courtroom and the prosecution will attempt to push workplace culture to the background, while foregrounding the

MISHAPS AND MISDEEDS THROUGH A LAW LENS

guilty intention and acts of the individual. In addition, the employing organisation and coworkers will generally attempt to distance themselves from the charged worker.

Moloney and Another v New Zealand and Another (2006) 235 ALR 159 is an illustrative example of the position of workers relative to the employing organisation (in time, media profile and legal action) when criminal behaviour is alleged. In this Australian Federal Court case, Fathers Moloney and Garshow of the Order of St John of God Brothers were appealing an extradition order that would see them returned to New Zealand to be tried under the *Crimes Act 1961* (NZ). They were facing charges for multiple offences allegedly committed more than 20 years ago when they were caring for disadvantaged boys at the Order's boarding school in Christchurch, New Zealand. The charges included committing sodomy and doing indecent acts on boys under 16 years. Madgwick J's judgement (at 162–3) recounts that the Order had in 1999 paid money to a victim of another former Brother in New Zealand for similar offences and in 2002 had agreed to pay more than $3 million to victims of similar behaviour of other staff in Victorian institutions run by the Order in Australia. Although these payments were attended by significant media attention, the negotiations about the details of the events and the damage that occurred would have been conducted in private. A criminal trial in New Zealand would, in contrast, have detailed in a public arena the minutiae of the Brothers' alleged behaviour with the boys. The result of the Australian case was the quashing of the lower court decision – the two Brothers were released to remain in Australia.

Mounting a defence in a criminal case can be emotionally and financially exhausting. It is reported that a youth policy officer who pleaded and was found not guilty in 2007 in South Australia of 20 counts of indecent assault and unlawful sexual intercourse with eight young boys in his care has to date accrued legal fees of $2 million dollars (Walker 2008).

Acquittal in a criminal case may leave lingering doubts about a worker's character, which will stall their career. A plea or a finding of guilt in a criminal case may result in a conviction and a penalty, which in the case of serious offences, can be a jail sentence. Both consequences are likely to compromise a worker's employment future, either through employer prejudice, or legal impediments. Those found guilty of specific offences in New South Wales and Queensland may be placed on the child protection registers under the *Child Protection (Offenders Registration) Act 2000* (NSW) and the *Child Protection (Offender Reporting) Act 2004* (Qld), respectively. Persons on these registers are precluded from child-related employment under Part 6 of the *Commission for Children and Young People and Child Guardian Act 2000* (Qld) and checks are required under the *Commission for Children and Young People Act 1998* (NSW).

Police checks that reveal offending history are now a regular feature of human service employment. Unsatisfactory criminal record notices can result in preclusion from work. Under the *Working with Children Act 2005* (Vic), people working with children must have a current assessment notice. It is a criminal offence for a holder of a negative notice to apply for child-related work (s 34). Negative notices arise from specified pornography, sex and drug offences.

The facts and finding in *XD v Department of Justice (Occupational and Business Regulation)* [2008] VCAT 118 illustrate how a criminal record can impede a later human service career or interest. The adult applicant in that case had committed serious rapes, one on a minor when he was about 20, and had spent a number of years in jail as a result. More recently he had been working in a voluntary capacity with a child-related charity. He was refused an assessment notice under the Victorian Act and in this 2008 case was asking the Tribunal to direct the Secretary to give him an assessment. Despite solid referees, including a positive one from both his welfare worker and the director of the charity in question, his application was refused, largely on the basis of the seriousness of his crimes. In contrast, the foster carer in *PEH v Department of Justice (Occupational and Business Regulation)* [2007] VCAT 470 did finally get an assessment notice that would allow him to continue in his work, despite a criminal record and a negative notice at first attempt. He had been found guilty of consensual carnal knowledge of a 13-year-old girl when he was 19 years old, 46 years ago. He had also been in jail for dishonesty offences before the age of 24, but had lived an 'exemplary life' (at para 18) since then. In the instant case, the assessment notice was awarded by the Tribunal, who determined that children in his care would not be at risk of sexual or physical harm. The seeking of the necessary assessment notice however resulted in the full disclosure of the details of his long distant criminal history.

Similar legislation was proclaimed in Western Australia in 2006 as the *Working with Children (Criminal Record Checking) Act 2004*, under which it is an offence for people without a current assessment or with a negative assessment to apply for child-related employment. It is also an offence for a child-related work employer to employ someone whom they know to have a conviction or pending charges for specified offences, someone with a negative assessment, or without a current assessment. It is not only child-related work that a criminal record may have an impact on – under

MISHAPS AND MISDEEDS THROUGH A LAW LENS

the *Aged Care Act 1997* (Cth) ss 10A.1 and 10A.2, a person convicted of an indictable offence is disqualified from being one of the key personnel in an approved provider service.

RISKS OF CRIMINAL CHARGES

There are many powerful reasons why human service workers, agencies and authorities may escape criminal charges – the standard of proof to be satisfied is 'beyond reasonable doubt', which requires compelling evidence provided by credible witnesses to persuade adjudicators or juries of guilt.

Many client victims of criminal behaviour do not report the acts, nor do they want the matter pursued (Wilson 2002) – this disinclination may be even more pronounced when people have been abused by a trusted person or one in authority. Moulden and her colleagues (2007) analysed care provider sexual offending against children through Canadian crime databases, and commented on the secret and trust circumstances of this offending and victims' reluctance to report. Reluctance by complainants to implicate individual workers is common because both positive and negative relationships between workers and clients can serve to stop clients from acting on concerns about human service activity. The client may need or fear the worker, feel sorry for them (Preston-Shoot 2000) or believe that the worker is only 'doing their job' (Jones and Alcabes 1989).

The activities and focus of investigating bodies and the legal processes involved may further weaken complainants' resolve to pursue criminal action, and lead to cases being compromised (eg on child complainants of sexual abuse, see Eastwood 2003). For example, as reported in the *Weekend Australian* 13–14 October 2007 (p. 1 and p. 7), it was alleged that a 14-year-old inmate of a youth detention centre in Queensland was raped by other inmates in 1988. She claimed that she was not interviewed properly by centre staff at the time, not given a medical examination and not interviewed by a later commission of enquiry.

> By the time the police became involved, she had decided to drop the complaint. 'I didn't think any one would believe me', [A] said, 'I was also getting all these threats in there. I was worried that something would happen to me if I spoke to the coppers' (p. 7).

Hall (2000 p. 164) tells of plaintiffs in residential sexual abuse cases being dissatisfied with criminal action against the workers involved because the process 'ignores the culpability of the "authorities" responsible for putting him [sic] in a position to be abused and then keeping him there... ignoring, even ridiculing, his efforts to get help'.

Even if a report is made, there may be few or no credible witnesses. Although evidence Acts in Australia have now generally abolished corroboration warnings to juries (eg *Evidence Act 1995* (NSW) s 164), the available evidence still may not be strong enough to convict. Many victims of human services conduct have already been damaged before contact with the human services and can present as confused and unconvincing witnesses.

There are often long periods of time and many intervening events between the criminal behaviour, the report and the trial. Sometimes the damage caused by the criminal act makes a plaintiff unable to come forward. If it is a summary offence, statues of limitations may apply, such that charges cannot be laid after a period of only a few months. For more serious, indictable offences, charges can be laid at any time, but evidential problems might include witnesses' memories fading regarding places, names, people and events; loss of records; and unavailable or untraceable witnesses. In the case outlined above – *Moloney and Another v New Zealand and Another* (2006) 235 ALR 159 (the *Moloney* case) – the offences alleged were committed between 1971 and 1980 and charges were laid in 2003.

The irony of the *Moloney* case is that intervening events – such as out of court settlements with other victims, encouragement of victims to go to the police, victims' support meetings and lobbying work done by advocates – all of which were carried out by the Order in good faith to satisfy current wisdom about healing, actually compromised conditions for a fair trial of alleged perpetrators. This was because of 'cross-fertilisation of complainant's statements' (para 101). The extradition was disallowed in the *Moloney* case because all of these things, along with the possibility of a joint trial in New Zealand (where delay warnings in trials are not present) would make it 'unjust or oppressive' (at para 142).

Efforts of the police and the Crown may also compromise a successful criminal prosecution. This was one of the matters considered in *Littler* [2001] A Crim R 512, which was an appeal against a refusal of stay of criminal proceedings. There the defendant was charged in 1996 with a number of sexual assaults on boys that allegedly occurred while he was working in the Marist Brothers Westmead Boys' home in the 1950s. At the time of the appeal, the defendant was 74 years old and ill. While detailing the health and memory problems of the defendant, and the evidential deficits caused by the time elapsed since the alleged offences, Adams J (at 515–6) commented on the gaps in the Crown case and the apparent failure to seek out and present relevant witnesses and evidence. It was unanimously decided in that case that a fair trial could not ensue and the indictments were permanently stayed.

A related point is that directors of public prosecution are reluctant to proceed with cases where a conviction is unlikely. Although cases may be morally deserving, resources may be too limited to risk on cases that are based on legally questionable evidence. The prosecution guidelines from the South Australian Office of the Director of Public Prosecutions provide an example of the matters that are taken into account in the decision to prosecute (South Australian Office of the Director of Public Prosecutions n.d.). These include the:

- possibility of evidence being excluded
- reliability of admissions by the accused
- reliability, credibility and impact of witnesses and their capacity to withstand cross-examination
- reliability and coherence of identification evidence
- degree of conflict between eye witnesses' evidence
- possibility of appearance of fabrication of a false story
- availability and competence of witnesses and statutory limitations placed on getting and evaluating their evidence
- public interest in prosecuting, considering issues such as seriousness of the alleged offence, aggravating or mitigating circumstances, the 'staleness of the alleged offence', the existence of public concern about the offence, the attitude of the victim and so on.

Finally, when criminal behaviour is evident, employers, employees and colleagues sometimes act in concert to avoid publicity. This is common when organisational corruption is involved; the culture supports both wrongdoing and silence, and the activity is "victimless" (Douglas 2006 p. 178). If an individual worker has transgressed, that person may agree to resign quietly – anecdotal evidence from human service employers suggests that some erring workers may even be provided with good references to help them on their way. This morally indefensible behaviour may also have legal consequences as exemplified in the education case of *VMT v The Corporation of the Synod of the Diocese of Brisbane* [2007] QSC 219. This case concerned a plaintiff sexually abused by a teacher in a state school 24 years previously. Before that, the teacher had taught in an Anglican school where he was also accused of touching girls inappropriately. At the first school, when confronted by the principal, he resigned and was given a positive reference that did not mention the sexual behaviour and in fact described him as 'maintaining the highest possible standards' (at para 4). This reference helped him obtain teaching work with the education department where the assaults referred to in the 2007 case allegedly took place. The plaintiff sought to sue the Anglican Synod in negligence for providing the reference, and her extension of time application was granted.

A 'culture of silence and fraternity' (Freckelton and Molloy 2007 p. 377) characterises most professional groups. Wilson (2002) reports studies in the United States that show that medical doctors often do not report misconduct by their peers for fear of reprisals or bad publicity for the profession. Sampford (2002) explains intra-professional tolerance for misconduct through fear for oneself in the same situation (ie through empathy or the idea that one may be in the same situation one day). Berliner (1989) notes the reluctance of National Association of Social Worker panels in the United States to substantiate sexual misconduct complaints against social workers. McMahon (1997) comments on the reluctance of Australian therapists to report colleagues if a criminal charge will ensue. Because human service agencies have been subject to damaging public scandals in recent years, they can face a dilemma when a staff member behaves criminally. Do they report and risk added public condemnation for their failure to select and manage staff properly, or do they come to a quiet agreement about resignation or termination?

OTHER STATUTORY LAW OF GENERAL APPLICATION

Human service bodies are subject to many legislative regimes proscribing and prescribing behaviour. Some provide for criminal penalties for breaches. Much of this legislation is of general application, but have particular relevance to human service work, including legislation on:
- occupational health and safety
- discrimination, vilification and harassment
- consumer protection
- information privacy and records management
- public service.

OCCUPATIONAL HEALTH AND SAFETY LEGISLATION

Every jurisdiction in Australia has legislation for safe workplaces and safe work practices. This legislation places obligations on both workers and employers about environments and conduct that can lead to or minimise the risk of injury at work. Serious injury and workplace death can lead to very severe penalties. In the case of death, there is the possibility of the organisation facing separate criminal charges under industrial manslaughter legislation or criminal law. Although some human service facilities meant to be 'home like' can be inappropriately constrained by this sort of legislation (eg Milligan and Stevens 2006), others are inherently dangerous so that the protective aim of this legislation is important.

If a worker engages in unsafe work practices, penalties will apply, and the employer is likely to step in and take remedial or disciplinary action. If the employer has breached requirements, the state may take action and fines may result. *Inspector Lewis v The Crown in the Right of the State of New South Wales (Department of Juvenile Justice)* [2006] NSWIRComm 8 demonstrates agency culpability under this type of law. Here youth officers in a juvenile justice centre were injured by residents who assaulted them with brooms and tools. This was the second such incident and the employer department had a previous conviction. It pleaded guilty to a charge under the *Occupational Health and Safety Act 2000* (NSW) s 8(1), which requires employers to maintain a safe work environment. It had failed to ensure that tools were removed from detainees, and safely stored and accounted for. The department was fined $165 000.

DISCRIMINATION, VILIFICATION AND HARASSMENT LEGISLATION

Human service actors may also fall foul of a number of pieces of legislation designed to prohibit discriminatory, offensive or harassing behaviour. Every state and territory has at least one anti-discrimination Act; several have religious vilification laws, and the Commonwealth has a number of relevant discrimination Acts.[2] The *Disability Discrimination Act 1992* (the DDA) (Cth) has a relatively wide scope of operation. Human service actors may face a complaint lodged under a Commonwealth or state discrimination Act if it is alleged that they discriminated directly or indirectly on the grounds and in an area (eg employment, service provision) within the scope of the relevant Act. These Acts are not fully rights based (Thackrah 2008), are limited in their coverage of grounds and areas, and are only activated by a complaint by the person believing him or herself wronged. As Brown FM said in *Power v Aboriginal Hostels Limited* [2004] FMCA

---

[2] *Sex Discrimination Act 1984, Racial Discrimination Act 1975, Disability Discrimination Act 1992, Age Discrimination Act 2004, Human Rights and Equal Opportunity Act 1986.*

PUBLIC LAW OF GENERAL APPLICATION | **61**

452 (at para 24) the 'DDA is not directed at achieving a fair outcome but rather is addressed at prohibiting discriminatory conduct on the basis of a disability'. Nonetheless complaints under this sort of legislation are relatively common and can embarrass human service actors, given their declared values of respect and inclusivity.

Generally, proceedings under these Acts take an investigation and conciliation approach, but penalties apply for noncompliance with orders made by the relevant tribunals or courts. It is common for the Acts to contain provisions that make employers vicariously liable for the actions of their workers in the course of authorised work, unless employers have taken reasonable steps to minimise the discrimination. Thus, agencies generally will be the target of the complaint, even though an employee or other agent may have been the offender but proceedings may be taken against both parties (eg *Anti-Discrimination Act 1991* (Qld) s 133). The Acts specify if civil or criminal liability applies to contraventions; for example, both are generally non applicable under the Victorian *Racial and Religious Tolerance Act 2001* (s 5) but the *Criminal Code 1995* (Cth) applies to all offences against the Commonwealth *Racial Discrimination Act 1975* (s 6B).

Under this sort of legislation, clients, carers and other affected parties take actions for perceived discriminatory or harassing omissions or commissions by human service actors. The case reports of the relevant state and territory tribunals, the Commonwealth magistrates and the Federal Court of Australia (and the Australian Human Rights and Equal Opportunity Commission prior to 2000) in respect to Commonwealth legislation, and the papers put out by the Australian Human Rights Commission (AHRC),[3] contain numerous examples of discrimination complaints by clients. The case of *McAlister v SEQ Aboriginal Corporation* [2002] FMCA 109 demonstrates individual client action under federal legislation, and the interplay of discrimination law and industrial consequences when a worker misbehaves. In that case, a woman claimed that she had been sexually discriminated against and sexually harassed by a field officer of an Aboriginal legal service when she sought assistance. She alleged that the employee agreed to help her if she would have sex with him and that he later stalked her. The AHRC was not able to conciliate her complaint and she pursued it in the Federal Magistrates Court of Australia. She was very distressed by the incidents, sought medical and counselling treatment and moved from the town. The worker denied the allegations. His employer argued that the claimant would not have been eligible for their services

---

[3] http://www.hreoc.gov.au

and thus any wrongful conduct on the part of the employee was not in connection with his employment. It was held that the worker's conduct was in contravention of the *Sex Discrimination Act 1984* (Cth) and, while he had been providing a service in connection with his work, the agency had a defence in that it had taken 'all reasonable steps to prevent sexual harassment happening' (at para 143). The field officer was dismissed. The action against the agency was dismissed and the field officer was ordered to pay $5100 in compensation to the complainant.

Employees and volunteers also lodge complaints against their human service employers for discriminatory behaviour. For example, *Perera v Commissioner of Corrective Services* [2007] NSWADT 115 illustrates a worker complaint about an immediate supervisor. In that case, a Sri Lankan-born corrective services officer was moved to a less desirable work location on a different shift in a prison because his area manager said 'I am not a racist but I cannot understand you' (at para 51). He complained that this comment and a set of related actions by the manager had discriminated against him on the grounds of race, and victimised him under the *Anti-Discrimination Act 1977* (NSW). The shift-change comment and complaint was substantiated, although his other complaints were not. The defendant department was ordered to pay him $1000.

In the case of *Walsh v St Vincent de Paul Society Queensland* (no. 2) [2008] QADT 32, a long-term volunteer, non-Catholic, and elected president of a St Vincent De Paul Conference working with refugees, alleged direct discrimination in her place of 'work' on the grounds of religious belief. She had been told by an area president of the Society that she must become a Catholic, or resign her position and leave the Society. The Society argued, among other things, that the *Anti-Discrimination Act 1991* (Qld) permitted it to impose genuine occupational requirements for a position and that it was a religious body under the Act in which the president was engaged in religious observance and practice. After careful analysis of the constitution documents of the Society, the Tribunal determined that it was not a religious body under the Act, that the president was not engaged in religious observance, and that being Catholic was not essential to the carrying out of the president's duties. The Society was ordered to pay the woman $27 500 general damages for pain, suffering, intimidation and embarrassment, and for expenses and ongoing psychiatric treatment.

Would-be service providers may also mount discrimination claims on the basis of their preclusion from involvement in the human services. For example, a gay couple recently succeeded in a claim under the *Anti-Discrimination Act 1977* (NSW) that it had been discriminated against by a Christian religious organisation which rejected it as a foster family on the grounds of sexuality (Public Interest Advocacy Centre Limited 2008). Discrimination cases appear throughout this book.

CONSUMER PROTECTION LEGISLATION

Human service agents who supply products, make claims about the results of intervention or represent their qualifications, specialisations and capacities, may be subject to the provisions of sale of goods Acts and fair trading Acts in each jurisdiction, or the *Trade Practices Act 1974* (Cth), if they operate as a corporation. Under these legislative regimes, products or goods that are sold must be as they are described, do what is claimed and be of merchantable quality. Those selling the services must not engage in misleading, unconscionable or deceptive claims or behaviours with clients/consumers. This sort of legislation is particularly relevant to private practitioners and profit-making organisations, as illustrated by the case of *Australian Competition and Consumer Commission v Rana* [2008] FCA. In this case, a company sold new age treatments made up of massage, vitamin supplements, coffee enemas and other alternative therapies for thousands of dollars and claimed that they cured cancer. The company directors were prosecuted under the *Trade Practices Act 1974* (Cth) and found to be guilty of misleading, unconscionable and deceptive conduct. The company director Rana, the initiator of the treatment regimes, was sentenced to six months' imprisonment. This was a serious case, but very many more modest spurious claims and sales may not have consequences under consumer protection legislation because of limited investigation and prosecution resources (ABC 2007).

INFORMATION PRIVACY AND RECORDS MANAGEMENT LEGISLATION

In Australia, there is a plethora of Acts across jurisdictions that address information privacy, record handling, storage, access, disposal, data linking, spent convictions and surveillance in health, mental health, adoptions, corrections, public welfare and more. These overlay civil actions challenging information mismanagement, to be covered in a later chapter. Many of these pieces of legislation focus on health and all of them are predicated on the value of discretion and privacy when it comes to sensitive personal information. They are of particular relevance to human services activity and form the core of Chapter 11.

The most significant piece of national legislation relevant to sensitive personal information is the *Privacy Act 1988* (Cth) (the Privacy Act) overseen by the Office of the Privacy Commissioner.[4] The Privacy Act contains 11 information privacy principles (IPP) covering consent, collection, quality, use, anonymity, security, and access to and disclosure of personal, including sensitive, information. The Privacy Act originally covered the information-handling operations of Commonwealth and ACT government departments, and was amended in 2000 to cover private organisations with an annual turnover of more than $3 million and all those offering health services.

Under s 6 of the Privacy Act, the meaning of health services includes assessing, recording, maintaining or improving an individual's health, diagnosing illness or disability, and treating illness or disability. Arguably, a range of human service activities, even those performed outside of conventional health agencies, would be included within these criteria. Schedule 3 of the amended Privacy Act contains 10 national privacy principles (NPP), which elaborate on the obligations detailed in the IPP. The Privacy Act is directed at organisations, but s 6C deems this term to include individuals. The Federal Privacy Commissioner is empowered to investigate complaints about privacy misdeeds by Australian and ACT government agencies and by private organisations that fall within the jurisdiction of the Privacy Act, and to make determinations about practices that may breach the Act or be permitted on the basis of public interest.

New South Wales, Victoria, Tasmania and the Northern Territory have general personal information protection legislation, and the other states and territories have administrative regimes with similar aims. In the ACT, the *Human Rights Act 2004* enshrines privacy as a human right. The ACT, New South Wales and Victoria have also enacted legislation devoted to health records and privacy. The *Health Records and Information Privacy Act 2002* (NSW), for example, specifies that offences other than corruption ones under the Act are to be dealt with summarily (s 74) and it provides for good faith legal immunity (s 72).

Statutory duties of confidentiality are imposed by a range of Acts in each jurisdiction that have relevance to human service operations in particular fields of practice beyond health (eg corrections and community services). Some examples of these appear in Chapter 4. Not all non-government human service organisations will be caught directly under Commonwealth, state or territory privacy-related legislation. However, privacy compliance

---

[4] For privacy rights laws, see http://www.privacy.gov.au

is required of many under their service contracts with government. Others, for example, in the job placement and rehabilitation areas, have voluntarily opted in to compliance with the Commonwealth Privacy Act, and register accordingly with the Office of the Privacy Commissioner.

If the recommendations of the most recent Australian Law Reform Commission (2008) review of the *Privacy Act 1988* (Cth) are accepted, a single, rationalised set of unified privacy principles (UPP) will apply to both government and private bodies. In addition, a nationally consistent approach to privacy will be taken, in which each state and territory agrees to enact legislation covering government operations in that jurisdiction, which mirrors the main features of the Commonwealth Privacy Act.

More commonly, organisations and their information management practices, rather then employees, fall foul of legislative regimes designed to protect sensitive information. However, individuals in private practice are vulnerable, and employees whose conduct compromises their employer may find themselves subject to internal disciplinary action. For instance, in *M v Health Service Provider* [2006] PrivCmA 12, a person lodged a complaint with the Privacy Commissioner under National Privacy Principle 2 alleging that a health service provider had disclosed to their partner the types of sexually transmitted disease tests the complainant had undergone. The health service provider admitted that the disclosure had been made by a new staff member, agreed that it should not have happened and apologised. The Privacy Commissioner conciliated a settlement between the complainant and the provider. It can be hoped that the worker concerned was the subject of some intra-organisational scrutiny and that new organisational induction protocols were subsequently put in place.

PUBLIC SERVICE LEGISLATION

Human service workers are bound by the provisions of the *Public Service Act 1999* (Cth) if they are employed by the Commonwealth, or by the equivalent state or territory Act if they are employed by those jurisdictions. Most of these Acts have clauses that prescribe specific behaviour. The *Public Sector Management Act 1995* (SA), for instance, in s 6ZA details duties of employees who have conflicts of interests and specifies civil liability for a contravention. These public service Acts or their regulations also commonly contain general provisions articulating public service values, principles or codes of conduct, all consistent with what would be considered good human service practice. For example, s 9(c) of the *Public Sector Management Act 1994* (WA) says that public sector bodies and employees 'are to exercise proper courtesy, consideration and sensitivity in their dealings with members of the public and employees'. Section 49 of the *Public Sector Employment and Management Act* (NT) specifies a range of behaviours that contravene the Act and will result in a breach of discipline. Proscribed behaviours include disobeying orders, being absent without leave, harassing or coercing other employees and being negligent or careless in the discharge of duties. Breaches, if very serious, may lead to summary dismissal under s 50 or a range of investigatory and less severe disciplinary actions under s 51.

The case of *Cassidy v Department of Corrective Services* [2007] QIRComm 15 illustrates the interaction of a statute specific to human services work, a state public service Act and industrial law. In this case, a prison officer was found guilty by a magistrate under s 112 (2) of the *Corrective Services Act 2000* (Qld), which covers the authorised use of force, for assaulting a prisoner during an over-vigorous physical restraint. He successfully appealed this finding. Meanwhile, the ethical standards branch of the department recommended that the prison officer's behaviour constituted a breach of s 87 (1) of the *Public Service Act 1996* (Qld) as it constituted disgraceful and improper conduct in an official capacity. The Deputy Director General of the department determined that the prison officer was guilty of misconduct and his employment was terminated. In the instant industrial case, where the much of the evidence heard in the criminal court was not available, it was found that the prison officer had used discretion permitted under s 112 (3) of the *Corrective Services Act 2000* (Qld) and that the dismissal was harsh, unjust and unreasonable. He was reinstated, as there was no evidence to suggest that reasonable working relationships could not be restored.

Section 13 of the *Public Service Act 1999* (Cth) contains the Australian Public Service Code of Conduct – breaches can lead to a range of outcomes, including termination of employment and salary reduction. There are provisions in s 13, among others, about honesty and integrity, care and diligence, maintaining confidentiality and proper use of resources. This section, like its state and territory counterparts, has given rise to only a few cases. Breaches do happen, but most are dealt with through the administrative processes set out in the Acts and do not get to court.

One case arising from an alleged breach of s 13 that did get to court is *Hensell v Centrelink* [2006] FCA 1844, involving a Centrelink social worker. She had been subject to a breach of the code of conduct (s 13) investigation as 'it is alleged that you may have dealt with Centrelink customers in an [in]appropriate manner and that you failed to treat fellow staff with courtesy and respect and that you failed to comply with a direction in relation to the wearing of an inappropriate lanyard' (at para 20). Other social workers had raised concerns about her supervision of them, and one lodged a complaint. The investigation considered a number of complaints about breaches of privacy, some from clients, and other matters. In the instant case, the social worker sought and obtained, on the grounds of procedural fairness, an interlocutory order preventing her employer from taking any disciplinary action resulting from the code of conduct investigation until a further court hearing on the matter.

In the *Public Sector Employment and Management Act* (NT) just cited, being found guilty in a court of an offence that affects the employee's employment (s 49 (b)) is also included. Thus, it is possible to see how falling foul of criminal law may have repercussions for the ongoing employment of a public servant beyond those of the criminal law itself (eg imprisonment). If an employee's employment is terminated on the grounds of a finding of guilt, and the termination is contested, there is likely to be a legal argument about whether or not the offence 'affects the employment'. Factors will be considered such as the type of offence, when it was committed and its connectedness to the work being done.

In this chapter, law of general application in society has been addressed. Statutory law of particular relevance to human service actors is turned to in Chapter 4. Its application to and definition of human service mishaps and misdeeds are both canvassed.

4

Public law of particular relevance to the human services

THIS CHAPTER OUTLINES legislation of more general application that places particular duties and obligations on human service actors among others and legislation that is directed primarily at human service activity. Some areas of mainly human service endeavour, especially those involving the exercise of executive government powers and duties through public authorities, are controlled by specific legislation. Obvious examples of these are corrections and juvenile justice, health including mental health, social security, immigration, child protection, family law and adult guardianship. In human services tradition, these were called 'statutory practice areas' – this is something of a misnomer, given the extent of legislative imperatives in all areas of human service practice. This chapter also briefly introduces administrative law, a major category of public law, which defines the powers of authorities (such as the state) and controls the administration of legislation. It ends with a comment on the absence of law concerning licence to practice in the human services.

Proscriptive and prescriptive legislation that is particularly relevant to human service work commonly specifies powers and permissible delegations (including the power to make subordinate legislation), duties, classes of people to whom the Acts are directed, prohibited acts and factors that must be taken into account when making decisions under the authority of the Acts. This type of legislation also declares types of breaches and penalties, and the legal immunities provided for authorised action under the Acts. It sometimes provides for administrative and judicial review processes. These matters are canvassed briefly in this chapter, using examples from child protection, residential care, corrections, social security and immigration legislation.

Child protection legislation is enacted in every Australian state and territory to provide for intervention where children may be subject to abuse and neglect. This legislation covers:

- definitions of the circumstances of concern
- reporting obligations and thresholds
- procedures for investigation, intervention and placement
- state guardianship.

In some jurisdictions, child protection legislation also covers juvenile justice (eg Victoria and the ACT). Each state and territory also has legislation and regulations that cover the administration of correctional services and the management of offenders. Social security legislation, which provides for income support and eligibility, and immigration legislation, which covers the granting of visas, are the province of the Commonwealth under its constitutional powers.

Most human service residential facilities (eg nursing homes, boarding houses, childcare centres, youth shelters, disabled accommodation) are also subject to legislatively based licensing regimes, which prescribe and prohibit acts and, in some cases, set service standards. Failure to comply with the requirements of the relevant Acts can result in loss or constraint of licence, defunding or public naming. However, facility closure is generally avoided if possible, as alternative care placements are so much in demand. Thus, licensing schemes commonly have provisions for the relevant authority to work with unsatisfactory facilities to improve their practices and services.

DUTIES

Human service-specific Acts commonly declare general and specific duties, some directed at individuals and some at statutory bodies. Although the discharge of duties is mandatory, Howell (1998) notes with disquiet that courts have on occasions found in favour of public authorities who have not carried out duties because of limited resources. The effect of this is to make the duty discretionary. New civil liability legislation, addressed in Chapter 5, may or may not mediate this situation. Section 12 of the *Prisons Act 1981* (WA) specifies that officers *shall* comply with law, rules and regulations, and direction, and that they have responsibility to maintain security and make records available to senior departmental staff.

Specific duties concerning security, confidentiality and the rights of prisoners generally are also included in human service-specific Acts. For example, s 11 of the *Corrections Management Act 2006* (Qld) requires that a prisoner, on admission to a facility under the Act, must be informed of their rights, entitlements and duties and that reasonable steps *must* be taken by the chief executive to ensure the understanding of people who are illiterate or do not speak English. The *Crimes (Administration of Sentences) Regulation 2001* (NSW) requires that correctional departmental officers *must* provide written advice to the Commissioner of their associations with offenders (reg 236). Regulation 247 requires that correctional officers *must* report misconduct (allegations or their own sincere beliefs) by other correctional officers.

Youth justice officers, under s 544 of the *Children, Youth and Families Act 2005* (Vic) *must* among other things carry out enquiries in a way that minimally prejudices the reputation of the child and parents. In contrast, the chief executive officer under the *Children and Young People Act 1999* (ACT) *may* take action in relation to reports of disciplinary actions by detainees. The director general under s 51 of the *Children and Young Persons (Care and Protection) Act 1998* (NSW) *must* inform parents about the taking of a child into care and keep them informed of the child's whereabouts.

In the aged care area, the *Aged Care Act 1997* (Cth) Part 4 gives force to 'quality of care principles' with which providers are expected to comply. These principles are further elaborated in accreditation standards monitored by the Aged Care Accreditation and Standards Agency, which may sanction non-compliant providers and services, and provide public reports on its findings.[1]

A range of legislative requirements exist for human service workers to report certain things. For example, in some jurisdictions, certain groups of workers (including social workers and counsellors) are obliged to report their opinion that a person to whom they have been providing professional services and who is in possession of a firearm poses a threat to public safety.[2] The reporting obligation is also generally accompanied by a legislative immunity clause, which protects the reporter from criminal or civil liability. There are also moves in the NT to make it mandatory under the *Domestic and Family Violence Act 2007* for all adults to report domestic violence (McCarthy 2008).

One of the better known legal obligations on human service personnel is that of reporting child abuse and or neglect under the *Family Law Act 1975* (Cth) s 76ZA, or state and territory child protection legislation, and child sexual abuse in Western Australia. The Acts of South Australia, Tasmania

[1] See 'Reports on homes' at http://www.accreditation.org.au
[2] *Firearms Act 1996* (ACT), s 115; *Firearms Act 1996* (NSW), s 79: *Firearms Regulations 1993* (SA), s 20 and r 44; *Firearms Act* 1996 (Vic), s 183; *Firearms Act 1973* (WA), s 23B.

Victoria, the Northern Territory, the Australian Capital Territory and New South Wales specify people who are obliged to report suspicions of abuse or neglect of any child. These provisions vary in detail and scope, but they generally cover a wide spectrum of human service workers and make the obligation mandatory. For example, the *Children, Youth and Families Act 2005* (Vic) specifies (s 184) that mandated notifiers *must* report their beliefs formed under the criteria set out in that section. Under the *Child Protection Act 1999* (Qld) (s 148), departmental and licensed care service staff *must* report suspicions of acts of harm to children in departmental or licensed care services.

Contrary to the belief of many human service workers, they are under no general legal duties to report crimes. Nor are they required to report peer misconduct or impairment. These matters are topical in the health sphere (Freckelton and Molloy 2007) and mandated reporting of doctors (of sexual abuse, drug or alcohol intoxication and behaviour that may harm others during the time that doctors are at work) by their peers has been introduced in New South Wales and is likely to follow nationally.

PROHIBITIONS

There are a great many statutory prohibitions against disclosing information, beyond the information privacy and records management Acts outlined in Chapter 3. Most of the human service practice areas that are highly statutorily regulated are covered by various confidentiality provisions. These may prohibit divulging information about the work of the authority or clients, or may target staff and the media. For example, the confidentiality clauses in the *Health Services Act 1988* (Vic) s 141 prohibit (subject to the exceptions listed) providers and employees in public and private hospitals, other health services and community health centres from giving any identifiable information about patients. The *Mental Health Act 1986* (Vic) s 120A contains similar provisions that are relevant to psychiatric service providers and employees. A breach of either provision is a summary offence. Family counsellors and family dispute resolution practitioners under the *Family Court Act 1975* (Cth) must not disclose information revealed by family members during professional work, unless the Act authorises such disclosures.

In corrections, the relevant Acts commonly detail prohibited conduct for staff members, prisoners, members of the public, corporations or contractors. Regulation 243 (1) of the New South Wales *Crimes (Administration of Sentences) Regulation 2001* states that correctional staff *must not*

MISHAPS AND MISDEEDS THROUGH A LAW LENS

use insulting or abusive language to prisoners or to each other. One can only speculate how many breaches there are of this regulation relative to disciplinary actions taken under it.

GRANTS AND EXERCISE OF POWERS

Corrections legislation generally grants wide powers of control, management and security to the relevant minister and chief executive. These broad powers are commonly delegable to other staff in the department; see, for example, s 271 of the *Corrective Services Act 2006* (ACT). Other powers commonly specified in the Acts cover searches, visits, seizures of properly and the use of dogs and force. Likewise, child protection legislation grants wide powers that are delegable. Section 250 of the *Children and Young Persons (Care and Protection) Act 1998* (NSW) declares that the director general *may* delegate any of his/her functions, with specified exceptions.

Under the *Social Security Act 1991* (Cth) the secretary has powers to make determinations about people's eligibility for benefits, and duties to consider certain aspects in the making of these decisions. These powers and duties are delegated to Centrelink staff, who make determinations about, among many other things, whether people are living singly or in a couple, or as a single person sharing accommodation, the value of assets, whether a person is renting, whether work falls within the definition of seasonal and so on. In contrast, under the *Migration Act 1958* (Cth), only the minister can vary or revoke a residence determination.

DECISION-MAKING CONSIDERATIONS

A good example of a decision-making consideration is provided by the *Social Security Act 1999* (Cth); in relation to forming an opinion about whether or not a person is living as part of a couple, the Act states in s 4 (3) that the decision maker is 'to have regard to all the circumstances of the relationship including, in particular . . .' and a long list, including financial, sexual and social indications follows. The Centrelink community service officer who makes the initial decision is provided with some guidance by departmental policy documents on how to balance and weigh these factors.[3] However, 'the nebulous articulation of the cohabitation rule' (Sleep et al. 2006 p. 143) remains, despite the Act and the decision guides (Tranter et al. 2007). The Commonwealth Ombudsman, faced with

---

[3] For examples of these guides, see http://www.facsia.gov.au

a great many complaints about determinations, has recommended additional policy changes (Commonwealth Ombudsman 2007). Thus, many final questions of determination get to the Federal Court of Australia on appeal from the review tribunals. For example, *Staunton-Smith v Secretary Department of Social Security* (1991) 32 FCR 164 concerns a separated woman who was appealing the cancellation of her sole parent's pension, after she returned to live in her husband's house so that he might share care of their disabled child. It was found that the reasoning of the previous decision maker, the Administrative Appeals Tribunal, did not show that it had considered six other matters specified in the Act, and her appeal was allowed. In the *Migration Act 1958* (Cth), s 54 states that the minister must have regard to *all* the information in a visa application when deciding whether to grant or refuse it.

IMMUNITY PROVISIONS

Human service-related legislation commonly includes immunity clauses. Child protection Acts, as mentioned earlier, generally contain immunity clauses that provide some legal protection for those who carry out work under the Act in good faith and those who make reports of suspected abuse or neglect. Correctional Acts often contain similar good faith civil immunity clauses; for example, s 223 of the *Corrections Management Act 2007* (ACT), and make clear an intention that employer vicarious liability will apply. Section 11D of the *Family Law Act* 1975 (Cth) specifies the immunity of a family consultant. However, the mere existence of an immunity clause will not preclude legal action.

STATUTORY BREACHES

Breaches of these and other Acts that regulate human service activity may be criminal or disciplinary (as specified in the Act itself or in the statutory interpretation Act of the relevant jurisdiction), and the penalties can be significant. For instance, under s 68 of the *Prisons Act 1981* (WA), breaches of the Act constitute disciplinary offences. Similarly, s 248 of the *Crimes (Administration of Sentences) Regulations 2001* (NSW) specifies that misconduct applies to the Regulation. In the case of *Gay v Department of Corrective Services* [2005] NSWIRComm 1212, a prison officer had disobeyed a lawful direction given pursuant to the New South Wales Act by refusing to take a drug test authorised under s 236F of the Act. Disciplinary action, as specified by the Regulation, applied and she was dismissed. That dismissal was not overturned in the instant case. The *Corrections Management Act 2007* (ACT) (s 222) declares that a breach of confidentiality under the Act is an offence that can lead to a 50-point penalty or six months' imprisonment, or both. Similarly the Queensland *Corrective Services Act 2006* under s 339 allows for a penalty of 100 units or imprisonment for two years for an employee who divulges information about prisoner criminal histories or correctional investigations. When individual worker breaches are legislated as criminal, there are likely to be disciplinary consequences as well.

There are also offences under child protection Acts with quite severe penalties. For example, s 241 of the *Children and Community Services Act 2004* (WA) specifies that an employee who divulges information obtained through the administration of the Act faces a fine of $12 000 or imprisonment of one year. Despite community concern about child abuse in recent years, prosecutions under the mandatory reporting obligations are all but non-existent. This sits curiously with evidence that professionals in the United States and Australia, generally aware of their legal obligations, often do not report (Besharov 1985; Bell and Tooman 1994; Blaskett and Taylor 2003). Besharov argues that there are few successful prosecutions in the United States for non-compliance with reporting obligations because of difficulties with proof, belief in the absence of criminal intent, and compassion for workers doing difficult jobs. Finally, he adds that the cooperation of the non-reporter is needed in action against the perpetrators of abuse, and this gives them some practical immunity. In Australia, the reasons for not reporting include lack of faith in child protection authorities, protection of confidentiality, fear of reprisals (Blaskett and Taylor 2003) and confusion about obligations (Goddard et al. 2002). Although there may be some cases in magistrates courts in Australia, and Swain (1998) has reported the commencement of a case against a teacher in New South Wales in 1994, no cases in higher courts could be found currently on the relevant sections in Queensland, the Northern Territory, Tasmania, the Australian Capital Territory or New South Wales. However, there are reports about disciplinary action for failure to report in the New South Wales Department of Education and Training (McDougall 2008).

There is one accessible case in Victoria under the now-repealed *Children and Young Persons Act 1989* (Vic). It is *Herald and Weekly Times LTD v Hassard* (unreported, VSC, Beach J, 8 December, 20 January 1998), which was an appeal against a suppression order, in which it was revealed that a primary school principal had faced a criminal prosecution under s 64 of the Act for failing to report suspected child sexual abuse. The charge had been dismissed over interpretation of the meaning of the words in the Act: 'belief on reasonable grounds' (Swain 1998).

There are two clearly relevant cases under s 11 of the *Children's Protection Act 1993* (SA), which mandates reporting. Both cases illustrate how different laws and penalties may be applied or not, or may invoke other law when misconduct is alleged. The medical practitioner in *Medical Board of South Australia v Chistopoulos (No 1)* [2000] SADC 47 failed to report as required. Although he was not charged with a breach of the statute, he was found by the Medical Practitioners Board of South Australia to have shown unprofessional conduct, including not reporting in respect of his treatment of the child, who subsequently died from injuries inflicted by others. His licence to practice was suspended for two months. The case of *EM v St Barbara's Parish School* [2006] SAIRComm 1 similarly concerns s 11 in a disciplinary (in this case industrial) context. In this case, the applicant teacher had been dismissed after she learned that her husband had been sexually inappropriate with a young boy and had requested the complainant student to remain silent. The court found that the teacher had not been obligated under s 11 in the circumstances to report because the knowledge of the allegation, even if was abuse under the Act, came to her in a social situation outside of work. However she did have obligations under her contract of employment to report her suspicions and to abstain from any sort of action that might suppress the allegation of abuse. It was further found that her attempt to silence the boy may have constituted serious and wilful misconduct. Her dismissal was upheld.

ADMINISTRATIVE LAW

Offences may be committed and penalties apply under the types and examples of Acts just canvassed, but more commonly their interpretation and administration will be disputed. This is the province of administrative law, that major area of public law that refers to the 'principles and procedures by which the exercise of executive government power is controlled and supervised' (Lane and Young 2007 p. 1). Administrative law is particularly relevant to, but not exhaustive of, the legislation covered in the previous section, and decisions about rights and entitlements made under it. Public authorities (and increasingly quasi-public and private bodies) that exercise powers and discretion are subject to provisions of relevant statutes as interpreted through the principles and processes of administrative law. This is a complex area of law that is evolving rapidly as the shape, character, roles and functions of government change, and the distinction between public

76 | MISHAPS AND MISDEEDS THROUGH A LAW LENS

and private bodies blurs. For current purposes, only the skeleton of the law is sketched.[4] The authority, not an individual worker, will generally be named as the defendant party in administrative action, but the functioning of service delivery systems, organisations and individual workers may well be exposed unfavourably in the review processes.

At the heart of administrative law is the requirement that public authorities make decisions that are lawful in their substance and process. These bodies are obliged to follow certain principles in their decision making. They must:

- exercise discretionary power appropriately and take into account only relevant considerations
- make their own decisions and not follow instructions from elsewhere
- not apply policy inflexibly
- work in good faith to further the objects of the legislation
- comply with mandatory legislative provisions
- not be biased or give the appearance of bias in their considerations
- enquire or investigate fully
- comply with the principles of natural justice – that is, they must give the subjects of their decisions a chance to be heard and to rebut negative information about themselves and their cases
- make reasonable decisions based on the evidence considered.

However, Douglas (2006) argues that review courts have become increasingly reluctant to take issue with decisions based on this last ground as it is hard to argue. Also, it may overlap with questions of government policy. Matters of how power has been exercised are more easily scrutinised.

Individuals and organisations aggrieved about the administration of an Act may, for example, allege that a power under the Act has not been exercised or exercised properly, or that it is not delegable. They may believe that a duty has not been fulfilled or that an action is beyond power, or that delegated legislation in the form of regulations and standard procedures has not been complied with. In areas of human service practice, allegations may, for example, claim the unlawfulness of:

- immigration detention
- unauthorised removal of a child from parents
- incomplete consideration of matters before visa refusal
- bias in a prisoner security classification
- withdrawal of a benefit without the chance to refute evidence.

---

[4] Comprehensive reference suggestions: Lane, W. and S. Young (2007). *Administrative Law in Australia.* Sydney: Thomson Lawbook Co.; Head, M. (2008). *Administrative Law: Context and Critique,* 2nd edn. Sydney: Federation Press.

Challenges to administrative decisions occur mostly through administrative review, and sometimes through judicial (ie court) or ombudsman review. Ombudsmen will be returned to in a later chapter. Administrative review bodies make determinations on the merits or facts of a case. In their broadest form, they consider all evidence, including new evidence, and make a decision afresh. They consider the facts of the case, policy issues it raises, relevant law and the challenged decision. In contrast, judicial review only canvasses questions of law and the legality of the decision. This distinction between administrative and judicial review of legal and other mistakes is imprecise and much more complex in practice (Lane and Young 2007 p. 236), but for current purposes it is sufficient.

Independent internal and external administrative review mechanisms are commonly a feature of legislative regimes that endow rights and entitlements. In these cases, relevant public decision makers regularly face actions by parties for alleged non-compliance with the legislation. In all fields of public work, there are increasing numbers of administrative review challenges (Germov 2003) and more and more, bodies not bound by a legislative scheme, are constructing their own internal review processes. All human service actors now and in the future, but particularly those exercising legislative powers, can expect to have their decisions questioned through administrative review challenges. Social security decisions made by Centrelink, for example, are subject to constant and expected administrative review challenges by citizens via a tiered system of review processes (see Carney 2006; Raper 2006). There is a similar review regime in relation to the Australian Government Department of Veterans' Affairs. Decisions made by the Australian Department of Immigration and Citizenship in relation to citizenship are also reviewed through bodies set up by the legislation for that purpose. The prevalence of administrative review is attested to by the existence and case lists of the Social Security Appeals Tribunal, the Migration Review Tribunal, the Refugee Review Tribunal, and the Administrative Appeals Tribunal.[5] Administrative review tribunals are themselves subject to review on questions of law by courts, because the legislative scheme that establishes them sometimes provides for it in a process akin to (but not the same as) judicial review. In the federal sphere, the appeal normally goes to the Federal Court, and in the states and territories to the supreme courts. Public authorities may also be subject to 'pure' judicial

---

[5] Social Security Appeals Tribunal (http://www.ssat.gov.au); Migration Review Tribunal and Refugee Review Tribunal (http://www.mrt-rrt.gov.au); Administrative Appeals Tribunal (http://www.aat. gov.au); Federal Court of Australia (http://www.fedcourt.gov.au).

review, although this is less common and less accessible than administrative review.

Judicial review has had a long history in common and constitutional law, as courts have evolved processes for regulating the actions of public bodies and officials, before the advent of administrative review regimes. Traditionally, the ground for judicial review was that the decision maker had acted beyond power and made a decision that was thus ultra vires. The grounds for judicial review have expanded over time and now include alleged breaches of procedural fairness, decisions made in excess of jurisdiction or in bad faith, and error of law (Clark 2007). Currently in Australia, judicial review and administrative review operate in tandem. In short, judicial review involves courts declaring and enforcing law without reconsidering the merits of the decision under review. It includes reviews of the exercise of statutory power by public bodies or the exercise of inherent prerogative powers by government ministers. Judicial review requires aggrieved parties to initiate a prerogative writ, or constitutional or equitable action, in the relevant court. A writ of certiorari cancels the decision of the official. A prohibition writ prevents a decision being made and a writ of mandamus compels a public body or official to carry out its duties. A writ of habeas corpus releases a person from detention that is illegal. Equitable declarations and injunctions declare the law and enforce legal rights, respectively. Human rights matters will often activate an application for judicial review. Increasingly these have been used to challenge the lawfulness and conditions of immigration detention in the United Kingdom (Sharpe 1989), and they have been used similarly in Australia. There are also examples of courts taking into account (rather than deciding on this basis) human rights principles and Australia's United Nations treaty obligations (O'Neill et al. 2004), in their administrative law judgements.

Legislation may attempt to limit the role of judicial review. Complex legal arguments about the relative powers of courts and governments follow if the limitation clauses are challenged. In recent years, for instance, the grounds for judicial review of immigration matters were limited by legislation as the federal government attempted to contain refugee immigration rights (Crock and Santow 2007). However, some cases still appeared before the courts despite these legislative restraints (Germov 2003), and despite the 'cumbersome, drawn out and expensive' judicial review system (Vrachnas et al. 2005 p. 330). The High Court is said to be limiting the applicability of these legislative limitations (Aronson et al. 2004; Crock and Santow 2007). Judicial review of executive and administrative action is a very complex area of law and legal activity. As stated earlier, courts have

PUBLIC LAW RELEVANCE TO HUMAN SERVICES | 79

traditionally been very reluctant to fetter executive governments' pursuits of policy objectives. As Hilson (1995) explains, they are exercised by what falls within the purview of judicial review and what does not, how to deal with administrative omissions rather than commissions, and the overlap between public and private actions in a world of contracted-out services. It takes a tenacious and well-resourced person, perhaps with the support of an advocacy group, to pursue judicial review.

The case of *Victorian Council for Civil Liberties and Vadarlis v Minister for Immigration and Multicultural Affairs* [2001] FCA 1297, concerning the refugees rescued from a sinking boat in the Indian ocean by the ship Tampa in 2001, illustrates both judicial review and other writs sought in respect of government actions in an immigration matter that has significant human rights implications. The ship had been boarded by Australian troops and had been refused permission to disembark the rescued people in Australia. In brief, in that case, the applicants argued that the *Migration Act 1958* (Cth) applied to the rescuees on the ship, and the government had a duty to bring them to shore and process their application for protection visas. They sought mandamus to enforce compliance under the Act and injunction to prevent the refugees from being expelled. They also argued for habeas corpus relief in that the refuges were detained without lawful authority and should have been released from detention. An injunction and mandamus were also sought by the lawyer Eric Vadarlis to allow him access to the refuges for the purpose of giving them legal advice.

On the first ground, the applicants failed because they did not have sufficient standing (ie connection with the issue in dispute) and it was held that the duties under the Act did not apply to the situation. On the second ground, it was held that the rescuees were held in detention and without lawful authority, and an order for their release onto the mainland of Australia was made. Justice North also noted that the decision was being made at a time of public debate about refugees and that the role of the court was not to interfere in matters of government policy but to 'determine if the government respondents have acted within the law' (at para 7). On appeal (*Ruddock v Vadarlis* [2001] FCA 1329) the majority of the full court of the Federal Court of Australia set aside the orders made by Justice North holding that the government was acting under the prerogative power conferred on it by s 61 of the constitution, which had not been abrogated by the *Migration Act 1958* (Cth). In addition, it had not restricted the freedom of the rescuees who were free to go elsewhere, although as Aronson et al. (2004 p. 758) point out 'this elides the issues of "restraint" and justification of that restraint'. The dissenting chief justice found that the Commonwealth had detained the rescuees unlawfully because their detention was not justified by powers conferred on it under the *Migration Act 1958* (Cth), the applicable source of power in the circumstances. The High Court of Australia refused Vadarlis' special leave to appeal the full court decision.

Disputed administrative decisions may or may not be solidly based in law and fact, and applications for review are certainly not synonymous with errors or poor practice at primary or secondary decision-maker levels. Douglas (2006) laments the absence of comprehensive data on the extent of administrative lapses, many of which are invisible, while canvassing statistics on successful appeals in social security and immigration. Clearly, there are significant numbers of errors made by primary decision makers – Douglas concludes that these are more likely to result from carelessness and ignorance, than what he calls 'extra-legal' (p. 12) intentions. Germov and Motta (2003) provide examples of tribunal members (ie secondary decision makers) who are biased, rude and disrespectful or who make errors of law and fact, some of which are appealed. They observe that there is insufficient training for tribunal members and that there is a pervasive influence of the political context that can undermine the independence of secondary decision makers.

Commentators on child protection work are more forceful about the existence and causes of administrative error at the primary decision-maker level. Public authorities in the United Kingdom are claimed to be regularly 'disregarding their statutory duties' (Braye and Preston-Shoot 2001 p. 48) and Besharov (1985 p. 156) said of United States child protection authorities 20 years ago 'agency regulations and manuals – when they exist – often do not conform to statutory requirements'. The current relevance of this claim to some Australian public authorities is attested to by recent high-profile investigations into the failures of child protection and immigration authorities. The reports for some of them are listed in Chapter 1 and by many of the cases in the following chapters.

The ordinary person faces many barriers to taking any form of administrative review action, despite positive developments in accessibility to administrative review mechanisms. Head (2008) lists among the obstacles limits in the law itself, cuts in legal aid, the rising costs of court and tribunal fees and the geographical inaccessibility of many review bodies. Douglas (2006 p. 59) adds in relation to judicial review that, even if people can afford to litigate, the time delay between the administrative decision and a judicial review court hearing 'could defeat the purpose of bringing the action'. It is well known that many service users and human service clients are intimidated by bureaucracies, unaware of their rights and lacking in the skills required to negotiate even the simplest of administrative appeal processes. Thus, while some tribunal members, ministers, departmental executives and front-line human services staff can experience very uncomfortable times in administrative review processes about their activities, many more who might and perhaps should, do not. As Carroll (2007) explains, although the courts engaged in judicial review cannot evaluate the merits of a decision by a public authority, in a private law case on the same facts, they often scrutinise such decision making in detail. A few people who claim significant harm at the hands of human service systems and actors do mount private law actions – these are turned to in the next two chapters.

REGULATION OF OCCUPATIONAL/ PROFESSIONAL TITLE OR INTERVENTIONS

Unlike the situation with lawyers, physiotherapists, psychologists, medical practitioners and a range of other professional groups in Australia (see Carlton 2008 for a list of allied health professions and legislation), unlike the situation with social workers in some provinces in Canada (Swain 2001), across the United States (Saltzman and Furman 1999; Barker and Branson 2000), and in New Zealand (Orme and Rennie 2006), and unlike the situation with the social care workforce in England (Orme and Rennie 2006; Cornes, et al. 2007; McLaughlin 2007), neither the titles nor core practices of social workers (or human service workers more broadly) are regulated by legislation in Australia. Despite the regulation culture in society (Freckelton 2006g) and the expansion of disciplinary law in other health professions (Freckelton 2004; Freckelton 2007c), the human services remain outside traditional professional regulatory regimes. In the context of the Australian omnibus national registration scheme, covering nine health professions, which commences in 2009 (Carlton 2006; Carlton 2008; Health Workforce Australia 2008), the Australian Association of Social Workers (AASW) has lobbied the Council of Australian Governments (COAG) for inclusion of social work, which is the largest allied health profession in Australia (Australian Association of Social Workers 2004). The AASW's arguments about risk posed by social work have not prevailed to this point, as outlined in Chapter 1, and it remains that anyone can assume the title of social worker. If a person's claims about their qualifications as a social worker are not fraudulent, the state will not act.

In contrast, a registered professional (eg a psychologist) who is charged with a crime or complained about and investigated by a state registration board, may lose their licence to practice. They will then be precluded from representing themselves as psychologists or doing anything that the legislation in that jurisdiction makes the exclusive province of psychologists. They will be publically named by the relevant board. If they do not comply with the prohibitions, they may be prosecuted under the legislation. The irony of the registration landscape in Australia is that the psychologist who acts unprofessionally and has their registration suspended may, with impunity, set up in private practice as a social worker, counsellor or psychotherapist. They may also obtain a job in the human services if an employer is willing to appoint them – they do not fall foul of any applicable criminal record check legislation and a complaints commissioner has not prohibited them.

The disciplinary activities that sit behind the registration cases that follow are not a feature of the human services, psychologists aside, although the misdeeds involved have resonance in this sector. In *Psychologists Board of Qld v Robinson* [2004] QCA 405, a psychologist unsuccessfully appealed suspension for six months and a subsequent 12-month period of supervised practice, for having a sexual relationship with a former client in a correctional centre. The medical practitioner in *A Practitioner v The Medical Board of Western Australia* [2005] WASC 198, who had been fined and suspended for 12 months for gross carelessness and infamous conduct arising from a situation in which he had a personal, religious and sexual relationship with a previous patient, appealed. His suspension was overturned as too severe, and a fine and a reprimand were ordered. In *Bhagwanini v Registrar of the Occupational Therapist Registration Board of South Australia* [2003] SASC 34, the appellant whose registration had been cancelled had been convicted of assuming the title 'occupational therapist' contrary to the *Occupational Therapists Act 1974* (SA), and fined. His instant appeal was dismissed. In *Health Care Complaints Commission v Moore* [2008] NSWPST 2, a psychologist was removed from the register for three years after being found guilty of unsatisfactory professional conduct, including failing to provide adequate and appropriate professional services to a client, and professional misconduct, including failing to observe professional boundaries – giving gifts to the client, entering into a sexual relationship with the client, inappropriately self disclosing, and passing on information about the client.

There are also no equivalent mechanisms in Australia for investigating, determining and making public social worker misconduct, as there is in England under the General Social Care Council registration scheme. Thus, there are no parallels in Australia with, for example, the media release by the United Kingdom General Social Care Council about a social worker who was admonished for breaching a code of practice for social care workers by failing to secure and record movements of the keys and money of a service user (General Social Care Council 2007). The social worker in England who was suspended from the register for two years after having been found guilty of misconduct by advertising herself as an escort through an internet agency with links to prostitution websites (General Social Care Council 2006), would not face this penalty in Australia. Her employer here in Australia may take action, there may be adverse publicity through the media, the AASW may take action if she happened to be a member, but otherwise there would be no legislative obstacle to her continuing work as a social worker.

There is some self and co-regulation in social work in Australia, in that the AASW does endorse some members as mental health social workers for Medicare purposes (Department of Human Services 2003; Macleod and McSherry 2007). Accreditation is allowed for or required of some human service workers under specific legislation that covers a field of practice. For example, migration agents may be registered under s 286 of the *Migration Act 1958* (Cth), and family counsellors and family dispute workers under the *Family Law Act 1975* (Cth) must be accredited through possession of specified vocational qualifications. In some jurisdictions, workers compensation counsellors must be accredited with the state workcover authority. Some legislative provisions specify particular qualifications for the performance of particular functions under the Act, as will be seen in later chapters. Notwithstanding these pockets of statutory regulation, the majority of the human service workforce remains free of state constraints on titles and practices.

Despite the absence of registration legislation, there is considerable concern among policy makers about conduct in unregulated workforces such as the human services (Wilson 2002; Carlton 2003; Department of Human Services 2003; Macleod and McSherry 2007). In addition, there are recent and potentially significant legislative developments in New South Wales, which Freckelton (2008c) and Wilson (2008) argue are likely to be replicated in other jurisdictions in the future. New South Wales has adopted a negative licensing approach to unregistered human service groups, including psychotherapists and counsellors. Under this model, professionals who are not licensed to practice, or who are engaging in unlicensed practices, can have their practice rights curtailed for unsatisfactory behaviour. Standards in the form of a code of conduct for unregistered practitioners are, since mid-2008, prescribed under the regulations of the *Public Health Act 1991* (NSW) and in the *Health Care Complaints Act 1993* (NSW). The code, among other things, proscribes practice while under the influence of drugs or alcohol, use of treatment that lacks an appropriate clinical basis, and sexual or other improper relationships with clients (NSW Health 2008). It prescribes compliance with privacy law, proper record keeping and the maintenance of adequate indemnity insurance. The New South Wales Health Care Complaints Commission is empowered to investigate breaches of this code of conduct and to take disciplinary action against practitioners, including banning them from practice and prohibition orders that place constraints on their practice. An example of what could happen to a human service worker under this regime is shown by the case of the radiographer (not registered in NSW) who was alleged to have indecently assaulted two patients while using an x-ray on them (Health Care Complaints Commission 2008). He was investigated by the Commission, found to be in breach of the code of conduct, and a public statement to this effect was made. This sort of action presumably will have some negative impact on a worker's current and future employment prospects.

There is extensive commentary and debate about regulation and registration models in the health and human services (eg Swain 2001; Allsop and Saks 2002; Baggott 2002; Freckelton 2006f; Cornes et al. 2007; Macleod and McSherry 2007; McLaughlin 2007). The exclusion of the human services from traditional regulatory regimes is based on matters of history, social legitimacy, status, gender, the pluralism of the sector and a belief that human service actors are relatively low risk (eg Jones 1999; Barker and Branson 2000; Healy 2004; Healy and Meagher 2004; Carlton 2006; Kennedy and Richards 2007). There is a prevailing view within the social work profession that it should be registered and the profession does consistently put this position before government (eg Swain 2001; Australian Association of Social Workers 2004). There are also more isolated calls for some form of registration of other sections of the human service workforce; for example, youth workers (Bessant 2004b), counsellors (Pelling and Sullivan 2006) and all mental health personnel (Macleod and McSherry 2007). In general, those aspiring to professional status and improved standards of practice assume registration to be a good thing.

In the context of a focus on misconduct and law, several points may be offered in support of a cautious approach to occupational regulation. Caution is not advocated because the risks of harm through human service activity are low – in fact this position is challenged by the content of this book – but rather, because registration per se does not eradicate misdeeds and mishaps (see Orme and Rennie 2006; see, on medicine relative to social work McInnes and Lawson-Brown 2007). Given the diversity of the human service workforce as outlined in Chapter 2, the registration of social workers alone (or social workers in health only), might advance the status and identity of the profession, but it would not have an impact on unsatisfactory conduct in the majority of human service workers. Nor would registration of social workers result in a social work qualified (and thus regulated) human service workforce, because there are insufficient social work graduates for jobs. Human service workforce and position diversity is on the increase and there is a well-established infrastructure in Australia for the training and education of non-social work human service graduates. Even with occupational regulation, misconduct in the non-regulated sections of the human service workforce is likely to be attributed to social workers by the layperson who does not make fine professional distinctions between those who 'help' or 'care'. These facts confront the social work profession with an ethical, moral and continuing public image challenge. The points made by Cornes et al. (2007) from the United Kingdom about the need to consider professional registration in the context of wider relevant workforce regulation, and the absence of empirical evidence on the effectiveness of registration schemes, are equally salient and persuasive in the Australian context.

Although occupational registration regimes do not prevent misdeeds and mishaps, they do provide mechanisms for investigating workers independently of the employer and for limiting their practice rights, as do negative licensing schemes. Professional registration does not solve the problem of how to determine fitness to practice or the good character of the individual worker. As Freckelton (2004; 2006e) notes, disciplinary boards and courts continue to face the same ethical and procedural difficulties confronted by professional associations in deciding how behaviour in one's private life should impact on one's professional status and rights. After reviewing a number of recent Victorian appeals against board decisions to curtail a practitioner's registration, Freckelton (2007b) concludes that courts sometimes deal very sympathetically with professionals who have misbehaved, to the consternation of the press and pubic.

Professionals who lose or have their practice rights limited often have the knowledge, resources, supports and financial incentives to pursue appeals and creative legal actions. For example, it is reported that a Victorian doctor charged with rape and indecent assault, and subsequently suspended and then restricted in his practice by the Medical Practitioners Board of Victoria is currently challenging that suspension under Victorian human rights legislation (AAP 2008a). In contrast, many of those who have suffered at the hands of professionals face all of the obstacles to legal action and complaint, under both positive and negative occupational registration schemes, outlined to date and in the following chapters. Last, but by no means least, occupational or workforce regulations that might (perhaps should) have a place in the future of the human services, focuses on misdeeds and mishaps at the level of the individual worker and risks minimising failures at system and organisational levels.

This chapter has summarised the extensive array of statutory law that applies to human service actors and acts. The state prosecutes when breaches of these laws, or of the laws outlined in Chapter 3, are alleged. What happens when it is not the state, but another citizen, who alleges a breach of some sort and seeks legal satisfaction? Private suits are the focus of Chapters 5–7.

5 | Private law and suits

RELATIONSHIPS BETWEEN CITIZENS, and private relation-
ships between citizens and the state and other bodies, are the province of
private law, in which individuals mount actions about private interests.
The main category of private law of relevance to the human services is civil
law, which includes family law, torts (ie the law of wrongful and actionable conduct), and contract law. The same set of facts may found both a
public and private law action, but the law applied in each area, the legal
procedure, the standard of proof and the possible outcomes will be different (see, for differences and overlaps in more detail Trindade et al. 2007
pp. 6–8). In civil law actions, the standard to be satisfied by the plaintiff is
'on the balance of probabilities'. Claims are generally heard in civil courts
and occasionally special civil tribunals. Most commonly, successful claims
result in compensation in the form of monetary damages, rather than some
form of required action, as in public law.

Much of the small amount of civil legal activity about alleged wrongdoing in the human services is conducted in private negotiations – very
few cases get to court. Anyone wanting to know about outcomes of private
settlements will need to rely on media and advocacy group reports for information. Although these private processes may be preferable for the plaintiff,
they do not, as Mann (2003) points out, ensure proper transparency about
wrongdoing and its consequences. High-profile cases on abuse in church
and charitable organisations, and immigration detention, often settle out
of court, without the facts declared or the legal questions tested. This may
be because the law seemed clear or the social and reputational imperatives
necessitated cessation of action and payment of damages. For example,
it is reported that Vivian Alvarez-Solon, the Australian citizen who was
wrongfully deported from Australia to the Philippines in 2001 settled for

$4 million out of court in 2006 (*Daily Telegraph* 2007). Victims of a Church of England paedophile priest and youth worker in South Australia are also said to have so far been awarded $4 million (ABC 2006b). Cornelia Rau's period in Baxter Immigration Detention Centre is reported to have resulted in her receiving $2.6 million in compensation (Merritt 2008). It has also been claimed that the delays in her compensation claim arose from complexities in the dual responsibility of the Australian Government and the private contractors operating Baxter Detention Centre (The *Australian* 2007). The privatisation of the human services brings with it additional legal complexities when suboptimal performance is alleged.

The sorts of events or behaviours in the human services that might give rise to a private law action are, as with public law, harm-causing commissions, misfeasance or malfeasance. Omissions (or nonfeasance) that cause harm also appear, although the law (particularly tort law) is traditionally uneasy about them (Brennan 2003; Trindade et al. 2007). Human service transgressions and resultant injuries alleged in civil law cases might include assaults, harmful restraint, imprisonment, invasion of personal space or body, infliction of psychological and physical distress, failing to prevent harm from occurring, causing harm through precipitous action, abuse and neglect in care, failure to follow up or refer, improper treatment, indiscretions with personal information and client death.

The list of possible grievances is enormous, although translating them into a viable civil law action is another matter. Areas of human service practice that are heavily regulated by statute feature largely, but not exclusively, in private law claims in Australia. Child protection (see McIvor 2006; Freckelton 2007a), corrections (Todd 1992), immigration (see Freckelton 2005; Mackay 2006; Penovic and Sifris 2006) and mental health (Freckelton 2003; Scott 2006) are all sources of private law cases, both overseas and in Australia. Likewise, failures in state, religious and charitable institutional care of children and young people have founded multiple civil suits (eg Olsson and Chung 2004; Senate Standing Committee on Community Affairs 2004). Civil law, particularly torts actions against child protection authorities and sometimes individual workers, are relatively common in the United States (eg Besharov 1985; Pollack 2003; Pollack and Marsh 2004). Civil actions against authorities are on the increase in the United Kingdom (Brammer 2003; Brayne and Carr 2003; Brennan 2003; Williams 2004; Arthur 2006; McIvor 2006; Carroll 2007) and evident in Canada (Regehr et al. 2001; Filippelli and Goodman 2005) and New Zealand (Tobin 1999; Todd 2004). There have been a number of recent significant civil cases in Australia concerning damage caused in child protection practice.

There are many different types of possible civil law actions. The distinctions between them, and the currency and character of each one, is evolving and often unsettled in critical areas. The nuances, developments and complexities of law in the civil law area are significant, and authoritative texts are best consulted for detailed information.[1] In the words of Trindade et al. (2007 p. 1):

> Sometimes one and the same act can constitute more than one tort; and because the various torts have different elements, there may be room for argument about which tort (if any) has been committed.

Torts actions may overlap with each other and with other civil causes of action. They may parallel public law actions on the same facts. Thus, it is not uncommon for many actions to be mounted in a single case – if a more advantageous legal claim fails, yet another may succeed. This is particularly so when a case is attempting to extend the law and the 'ingenuity of the legal profession' has been activated (Spigelman 2006 p. 15). In cases testing and claiming human and civil rights, creative and unusual actions are often mounted, as in public law, sometimes because this may be one of the few legal avenues available to the plaintiffs. For example, when the Bakhtiyari children escaped from immigration detention at Woomera in 2002, their subsequent legal action was mounted under family law. The High Court, in *Minister for Immigration and Multicultural and Indigenous Affairs v B* (2004) 219 CLR 365, eventually ruled that the Family Court did not have jurisdiction to order the release of children from immigration detention. The stolen generation case of *Trevorrow v State of South Australia* (no 5) [2007] SASC 285, which is covered in more detail in the next chapter, also illustrates the use of multiple actions. On the one set of facts, the plaintiff argued misfeasance of public office, false imprisonment, breach of duty of care, and breach of fiduciary and statutory duties.

This chapter addresses the present state of torts law, the place of public authorities in private law action, targets of private legal action and the risks of a civil suit in the human services.

---

[1] For example, see McGlone, F. and A. Stickley (2009). *Australian Torts Law*, 2nd edn. Sydney: LexisNexis Butterworths. Trindade, F., Cane, P., et al. (2007). *The Law of Torts in Australia*, 4th edn. Melbourne: Oxford University Press. Walmsley, S., Zipser, B., et al. (2007). *Professional Liability in Australia*, 2nd edn. Sydney: Lawbook Co.

FLUIDITY OF TORTS LAW

Torts law is in flux – its future trajectory in a number of areas pertinent to human service claims is uncertain. As the courts have struggled over time with difficult social questions of fault, blame, liability and restitution, they have expanded the recognised range of legal duties, conduct and relationships that can sustain a torts action. This natural evolution of the common law has led to community concerns about increased insurance and professional indemnity costs. In the 1990s in Australia, this concern culminated in the report, *Review of the Law of Negligence* (Ipp Report) (Commonwealth Treasury 2002), which, among many other things, recommended legislation that would:

- make it harder for people to sue
- confine types and amounts of damage
- limit the liability of public authorities, good Samaritans and volunteers
- expand the defences available to defendants.

Subsequently, each of the states and territories enacted civil liability legislation (Table 5.1), along with provisions relevant to duty of care, causation, mental harm (which is extremely relevant to human service activity), standards of practice for professionals and the liability of public authorities. The significant details of this legislation vary across jurisdictions.

Thus, a pattern of subtly non-uniform and quite restrictive legislation has been superimposed on an expanding common law base, and there is consternation among law commentators regarding the new legislation and how it will be interpreted in relation to pre-existing common law developments (eg Cappa et al. 2003; Mendelson 2004; Dietrich 2005; Spigelman 2006; Carroll 2007). As Cappa et al. (2003) say:

> The High Court has sought and continues to develop a principled approach to negligence that denies tenuous claims. It is perhaps ironic that, at the very moment the High Court is succeeding in developing a coherent and predictable common law, the legislature has sought to take the initiative and to retreat from some of the Court's initiatives (p. 215).

It will be some time before cases interpret the clauses of the new Acts and the status of significant pre-legislation human services cases are tested (Freckelton 2002). In this volatile and murky environment, this and the next two chapters endeavour to map themes and cases relevant to the human services. Many of the cases have been heard, or concern events that occurred, prior to the enactment of the civil liability legislation.

Table 5.1 *Civil liability legislation in Australia*

Jurisdiction	Civil liability legislation	Duty of care provisions	Causation	Mental harm	Standard of care for those professing skills and professionals	Liability of public authorities
ACT	*Civil Law (Wrongs) Act 2002*	ss 42–4	ss 45–6	ss 32–6	–	ss 108–14
NSW	*Civil Liability Act 2002*	ss 5B, 5C	ss 5D, 5E	ss 27–33	s 5O, s 5P	ss 40–6
NT	*Personal Injuries (Liabilities and Damages) Act 2003*	–	–	–	–	–
Qld	*Civil Liability Act 2003*	ss 9–10	ss 11–12	–	ss 20–2	ss 35–7
SA	*Civil Liability Act 2002*	ss 31–2	ss 34–5	ss 33, 53	ss 40–1	–
Tas	*Civil Liability Act 2002*	ss 9–12	ss 13–14	ss 29–35	ss 21–2	ss 36–43
Vic	*Wrongs Act 1958*	ss 48–50, 72	ss 51–2	ss 67–78	ss 57–60	ss 79–87
WA	*Civil Liability Act 2002*	s 5B	ss 5C, 5D	ss 5Q–5T	ss 5PA, 5PB	ss 5U–5Z, 5AA

– = no comparable clauses.

PUBLIC AUTHORITIES

There are vigorous legal debates, which have been referred to a number of times already in this book, about the extent to which public authorities should be held liable for the intentional or unintentional harms that occur under their auspices. In coming to decisions about public authorities, courts have sometimes distinguished between political or policy matters, which they argue are the purview of governments and their instrumentalities, and operational matters, which they argue are subject to court consideration. In practice, this distinction is blurred and courts do sometimes make policy-based decisions.

Arguments about public bodies were canvassed extensively by the High Court in *Graham Barclay Oysters Pty Ltd v Ryan* [2002] HCA 54, in which a person who ate and was made ill by contaminated oysters sued the oyster grower, distributer, the local council and the state; the latter two for failing to take action in relation to the contamination outbreak. Chief Justice Gleeson said (at para 6): 'courts have long recognised the inappropriateness of judicial complaints about the reasonableness of governmental conduct where such complaints are political in nature'. It was said in this case that government priorities for revenue raising and resource allocation are political matters and not justiciable, or only in a very limited way, and that whether or not a body is in breach of its common law duty will depend on the wording of relevant legislation. In relation to public authorities, it was held that a duty might exist in a situation based on salient features, such as the degree of control the authority has over the risk of harm, the vulnerability of those who depend on the exercise of the body's powers, and the consistency of a duty with the intent and scope of the relevant statute. A duty of care did not lie in *Graham Barclay Oysters Pty Ltd v Ryan* [2002] HCA 54 against the state or the local council.

The new civil liability legislation provisions concerning public authorities are quite complex, vary across jurisdictions on fine but significant points, and to some extent remove the common law distinction between policy and operation. New civil liability legislation in Tasmania, Victoria, New South Wales, the Australian Capital Territory and Western Australia does mirror the common law position: the fact of a public authority exercising a function does not indicate that the authority is under a duty to exercise that function, or to do so in a particular way or in a particular situation (Mendelson 2007). The legislation in Tasmania, Victoria, New South Wales, the Australian Capital Territory, Western Australia and Queensland places limits on the liability of public authorities for breach of statutory duty, unless they are judged to have been acting so unreasonably in the view of any other authority exercising the same powers and performing the same functions.[2] In addition, in New South Wales, there are limits on liability for failure to exercise a power unless that failure is unreasonable.

Dietrich (2005 p. 33) says of these provisions about public authorities, 'the precise meaning and operation of sections such as these, and how they interact with the other public authority provisions, is difficult to predict'. The legislative clauses about the liability of public bodies commonly include consideration of the functions to be exercised by the authority and the resources that are reasonably available to it, and recognition of functions and responsibilities beyond the case being considered. All jurisdictions that have such provisions, except Victoria, exclude challenges to the way in which the body allocates its resources. The impact of the new provisions will be mediated by their interaction with the relevant statutes under which the authority operates, immunity clauses, and the availability of other means of redress such as judicial review (CCH 2007).

In many situations involving public authorities and people in difficulty, injury is probable unless extensive and expensive surveillance, support and intervention services are put in place, and statutory powers exercised. However, such actions would absorb scarce resources needed elsewhere, may not be required under another interpretation of the relevant Act, and moreover may compromise civil liberties. Several police and mental health cases that show how courts attempt to negotiate these finely balanced imperatives are surveyed briefly here.

The police case of *Batchelor v State of Tasmania* [2005] TASCC 11, heard prior to the new civil liability legislation, shows how courts might emphasise the policies and procedures of the public authority in judging its actions. In this case, a woman who had evidence that her partner would shoot her and then suicide, approached police for help and a restraint order. The police took her home, with her partner's knowledge, and while all were at the house he shot and killed her and then himself. The young son of this relationship commenced a negligence claim against the police and in this action the state attempted to have his claim struck out. The Tasmanian Supreme Court held, among other things, that it was arguable that police immunity would not hold if police officers had not acted in accord with their training and instructions. In addition, it was arguable on the facts of the case that the police had not complied with the robust

---

[2] *Civil Liability Act 2002* (Tas) s 40; *Wrongs Act 1958* (Vic) s 84; *Civil Liability Act 2002* (NSW) s 43(2); *Civil Law (Wrongs Act) 2002* (ACT) s 111(2); *Civil Liability Act 2002* (WA) s 5X; *Civil Liability Act 2002* (Qld) s 36.

charge and arrest policy then in force. The Court allowed the child to go ahead with an amended statement of claim.

In the case of *Presland v Hunter Area Health Service* [2003] NSWSC 754, also heard before the civil liability changes, a man who was not detained involuntarily in a psychiatric hospital, immediately after discharge murdered his brother's fiancé while in a psychotic state. He was charged with murder, found not guilty on the grounds of insanity and incarcerated. He sued the mental health service in negligence and argued that his behaviour and clinical signs should have resulted in his involuntary detention under the *Mental Health Act 1990* (NSW), in which case the subsequent killing would not have taken place and he would not have been incarcerated. It was held at first, among other things, that the adverse consequences which followed his release from hospital were foreseeable and that the *Mental Health Act 1990* (NSW) required his detention. On appeal (*Hunter Area Health Services v Presland* (2005) 63 NSWLR 22) this judgement was set aside on a different reading of the *Mental Health Act 1990* (NSW) and on various public policy grounds, among which was concern that a plaintiff might benefit from an unlawful killing (see Scott 2006), even though there was evidence that the service system had not responded efficiently and effectively.

An example of the interaction between the new civil liability and other legislation is provided by the mental health case of *Walker v Sydney West Area Health Service* [2007] NSWSC 526, which was heard under the *Civil Liability Act 2002* (NSW). In this case, a young man with a known mental health history and suicidal tendencies had not been admitted as an involuntary patient after jumping in front of a train, not placed on a community treatment order, and not prescribed medication. He had however been assessed and followed up several times at home by a case manager. Some weeks later, the man, while drunk, attempted to hang himself, and in the process fell from a tree and suffered spinal injuries that resulted in quadriplegia. He sued the health service in negligence for failing to provide him with adequate care. In this case, the court had to consider and balance the *Civil Liability Act 2002* (NSW) provisions concerning contributory negligence, intoxication, s 43A (which limits the liability of public authorities exercising statutory powers), standards of practice, and the powers conferred on the body under the *Mental Health Act 1990* (NSW). It found in favour of the public authority. There was no proof that the care was substandard and there was no evidence that the mental health service's failure to exercise its powers under the *Mental Health Act 1990* (NSW) 'was so unreasonable that no Area Health Service could have regarded it as a reasonable exercise of power' (at para 168). Thus, liability was precluded by s 43A of the *Civil Liability Act 2002* (NSW).

TARGETS OF PRIVATE LEGAL ACTION

In effect, individual human service workers have been almost free of civil claims in Australia, although as Rogers (1994) from the United Kingdom points out, there is no doctrinal reasons why they should be. The reasons are largely practical and strategic. These workers are generally employees, are not seen as financially well endowed and commonly do not have professional indemnity insurance. If their actions were not intentionally harmful, they may also be protected by good faith statutory immunities of the kind outlined previously. Thus, they are unattractive targets for a plaintiff seeking damages. The 'deeper pockets' of their employer organisations, or treasury in the case of public bodies, are bound to be more inviting.

Thus, human service bodies, including public authorities, are more likely than individuals to be sued. This is notwithstanding the difficulties courts face with policy questions, the Crown's traditional common law immunity from vicarious liability for its employees' actions, and the presence of statutory immunities. Organisations may be sued directly for the harm they have caused or through their vicarious liability for the torts of their workers. Workers in most jurisdictions will have some legislative immunity from suits directed at their employer, or from suits against them by their employers who have incurred vicarious liability. The ability of public authorities in general to avoid risk of suits and vicarious liability by using contractors, rather than employees, is unclear – authorities here and in the United Kingdom take different approaches (Trindade et al. 2007). If vicarious liability is argued, courts will be concerned with questions of whether the worker was an employee, as opposed to a contractor, and whether or not the transgression was within the scope of work. Intentional, unsanctioned and illegal conduct by employees poses some particular problems (Feldthusen 1998; Trindade et al. 2007) and often (but not always) negates the vicarious liability of the employer as the *O'Sullivan* case (below) shows.

Employers who are sued successfully can theoretically sue their workers for recovery of damages, unless as indicated above, the worker has legislative immunity from the employer. Such suits are not common, largely because employers' insurance usually covers their costs. However, they do happen, as evidenced by the following pre-civil liability legislation case, which also illustrates the complex interaction of legislation in this area. In *O'Sullivan v the Queen* [2002] NSWCCA 98, New South Wales had accepted vicarious liability under the provisions of the *Law Reform (Vicarious Liability) Act 1983* (NSW) and paid damages for the actions of its police officers who maliciously prosecuted, wrongfully arrested and falsely imprisoned a person. The state then sought contribution from one of the police officers in *State of NSW v Wayne Eade* [2006] NSWSC 84. Section 5 of the *Employees' Liability Act 1991* (NSW) indemnified the officer against his employer for the tort, unless his behaviour was serious and wilful misconduct, or did not occur in the course of or arising through employment. It was found that the officer, in committing the torts, had been performing the functions of a police officer, albeit improperly, so the wrong conduct occurred in the course of work. The officer was ordered to pay 80% of the damages, an amount of $286 828.80. The test used here to determine whether the actions were in the course of employment was that of authorised functions being carried out in an unauthorised manner.

Courts have used a variety of tests to determine if someone is an employee. These include the extent to which the employer controls the work of the person and the extent to which the person is integrated into the organisation. A variety of tests are also applied in determining whether or not conduct was carried out in the course of work, including the connection between the employee's misconduct and the employer's enterprise and its risks. The choice of test concerning work relatedness, to be used by courts in the case of sexual misconduct in non-residential facilities, is unclear as a result of *New South Wales v Lepore; Samin v Queensland: Rich v Queensland* (2003) 77ALJR 558. In this case, the High Court considered the question of the liability of schools for sexual assaults by teachers on pupils, and was divided on the applicability of and approach to vicarious liability. It did not find any general reason why intentional wrongdoing would always preclude vicarious liability, but conduct that was so grossly beyond the employee's authority and interests of the employer would probably not, on policy grounds, attract the vicarious liability of the employer. *Lepore* was considered in *Sprod BNF v Public Relations Oriented Security Pty Ltd* [2005] NSWSC 1074, where a person assaulted by security officers alleged negligence on the part of their employing firm for failing to train and supervise them adequately. The court found that the improper acts of the guards were done to further the employer's interests and in the course of carrying out employment. The unauthorised acts were sufficiently close to employer authorised acts, and the respondent was found vicariously liable for the intentional wrongdoing of the guards.

In similar overseas cases, authorities have been found vicariously liable for the sexual misconduct of employees through application of the test that finds a 'close connection' between the work and the tort, and where the work puts the person who commits a tort in a better position to do so, regardless of whether or not it happens in work time and at a workplace. Trindade et al. (2007) argue that this test provides a fair way of determining vicarious liability. Feldthusen (1998 p. 234) agrees on the work/private time point saying 'if an adult has job-created power over a child, or a therapist over a patient, or a member of the clergy over a parishioner, it is unrealistic to suppose that power can be constrained within its formal boundaries of space, time and subject matter'. Although courts commonly see sexual misconduct as antithetical to work in institutions and schools, there are those who contend that it may be inherent to that kind of work. Wangmann (2004) argues that the High Court in the *Lepore* case demonstrated an inability to come to grips with the character of sexual misconduct in environments (beyond institutions) where children are in the care of and in close proximity to adults, and says that the work context should be the focus as much as the wrongdoer. Hall (2000 p. 162; 2006), in relation to institutional abuse, similarly argues that the workplace is not the 'honey pot' that attracts sexual predators but a 'crucible' in which the culture can work to nurture and release (if not create) them.

RISKS OF PRIVATE LAW SUITS IN THE HUMAN SERVICES

Civil law and the courts are not well placed and are not the place (in the view of many) to resolve human hurts and distress (eg Mann 2003). In the prison search case in the United Kingdom of *Wainwright*, which is covered later in this book, Lord Hoffman (at para 46) said in relation to even intentional hurt:

> In institutions and workplaces all over the country, people constantly do and say things with the intention of causing distress and humiliation to others. This shows lack of consideration and appalling manners but I am not sure that the right way to deal with it is always litigation.

However, there are publicly and politically noteworthy cases that demonstrate how civil law, ill equipped as it is, sometimes becomes the main and even the best mechanism for dealing with human traumas caused by human failure, particularly in the absence of other enforceable private rights (McLay 2004); as, for example, when permanent resident Cornelia Rau or valid visa holder Tony Tran (AAP 2007b) were wrongfully held and treated very badly in immigration detention. Freckelton concludes (2005 p. 11) 'when caring is replaced by breaches of duty of care and by inhumanity, there are times when the legal system, in spite of its bluntness as an instrument of social change, can serve a constructive purpose'. The same sentiment may be applied to child protection and stolen children cases. Besharov (1985), in canvassing the arguments about the place of civil suits in child protection failures in the United States, differentiates between individual compensation and systemic reform actions and outcomes. He advocates the latter, but acknowledges the predominance of the former in legal action.

Nonetheless, even in the United States, where there are more civil malpractice suits in the human services than in Australia, there are still few suits relative to other professions (Jones and Alcabes 1989). In Australia, despite a few high-profile individual cases that are detailed in this and the following chapters, human service civil cases of the individual or the advocacy kind are the exception. Not perhaps 'almost unknown' as Swain (2001 p. 64) asserted in 1996, but certainly very rare indeed. In the words of Collingridge et al. (1991 p. 12) 'Australian social workers and social welfare workers do not work in a culture of litigation'. If medical negligence, product liability and road accident figures are anything to go by (Mann 2003), only a tiny fraction of victims ever pursue or succeed in torts cases. Most who commence an action drop it or settle early, and according to Luntz (2006) often for less than they might have received in court.

There are multiple reasons, some already outlined in relation to criminal and other public law, explaining why those harmed in human service operations generally do not take civil legal action. The first of these reasons concerns the substance of the law. Various legal tests must be satisfied under each civil legal action and interpretations of relevant legislation may pose obstacles. For example, it may be difficult to argue a duty or damage acceptable in law, or that a breach caused the damage that is alleged, or that the plaintiff is in the class intended by the statute to be protected. It is also likely that defences (eg contributory negligence where the defendant argues that the plaintiff was responsible for some of the harm they experienced) will be available to defendants, as many client plaintiffs have turbulent lives and indulge in risky behaviours. Moreover, it may be argued that the new civil liability legislation has set higher barriers for smaller claims and claims involving non-financial damage (Bennett and Freckelton 2006). In other words, the plaintiff may not be able to surmount substantive law hurdles.

In addition, plaintiffs may lack access to the best legal advice to help them negotiate hurdles of substantive law. Luntz (2005 p. 395), in musing on a lifetime's experience as a torts lawyer and academic, says of an early case:

> ...it taught me one thing that was reflected in many more important [cases]...namely, that the outcome of litigation is often not dependent on the merits of the law, but on the forensic tactics adopted, which may in turn be dependent on the experience and skill of the legal representatives the parties are able to afford.

Many damaged human service clients are potential litigants in areas where the law is evolving, and courts are wary of interfering in government policy, or of being seen as too activist, or of 'opening the floodgates'. The courts and the clients in these situations need the assistance of committed, knowledgeable, creative and confident counsel. Finding such people is difficult at the best of times, and particularly so if the plaintiff is socially and in other ways disadvantaged or does not present well. Many damaged individuals do not make good plaintiffs – they may not be attractive propositions for civil lawyers. Nonetheless, there have been some extraordinary efforts by lawyers, legal advocacy groups and legal centres in some of the high-profile cases mentioned in this book, but their resources are finite and most likely directed to the most meretricious cases (eg Williams and Nash 2001). One Western Australian law firm claims to have 1000 stolen generation claimants on its books and to be working pro bono (AAP 2008b).

Luntz (2005) also raises the apposite matter of money, as litigation is extremely expensive. Public legal aid for civil actions is extremely limited or non-existent and organisational defendants generally mount very robust defences (Senate Standing Committee on Community Affairs 2004). In attempting to secure legal advice, human service plaintiffs may face a legal perception that human service defendants do not have the wherewithal to make a suit worthwhile. Rogers (1994), in discussing child abuse claims in the United Kingdom some years ago, challenged this assumption with an interesting argument that still has currency. His position was that non-pecuniary losses in human service torts cases are generally modest; in relation to individual worker defendants 'a very large number of people, even of quite modest means, are good for £10,000 or £20,000'. In Australia today, many human service workers and other individual perpetrators of damage would have assets of some sort, including equity in real estate of a value commensurate with the amounts of the damages outlined below.

However, they are seldom targeted for all the reasons mentioned earlier and their assets would be absorbed by their legal defence.

The plaintiff in the *Trevorrow* case, to be discussed in Chapter 6, was awarded around half a million dollars damages for a life which was comprehensively and irretrievably wrecked by human service activity. The plaintiff in *SB*, discussed below, who was abused in both foster care and by her father, received around $200 000 for a life destroyed by unimaginable horrors. These amounts could hardly be seen as excessive compensation in view of the extent of injuries. Both amounts are less than is commonly seen in business-related litigation, although the size of some of the Australian immigration detention civil claims may change perceptions that human service damages are modest. As Mann (2003 p. 217) says of torts actions in general, 'damages themselves perpetuate inequality insofar as those with greater wealth, higher wages (or earning potential), greater "reputation", better health and longer lifespan (by virtue of social privilege) receive correspondingly higher payments'.

A defendant must also be identified and this is often not a straightforward matter. The relative, practical immunity of individual workers has been mentioned. If an unincorporated organisation is involved, there is no legal entity to sue (as with some charitable bodies in institutional abuse cases, Senate Standing Committee on Community Affairs 2004). Public bodies present their own problems to a litigant. Public policy and or good faith statutory immunities have resurfaced throughout this book. Although it is evident that courts in some recent civil child protection, immigration and stolen generation cases have been willing to find for the plaintiff against both public policy and statutory immunity arguments, both immunities continue to exist, should exist (McIvor 2006), and are likely to apply in all but exceptionally egregious situations. 'Good faith has accommodated many errors in judgment' (Filippelli and Goodman 2005 p. 74) and service system failures. Many potential client plaintiffs will find it difficult to convince courts that their damage is so significant, that the conduct that caused it is so wrongful, and that the absence of good faith is so evident, that their rights to compensation should prevail over concerns about future defensive practice.

All of the evidential obstacles faced by plaintiffs in relation to criminal cases, summarised in Chapter 3, apply equally in potential civil cases. In addition, various public interest and statutory immunities may prevent access to necessary records (Kelly and Lewis 1994). All of the personal, social and knowledge resources required of a victim agreeing to participate in a criminal action are even more relevant in a civil action, where the state does not lead, the plaintiff commonly acts alone, and years may pass before a case is finally determined. Many clients injured at the hands of human service actors do not wish to or are not in a position to mount a case that will expose the details of their lives, reopen their scars and where the outcome is unknown. Many do not know that they have any legal rights. In *Rundle v Salvation Army* NSWSC [2007] 443, a man had been placed in a Salvation Army home as an eight-year-old and thereafter, until the age of 13, was allegedly subject to several hundred severe sexual assaults by other residents and a staff member. On the two or three occasions in which he attempted to report the abuse, or stop other children from being abused, he was beaten by other officers, often senior ones. The plaintiff did not know until 2001 that he might have a legal claim and only then because others who knew his story had suggested the possibility. Nor did he realise until then that his unhappy adult life and psychiatric condition may be linked to his childhood experiences.

Statutes of limitations apply to all actions in tort law and, as with criminal law, these can discourage or bar potential human service cases. The statutory periods vary according to the type of action, damage and defendant, the circumstances under which the damage occurred and the point at which the periods start to run. They also differ across jurisdictions. In general, tort actions must be commenced within three to six years. Claims for death or personal injury are generally statute-barred after three years (Walmsley et al. 2007). These statutes are in part aimed at ensuring that defendants will not be unfairly prejudiced in mounting an adequate defence given the passage of time. There is a great deal of court interpretation about the meaning and intent of the statutes, particularly in relation to damage that may not be understood or acknowledged until long after the causal events. This is often pertinent in cases of damage caused to clients by human service failures. Among the cases included in this and the next two chapters, there are several where applications were made to extend the statutory period for actions in which the damage had been inflicted many years before, but only appreciated more recently. For example, in *SB v New South Wales* (2004) VR 527; VSC 514, the plaintiff was not statute-barred as the court determined that she had been under a disability at all significant times until the commencement of her actions (Freckelton 2007a).

A number of British child migrant cases in the mid 1990s demonstrate how human service cases may be statute-barred. These cases arise from the British children bought to Western Australia in the 1940s and 1950s, who were placed in and abused in Christian Brothers' orphanages. Two actions were initiated in Victoria where the statute of limitations was more accommodating than in Western Australia. The Supreme Court of Victoria held that the cases would have to be heard in Western Australia (*Taylor v Trustees of the Christian Brothers and Ors*; *Reidy v Trustees of the Christian Brothers and Ors*. VSC 9753/4 of 1993). This was confirmed by the Western Australian Supreme Court in *Reidy v Trustees of the Christian Brothers and Ors* (1994) 12 WAR 583, and they were statute-barred in that state. Another case was mounted in New South Wales, which had limited success in the procedural complexities argued at first instance and on appeal (*Archbishop of Perth v 'AA' to 'JC' inclusive*; *'DJ' and others v Trustees of the Christian Brothers and others* (1995) 18 ACSR 333). However, it is reported that this case was soon thereafter settled out of court (Handford 2006).

Werren (2007) argues that courts have become increasingly sensitive to problems faced by child abuse claimants and more willing to extend limitation periods when they do have the discretionary power. The recommendation of the Senate Standing Committee on Community Affairs for revision of statutory time barriers in this area, if followed, should take the onus off courts to exercise their discretion (Senate Standing Committee on Community Affairs 2004). Certainly, the more recent *Trevorrow* and *SB* cases survived, despite the apparent constraints of the statutes of limitations. Similarly in the *Rundle* case outlined above, arguments by the defendant against an extension of time were dispatched firmly by the court, an extension was granted and a civil case could then go ahead for damage allegedly resulting from events in the 1960s. The High Court in *Davison v Queensland* (2006) 226 CLR 234 reversed a Queensland Court of Appeal decision on statutory interpretation of the *Limitation of Actions Act 1974* (Qld), in favour of the six adult appellants who wished to sue in tort for abuse they suffered as children while in the care of that state. Freckelton (2006d) is also of the view that, despite the new civil liability Acts, there is some room for optimism in relation to extensions of time for intentional torts and psychiatric injuries.

Many potential child abuse claimants lack faith in the legal system to deliver them justice (Senate Standing Committee on Community Affairs 2004). Plaintiffs who have suffered grievous personal wrongs may really be seeking psychological restitution, incidental to or incompatible with a legal claim. Some potential litigants may want an explanation, a declaration of a wrong, an apology, or retribution against the alleged wrongdoer through the latter's exposure and humiliation (Merry and McCall-Smith 2004). Others may be dissatisfied with the substantive and procedural constraints that the law places on the narrative and subjective experience of their story. Rogers (1994 p. 272) says, in relation to child abuse, that civil claims play more of a symbolic role in 'express[ing] the ideas of personal responsibility for grievously wrongful acts' than anything else. These profound psychological imperatives have underpinned an increasing acceptance of the role of apology in law (see Bennett and Freckelton 2006; Allan 2007), including the more recent civil liability legislation and developments in restorative justice (eg Daly and Hayes 2001; Strang 2001; Madden and Cockburn 2007).

Compensation schemes may reduce litigation. For example, criminal injuries compensation schemes, even though inadequate in many ways (Freckelton 2001a; Forster 2002), including modest payouts may satisfy victims. Victims may also seek compensation from the Commonwealth's 'Compensation for detriment caused by defective administration' scheme (which is itself defective according to Department of Parliamentary Services 2005), the state system redress schemes in Tasmania, Western Australia and Queensland, or compensatory funds set up to deal with widespread intra-organisational abuse (Senate Standing Committee on Community Affairs 2004) (in relation to the Anglican Church, see ABC 2006a; ABC 2006b). In future, children damaged in institutional and welfare care may have access to reparation schemes of the kind outlined by Hall (2006) in Canada, the Senate Standing Committee on Community Affairs (2004), the Senate Legal and Constitutional Affairs Committee and the Public Interest Advocacy Group (O'Neill et al. 2004). For Indigenous children, schemes of some sort may follow the Apology and some are already in place in Tasmania (*Sydney Morning Herald* 2008). Other victims may not sue because their cases have already come to the attention of other bodies and have been dealt with in different ways. This is a topic to be returned to in Chapter 8.

Despite these many impediments, some private law cases about human service activity have been initiated, and a number of these have progressed into the courts. Examples of these cases and the law that sustains them are detailed in the next two chapters.

6 | Private law – negligence

THE MOST COMMON tort law action in the human services has been negligence. Negligence involves unintentional but blameworthy wrongs done to others, for which the wrongdoer can be held responsible in law. At the core of negligence is a failure to meet the standards of the time.

For a negligence action to succeed, three critical elements must be established by the plaintiff and for each element much will hang on the nature of the relationship between the plaintiff and the alleged wrongdoer. The elements are:

- the plaintiff was owed a duty of care by the alleged wrongdoer
- the wrongdoer breached the duty of care
- the breach caused the reasonably foreseeable harm to the plaintiff.

This chapter considers these three elements of negligence in relation to child protection, stolen generations, correctional and immigration detention cases.

DUTY OF CARE

The phrase 'duty of care' is in the title of this book due to widespread use in the human services. However, as argued elsewhere (Kennedy and Richards 2007), the meaning of duty of care in the human services is inchoate and probably bears little resemblance to the very particular way in which it is used in the law. Duty of care in law concerns the relationships between parties and is a question of law at any one time – it is not a question of fact, of the views of the parties involved, or of morality or ethics. Duty of care is a mechanism by which courts determine legal obligations and appropriate conduct between parties. Courts have developed, accepted,

104

rejected and later revisited a variety of tests for determining who is owed a duty in law and the scope of that duty. Concepts such as proximity of the parties have been applied and abandoned, although the word still appears in judgements. Currently, reasonable foreseeability of damage to the plaintiff in the absence of reasonable care by the defendant is used by courts to decide if a duty exists in any particular situation. However, as the High Court argued in *Sullivan v Moody* [2001] HCA 59, a case which will be returned to later in this chapter, foreseeability of harm alone is insufficient to give rise to a duty of care. As explained earlier in relation to the *Graham Barclay* case, salient factors in different fact situations will influence the finding of a duty and its scope. In the *Sullivan* case, factors were held to include the harm suffered and its cause, the details of the statutory regime under which the defendant operates, difficulties in limiting the size of the class of people to whom the duty is owed, and conflict between a duty and the coherence of the whole body of applicable law.

Walmsley et al. (2007 pp. 31–4) summarise four points from the salient factors currently canvassed by courts in finding a duty, and four in decisions where there is no duty. Thus, a duty is more likely to be found if:

- the plaintiff's vulnerability to harm from the defendant's conduct is a significant feature of the situation
- the defendant has a significant degree of control over the risk of injury to the plaintiff
- the plaintiff relies on the defendant and/or the latter assumes responsibility – this is particularly important in cases involving the giving of advice
- there was reasonable foreseeability of harm – the liability of the defendant is more likely if they knew of the risk and particularly if they knew the risk was high.

A duty is less likely to be found where:

- liability is indeterminate and any member of the public might have a claim
- serious burdens would be imposed on people engaged in legitimate business and social activities
- a conflict with other duties, especially statutory duties, would result
- a conflict with other legal principles would arise.

CHILD PROTECTION AND DUTY OF CARE

It may be argued that finding a duty of care is now less of a problem in child protection cases in the United Kingdom (Williams 2004) and

Australia (Freckelton 2007a), than finding beaches and or causation. This is significant because civil child protection actions in the United Kingdom and Australia for a time foundered on the United Kingdom precedent *X (Minors) v Bedfordshire County Council* [1995] 2 AC 633, where five child plaintiffs alleged negligence and breach of statutory duty because they had not been taken into care and thus protected from serious and prolonged parental abuse and neglect. No duty to the children was found in that case. It was held that the task of child protection authorities was complicated and delicate, and the authorities would become defensive in their practice if the claim succeeded. In addition, the danger of vexatious litigation would be increased and other remedies were available. In other words, in the view of the House of Lords at that time, the case raised questions of public policy that were not appropriately justiciable by courts. This case caused unease in commentators (eg Hilson and Rogers 1995) and later cases in the United Kingdom have read down its findings. For example, in *Barrett v Enfield London Borough Council* [2001] 2 AC 550, a plaintiff who had been taken into care as a child alleged psychological, emotional and social damage as a result of unsatisfactory placements and ongoing monitoring. The refusals by lower courts to allow his claim were dismissed by the House of Lords. His removal into care distinguished him from the *Bedfordshire* claimants who were not taken into care, and the public policy considerations that undermined the *Bedfordshire* case had less force in his circumstances. It was found that he may have been owed a duty of care on the facts of his situation which, along with causation, should be tested at trial.

After the enactment of the *Human Rights Act 1998* (UK) the *Bedfordshire* claimants went to the European Court of Human Rights in *Z v United Kingdom* (2001) 34 EHRR 97 or [2001] 2 FCR 246, which found that the local authority did have a statutory duty to protect them, including taking them into care. Later, the UK Court of Appeal, in *D v East Berkshire Community NHS Trust* [2004] 2 WLR, found that the policy arguments underpinning the *Bedfordshire* case had been negated by the incorporation of the Human Rights Convention into law, and that the three children in that case were owed a duty by child protection medical investigators who had wrongly concluded that they evidenced separately, sexual abuse, non-accidental injury and medical conditions fabricated by the mother. The majority of the House of Lords affirmed this decision in *D v East Berkshire Community NHS Trust* [2005] 2 AC 373. The court canvassed, but did not find on, the idea of the facts of a breach supplanting the element of duty in such cases.

In Freckelton's (2007a p. 443) words, 'the tide has turned' now in Australia, New Zealand and the United Kingdom in relation to courts' receptiveness to a duty owed to children in child protection claims, although cases in the United Kingdom have limited application in Australia because of different legislation and common law tests for establishing a duty of care. Arthur (2006) also agrees that the tide has turned, particularly in the United Kingdom, following *D v East Berkshire Community NHS Trust* [2004] 2 WLR, in which a duty was owed to the child taken into care after a wrongful accusation that she had been sexually abused by her father. In *TC by his tutor Sabatino v New South Wales* [2001] NSWCA 380, the plaintiff argued that he would not have suffered sexual and physical abuse while in the care of his mother if the Department of Youth and Community Services (DOCS) had properly followed up notifications made to them about him. The original *Bedfordshire* case was distinguished on the grounds of a different statutory framework in New South Wales, which did impose a duty. It was said that a private duty could be found in relation to the exercise of powers under the then *Child Welfare Act 1939* (NSW) and that it was reasonably foreseeable that any failure by DOCS to investigate allegations properly could lead to damage to TC. TC's appeal failed, but on causation and not duty grounds.

A more recent and significant Australian child protection case is that of *SB v New South Wales* (2004) 13 VR 527. SB was made a ward of the state and then placed in foster care in New South Wales in 1972. She was sexually and physically abused while in foster care and DOCS subsequently removed her from that placement. In 1984, at the age of 16, after a temporary foster placement collapse, she was abruptly placed with her natural father with whom she had been in minimal contact in the preceding 10 years. Thereafter for 10 years she was forced into regular sex with him, and bore him two children. DOCS knew of difficulties in this placement too and did make some attempt to investigate reports of sexual assaults, but no action was taken and SB was discharged from guardianship in 1986. In 1994, after moving to Victoria, SB notified the police about her father's conduct. Her children were removed from her permanently, she self harmed and became intermittently an involuntary psychiatric patient. Her litigation guardian sued New South Wales in 2001 for negligence and breach of fiduciary duty in relation to the placement with her natural father and her subsequent psychiatric damage.

Thus, DOCS was found to have been in breach of its duty in that the placement with her father (at para 526):

108 | MISHAPS AND MISDEEDS THROUGH A LAW LENS

... increased the risk of harm and called for the exercise of reasonable care by her guardian. The Department breached its duty by failing to exercise its powers under the Act to protect its ward by terminating that restoration [to her father] and removing her from what the Defendant's own officers believed to be a sexually abusive situation in which the plaintiff was isolated, dominated and denied therapy.

Redlich J canvassed contemporary arguments about liability of public authorities and salient features indicative of a duty of care. The good faith clauses in the Act did not indemnify DOCS because it had not made genuine attempts to perform its functions properly. He took it as agreed that a public authority could be subject to a common law duty of care in the exercise of its powers. In relation to the non-exercise of powers, a duty may arise if the act not done was within power, and operational in character as opposed to a matter of core policy. He addressed vulnerability, indeterminacy of liability, control over risk, knowledge of risk, specificity of the duty, policy considerations, immunity and child welfare case precedents.

Redlich J found that in the context of the special relationship between DOCS and SB, the former had a duty to take reasonable care to protect her once it knew of the incest with her father. Her vulnerability was known, the risk to her foreseeable, there were no policy factors excluding a duty, the duty was not owed to the public at large and it was identifiable. The failure of the Department to exercise its powers was not a policy matter, and there was no incompatibility between the existence of a duty and the statutory responsibilities of DOCS.

However, the courts in Australia and the United Kingdom have not been willing to extend the scope of a duty of care to parents who have been accused of negligence or abuse by child protection authorities. Some legal commentators dispute the logic and fairness of this outcome, as wrongly accused third parties in child abuse investigations can suffer significant damage (eg Bates 2002). In the case of *D v East Berkshire Community NHS Trust* [2005] 2 AC 373, the primacy of the duty to the child was seen as incompatible with a duty owed to parents, although their distress and the damage they experienced was acknowledged. The *Berkshire* appeal was influenced by the previously mentioned Australian case of *Sullivan v Moody* [2001] HCA 59 (2001) 207 CLR 562. There, two fathers had been the subject of sexual abuse allegations concerning their children. Criminal charges were not laid for one and were dropped for the other father. The fathers claimed that various medical and human service child protection staff had been negligent in carrying out their investigations and that as a result they had suffered shock, psychiatric damage and financial and personal losses through family breakdown. Their appeal from earlier failures to establish legal claims was dismissed by the Australian High Court. Even though it was recognised that harm to the fathers who were investigated might be foreseeable, that alone could not found a duty. In fact, the finding of a duty to them would open up an unlimited range of possible claimants. It would be inconsistent with the authorities' statutory duties to give paramountcy to the interests of the child in such investigations and a duty would be inconsistent with other relevant legal obligations.

Some commentators have argued, on the basis of a handful of English cases, that the question of duty owed to parents in these situations may not be closed – it depends on the particular facts of a case. Handford (2006) suggests that the minority judgement in the case of *D v East Berkshire Community NHS Trust* [2004] 2 WLR keeps the matter alive and, while the majority of the House of Lords in *D v East Berkshire Community NHS Trust* [2005] 2 AC 373 dismissed the parents' appeal, the dissenting judgement argued that the interests of parents and children could be compatible in situations where abuse is investigated, but has not occurred. The parental claim is being pursued in the European Court of Human Rights (Gumbel et al. 2006).

Luntz (2006) observes that the High Court in *Sullivan and Moody* did not refer to the cases of *W v Essex County Council* [2000] 2 ALL ER 237 and *L (A Child) v Reading Borough Council* [2001] 1 WLR 1575. In the first case, foster parents had made it clear that they would not put their own children at risk by fostering a known sex abuser. The council social worker, who knew this, placed a boy who had previously committed sexual abuse acts with the foster parents – he subsequently abused their children. The parents sued the council in negligence for the psychiatric damage that they had suffered. Their claim, while not determined by the House of Lords, was not struck out as the facts might support it. In the second case, a mother fabricated a claim that the father of her child was sexually abusing the child. This was accepted by a social worker and a police officer, who were said at trial to have improperly conducted and misrepresented the interview with the child. The father was arrested and later exonerated. He sued the council and police in negligence, for misfeasance in public office and conspiracy. The UK Court of Appeal held that a duty to the father arguably arose when the officers continued to pursue him in the absence of evidence to support criminal action against him. However, the UK Court of Appeal later at trial rejected the father's claim in negligence against the council, again on the grounds that a duty owed to him would conflict with that of its duty to his child (*L (A Child) v Reading Borough Council* (No 2) Times Law Reports 27 December 2007).

CORRECTIONS AND DUTY OF CARE

It is now fairly well established that prison authorities owe a duty to take reasonable care of the safety of prisoners, at least from fire (*Howard v Jarvis* (1958) 98 CLR 177), and from assault by other prisoners (*L v Commonwealth of Australia* 1976 10 ALR 269 and *New South Wales v Bujdoso* (2005) 222 ALR 663). Several cases claiming that intolerable conditions in immigration detention may render the detention unlawful have not succeeded on that ground. However, there are some comments in the judgements to the effect that immigration authorities may owe a duty to detainees (as prison officials do to prisoners) and if the duty exists, intolerable conditions may constitute a breach (Aronson et al. 2004; Mackay 2006).

As it is in child protection, the question of secondary victims in corrections is fraught. There are a few cases in which relatives of prisoners who committed suicide in prison have made successful claims against prison authorities for psychiatric harm they suffered after hearing the news (Handford 2006 p. 600). In contrast, in *New South Wales v Godfrey* [2004] NSWCA 113, it was found on appeal that no indeterminate duty was owed by the state to the public at large. Thus, no duty was owed to a newsagent and her unborn child who were both harmed in a robbery committed by an escaped prisoner. There was some evidence that it was foreseeable that he might escape and reoffend but *Sullivan v Moody* had established that this alone is not enough to establish a duty. The prison authorities had no control over the prisoner once he had escaped. Establishing a duty here would conflict with the statutory duties of the corrective services concerning changes over sentence time in prisoner security classifications. The lower court's view that a duty was owed the newsagent because of the special relationship between prisoners and prison authorities, their ability to control prisoners and their knowledge of the likelihood of this prisoner escaping and offending, did not prevail.

Another case that illustrates courts' struggles with the liability of public authorities is that of *X v State of South Australia* (No 3) (2007) 97 SASC 125. In this case, a man with an extensive sexual offending history was released from prison on licence. While working in a community centre teaching children computing, he allegedly sexually abused the plaintiff. It was found by the majority on appeal that the parole board owed no duty to the plaintiff. Duggan J in the majority said (at para 196) that a public law remedy might be more applicable. Debelle J, also in the majority, itemised the salient features in the case and found that the parole board did not owe a general duty of care to the community, as this would be inconsistent with the statutory scheme under which it operated, it had no real control over people released on licence, and its liability would be indeterminate. In addition (at para 193) there was no irrationality in the non-exercise of power here by the parole board, and no exceptional grounds to find a policy in the relevant legislation requiring compensation for damage through the non-exercise of power. Gray J, the judge in the *Trevorrow* case, and in the minority here, found that a duty did exist as there was nothing in the relevant legislation that precluded a common law duty. The salient factors in this case, in his view, were vulnerability and dependence of the children, foreseeability because the parole board had knowledge of the offender's activities, control and proximity. He argued that the parole board had breached its duty by not pursuing the offender's non-compliance with his licence conditions. Similar reasoning to that of the majority found no duty in *L v State of SA* [2004] SADC 110, where a prisoner was released on parole by mistake, earlier than he should have been, and committed a number of rapes.

IMMIGRATION DETENTION AND DUTY OF CARE

In immigration detention and duty of care, the law is evolving. Various commentators have noted that the question of delegability of a duty is central as the immigration centres are privatised (Bagot 2002; Groves 2005; McSherry 2006), and the medical services in them are subcontracted by the contractors (Mackay 2006). This complexity has already been revealed in the delays in the resolution of the Cornelia Rau case, mentioned earlier in this chapter. The courts are faced with the dynamic character of responsible government in contemporary society, and with determining where a duty might lie between government and private providers. The reputable evidence demonstrating that the psychiatric harm caused by immigration detention outweighs and compounds previous experiences (Human Rights and Equal Opportunity Commission 2004), has no doubt had some impact on courts' attitudes. In *Behrooz v Secretary, Department of Immigration and Multicultural and Indigenous Affairs* (2004) 208 ALR 271, (at para 303) Gleeson CJ said in the context of comments about punishment

MISHAPS AND MISDEEDS THROUGH A LAW LENS

in detention 'if those who manage a detention centre fail to comply with their duty of care, they may be liable in tort'.

This view was confirmed in *S v Secretary, Department of Immigration and Multicultural and Indigenous Affairs* (2005) 216 ALR 252. In this case, two Iranian men who had been held in immigration detention for several years applied for an order to transfer them from Baxter Immigration Reception and Processing Centre for psychiatric treatment. They claimed that the duty to ensure their safety had been breached as both had untreated psychiatric conditions. In this case, the Commonwealth did concede that it owed a non-delegable duty. This concession, according to Groves (2005) is surprising and has possible ramifications for future prison cases. In the *S* case, Finn J found that the Commonwealth had a clear and non-delegable duty to take reasonable care of people in detention. In the case of *Shayan Badraie by his tutor Mohammad Saeed Badraie v Commonwealth* [2005] NSWSC, a young Iranian boy who had been hospitalised many times from immigration detention, sued the Commonwealth and the detention centre providers, alleging negligence through omissions and commissions. It was claimed that the boy had posttraumatic stress disorder (PTSD) resulting from witnessing violent and traumatic events in the Woomera Immigration Reception and Processing Centre. The Commonwealth accepted that it had a non-delegable duty, but argued no breach and attempted to present evidence that the damage had been caused by the father's mistreatment of the child in Iran, and by his bringing him to Australia and extending his time in immigration detention. The claims were never fully tested as the Commonwealth settled out of court by paying compensation of $400 000 plus legal costs and granting permanent residence visas to the child and his family (Penovic and Sifris 2006). As Penovic and Sifris argue (2006 p. 37), this outcome indicates that the Commonwealth accepted, to some extent at least, the strength of the plaintiff's legal case.

INDIGENOUS STOLEN CHILDREN AND DUTY OF CARE

Negligence law has also been invoked in a number of cases in the last 25 years or so by Indigenous people claiming multiple harms as a result of removal from their families and placement in non-Indigenous foster or institutional care (the stolen generations), where they were often maltreated or abused. Some of these cases have foundered on statutes of limitations as the plaintiffs have been adults when they have taken action. They can also face the problem of acceptable standards of practice changing over time. In *Williams v Minister, Aboriginal Land Rights Act 1983* (2000) Aust Torts Rep 81 578, an Aboriginal woman born in 1942 and then placed in a home with her mother's consent, claimed in 1999 to have borderline personality disorder as a result and mounted an action for negligence, breach of statutory duty and wrongful detention. The case went through several appeals, which showed the courts' difficulties with questions of time limitations, causation, matters of personal relationships and imposition of duties on public authorities. Finally, in the New South Wales Court of Appeal, her extension of time claim was refused and the question of duty, not found at trial, was left open in recognition of this being an unsettled and developing area of law.

In the much publicised and criticised (eg O'Connor 2001; Bessant 2004) stolen generation case of *Cubillo v Commonwealth* (2000) 103 FCR 1, [2001] FCA 1213, two Aboriginal children alleged that they were removed from their families (with the question of informed consent contested), kept in charitable institutions against their will until late adolescence, and mistreated therein. As adults, they lodged claims against the Northern Terrritory Director of Native Affairs arguing the vicarious liability of the Commonwealth for breach of statutory and fiduciary duty, breach of a common law duty of care and wrongful imprisonment. For technical and strategic legal reasons, actions were not taken against the directors or the religious bodies responsible for the institutions where they had been abused and mistreated. At trial the Commonwealth was successful in having the claim struck out and the action dismissed.

O'Loughlin J, relying on early child protection case policy arguments, commented that the court would not review government policies in general, or fetter their implementation. He found that there was no government removal policy underpinning the false imprisonment claim, there was no statutory duty to do or refrain from doing something that could give rise to a common law duty, and that even if there was, the duty would lie with Northern Territory public servants and not vicariously against the Commonwealth (which was not in control of their care). He conceded that there might be a statutory duty once the children were taken into care. However, they did not tell anyone of the assaults at the time and the directors were not aware of them in relation to Cubillo at least. Although much of the evidence the plaintiffs submitted was accepted, they could not sustain their legal arguments. Their appeal on narrower grounds in *Cubillo v Commonwealth of Australia* (2001) 112 FCR 455, [2001] FCA 1213 also failed and they were refused leave to appeal to the High Court of Australia.

114 | MISHAPS AND MISDEEDS THROUGH A LAW LENS

There was some movement of the law in *Johnson v DOCS* (No 2) [1999] NSWSC 1156. This was an appeal against a refusal to extend limitation periods to allow proceedings against DOCS for negligence and breach of statutory and fiduciary duty. It was upheld as the plaintiff did have available causes of action. He was an Aboriginal man who had been made a ward of the state at age four in 1968 and placed in white foster care. There he was harshly physically disciplined, about which a report was made to DOCS. Eventually the placement broke down and he was sent to institutional care, where he was sexually abused by a person who took him out for weekends. From 1986 onwards, he fended for himself on the streets, was prone to violence, charged with murder, and suffered from chronic depression and PTSD. He had no education and significant identity problems. In both the lower court and on appeal, it was said to be arguable that he was owed a common law duty of care. The appeal court distinguished the *Williams* case because there were no specific acts that constituted negligence, as were evident in the instant case. Rolfe J said (at para 88) 'I do not see why, if tortious conduct causes a person to develop a psychiatric illness, that person, at least prima facie, is not entitled to recover damages in consequence thereof'.

A significant advance in this line of cases occurred with *Trevorrow v State of South Australia* (No 5) [2007] SASC 285, concerning the removal in 1957 of a Aboriginal infant from his family and placement in a white middle-class foster home without the consent or knowledge of his family. The removal was unlawful and the foster family was not properly registered at the time of his placement. After 10 years in that foster family and having had no contact with his natural family, he was abruptly and without farewells, returned to his natural family. He and his natural family found it very difficult to re-establish relationships, and he thereafter moved in and out of different foster arrangements, institutions for offenders and psychiatric facilities.

Fifty years after the original removal, the plaintiff bought an action against the state claiming misfeasance in public office, false imprisonment, breach of duty of care, and breach of fiduciary and statutory duties. The Supreme Court of South Australia found that he was the subject of misfeasance in public office, falsely imprisoned, the subject of a breach of common law duty of care owed him by the state, and that the state's actions had contributed materially to his depression, loss of family bonds and confused identity. Gray J agreed with Redlich J in the *SB* child protection case, that the law was developing in this area. Gray J applied the salient features test in *Trevorrow* and found that:

PRIVATE LAW – NEGLIGENCE | **115**

- the relevant legislation did not exclude a duty of care
- there was no incompatibility between the legislation and a duty
- the class of plaintiffs was not indeterminate as there was 'no risk of a flood of claims' (at para 1044) if the current plaintiff should succeed
- there were no conflicting legal duties
- the consequence of harm from removing the child was reasonably foreseeable
- the vulnerable plaintiff was placed in harms way by the actions of the state, which had a high degree of control over the situation and power to reduce the risk of that harm
- there was proximity between the state and the child.

He found that the test for a duty was satisfied in respect of the child's removal from his parents, the monitoring of his ongoing foster care, the circumstances of his return to his mother and throughout his adolescence.

BREACH OF DUTY

A plaintiff must prove on the balance of probabilities that the duty owed them was breached. This requires identifying the appropriate standard to be applied in the situation and providing proof that it was not met. In common law, the standard is 'the exercise of reasonable care to avoid foreseeable risks' (MacFarlane 2000 p. 116) and it is determined objectively based on what would be done by a reasonable person. The likelihood of the risk, the significance of it and the gravity of the likely resultant harm, the cost and practicability of reducing the risk, and the social utility of the activity that creates the risk, will all be factored into reasoning about a breach under both common law and civil liability legislation. Law does not require or expect perfect practice. The possibility of error is acknowledged in court commentaries on breach. In the final analysis, court decisions will hang very much on the facts of each situation.

Breach is a thorny matter in relation to public authorities because of the fear of courts of placing too onerous and restrictive a burden on them. In human service work, it is additionally thorny because practice research is underdeveloped and the effectiveness of interventions seldom known (Gibbons 2001). As Reamer (2003b p. 14) argues in relation to social work, standards are ill defined and it is often very difficult to get any number of workers to agree on the most appropriate course of action in a particular practice fact situation. For this reason, he says, courts will often focus on the propriety of the procedural steps that led to the decision in question, more than the decision itself. Thus, in his view, procedural standards of care may be as important as substantive ones. This is a critical point that reverberates in later chapters. Courts may look to such things as professional association material on standards, expert evidence, and procedural and practice guidelines, for assistance in determining appropriate conduct at a particular time and in the particular circumstances.

There are a number of other points about questions of standards and breach made by Walmsley et al. (2007), which are particularly relevant to the human services, given the make-up of the workforce and many of its clients. These commentators suggest that for new graduates a lower standard, still objective, for people of that level of experience may be accepted by the courts. People with inadequate experience and qualifications should warn their clients of their limitations and refer on where necessary. Whether the professional test or a lower one will apply in regard to unqualified people doing qualified work is unclear. Where people work in teams or as employees, they will be evaluated against the standard for their particular profession, and questions of supervision and vicarious liability will predominate. In addition, particular care needs to be taken with unskilled and vulnerable clients. For human service individuals in private practice and for human service employers, the points about lower standards, warnings and the standards of the profession are particularly pertinent. For most areas of human service work the point about vulnerable clients is very relevant.

Table 5.1 displays the clauses in the civil liability legislation of each jurisdiction that are relevant to standards of professionals and others professing particular skills. This legislation attempts to encapsulate many of the common law principles, but the provisions on professional standards vary across the jurisdictions and will only be clarified by precedents. Despite the different phrasing, there is unanimity in general that practice that is widely accepted by peer professional opinion as competent will not be in breach. Standards in relation to diagnosis and treatment are commonly worded as those which could reasonably be expected of someone professing that particular skill. This is a move back from the common law position (stated in the medical case of *Rogers v Whitaker* (1992) 175 CLR 479) that it was for the courts, not professionals, to determine the appropriate standard to be applied. However, the *Rogers* approach still applies to advice about risks of treatment. The legislation, in general, also allows that differing professional opinions may exist and be relied upon, but not if they are 'irrational' or 'unreasonable'. Section 5O of the *Civil Liability Act* (2002) (NSW), which enumerates the standard of care for professionals, was considered by the Supreme Court of New South Wales in *Walker v Sydney West Area Health Service* [2007] NSWSC 526 (see Chapter 5). It was found, notwithstanding some contrary expert evidence, that the standard of mental health care that the suicidal young man had received was commensurate with accepted competent professional practice. However, the young man was clearly very troubled, his parents were frustrated by and critical of the service received, and he continued to attempt suicide with drastic results. A lay observer or an academic commentator might conclude that these indicia implied unsatisfactory service provision, but the court accepted that the service was performing in a competent way as measured against the opinion of front-line psychiatric service peers.

It is generally declared in the new legislation, as in common law, that actions will be assessed against standards that applied at the time in question. This is a particularly relevant point for human service cases, which may arise many years after the allegedly damaging human service activity. As Stein (2006 p. 13) points out in relation to children's homes, what is now seen as abuse was often at the time accepted practice, or '"approved" treatment methods'. He lists a range of practices, some seen as therapeutic, including isolation and restraint, removal of clothing, refusal of visits and schooling, toilet restrictions, and oral and physical provocation, which were endorsed and pursued not so many decades ago. The same analysis could apply to stolen children situations, and to cases where children were adopted by abusive families – at the time, these were assessed only on the grounds of domestic hygiene and facilities. Two such adoption cases will appear later.

In many human services cases, courts have laboured over questions of the standards that should apply to the practices under question and whether or not those standards have been breached. This is not surprising, given the complex personal situations generally under consideration, the multitude of service providers, the incompleteness of the available evidence and the lapse of time since the alleged commissions or omissions. It is for these reasons that the House of Lords in the *Bedfordshire* case had thought that the child protection cases before it should not be the subject of court review.

The *SB* and *Trevorrow* cases illustrate how, more recently, courts can comprehensively and carefully deal with questions of breach. In *SB*, Redlich J closely scrutinised a detailed chronology of DOCS actions and omissions over the later period of the plaintiff's time in foster care, in order to understand the reasoning (or lack of it) behind the decisions made. He did not find that DOCS had breached its duty by returning SB to her father, as judged by the standards of the day and the options then available. This was despite the fact that DOCS had not complied with its own interim guidelines, which required a case conference and the development of a case plan before SB was placed with her father, neither of which happened. He also accepted that the hasty, ill prepared and possibly non-consensual return of SB to her father did not comply with the DOCS ward manual directive, as the return was neither authorised nor endorsed by a case plan. He did find a breach in DOCS substandard monitoring of SB's placement with her father, again after very detailed inspection of the evidence available to DOCS, its actions and, more commonly, inaction.

Similarly in *Trevorrow*, Gray J carefully detailed departmental activities and failures to act. He said that the risk of rupture of maternal attachment was high when the infant was removed from his natural family, and that the department did or should have known of this risk. Gray J's assertion was based on a review of attachment theory literature of the time, which he used as the standard of medical knowledge at the time of the removal. This is pertinent in view of Barker and Branson's (2000) observation that there are low expectations about keeping up to date in the social work practice culture. Also, many current human service intervention approaches and practices are not well founded in contemporary research and literature. Gray J also found that the department did not follow its own procedures in the plaintiff's removal from his original family, which would have provided some safeguards. Once the plaintiff was in a foster family, 'matters were left to drift' (at para 1086) and the manner of his abrupt return to his natural family fell below the standard of care required. A very vulnerable person thus suffered terrible damage.

In relation to prison authorities, it seems settled that the standards for looking after prisoner safety will not be set too high and not as high as those owed by schools to pupils (McGlone and Stickley 2009). Assaults alone do not invoke organisational liability, unless there was no supervision system or it was not being implemented (Mackay [2006] referring to *Nada v Knight* [1990] Aust Torts Reports 81–032). However, the supervision duty is clearer if a prisoner is known to have psychiatric problems or be suicidal (Groves 2005).

McSherry (2006; 2007) asserts that complex outsourcing and subcontracting arrangements in immigration detention do not negate the Commonwealth's responsibility for ensuring adequate standards of health care in detention centres. Finn J, in *S v Secretary, Department of Immigration and Multicultural and Indigenous Affairs* (2005) FCA 459, noted that appropriate subcontract arrangements were not in evidence, and that the Commonwealth had not audited the level and standards of psychological and psychiatric services delivered by the devolved and fragmented system, for which it had responsibility. The services were inadequate. McSherry (2007) argues that this case sets an important precedent for future actions against the Commonwealth. Mackay (2006) notes that the existence of the immigration detention standards may provide a useful mechanism for supporting a breach argument.

CAUSATION AND DAMAGE

Finally, after establishing duty and breach, a plaintiff must show that the breach was the cause of their damage. If there is no damage, despite the gravity of the breach, there is no claim in negligence. Neither is there a claim if the same damage would have happened without the breach. A claim is compromised if intervening and damaging events occur between the original wrongdoing and the taking of legal action, and if there are multiple causes, only some of them attributable to the transgressions. However, conduct that is a material or substantial cause may be sufficient to sustain the case. In common law, the question of whether or not the wrongdoer caused the damage is one of fact, which common sense will help determine. Issues of contributory negligence may also be canvassed and many human service client plaintiffs may well act in ways that compound if not contribute to their own distress and ill health. In many human service cases, the damage is 'pure' mental harm – this has not been as well accepted in law as psychiatric or psychological damage consequential on physical harm caused by the wrongdoer. However, once the common law started accommodating claims for pure mental harm, policy concerns about opening the floodgates of claims were raised (Freckelton 2001b; 2002).

As previously explained, common law causation and damage principles are superimposed and mediated by civil liability legislation. The 'but for' test of causation (ie the breach was a necessary condition of the occurrence of the harm) has been rejected at common law, but something similar appears in the civil liability legislation that states that the negligence is a necessary condition of the harm, and that it is appropriate to include the harm in the scope of the defendant's liability (see Table 5.1).

The civil liability legislation also limits claims for mental harm (Table 5.1). Only a recognised psychiatric illness will be accepted as damage for the purpose of negligence actions. Distress or psychological anguish will not be claimable, other than in Queensland and the Northern Territory where mental harm resulting from physical harm (as at common law) is still acceptable (McGlone and Stickley 2009). Freckelton (2002) contends that psychological claims are likely to be limited to posttraumatic stress, adjustment, dysthymic and anxiety disorders. In the words of Butler (2004 p. 127) 'at a time when so much is now known about psychiatric medicine, the law governing psychiatric claims in Australia has never been more divided'. Even so, Handford (2006 p. 601) believes that possibilities in this area will emerge over time.

In most jurisdictions, there has also been an attempt to reinstate the 'normal fortitude' rule from which the common law has resiled. This has particular relevance to human service activity, where very susceptible clients are being managed. The intent of the legislative provisions is to impose a duty if it is reasonably foreseeable that a person of normal fortitude may suffer psychiatric harm as a result of the defendant's conduct. However, the principle still stands that a defendant is liable if they knew that the plaintiff had particular susceptibilities (Trindade et al. 2007). In addition, once it is established that there was a duty, reasonable foreseeability of psychiatric damage, and a breach, the defendant must take the plaintiff as they find them, including their susceptibilities. Plaintiffs have to prove that it was reasonably foreseeable that they would suffer psychiatric illness as a result of the defendant's conduct. There are many complexities here, not the least of which is the recognition that normality is a social and cultural construct (Trindade et al. 2007), and that there is great diversity in human responses to trauma (Freckelton 2002).

For many clients who have been damaged through human service activity, causation and damage are major hurdles in a civil suit. Many of them will be arguing mental, rather than physical and economic damage, many of them will have pre-existing psychological conditions and particular vulnerabilities, and many will have experienced more of the same, after the human services intervention. One can only sympathise with courts attempting to untangle the relevant contributions of the human service activity from the contributions of other tortfeasors and general life circumstances. In the case of *SB v New South Wales* (2004) 13 VR 527, the plaintiff was probably psychologically damaged when she was taken into care, she was damaged in foster care and then she was further damaged in the placement with her father. She was damaged again on leaving his care. She sued on the matter of the placement with her father and it would have been ironic indeed if DOCS had succeeded in arguing that the damage caused in their foster placement precluded her claim on the later placement damage. Redlich J found that DOCS had to take her and her vulnerability as they found it. As long as their negligence after her placement with her father had aggravated and contributed to her PTSD and other psychological difficulties,

PRIVATE LAW – NEGLIGENCE

they were liable. The negligence did exacerbate her symptoms and she was awarded $195 000 plus $26 400 for loss of earnings.

In *Trevorrow*, the defendant department argued among other things that the plaintiff 'may well have suffered the same constellation of problems if he had stayed with his natural family' (at para 1113). Gray J rejected these claims in a critique of the evidence put before him by psychiatrists and other professionals. He applied a common sense test of causation and found that the plaintiff developed an anxiety state and depression as a result of his removal from his family and placement in white foster care. His unlawful removal 'was a material cause of his serious lifelong depression and its sequelae' (at para 1139). The plaintiff was awarded damages of $450 000 for loss and injury, exemplary damages of $75 000 for misfeasance in public office and false imprisonment, and an additional $250 000 in lieu of interest on the damages (Roberts 2008). The plaintiff died in 2008, but the South Australian Government is pursuing an appeal on some elements of law, in order to limit the status of the case as a precedent (The *Australian* 2008).

Physical damage resulting from human service activity is evidenced in the following case, which also illustrates how courts deal with questions of intervening events when causation is being considered. In *Bennet v Minister of Community Welfare* (1993) 176 CLR 408, a child ward of the state in Western Australia, while working a circular saw in a detention centre in 1973, had his fingers amputated. He was not properly supervised or instructed in the use of the saw, and he was not given independent legal advice about the injury and his legal rights. Soon after the injury, while still a state ward, he sought and received erroneous legal advice and consequently did not pursue his common law rights to claim. When he did commence action in 1983, his claim was out of time and the department argued successfully that it was the wrong legal advice and not its breach that had resulted in the loss of the plaintiff's right to claim damages. His appeal to the Supreme Court of Western Australia was dismissed. The High Court unanimously allowed his appeal and remitted the case to the Supreme Court of Western Australia for determination of damages. The court found that there was a common law and fiduciary duty owed by the state. On the question of causation, it was emphasised that all the facts of the situation needed to be considered and both Gaudron and McHugh JJ referred to the common sense test. The failure of the departmental director to ensure that the plaintiff had proper legal advice at the time was material in his loss of claim. The wrongful legal advice did not break the chain of causation that existed between the department and his loss of claim.

NEGLIGENT ADVICE OR INFORMATION

A civil action can be taken for loss, usually economic, resulting from negligent advice. In these situations, there may also be contractual and fiduciary duties. Outcomes will depend on the full circumstances and the following will be under consideration:

- the relative positions and relationship of the parties
- the reasonable reliance of one on the other
- the holding out of one as having expertise and the content of the advice or information.

In respect of the human services, it is possible to think of many situations where advice may cause loss or lost opportunity. In the social security and immigration systems, the administrative review processes discussed in Chapter 5 can be used to remedy losses caused by wrong advice or information from within the departments, or decisions based on them. The question of wrong advice about entitlements by workers outside of these departments may give rise to civil liability, due to the possibility of advising beyond an area of expertise. In fields such as aged care, where significant amounts of money may be involved in arrangements for alternative housing and care, it is quite conceivable that substandard advice could result in a negligence suit.

Inappropriate relationship advice may also found a negligence claim, as occurred in *Pickering v McArthur* [2005] QCA 294. In this case, it was alleged that a massage therapist/counsellor in private practice had been advising a long-term client to end his de facto relationship. The client relied on the advice, subsequently ended the relationship, and suffered psychiatric damage as a result. The court refused at first instance, and on appeal in this case, to strike out the client's claim – it was held that the counsellor did owe a duty to the client. This story has a sequel that suggests at the very least that the counsellor concerned had some recurring difficulties. He faced a similar, later legal claim by another client who alleged, in addition, that he had engaged in inappropriate sexual behaviour with her during their professional sessions. Her appeal against an earlier striking out of claim was unsuccessful in *Uzsoki v Macarthur* [2007] QDC 110, but the court held that she did have a reasonable cause of action.

DUTY TO WARN OR INFORM

It is well established from the medical case of *Rogers v Whitaker* that a negligence claim may lie against a professional who does not warn

PRIVATE LAW – NEGLIGENCE | **123**

their client of the material risks of planned intervention. However, matters of information provision and informed consent are always complex and very difficult in emotionally charged situations, particularly where 'barriers of language, culture, gender or ethnicity exist' (Swain 1996 p. 48). The Indigenous removal cases often reveal this issue when the consent on the part of a mother who is illiterate, confused and under pressure, is asserted.

In the human services, the question of whether or not to warn about a risk posed by someone, perhaps a client or a student (eg Hicks and Swain 2007) to third parties often arises, attended by the tension between breaching confidentiality and promoting the safety of others. Various statutory reporting obligations have been outlined in previous chapters of this book, but in civil law the case of *Tarasoff v Regents of the University of California* 526 P2d 553 (1974) and 551 P2d 334 (1976) has mythical status in the human services as it is so often cited in human service law and ethics texts (eg Corey et al. 2007). In that case, the university student counsellor did not warn a student client's girlfriend that the student was threatening to kill her. He did kill her, despite the university police and the girl's brother being made aware of the threats. The girl's parents successfully sued the counsellor. He became the target, according to Mendelson (1993), because the police had immunity, the brother was part of the family and the counsellor had indemnity insurance. The extent to which this case is good law in Australia is still unclear (McMahon 1992; Mendelson 1993; Abadee 1995; McSherry 2001; McMahon 2006a; McMahon 2006b, Freckelton 2009). However, research with psychologists indicates that most of them think that they do have a legal duty to report information about dangerousness in their clients (Kampf et al. 2008).

Similar results could be predicted for other human service workers familiar with text books that include the *Tarasoff* case. The *National Privacy Principles* do allow for, but do not compel unauthorised disclosure of information when there is a significant danger to others.[1] There are cases in Canada and the United Kingdon (*Smith v Jones* [1999] 1SCR 455 and *W v Egdell and others* [1990] 1 ALL ER 835) in which prison psychiatrists breached confidentiality without consent because of the dangerousness of their clients. The courts in both cases confirmed the primacy of the public interest. In fact, Freckelton and Selby (2009; p. 433) conclude that these cases 'appear to leave a significant hole in terms of the obligation of a

[1] Available from http://www.privacy.gov.au

mental health practitioner to maintain' the confidentiality of information revealed by the client in the professional relationship.

Clark and North (2007), discussing the responsibilities of psychiatrists, also outline a small body of cases that are suggestive of a common law duty to disclose (perhaps to a carer), to prevent a patient suiciding or self harming.

Other possible, albeit less familiar, civil law actions are the focus of the next chapter, some of which appeared alongside negligence in the cases discussed in this chapter.

7 | Private law – other torts and civil actions

B<small>EYOND NEGLIGENCE THERE</small> is a range of other tort and civil actions that have current or emerging relevance to human services conduct. Some of them, such as the tort of false imprisonment, have already appeared alongside the negligence actions mentioned in a number of cases in the previous chapter. Luntz (2005) has argued that the intentional torts are more effective in protecting civil liberties than is negligence. It may be that human services cases in the future will feature these alternative torts or other civil actions more frequently. These actions have different requirements and advantages; for instance, in relation to onus of proof, necessity for damage, and statutory limitation periods, which may make them feasible when other claims, such as negligence, are not.

There are other possible developments or more obscure civil actions that may also be important in future legal responses to human services failures. Only a few are mentioned briefly in this chapter. 'Actions on the case' is an archaic umbrella term referring to a wide range of torts, of which negligence is one (Mendelson 2007). There is a subgroup of innominate actions on the case for acts that consequentially cause physical or mental harm (McGlone and Stickley 2009). A major example is where a defendant makes statements to another with the intention of shocking or frightening them, perhaps as a joke, and as a result mental or physical damage is caused. These causes may be useful where specific conditions of directness and intentionality required for other torts are not satisfied. Directness concerns the immediacy of act and interference. These innominate claims are infrequent but, as Mendelson (2007) says, may become of greater interest as courts face and attempt to negotiate contemporary issues and new fact situations within the limits of the new civil liability legislation. Trindade et al's (2007) example of how threats to someone may consequentially frighten and

125

harm another nearby person is easily imagined in many human services settings. In contrast, Handford (2006) is of the view that in future this sort of action is more likely and appropriately dealt with under negligence.

If the recommendations of the Australian Law Reform Commission (2008) in its recent review of privacy law are accepted, there will also be a new tort of breach of privacy in Australia. As this involves intrusion on personal space and personal life, it may be significant for the human services. Hall's (2000, 2006) notion of a tort of institutional abuse has even more potency for the human services should it ever be adopted in Australian law. The main point here is that actions are forever evolving or emerging and astute lawyers will find and test them, especially in the face of egregious wrongs.

In this chapter, the contours of the direct and nominate torts of trespass, and actions on the case of misfeasance in public office and defamation, are outlined, along with those of breaches of fiduciary and statutory duty. The law of contract is then briefly sketched and its past and potential role in human services-related actions considered. Yet again it is stressed that the summary herein does not substitute for authoritative sources that elaborate the details and subtleties in these areas of law.[1]

LAW OF TORTS

This section provides a discussion on the law of torts, including trespass to the person, misfeasance in a public office, defamation and breach of statutory duty.

TRESPASS TO THE PERSON

Trespass to the person includes direct and intentional wrongful acts, such as battery, assault and false imprisonment; actions that may also give rise to criminal charges. A negligent trespass cause may also lie in Australia if the acts that result in damage are unintentional or the intention is unknown. Negligent trespass to the person is the same as trespass without the intent. Negligent trespass does not require a duty of care to be in existence.

Trespass claims, unlike those in negligence, do not require damage to have occurred, although in practice most plaintiffs will allege it. Trindade

---

[1] For example: Handford, P. (2006). *Mullany and Handford's Tort Liability for Psychiatric Damage*. Sydney: Lawbook Co. Mendelson, D. (2007). *The New Law of Torts*. Melbourne: Oxford University Press. McGlone, F. and A. Stickley (2009). *Australian Torts Law*, 2nd ed. Sydney: LexisNexis Butterworths. Trindade, F. and P. Cane, et al. (2007). *The Law of Torts in Australia*, 4th ed. Melbourne: Oxford University Press. Walmsley, A. and A. Abadee, et al. (2007). *Professional Liability in Australia*, 2nd ed. Sydney: Lawbook Co.

PRIVATE LAW – OTHER TORTS AND CIVIL ACTIONS

et al. (2007) contend that this rule makes the action useful when the damage suffered will not prevail under a negligence claim; for example, humiliation or a non-recoverable psychological reaction. There are a number of other reasons why these sorts of actions may have advantages over negligence. Cockburn and Madden (2006 p. 315), writing of these advantages in relation to medicine, say in summary that 'trespass is actionable per se; the defendant bears the onus of proof; the rules of causation and remoteness which relate to negligence actions may not apply to trespass actions; and exemplary and aggravated damages may be awarded'. Thus, the damages may be both punitive and compensatory. These commentators add that in all jurisdictions in Australia, these torts are to varying degrees not included in the new civil liability legislation, and may be free of its constraints.

Battery is 'a direct act of the defendant that has the effect of causing contact with the body of the plaintiff without the latter's consent' (Trindade et al. 2007 p. 36) and assault 'occurs when one person deliberately creates in another an apprehension of imminent harmful or offensive direct contact and there is a reasonable belief that they have the ability to carry out that threat' (McGlone and Stickley 2009 p. 37). Battery is thus an act and assault is a threat to act. An act to be battery must be unlawful and with consent absent. Both actions must be intentional or negligent. Both of these actions have obvious possibilities for almost any human services setting. Physical interference or threat can be imagined in services as diverse as child care, juvenile justice, community work, residential and in-home aged care, mental health and disability.

The case in the United Kingdom of *Wainwright and Anor v Home Office* [2003] UKHL 53 illustrates how ordinary 'sloppiness' (at para 50) in human services operations may result in legal action and a claim of battery. In this case, a mother and her young son were strip searched, contrary to internal prison rules, before being allowed to visit their son and brother in prison. The prison search rules addressed matters of privacy and consent, and prohibited touching and full removal of clothes. The searches in question were conducted without proper consent, with limited privacy and the visitor son's penis was touched and his foreskin lifted. Both mother and son were distressed and the latter suffered posttraumatic stress disorder. Damages were initially awarded to both mother and son, and most of them later overturned. The House of Lords in the instant case canvassed, but did not find, that there was a tort of invasion of privacy. But it was conceded early on by the Home Office and never thereafter challenged in the courts, that damage would lie for battery in the touching of the penis.

False imprisonment, a tort of strict liability, requires that the defendant directly restrained the plaintiff's liberty (Luntz and Hambly 2006). A restraint that is lawful, for example, imprisonment or detention under mental health legislation, will not incur liability here. *Ruddock v Taylor* (2003) 58 NSWLR 269 is a recent immigration detention case canvassing this action. Here the plaintiff's visa was cancelled after he was found guilty of sexual offences against children. He was detained as an alien in immigration detention and prison. He sued for false imprisonment and was awarded damages. He survived one appeal, but a further appeal to the High Court (*Ruddock v Taylor* [2005] HCA 48; 79 ALJR 1534; 221 ALR 32) was allowed. A majority of the High Court found his visa cancellation and subsequent detention lawful under the provisions of the *Migration Act 1958* (Cth). In contrast, the plaintiff in *Goldie v Commonwealth of Australia* (No 2) [2004] FCA 156 succeeded in his false imprisonment claim and the court found that detaining someone on suspicion of them being unlawfully in Australia requires an objective scrutiny of the material available. That is, the scrutiny must be comprehensive and based in fact. The plaintiff there had been arrested and detained on suspicion as an alien when he had a valid visa. He was awarded $22 000 in damages, but also incurred liability for some of the costs.

Police and correctional cases in which plaintiffs have alleged that they were unlawfully detained are not uncommon and sometimes they demonstrate attempts to set human rights precedents. For example, in *Sleiman v Commissioner for Corrective Services; Hamzy v Commissioner for Corrective Services* [2009] NSWSC 304 the plaintiff prisoner Sleiman sought administrative law relief for what he argued was his unlawful incarceration in solitary confinement in Goulburn Correctional Centre. The New South Wales Supreme Court found that the role of law in protecting personal liberty is so important and the legislative constraints on segregated custody so particular, that complete compliance with it is essential. For this reason the court granted the prisoner leave to commence proceedings for a declaration on the place and circumstances of his imprisonment.

There are many reasons why detention by authorities may be unlawful. For example, prisoners held in error beyond their legal release date were successful in *Cowell v Corrective Services Commission of New South Wales* (1998) 13 NSWLR 714. Removal from his family and placement in a foster family was found to be false imprisonment in the *Trevorrow* case. It was of particular significance in that case that the Crown Solicitor had advised that removals of Aboriginal children were not lawful, other than under very specific circumstances, and that the relevant ministers and officers of the Aborigines Department were aware of this advice. As the removal was unlawful and not consented to by the child or his parents, the child had been falsely imprisoned by the state.

A number of defences to trespass actions may have particular applicability to human services actors. For example, necessity might be argued. That is, restraint or some other conduct, consistent with policy and community attitudes, was necessary to prevent harm to the plaintiff. However, courts are very cautious with this argument (Stuhcke 2005). A right to discipline might be a defence, but less so if it is inconsistent with social norms and the regulations of the relevant employer. The defence of self-defence and defence of others may also be available. Consent could also be a defence if it is voluntarily given, and if it is consent to the injury as compared with consent to a risk, as in negligence. Neither mistake nor contributory negligence is a defence (Stuhcke 2005).

MISFEASANCE IN A PUBLIC OFFICE

This tort action allows a plaintiff to sue for compensatory damages if a public official recklessly or maliciously, in the exercise of public duty, does acts that are unauthorised or invalid, and that cause the plaintiff harm. Trindade et al. (2007) say that the limits of the tort in Australia are not yet defined, although a wide approach has been taken as to who might be a public officer. It seems clear that the officer must have intended harm or known that their unlawful acts were likely to damage the plaintiff or the group that they belong to, and the plaintiff must suffer loss or harm. Todd (1992) cites English cases where prison officers who acted in bad faith in their treatment of prisoners were personally liable in this tort. Vicarious liability against their employers did not hold because the prison officers were engaged in intentional wrongdoing. Trindade et al. (2007) suggest that vicarious liability may now lie against the state in tort actions of this kind in Australia if the relationship between the wrongdoer and the state is able to found it. Freckelton (2005) is of the view that Cornelia Rau may have had a valid action in this tort, among others, against the Commonwealth. *Trevorrow* succeeded on this ground because the state knew that removals of Aboriginal children were taking place contrary to Crown Solicitor advice, that there would be a risk of harm to the children so removed, and that the risk was reasonably foreseeable.

In *Cornwall and Ors v Rowan* [2004] SASC 383, the state minister of community welfare was not successful in his appeal against a finding that he had committed misfeasance in public office. That case exposes a time in

South Australia characterised by acrimonious intra-sectorial and political debate about the funding of women's shelters. The minister initiated a review of the shelters, which was duly carried out by his appointed review committee. He also cancelled the joint Commonwealth–state funding of a particular shelter that had refused to sign a funding agreement. In its report to the minister, the review committee included reference to a number of unsubstantiated allegations about the personal and financial misconduct of the social work administrator of that shelter. The minister tabled the report in Parliament and the review chairperson subsequently answered questions about the report in television interviews. The shelter administrator sued the review committee and its chairperson, the minister, the television stations and the Commonwealth for vicarious liability, on a number of grounds including misfeasance in a public office in relation to the minister and defamation in relation to most of the other actors. The applicant was successful in her misfeasance claim and the defamation claim against the minister and the review committee chairperson.

Most of the original judgment for the plaintiff in that case was upheld on appeal. It was held that the minister had committed misfeasance in public office, not because he had tabled the report in Parliament as that was privileged, but because he chose to leave the allegations in the report with the intention of damaging the coordinator's reputation, justifying his decision to withdraw the shelter's funding, and mitigating the political controversy that was likely to follow his decision. It was further found that the administrator was not owed a duty of care in the circumstances and that the Commonwealth was not vicariously liable for the actions of state authorities, as there was no evidence that the review activity was a joint enterprise between the two levels of government. The plaintiff was awarded damages of \$280 425.10, for which the minister and the chairperson were jointly liable. No judgment was made about the vicarious liability of the state, as it had not been pleaded.

The case of *Chan Yee Kin and the Minister for Immigration, Local Government and Ethnic Affairs and the Commonwealth of Australia* (1991) 103 ALR 499 illuminates misfeasance through another set of facts. In this case, the minister's delegate had refused a Chinese man a refugee visa, who was then detained while waiting deportation. The visa refusal had been overturned by the High Court and in the instant case the plaintiff sued the minister on a number of grounds, including misfeasance in public office. The Federal Court of Australia held that although there had been administrative error in the visa decisions, they had not been made with malice or bad faith. Einfeld J said (at para 51):

PRIVATE LAW – OTHER TORTS AND CIVIL ACTIONS | 131

I can find no support for the proposition tha[t] a genuine good faith decision of an administrator, which is held on administrative law principles or in the exercise of a supervisory jurisdiction to be legally erroneous, can attract a liability in tort for damages.

DEFAMATION

Doyle and Bagaric (2005 p. 64), relying on common law precedents, define the general rule of defamation as 'any publication or imputation which tends to injure a person's reputation in the estimation of others by making them think less of that person, usually by bringing the person into hatred, contempt, or ridicule'. The tort of defamation is a particularly complex and technical area of law because different legislation in each jurisdiction has been, over time, superimposed on the common law (Trindade et al. 2007). This composite landscape has, in turn, been resurfaced by a Commonwealth-led initiative resulting in the enactment of the *Uniform Defamation Act* which came into operation in each of the state jurisdictions in 2005 and 2006, with the territories to follow (Mendelson 2007).The common law still applies in each jurisdiction, other than as modified by this new Act. Legal cases based on actions that took place prior to the application of the new Act will be heard under the previous law in the relevant jurisdiction and the Uniform Acts will have to be read in conjunction with existing laws in each jurisdiction (LexisNexis 2007). The new Act also removes the common law distinction between slander (ie speech) and libel (ie written including electronic), as methods of harming reputation.

The *Cornwall* case covered above was decided before the enactment of this new legislation. In that case, the social worker argued successfully against the minister and the review committee chairperson that her reputation as a shelter manager had been damaged by the unsubstantiated allegations in the report and referred to in the television interviews. However, the television channels were not guilty of defamation because their reliance on the defence of qualified privilege was accepted. They were covering a matter of public interest and one which both the common law and the new Act, presumably, would aim to protect.

A great deal of human services activity is concerned with making, stating and writing assessments of others, particularly clients, which have defamation implications. At common law and under the Defamation Act, substantial truth is a defence to defamation, so accurate recording and reporting has always been and remains accepted as necessary and fair.

MISHAPS AND MISDEEDS THROUGH A LAW LENS

There is statutory protection, too, for many public documents that will have qualified privilege. Defamation law is concerned with protecting reputations that are solid and thus can be damaged, but not with preventing truthful and non-malicious commentary. It has already been shown in Chapter 6 that many human services reporting activities will be conducted under the rubric of a particular piece of legislation regulating that field of work, within which there is generally a good faith indemnity clause. Certainly most client-related material will never be published, although organisational and policy reports, as witnessed in the *Cornwall* case, might be. Generally, in government work, Crown law advice will be sought before a document is published if there is a question of potential litigation. The shelter review report in the *Cornwall* case had been referred to Crown law, but more on the question of cessation of funding than defamation. The advice given was followed only in part. The Defamation Act contains a number of provisions designed to encourage potential litigants to negotiate making amends rather than going to court.

Finally, the Act also enumerates an extensive range of defences to a defamation claim beyond that of truth. A complaint about published comments may fail if those comments are set within a contextual commentary that is substantially true. There is a defence of absolute privilege that relates to parliamentary and court operations and it was the common law version of this that protected the minister in the *Cornwall* case for the tabling of the shelter review report in Parliament. The defence of publication of public documents also relates to parliamentary, court and government documents that are open to the public. There is a defence of fair report of proceeding of public concern, and one of qualified privilege for dissemination of certain information. The latter defence in its common law form protected the television channels in the *Cornwall* case, but it will not hold if malice is proved. There is also a defence of honest opinion that allows for honest commentary that is based in solid material, of public interest and not claimed to be factual. Finally, there are defences of honest dissemination and triviality. The latter applies if the plaintiff was unlikely to be harmed. For successful defamation actions, the remedies are damages or injunctions.

BREACH OF STATUTORY DUTY

This action in tort may indicate the existence of negligence, but is not synonymous with it. It is a distinct action that may or may not accompany one in negligence. One of its advantages over negligence is that injunctions against threatened breaches can apply as well as the usual damages for

PRIVATE LAW – OTHER TORTS AND CIVIL ACTIONS

breaches (CCH 2007; Trindade et al. 2007). Facts that found this action may also give rise to a number of the offences explained in Chapters 3 and 4 on public law. The fundamental issue in this action is determination of the intent of the relevant statute. A private right of action is unlikely to be found if the statute imposes only a public duty. However, a statute is seldom clear about whether a right to private action under it was envisaged, so intention must be inferred (Mendelson 2007; Walmsley et al. 2007). An action for breach of statutory duty may lie if the defendant can prove (based on Luntz and Hambly 2006 p. 638):

- a tort action is allowed by the legislation
- the defendant is one of the people on whom a duty is imposed and has some control in the situation
- the plaintiff is one of the people protected by the statutory duty and is particularly vulnerable
- the defendant has breached the duty
- the plaintiff has suffered harm as a result
- the harm is in a form envisaged by the legislation.

This action may also be more acceptable where there are no other legal means, such as negligence, of enforcing a duty.

The tension between private rights and the duties and responsibilities of public authorities is evident in the *Chan* case and its predecessor. In *Chan v Minister for Immigration and Ethnic Affairs* (1989) 169 CLR 379, the High Court allowed an appeal against the minister's refusal, held to be unreasonable, to grant the visa. The plaintiff later sued the minister for false imprisonment, assault and trespass, and misfeasance in public office, among other things, on the grounds that the detention was illegal (*Chan Yee Kin and the Minister for Immigration, Local Government and Ethnic Affairs and the Commonwealth of Australia* (1991) 103 ALR 499). A breach of statutory duty was also alleged in relation to s 38 of the *Migration Act 1958* (Cth), which requires the minister to bring a person about to be deported before a magistrate within 48 hours of arrest. The Federal Court held, in very few words, that the breach gave no private cause of action.

Carroll (2007) claims that the tort was always of limited relevance, even before its attempted reading down by the Ipp reforms (see Chapter 6), as there are too many elements to satisfy. She argues that it should be abolished. Todd (1992) also contends that it will not provide much joy for prisoners seeking to take civil actions against prison authorities. However, Freckelton (2005) is of the view that it could have been one of the actions open to Cornelia Rau.

LAW OF EQUITY

This section provides a discussion on the law of equity, including breach of fiduciary duty and breach of confidence.

BREACH OF FIDUCIARY DUTY

Within the law of equity there are fiduciary relationships and obligations that if breached may found a civil action. These have traditionally concerned economic interests where conflicts about the accumulation of benefits arise. There are accepted categories of fiduciary relationships, such as those between solicitor and client, between employer and employee and between trustee and beneficiary (Walmsley et al. 2007). For new categories to be accepted, the courts will consider a number of indicia, which include a relationship of confidence, unequal bargaining power, the vulnerability of one party, and the capacity of one party to unilaterally exercise a discretion that will affect the interests of the other (Walmsley et al. 2007). The existence of a duty of care does not automatically imply a fiduciary duty and it is said that the courts are reluctant to impose fiduciary duties on existing common law ones when plaintiffs are pursuing preferred remedies (Walmsley et al. 2007). However, the High Court found both duties in *Bennet v Minister of Community Welfare* (1993) 176 CLR 408, outlined in Chapter 6 where a boy in detention lost his fingers in a saw accident. The remedies under this action include compensation, accounting of profits, and injunctions that stop a particular action.

Breach of fiduciary duty is sometimes argued in North American child abuse and neglect cases, although courts in Australia have not traditionally been receptive to the finding of fiduciary relationships in human services situations (Werren 2007). In *Cubillo v Commonwealth* (2000) 103 FCR 1, a fiduciary relationship between the Commonwealth and the Directors of Native Affairs was rejected on the grounds that the law of torts and not equity applied. The same reasoning was applied in the case of *SB v New South Wales* (2004) VR 527; VSC 514, which was outlined in Chapter 6. SB was successful in her common law claims, but equitable duties were held to be inapplicable. Significantly and more recently, both fiduciary and common law duties were found in *Trevorrow*. The breach of fiduciary duty there arose from failure on the part of the state to give the plaintiff 'full information as to the circumstances of his removal . . . and access to professional advice as to his legal rights to bring an action against the Crown in respect of its breaches of duty and unlawful conduct' (at para 1007).

PRIVATE LAW – OTHER TORTS AND CIVIL ACTIONS

Gray J said (at para 1008) that breaches of fiduciary duty are particularly relevant in extension of time cases where the state had a fiduciary duty and opposed applications for extensions. However, the plaintiff in *Trevorrow* was not awarded equitable damages in that case, as he received them for the parallel common law claims.

BREACH OF CONFIDENCE

Breach of confidence is another equitable action which, although traditionally used to protect commercial material from disclosure, can also be applied to personal information (Doyle and Bagaric 2005). Confidentiality is the protection of information given with an understanding of non-disclosure and received by a worker in a relationship of trust (McMahon 2008). A breach occurs when the information is used in an unauthorised way. Most worker–client relationships in the human services would thus be covered, as intimate information is being addressed in a context in which the value of confidentiality is affirmed by professional ethics and accepted practice standards. It is the client and not the worker who has the privilege when information is confidential, and it is the general rule that only the client can waive the privilege (ie consent to disclosure). It may also be possible to mount a negligence claim when confidentiality is broken if a duty is breached, harm is foreseeable and harm does in fact occur.

As seen in Chapter 3, immunity from civil action is often provided by legislation that mandates reporting of some kind or allows for discretionary reporting in the interests of public safety. Other defences are that the information was not given in confidence or that disclosure was consented to. There is also a defence of public interest in an action for breach of confidence and this may well apply where a worker divulges information about a client in the interests of public safety. A number of cases in which the public interest prevailed over private confidentiality were outlined in the Chapter 6 in the section on duty to warn (eg *W v Egdell* [1990] 1 ALL ER 835).

The Australian case of *R v Lowe* (1997) 2 VR 465 also confirms the primacy of the public interest when serious questions of public safety are at issue. The facts in this case are of the more exceptional kind in human services experience. An 'unqualified and self styled psychotherapist' (at para 483) was counselling a client simultaneously being investigated by police for the sexual assault and murder of a six-year-old girl. The psychotherapist had told the client that the sessions were confidential. Unbeknown to the psychotherapist, her counselling sessions with the client were being taped by the police. Later, after she had become disturbed by some of the client's revelations, she agreed to cooperate with the police, without the client's consent, by continuing the counselling sessions knowing that they were being taped. During these sessions the client made further admissions about the killing and was subsequently charged with murder. The counsellor breached the client's confidentiality and in theory could have been sued by her client. In theory, she could have mounted a public interest defence, and a public interest argument prevailed when her information became the subject of legal argument in the criminal case against her client. However, even if a public safety argument wins, as Freckelton and Selby (2009) suggest is increasingly indicated, it may not, according to Mendelson (1993), offset the humiliation and professional consequences of an action for breach of confidence.

In the *Lowe* trial the client's lawyers failed in their argument that the evidence from the counselling sessions should be inadmissible on the grounds that it had been gained in a context of trust and confidentiality. The Victorian Court of Appeal also later rejected this argument on the grounds that confidentiality was subordinate to the public interest, that confidentially in this sort of client–worker relationship is not absolute and that in general it is not privileged either. The confidentiality in this case was also not one protected under various and limited statutory provisions. The court said (at 485):

> . . . it has not been, and cannot be, suggested that health service providers are under a duty (in the interests of the patient) not to disclose confidential information if such disclosure will aid the protection of the public from a specific and identifiable threat.

McMahon (1998) argues that different issues may apply if the psychotherapist had been qualified, but it is difficult to see why this should be so, given that the fundamental issue was solving a serious crime and ensuring future public safety. She may be referring to some of the limited statutory protections for confidentiality in Victoria mentioned by the Court of Appeal, as these cover psychiatric and health services and clergy, and would thus generally involve qualified workers. However, statutory protections of this kind often skirt the qualifications question; for example, a 'counsellor or therapist' under the *Evidence Act 1929* (SA) s 67D is defined by the work done and includes volunteers. Statutory protections also often include a provision for dealing with conflict with other law. In addition, National

PRIVATE LAW – OTHER TORTS AND CIVIL ACTIONS | **137**

Privacy Principle 2.1 allows for disclosure of confidential information without consent on public safely grounds.

Confidentiality, like duty of care, is something of an omnipresent mantra in the human services (Kennedy and Richards 2007), although the rhetoric is not matched in practice (Clark 2006a). McMahon (2006 p. 603) contends in respect of health that much confidentiality activity is 'modern, secular ritual'. Despite these assertions, no human services civil court actions in Australia alleging breach of confidence have been found. This is not indicative of an absence of breaches in the human services. Many breaches are not known to the potential plaintiffs. Some breaches may have statutory immunity, either of the good faith or mandatory reporting kind outlined in Chapter 3. A few, in exceptional situations of the *Lowe* case type, may have public interest immunity. In addition, aggrieved people are less likely to take legal action than to make complaints either under privacy legislation as outlined in Chapters 3 and 5 or through complaints bodies, which are covered in the next chapter.

CONTRACT LAW

Contract law is a vast area of civil law separate from, but often used in conjunction with, torts actions (for differences between contract and torts see Trindade et al. 2007 pp. 8–11; McGlone and Stickley 2009 pp. 7–8). It has evolved mainly through commercial and financial activities, and as Brammer (2003) says of the United Kingdom but with relevance to Australia, it has not been much relied on in human services client cases to date. Saltzman (1999 p. 483) from the United States summarises a case in which a marriage counsellor was sued for breach of contract through failing to deliver competent services to a married couple. The counsellor fell in love with and was intimate with the plaintiff's spouse. Despite the few cases raised to date by clients, contracts are very relevant in the human services (Kennedy and Richards 2007). They are critical in the employer–employee relationship when disciplinary cases are reviewed. They are fundamental in the private professional–client relationship (eg Cordon and Preston-Shoot 1987), and also in the outsourcing of services, and particularly social services, by the state (Brown et al. 2006; VanSlyke 2007). The significance of ambiguous terms in contracts between the Commonwealth and detention centre providers in the immigration cases has been noted already in this and the previous chapter (see Australian National Audit Office 2005; 2006). Little will be said here about contract law beyond a very brief sketch of some main legal principles and a comment about its future potential in the human services. Authoritative texts on contract law should be pursued for more comprehensive information.[2]

Contracts are legally enforceable agreements. Contracts between parties may be express or implied; that is, they may be consciously constructed and agreed to or they may be construed by a court from the conduct of the parties. For a contract to be found, it must be clear that the parties intended to create legal relations (ie an offer was made and accepted). All parties to the contract must also promise something in the arrangement and this in law is called providing consideration. Contracts in turn contain terms that are express, not necessarily in writing, or implied. Implied terms may derive from legislation that mandates conduct or they may be imputed by the conduct of the parties (Walmsley et al. 2007). If terms of a contract are breached, a party to the contract may sue for damages that would restore them to the position they would have been in if the contract had been properly performed. Occasionally the offended party may also seek specific performance (ie an order from a court for the contract to be performed) or an injunction to prevent something happening that is contra to the contract. If it can be shown that it was in the terms of a contract for a party to exercise reasonable care and skill in fulfilling their contractual obligations and they fail to do this, it may be that an action in both contract and torts will lie against them.

Given the extent of outsourcing and privatisation in the human services and 'the complicated and politically charged' contracting processes (Brown et al. 2006 p. 323) along with limited public service contract management skills (Brown et al. 2006; VanSlyke 2007), the conditions are set for an increase in legal actions for performance failures or other breaches, despite the financial and political disincentives against litigation. Van Slyke (2003) notes that some government agencies in the United States recognise their vulnerability to allegations of fraud because of their inability to manage their contracts and contracted service provision. At the individual level, it is also just possible that contract law may provide a new avenue of redress for service users harmed in human services operations. Bagot (2002), for example, canvasses the idea of individual prisoners suing prison authorities directly for breach of contract or attempting to enforce the terms of contracts between governments and private prison operators. She argues that

---

[2] For example, Gooley, J., Radan, P., et al. (2006). *Principles of Australian Contract Law.* Sydney: LexisNexis Butterworths. Chen-Wishart, M. (2008). *Contract Law,* 2nd edn. New York and London: Oxford University Press.

the first contractual action is likely to be hampered by lack of consideration at least. On the second option, there are problems for prisoners in privity principles (ie their claim to be a party to the contract), in knowledge of the contract details and in choice of remedies. In conclusion, she is pessimistic about the role of contract litigation in enhancing accountability in prisons, but she does not close it off entirely.

In the chapters to date, the public and private law actions that have or are likely to be activated by human services mishaps and misdeeds have been covered. However, this does not exhaust the range of legal possibilities faced by human services transgressors. Legal processes themselves can trip human service actors, and there is a large array of legal bodies, most operating under some form of public law, that may scrutinise or discipline human services actions and actors.

8

Legal processes, quasi and indirect legal scrutiny

IF A PUBLIC OR PRIVATE law action for unlawful or substandard service delivery is not raised against human service actors, this may not be the end of the story in terms of the law and human services shortcomings. Legal processes, rather than substantive law, can found tales of woe for human service actors. Bodies with investigatory legal authority may be activated by human services transgressions. Perhaps most importantly, mishaps and misdeeds may attract legally based disciplinary responses.

This chapter begins with a comment on legal processes, but deals largely with quasi-legal bodies in relation to flawed human services activity. It concludes with an overview of legally founded disciplinary actions and sanctions that may confront individual human service workers who have acted unlawfully or inadequately in some way.

LEGAL PROCESSES

This section discusses collateral exposure through legal action and court work for human service actors.

COLLATERAL EXPOSURE THROUGH LEGAL ACTIONS

As stated earlier, human service workers and their employing organisations whose service appears less than exemplary although not criminal, may be exposed through the criminal behaviour of others. This is particularly likely in areas of work such as corrections, child protection and mental health, where the criminal actions of clients cause public outrage and the work of the relevant statutory authorities is scrutinised and criticised, fairly or otherwise. For instance, when a two-year-old child was allegedly tortured and killed by his father in 2007 in Queensland soon after being returned to his parents by the Queensland Department of Child Safety, the criminal charges against the father were paralleled by press and ministerial comments about the age, lack of experience and inadequate skills of child safety officers (AAP 2007a). Such human services trials by press have been observed in the United States (eg Brawley 1995) Canada (Regehr et al. 2001) and in Australia (eg Mendes 2001).

Similarly, human services actors may be exposed through court scrutiny in a civil action. The negligence cases of *SB v New South Wales* (2004) 13 VR 527 and *Trevorrow v State of South Australia* (No 5) [2007] SASC 285, addressed in Chapter 6, are good examples of the way in which the failures of a human services agency and its staff at all levels may be exposed through an action in which only one of them (the department) is named as the defendant.

COURT WORK

In the normal course of human services activity, workers may prepare reports for courts, or appear as witnesses. The tribulations experienced by human service workers whose written material or testimony fails to impress courts and lawyers are extensively documented (eg Braye and Preston-Shoot 1997; Cull and Roche 2001; Vogelsang 2001; Barsky and Gould 2002; Swain 2002b; Brammer 2003; Brayne and Carr 2003; Gould and Barsky 2004; Swain 2005; Freckelton 2006c; Kennedy and Richards 2007; Seymour and Seymour 2007; Stevens 2007; White et al. 2007). It is sufficient for current purposes to observe that while cultural differences between legal and human services spheres may contribute to what is perceived by human services actors as legal savaging, more is attributable to the poor quality of the reports and the evidence given. Any deficiencies in court performance are likely to be publicly noted and recorded.

Courts are not shy of commenting unfavourably on the testimony and credibility of human services witnesses in civil and criminal actions. For instance, in the defamation and misfeasance case of *Cornwall and Ors v Rowan* [2004] SASC 383 outlined in Chapter 7, the appeal judges record the views of the original judge about the testimony of witnesses, one of them a minister and many of them very senior public servants. Quotes include 'plainly wrong', 'most unimpressive', 'careless and on occasions, quite inappropriately flippant', 'unconvincing', and 'clearly opportunistic'. The appeal judges paraphrase the judge's concerns about witness 'self-justification' and 'prone[ness] to exaggeration' (at paras 48–56). In the industrial case *The Salvation Army v Mejia-Rodriguez-Appeal* [2003] SAIRComm 65, the commissioner's findings about the human services witnesses, both peers and managers, are summarised (at para 7) with words such as 'honest but vague', 'evidence was coloured', 'unreliable in several respects because of inconsistencies' and 'overtly negative manner'.

While social workers are used as expert witnesses in courts in the United States (see Vogelsang 2001; Barsky and Gould 2002; Pollack 2003), for a number of reasons this has not been common practice in Australia, and it is even less likely that a more generic human service worker would be called. Generic human service workers have less identifiable professional identities, fewer years of training, and possibly lower status in the legal system. Human service workers of any kind are likely to contribute information and knowledge that falls foul of the traditional common knowledge and ultimate issue rules in law. While these have been largely amended by legislation over time, their echoes remain in legal attitudes towards human services expert witnesses and their evidence (Kennedy with Richards 2007).

In Australia, social workers are called on occasion as expert witnesses; for example, *W v W* (2005) 34 Fam LR 129 was an appeal from a finding that the appellant could not have unsupervised contact with his young daughter on the grounds of evidence of sexual abuse. A social worker who had worked with the child was called as an expert witness and, while her capacity was challenged by the appellant because 'she was a social worker not a psychologist or psychiatrist' (at para 152), the court accepted her evidence. It said (at para 153): 'Ms M had 23 years experience in family therapy and sexual abuse cases. She was a suitably qualified expert, giving evidence within a specialised area of skill and knowledge'.

If a human services worker is accepted as an expert, court performance and evidential flaws will be observed. In the case of *SB v New South Wales* (2004) 13 VR 527 detailed in Chapter 6, in which a client successfully sued the New South Wales Department of Community Services for leaving her in a sexually abusive placement with her father, a social work expert was called. The department briefed an academic social worker who gave evidence on the department's intervention processes and its knowledge of child sexual abuse. Redlich J said of that expert's evidence (at para 438):

> I did not find [her] opinion persuasive that prior to 1986 the Department had little knowledge or understanding of child sexual abuse within a family setting. I could find no support in the evidence for the arbitrary line which she had drawn in the year of 1986.

LEGAL PROCESSES, QUASI AND INDIRECT LEGAL SCRUTINY | **143**

Psychologists are called more commonly than social workers as experts in human services cases and salutary lessons can be learned from their experiences in courts. For example, in the murder case of *R v Lem* (No 1) [2004] SASC 416, a psychologist was called to give expert evidence on the intellectual capacity of the defendant, a Cambodian man who had limited English. Nyland J, in ruling on a voire dire (at paras 78–86), detailed the psychological testing processes and interviews, expressed amazement that an interpreter had not been used in these processes and found the psychologist to have a defence bias. She concluded in relation to the psychologist's evidence, 'I therefore place little reliance on it' (at para 86). The Family Court in *W and W* (2001) 28 Fam LR 45 was even more damming of the child psychologist expert in the lower court hearing. In this contested custody appeal, the court found the psychologist to be biased in favour of the husband, to have drawn conclusions about people without having had contact with them, and to have made farfetched linkages and claims. The majority judges, in allowing the appeal, said (at 69): 'Dr W was prepared to go well beyond the position of an expert commenting on facts that were common ground or the opinion of other experts and was stepping into the ring himself' and later on the same page, 'We believe that a careful reading of Dr W[s] evidence reveals him to have been extremely partisan to the point where we find it difficult to accept his professional objectivity'. Misplaced advocacy of this kind by human service workers is at the least embarrassing and probably damaging to one's professional reputation.

Ordinary and expert human services witnesses who perform unconvincingly in courts may be merely discomfited by the sorts of comments just enumerated. Expert witnesses who breach codes of conduct relevant to witness functions may be subject to disciplinary procedures through professional associations or registration bodies if they are registered. Registered or not, would-be expert witnesses may experience a decline in referrals. Expert witnesses are, however, traditionally immune from civil action for the opinions they express in courts (Freckelton and Selby 2009).

STANDING COMPLAINTS AND INVESTIGATORY BODIES

While most agencies and workers whose performance is substandard will never be named as parties in a direct legal action or appear before courts or tribunals, many will be dealt with by complaints mechanisms internal to the agency concerned, and all are subject to the scrutiny of external state-sponsored special and ongoing investigation and complaints bodies. These external bodies are increasing in number and impact in health in particular (Devereux 2002), and across the human services. The close attention of an investigatory or complaints body may be no less revealing and exposing of unsatisfactory conduct than a legal action and its outcomes, and in many cases, no less consequential.

A range of tribunals and commissions that deal with administrative error and discriminatory conduct were referred to in the public law chapters, which outline standing and special bodies of major relevance to the human services. The list is not exhaustive as there are many state bodies that have monitoring, investigation, compliance and enforcement responsibilities, some of them overlapping. Some of these bodies were mentioned in earlier chapters; for example, Auditors General (ie Australian National Audit Office), parliamentary committees, and the Aged Care Standards and Accreditation Agency. There are also protective commissioners, such as those for children and young people, and the aged and disabled, who have watching and advocacy briefs. The following list includes the major investigation and complaints bodies for which allegations of inadequate and improper human services conduct are core business.

THE AUSTRALIAN HUMAN RIGHTS COMMISSION

The Australian Human Rights Commission (AHRC), previously known as the Human Rights and Equal Opportunity Commission (HREOC), is empowered under Commonwealth legislation to administer the Commonwealth discrimination Acts outlined in Chapter 3 and reports to the Australian Government through the Attorney-General. It investigates and conciliates complaints and human rights breaches under these Acts, investigates human rights issues of national importance, including alleged breaches by the Australian Government of international human rights standards, develops human rights educational resources, provides advice to courts and governments on human rights matters and conducts human rights research (Australian Human Rights Commission n.d.). The AHRC attempts to conciliate complaints about unlawful discrimination under the above Acts, but if conciliation fails, complainants may pursue the matter in the federal courts.

The AHRC is a body with particular significance for the human services, in connection with misdeeds and mishaps and beyond. It hears individual

LEGAL PROCESSES, QUASI AND INDIRECT LEGAL SCRUTINY | **145**

complaints of the kind outlined and illustrated in Chapter 3. However, it also investigates and attempts to conciliate complaints brought by human services advocates and individuals pursuing precedents of relevance to a class of people. It also investigates and reports to government on significant human rights matters. Although this function may be harnessed by human services advocates, other human service actors, particularly at the organisation and system level, can find themselves the subject of extensive, critical and public commentary. For example, in relation to immigration detention, the AHRC has reported to government on violations of the *International Convention on the Rights of the Child*, the *International Covenant on Civil and Political Rights* and the *International Covenant on Economic, Social and Cultural Rights*, in respect of arbitrariness of detention, children in detention, conditions in detention, access to legal advice, appeal rights, rights to services in the community, and so on (Australian Human Rights Commission 2008).

OMBUDSMEN

The existence of an ombudsman in each jurisdiction, including the Commonwealth,[1] who investigates the administrative actions of public authorities, has been mentioned previously. Ombudsmen are appointed by parliaments to investigate complaints of a wide range of wrong actions or inactions by public bodies and officials. They are independent of government and have the power to investigate, critique, recommend remedial action and publicise their findings, but they do not have determinative power and their recommendations are not enforceable. Ombudsmen must act within the powers specified in the legislation that creates them in each jurisdiction, but the Acts are similar in endowing them with power to investigate administrative acts (Douglas 2006). Generally, they have wide powers of conflict resolution and investigation. Ombudsmen are also able to investigate on their own initiative.

---

[1]
Australian Capital Territory	http://www.ombudsman.act.gov.au
New South Wales	http://www.ombo.nsw.gov.au
Northern Territory	http://www.omb-hcscc.nt.gov.au
Queensland	http://www.ombudsman.qld.gov.au
South Australia	http://www.ombudsman.sa.gov.au
Tasmania	http://www.ombudsman.tas.gov.au
Victoria	http://www.ombudsman.vic.gov.au
Western Australia	http://www.ombudsman.wa.gov.au
Commonwealth	http://www.ombudsman.gov.au

146   MISHAPS AND MISDEEDS THROUGH A LAW LENS

Ombudsmen generally resolve matters, but if an action is unlawful or in other ways unreasonable or unjust, they can report formally to the department and minister concerned. They also play an expanding and significant role in monitoring and commentating on the health of the public sector through their good administration guidance and special report functions (Kirkham 2004; Stuhmcke and Tran 2007). They have the capacity, much more so than courts, to assess the respective contributions to dysfunction of the system, the organisation and the worker.

The Commonwealth Ombudsman's special investigation in relation to the Welfare to Work reforms, and its policy recommendations on the 'marriage-like' relationship social security test, have already been mentioned. Douglas' (2006) review of complaints to the Commonwealth Ombudsman indicates that most compaints concern perceived unsatisfactory, rather than unlawful, behaviour. In fact, over-rigid compliance with the law can produce this dissatisfaction. It is not surprising that the agencies or departments with the highest levels of contact with the public generate the most complaints. The 2006–07 annual report of the Commonwealth Ombudsman shows that 75% of all complaints dealt with in that year emanated from five agencies, including Centrelink, the Child Support Agency and the Department of Immigration and Citizenship (Commonwealth Ombudsman 2007).

Human services departments, agencies and workers are subject to very close attention when an ombudsman investigates a complaint or a more general deficiency in their service. Their behaviour or service actions may also be detailed and evaluated in publicly accessible written reports or in public statements (excluding full names). For example, Ombudsman Tasmania's investigation into a complaint about calculations of remission in Risdon Prison remarks on the inadequacy of the Department of Justice Corrective Services' remission policy documents (Ombudsman Tasmania 2007). An example of a less benign and more individually targeted report, by Ombudsman Victoria, relates to a complaint about excessive use of force in the privately run Melbourne Custody Centre (Ombudsman Victoria 2007). It was found that unwarranted excessive force had been used against a prisoner and the *Charter of Human Rights and Responsibilities Act 2006* (Vic) breached. Unfavourable observations about incident monitoring systems in the prison, prisoner access to telephone contact with solicitors, and an unhealthy staff culture, among other things, are recorded. Among the recommendations made is one to review the suitability of officers X, Z and Y for ongoing employment. Unlike a court finding, this is only a recommendation, but it is likely to result in some form of disciplinary action or damaged career prospects for the officers (whose identity would be known to the employer and others in the corrections field).

In another human services example, the NSW Ombudsman presented a special report to parliament on monitoring and licensing of boarding houses in that state (NSW Ombudsman 2006). The report makes a number of findings about serious problems, including comments about licensing gaps that leave some young people and some people with a disability unprotected. It provides a critique of the monitoring system and observes that particular Department of Ageing, Disability and Home Care regions have not carried out their responsibilities. Again, no outcome is compelled, but the spotlight turned on one or two regions may cause job discomfort, if not career disruption, for some managers. The New South Wales Parliament may also be moved to amend the relevant legislation and devote more resources and attention to boarding house regulation and development in that state.

COMPLAINTS COMMISSIONS

There is now in each Australian state and territory a mechanism created to receive, investigate and sometimes impose sanctions in relation to complaints about health and sometimes community services.[2] These bodies, referred to in Chapter 2 and listed in Table 8.1, are an increasingly significant presence in the lives of human service actors. All human services agencies and workers in the private and public health arena will be covered and large numbers in the other human services, either because health is broadly defined in the health-only jurisdictions or because the legislation in the other jurisdictions specifically includes the human services.

Complaints bodies are generally independent of government, do not charge fees, take an informal, cooperative and conciliatory approach to complaints handling and have a range of outcomes including apology, remedial treatment, explanations, and referrals to professional registration boards. Although these bodies have traditionally had limited powers in

---

[2] Australian Capital Territory   http://www.hrc.act.gov.au
New South Wales   http://www.hccc.nsw.gov.au
Northern Territory   http://www.nt.gov.au/omb_hcscc/hcscc/index.htm
Queensland   http://www.hrc.qld.gov.au
South Australia   http://www.hcscc.sa.gov.au
Tasmania   http://www.healthcomplaints.tas.gov.au
Victoria   http://www.health.vic.gov.au/hsc
Western Australia   http://www.healthreview.wa.gov.au

148 | MISHAPS AND MISDEEDS THROUGH A LAW LENS

Table 8.1 *Health and human services complaints bodies*

Jurisdiction	Body	Services/providers covered
Australian Capital Territory	Human Rights Commission Health Services Commissioner Human Rights and Discrimination Commissioner Disability and Community Services Commissioner Children and Young People Commissioner	Aged care, disability, children and young people and health services
New South Wales	Health Care Complaints Commission	Health services and providers (eg health clinics, hospitals), registered health professionals and unregistered health providers (eg psychotherapists, acupuncturists)
Northern Territory	Health and Community Services Complaints Commission	Health and community services such as hospitals, nursing homes, supported accommodation, disability and aged services, counsellors, masseurs, carers and home care
Queensland	Health Quality and Complaints Commission	Services for benefit of human health including hospital, community and mental health, allied health, disability, social work and welfare services within health service, psychotherapists, counsellors, and health promotion
South Australia	Health and Community Services Complaints Commissioner	Health and community services such as health clinics, alternative health therapists, registered health professionals, child protection services

Table 8.1 *(cont.)*

Jurisdiction	Body	Services/providers covered
Tasmania	Health Complaints Commissioner	Services for benefit of human health including hospital, nursing home, community health, mental or physical disability services
Victoria	Health Services Commissioner	Health services such as doctors, hospitals, psychiatric services, physiotherapists, alternative therapists, counsellors, health social workers
Western Australia	Office of Health Review	Health and mental health services and professionals, including social workers and disability services

relation to unregistered workers (Wilson 2002; Carlton 2003), this may be changing with the developments in New South Wales, outlined in Chapter 4. The New South Wales Health Care Complaints Commission has prohibition and public warning powers under s 41A of the *Health Care Complaints Act 1993* (NSW). This point will be returned to later in this chapter. Within the ranges of their diverse legislative mandates, these bodies examine individual complaints and undertake investigations of systemic problems. Individual workers and agencies may find themselves the subject of a complaint and considerable scrutiny. If the complaint has substance, they may be encouraged to make good in some agreed way (ie in a way that has some relevance to the circumstances of the complainant that prompted the complaint).

Individual and agency deficiencies may contribute to the statistics or underpin the case studies cited in the annual reports of complaints bodies. Individual workers, agencies and service systems may also be exposed when systemic problems are alleged and investigated. This is evidenced in the Health Complaints Commissioner Tasmania's investigation into mental health services in northern Tasmania (Office of the Health Complaints Commissioner 2005). The report details particular allegations of sexual misconduct as well as chronic service failures in safety procedures, regional management, professional judgement and discharge planning, among other things.

150 | MISHAPS AND MISDEEDS THROUGH A LAW LENS

Individual workers may be the main focus of a report as exemplified by a medical doctor in Western Australia who performed a vasectomy on a patient with Down syndrome when the patient did not have the capacity for informed consent, and in ignorance of the requirements of the *Guardianship and Administration Act 1990* (WA) (Office of Health Review 2000). That doctor was referred to the Medical Board of Western Australia. Workers and agencies may appear unfavourably or have their practices affected by reports on specific techniques. In 2005, the Victorian Health Services Commissioner reported on the practice of recovered memory therapy (Health Services Commissioner 2005). Of particular import for human service workers, particularly those in private practice, are the expressions of concern and recommendations in the report about unregistered professionals using recovered memory therapy while functioning in isolation, without adequate peer review or support, or access to professional development.

RISK OF COMPLAINTS TO STANDING BODIES

Standing investigation and complaints authorities are intended to be more complainant-friendly than courts, as they take an inquisitorial approach, are less formal, require a less demanding burden of proof than criminal courts, and take responsibility for managing the investigation (in courts, the complainant must take this responsibility). However, many of the factors that inhibit legal action also apply to standing investigation and complaints authorities – similarly applicable obstacles to complaint were mentioned in Chapter 2. Lack of knowledge, capacity, and trust in the potential complainant, along with anxiety about retribution, disbelief in the processes and statutory time limitations, may all impede the lodging of a complaint.

SPECIAL COURTS, INQUIRIES AND COMMISSIONS

Human services activities that have attracted negative public attention may become the subject of special inquiries, many already mentioned in this book, or even royal commissions. These government-initiated inquiries are conducted by bodies of the kinds listed earlier in this chapter or may be internal to a private organisation (eg the Anglican church, see Olsson and Chung 2004). They may be conducted by special-purpose bodies or standing bodies that have wider legal mandates beyond health and human services. Child protection, immigration, mental health, disability, corrections, Indigenous affairs, social security and aged care are some areas of practice that have been, and will probably continue to be, scrutinised by special-purpose investigations.

Some of these inquiries have national scope, significance and lengthy reverberations. An example is the *Bringing Them Home* report on the taking of Indigenous children from their families (Wilson 1997). Some inquiries focus on practices within a sector in a state – two examples of these are the Layton Report (a review of child protection in South Australia) (Layton 2003) and the Wood Commission (into child protection in New South Wales) following the high-profile deaths of several children in 2007 (Wood 2008). Some inquiries have narrower terms of reference, but may be targeted (and thus have more impact on individual workers). For example, a New South Wales inquiry in 2006 investigated 29 juvenile justice workers who had been viewing pornography and circulating it by work email (AAP 2007d). The same source reported that members of the group were fined and the matter referred to the Independent Commission Against Corruption.

Inquiries, often themselves flawed by limited terms of reference, multiple agendas and other constraints, can seriously expose and question the competence of individuals (eg Swain 1996) and service systems. Their capacity to bring about significant change is another matter, but the repeat character of some of them suggests limited effectiveness, particularly in respect of implementation. Problems with implementation of recommendations were noted in the second Senate Standing Committee on Community Affairs inquiry into children in institutional or out-of-home care (Senate Standing Committee on Community Affairs 2005).

CORONERS' COURTS

If a death that appears unnatural, suspicious, unexpected or violent (Freckelton and Ranson 2006a) occurs during human services activity, a coroner's investigation or inquest into its cause is likely. Whether an inquest is legislatively mandated or not, family members and advocacy groups may agitate for one to be held and this is increasingly the case in relation to nursing home deaths (Freckelton and Ranson 2006a) and in Victoria soon in relation to deaths subsequent to discharge from an approved mental

152 | MISHAPS AND MISDEEDS THROUGH A LAW LENS

health service (Freckelton 2009). There are legislative differences between jurisdictions about the circumstances under which an inquest is mandatory or discretional (see for differences and similarities MacFarlane 2000 pp. 243–4). There is also a large body of coronial law for which a comprehensive authority should be consulted for full details.[3] Deaths in institutions such as prisons, nursing homes and in alternative care have contributed significantly to coronial case law (Freckelton and Ranson 2006a).

Coroners generally have wide powers in commanding evidence and are not bound by the rules of evidence. Their processes are inquisitorial rather than adversarial, which means that they can range freely across evidence that they believe will throw light on the circumstances of the death. Thus, human service workers who are involved with the coroner in inquests can expect to have their practices, records and memories carefully examined and to be questioned robustly during inquest hearings.

Other than in New South Wales, coroners do not have powers to commit people for trial (Freckelton and Ranson 2006a) and they are also proscribed from findings of civil liability, even though much of the evidence they hear may support a civil case. 'However the preclusion from making findings that a person is or may be guilty of an offence, or findings as to civil liability, does not include censorious criticism by coroners' (Freckelton and Ranson 2006a p. 650). Moreover, coroners can make findings about inadequate standards of conduct or practice, and their reports may expose and discomfort those involved. When a 17-year-old resident of a secure centre for young offenders in South Australia died soon after having seizures in 2006, the subsequent coroner's report detailed allegations about staff members bringing illegal drugs into the centre, criticised the quality of the police investigation into these allegations, and described the administration by staff of prescription drugs to the boy in the centre as 'less than ideal' (at para 4.7) (South Australian Coroner 2009).

Coroners also commonly make comments and recommendations about the circumstances of a death in an effort to avoid such deaths in the future. A commentary of this kind is illustrated in the inquest finding for Gerard McGrath, who was fatally shot by police in Melbourne in 1995 while police were attending a disturbance call from his parents (Freckelton and Ranson 2006a). McGrath had a known personality disorder and other difficulties. The coroner reported a lack of communication between police and psychiatric services, the absence of appropriate support to the family,

---

[3] Freckelton, I. and D. Ranson (2006). *Death Investigation and the Coroner's Inquest.* Melbourne: Oxford University Press.

LEGAL PROCESSES, QUASI AND INDIRECT LEGAL SCRUTINY

and various other intra- and inter-service inadequacies. The report also made specific service recommendations.

Generally there has been no mandated requirement for coronial reports and recommendations to be acted on, although media and political attention may demand changes of some sort, particularly if family members are dissatisfied with the report (Freckelton and Ranson 2006b; ABC 2008a). However, Victoria has taken a lead with a new Act, the *Coroners Act 2008*, which comes into force in late 2009. This Act imposes a range of new obligations on coroners and increases their powers in relation to recommendations (Freckelton 2009). The coroner in Victoria under the new Act must recognise the distress of family members, particularly when there are delays, must keep them informed and must be sensitive to and respectful of cultural differences around death. The coroner will also be empowered to make recommendations to any minister or public authority on a matter that they have investigated, and the recipient must provide a written response within three months explaining the actions that they have taken in respect of those recommendations (Freckelton 2009).

Swain's (2003) review of coronial reports on child protection deaths in Victoria in the years 1999–2000 found no policy or practice recommendations therein. In relation to child protection inquests, Swain is of the view that their protracted nature has often rendered them 'history' by the time their findings finally appear, and internal investigations and policy and procedure changes may have preceded them. The public appetite for such stories may also have faded. Given the spate of deaths of young children in recent years and the changed legislation in Victoria, a repeat study would no doubt come up with different findings.

In some jurisdictions, the legislation requires coroners to report to the Attorney-General on the circumstances of deaths of certain classes of people (eg children in care, prisoners, psychiatric inpatients). As indicated in the quote below, their commentary can be quite savage. However, Freckelton and Ranson (2006a) add that they generally focus on systemic problems and attempt to avoid blaming individuals in situations where the contextual factors have contributed to a death. Nonetheless, coroners' verdicts or findings often generate strong emotions and attract considerable media attention:

> For this reason they can devastate reputations . . . and can have major ramifications for affected persons and bodies in terms of both commercial and vocational viability. They can also have an indirect effect on secondary criminal, civil and disciplinary actions (Freckelton and Ranson 2006a p. 616).

MISHAPS AND MISDEEDS THROUGH A LAW LENS

Organisations and those responsible for service systems may thus have an interest in limiting the scope of an inquest. This is demonstrated in the English case of *Plymouth City Council v Her Majesty's Coroner for the County of Devon* [2005] EWCH 1014 (Admin), in which the details of the death of an infant from a family well known to the Plymouth child protection service are revealed. The child died from bronchopneumonia exacerbated by dehydration in the last two days of his life. Tragically, he was dying while a case conference about his situation was underway.

The authority and health services in the *Plymouth City Council* case had been working extensively with the family, who had several other children in care. The coroner had determined that the inquest should investigate broadly the operation of the child protection system and the knowledge, actions and omissions of the authorities in relation to that child. The coroner is quoted as having said that the 'system is judged by its results' (at para 5) and he intended to investigate fully so as to make recommendations that would reduce the risk of similar deaths in future. Plymouth City Council sought judicial review in the instant case, arguing the unlawfulness of the planned scope of the inquest and a narrowing of the scope of the inquest to the last two days of the baby's life. The coroner's determination was quashed on the grounds that there was no evidence that the authority should have known that there was a real and immediate risk to the child. The judge's comments indicate that he was sympathetic to the efforts of the authority to support and monitor the family.

CRIME AND MISCONDUCT COMMISSIONS

Public officials, agencies and service systems demonstrating corrupt, criminal or possibly criminal conduct in three states may be investigated by what Douglas (2006 p. 178) calls 'anti-misconduct commissions'. These are displayed in Table 8.2. These three bodies aim to prevent official misconduct as defined in each of the relevant Acts in the jurisdictions, and they are empowered variously by the Acts to investigate, report and make recommendations.

Human service actors, both individuals and organisations, have come to the attention of each of these misconduct investigatory bodies. For example, the Crime and Misconduct Commission inquired widely into abuse of children in foster care in Queensland (Crime and Misconduct Commission 2004), examined systemic inadequacies and made recommendations about extensive changes in organisation and culture. A new section of Child Safety Services in the Department of Communities resulted. The extent to which the root causes of the problems were satisfactorily identified and

LEGAL PROCESSES, QUASI AND INDIRECT LEGAL SCRUTINY | 155

Table 8.2 *Corruption and misconduct investigatory bodies*

Jurisdiction	Corruption and misconduct investigatory body	Legislation	Examples of human service-related investigations
New South Wales	Independent Commission against Corruption (ICAC)	*Independent Commission Against Corruption Act 1988* (NSW)	*Report on Investigation into the Case Management and Administration of community Service Orders* (2006)
Queensland	Crime and Misconduct Commission (CMC)	*Crime and Misconduct Act 2001* (Qld)	*Protecting Children: An Inquiry into Abuse of Children in Foster Care* (2004)
Western Australia	Corruption and Crime Commission (CCC)	*Corruption and Crime Commission Act 2003* (WA)	*Misconduct Handing Procedures in the Western Australian Public Sector: Department for Community Development* (2007)

accountability properly attributed by the inquiry is arguable (Lonne and Thomson 2005). However, there is no question that some senior human services managers at least would have experienced discomfort, if not had their career prospects damaged.

The Corruption and Crime Commission (CCC) conducted a review of the Western Australian Department for Community Development's misconduct management processes and found them wanting (Corruption and Crime Commission of Western Australia 2007). The department was responsible for vulnerable groups such as disadvantaged children, young people and families. It delivered services, managed large amounts of financial assistance to clients and funding to support organisations, and licenced child care. As the CCC report makes clear (p. 19), it operated in a high-risk environment and was legislatively endowed with enormous power. Nonetheless, the department could not properly quantify existing misconduct, reported 'unrealistically low' (p. 5) notifications of misconduct and had 'no systematic approach to misconduct management' (p. 5). Various recommendations about a misconduct strategy were made by the CCC.

Not all of the activities of these sorts of commissions result in disembodied investigations and reports. It is within their powers to review the behaviour of transgressing individuals in public authorities. The Independent Commission Against Corruption (ICAC) investigation and report, shown in Table 8.2, is one such example. The conduct of three named staff and their associates in relation to the management of community service orders is detailed in the report. Time sheets were falsified, confidential information from the New South Wales Department of Corrective Services database accessed, false references given, and work done on private houses. The ICAC made adverse findings about conflicts of interest, roles, responsibilities and line management, supervision, and record keeping in the community service order system. Recommendations included advice about departmental training procedures, induction programs, practice guidelines, communications, auditing of staff and performance appraisal. In addition, a number of staff and associates were recommended for referral to the Director of Public Prosecutions for consideration of criminal prosecutions.

Another example, this time from education, is provided by the CCC report in 2006: *Sexual Contact with Children by Persons in Authority in the Department of Education and Training of Western Australia* (Corruption and Crime Commission of Western Australia 2006). The report details the illegal behaviour of individual teachers, some of whom had also faced criminal charges, and the departmental response to their conduct. Unfavourable comments are made about senior and local managerial accountability, failure to comply with policies and procedures, poor record keeping, insufficient referrals to police and a concern for the welfare of staff over that of a safe education environment.

DISCIPLINARY ACTION AND SANCTIONS

For most human services workers who transgress, disciplinary action of some sort is the most likely consequence, if there is any consequence at all. This action may be taken by a professional association, but is much more likely to be by the worker's employer. Very few workers in the human services will be of interest to a professional registration board because occupational registration is not very common in the sector.

PROFESSIONAL ASSOCIATIONS

A tiny number of individuals who violate the rules and particularly the code of ethics of a professional association may face disciplinary action by that body. This action is dependent on the individual concerned being or remaining a member of the association, which in turn must have procedures for receiving, processing and adjudicating complaints against its members and capacity for enforcement of its dispositions. Moreover, potential complainants need to be aware of the grievance avenue and the membership status of the worker concerned, and must make the complaint within time limits and in accord with the by-laws of the body. Aggrieved people must, as in legal actions, have personal and knowledge resources to pursue a complaint through professional bodies that to the public may be obscure, mysterious and potentially self-protective. All these factors combine to reduce the risk of a successful grievance action against an individual worker.

In Australia, the fragmented and deregulated character of the human services workforce outlined in Chapter 2 reduces even further the likelihood of professional sanctions. The Australian Association of Social Workers (AASW) and Australian Institute of Welfare and Community Workers (AIWCW), the two most obvious professional bodies, capture only fractions of their potential memberships. Going by 6200 AASW members in 2004 and estimates of 12 000–14 000 graduates of social work in Australia in total in 2001 (more in 2004 if growth rates given by [Healy 2004] continued) (Australian Association of Social Workers 2004), less than half of the social work graduates in Australia are members of their professional association. On Gillingham's (2007) figures, AASW membership represents about 34% of the welfare and social work workforce and even less of the entire human services workforce. Cooper's (2007) figures on the proportion of university social work field supervisors who have AASW membership are much lower, and are falling relative to welfare worker numbers (Healy 2004; Healy and Meagher 2004). Even if eligibility for membership of AASW is required for employment, employers do not always check the applicant's claims (Australian Association of Social Workers 2004).

In relation to the AASW it is argued that the mechanisms for managing code of ethics violations are 'effectively toothless' (Swain 1996 p. 51) because non-members and those who relinquish membership while under investigation can continue to practise as social workers beyond the jurisdiction of the AASW (Murray and Swain 1999; Australian Association of Social Workers 2004). In addition, the code (Australian Association of Social Workers 2002) is non-specific, such that alleged violations are readily open to legal challenge. This commentary about violations is of even more relevance to AIWCW, which is an even less homogenous and well-resourced body with an even more generally worded code of ethics

(Australian Institute of Welfare and Community Workers n.d.). The ultimate sanction of a professional association is suspension of membership – this does not impede employment in the human services in Australia.

These professional bodies do conduct investigations into alleged unprofessional conduct (Murray and Swain 1999; Australian Association of Social Workers 2004), but the numbers and results showed that they are only exposing the tip of the mishap and misdeed iceberg. In the period 1999–2004, nine social workers determined by AASW to be ineligible for membership of AASW were still practising (Australian Association of Social Workers 2004 pp. 8 and 11). Many of those complained about are not members of AASW, or resign on investigation. It is likely, as suggested earlier in relation to registration board decisions, that professional people will be more protective of their reputations and inclined to seek and exhaust all possible impediments to an investigation or negative determination. The same can be said of members of a professional association, although professional association sanctions have less impact than those of a registration board. Although legal action in respect of AASW decisions is almost non-existent, the one known case that reached court shows a professional determined to challenge procedural injustices. In *Robinson v Australian Association of Social Workers Ltd* (2000) 206 LSJS 209, a family counsellor and member of AASW was subject to a complaint investigation that he contended was not conducted in accordance with the AASW's by-laws. He sought an injunction to halt the investigation and prevent a determination, both of which were refused on the grounds that the by-laws had been substantially complied with and that there had been no bias and no procedural unfairness. The counsellor appealed successfully on the question of costs in *Robinson v Australian Association of Social Workers Ltd* [2000] SASC 239 and the AASW was ordered to pay 50% of his costs.

EMPLOYERS AND EMPLOYEES

Unsatisfactory worker conduct will be noticed mostly, if at all, by employers, through internal investigation, audit, supervision or complaint processes. This may result in disciplinary action. However, it has been shown in this and the previous chapters, that unsatisfactory if not criminal behaviour may occur, but also be ignored or insufficiently attended to by supervisors and managers. However, these chapters have also been peppered with industrial cases and reports recommending disciplinary action, and chapters that follow show these as well. The range of possible disciplinary actions and their degree of formality will depend on which employment legislation

LEGAL PROCESSES, QUASI AND INDIRECT LEGAL SCRUTINY | 159

covers the workplace and worker, on relevant award and agreement conditions, the terms of the employment contract and the human resources policies and procedures of the employer. The public service Acts referred to in Chapter 3 determine the destinies of human service workers employed in the public sector. In respect of seriousness and formality, disciplinary actions may range from relatively casual oral feedback about performance deficiencies through to salary reductions, demotions, notes on personnel files, warnings and termination. The accurate details of almost all of these actions remain private, apart from workplace gossip, unless they too are contested.

A few workers are dismissed. Some examples of the unfair dismissal cases that not uncommonly result have been seen in previous chapters. The representativeness of the cases cited in these chapters is unknown – for every case that gets to an industrial court, innumerable others are not contested or are conciliated, arbitrated or finalised at the commission level. Nonetheless, human services unfair dismissal cases provide a revelatory window into supervisory and staff behaviour and credibility, workplace culture, staff dynamics, staff training and induction, and forms of transgressions. They also show glimpses of a substratum of histories, agendas and conflicts, which will be recognisable to human services readers, through the legal debates. These will be returned to in Chapter 12. Some of the cases reveal unsophisticated human resources management practices as much as they do worker misconduct. For example, in *Stuart Hill and the Department of Juvenile Justice* [2000] NSWIRComm 128, Sams DP concluded (at para 88) 'This case displayed a litany of procedural defects – the number, and seriousness, of which I regard as a disgrace, unbefitting any employer; let alone a major public employer in New South Wales'. Several different and illustrative unfair dismissal examples are outlined below.

Dismissal triggers may range from breakdowns in staff relationships, as will be seen in Chapter 12, to allegedly criminal behaviour. In the *Stuart Hill* case, a casual senior youth worker at the Riverina Justice Centre had been dismissed for allegedly supplying detainees with marijuana and cigarettes, attempting to purchase illicit drugs from the parents of a detainee, and failing to intervene in a sexual assault on a detainee. In the instant case, it was found that the dismissal was harsh because it was disproportionate to the gravity of the alleged conduct, unjust because the employer department had not proved the allegations and unreasonable because it relied on wrong inferences. Sams DP, who was patently unimpressed by the department's case, reinstated the worker at a location nearer his new home and ordered that he be back-paid from the time of his dismissal. Thus, poor human resources practices appear to have compromised action against what might well have been an unsatisfactory worker. In contrast, in *Thomson v Intellectual Disability Services Council* [2006] SAIRComm 21, the care worker was charged for assaulting an intellectually disabled resident during a restraint incident, and sacked. Criminal charges were subsequently dropped, but in the instant case the unfair dismissal application was dismissed. It was found that the care worker had not complied with the agency's procedures, had been trained, was not acting in self-defence and was not inexperienced in restraint situations. Likewise, the program coordinator from the same workplace who, on the balance of probabilities, had a sexual relationship with an intellectually disabled client, failed to have his dismissal overturned in *Squire v Intellectual Disability Services Council Inc – Appeal* [2006] SAIRComm 14.

Dismissal and its possible legal ramifications have particular significance in the human services context. The shallowness of supervisory and human resources capacity in the human services was noted in Chapter 2. Investigations of performance inadequacies require special skills and knowledge (Cambridge 2001). In addition, human services supervisors are often acculturated into a helping and toleration response mode. Thus, human resources processes and practices can be rudimentary and the discipline or termination of a colleague daunting. If a decision to dismiss is based on good evidence, particularly evidence about risk to clients, there are moral, ethical and possibly legal imperatives to pursue it. Failure to act on a genuine 'bad apple' or a major staff problem is unprofessional at least and possibly negligent, as will be shown in Chapter 12. However, the pursuit will require time, expertise and financial resources, which are not available in many human services agencies, and must be played out in an alien legal arena.

Inexpert legal advice, an unsympathetic commissioner or judge, poor witness skills and unequal tenacity between the parties can all contribute to employer failure in an unfair dismissal case, even when a worker has misbehaved seriously. The particular problem for the human services, in contrast to many other areas of work, is that a high-risk person is vindicated and returned to work with vulnerable people. However, although they should never be, cases of this type are frequently lost on the grounds of insufficient and poor evidence (eg the *Stuart Hill* case). Observation, recording, analysing and reporting on data are in theory the bread and butter of human services work. These skills applied properly can go a long way to offsetting some of the external difficulties in dismissal situations.

Employer organisations are no less liable to real or threatened industrial action by employees. Although the consequences may not be as personally devastating as they are when individual workers are targeted, the reputations of managers and the agency itself may be hurt by exposure in these conflicts. For example, it is reported that the Australian Services Union (ASU) took action in 2008 on behalf of a group of youth workers employed by the Marist Youth Centre in New South Wales because their shift rosters had been rewritten, albeit legally, in a way that significantly reduced their salaries (AAP 2008f). The same source reported the name of the chief executive and ASU allegations that mismanagement in the organisation had created a financial crisis, which in turn resulted in the roster changes. These changes were said by the union to put the safety of staff and residents at risk. This sort of publicity is never welcome and in some cases it may put ongoing government funding at risk.

It is now time to turn from a primarily legal perspective on shortcomings as applied to the human services, to a primarily human services perspective in which human services activity that has or might invoke legal interest is canvassed in relation to the law covered to date. Human services endeavours and the mishaps and misdeeds that attend them are the focus of the next four chapters.

Part 3

Mishaps and misdeeds through a human services lens

9

Service delivery – screening, assessment and planning

On the first page of the report, of the inquiry into Vivian Alvarez's unlawful removal from Australia to the Philippines in 2001, is the following finding: 'On the basis of information Vivian provided, a social worker at the Richmond Clinic [psychiatric Unit] advised the Department of Immigration and Multicultural and Indigenous Affairs (DIMIA) office in Southport . . . that Vivian might be an illegal immigrant' (McMillan 2005 p. ix). Thereafter ensued a litany of 'catastrophic' (p. xv) and 'systematic failures in DIMIA' (p. xiii) which resulted in Ms Alvarez's 'disappearance' from Australia. Here is irrefutable evidence of the power and potential impact of the earliest presumptions and decisions, righty or wrongly made by human services agents in their interactions with those who enter their service networks.

The earliest phase of human services activity with potential clients involves a process of interpersonal engagement, information gathering and screening for agency–client fit or referral elsewhere. In this first contact, human services actors are ideally conducting a complex dual process; appraising the person in terms of service criteria and resources, while simultaneously and as objectively as possible observing behaviour and need, independent of agency demands. Workers' first appraisals are critical in determining much of what follows in the way of service activity. As Schön (1991) has so seminally argued, and others elaborated (eg Camilleri 1996; Gambrill 2006), the finding and framing of a problem is as important as any intervention intended to solve it. Workers, and sometimes administrative workers in the first instance, make these initial appraisals within an organisational context which either enhances or hinders genuine personalised assessment through, for example, its data-gathering tools, frameworks, recording systems and supervisory and administrative support. Workers

166 | MISHAPS AND MISDEEDS THROUGH A HUMAN SERVICES LENS

also make appraisals within the limits of their own training and competence. Soon after first contact, if the client is accepted into the service system, some form of more comprehensive assessment is generally undertaken and this in turn leads to referral or service planning activity. Depending on the nature of the agency and service, these initial and more detailed assessments may overlap, be emphasised or be de-emphasised, but such variations do not matter for present purposes.

This chapter considers problems particularly relevant to these early phases and activities which have led to or could found legal risk. Some of these problems span all or several phases of human services intervention but are positioned herein at junctures where they are often most evident or particularly significant. It also offers some considerations about legal liability. These too have relevance across the chapter but are included at points of particular pertinence.

INITIAL SCREENING

During the earliest contact between agency, worker and potential client a number of eventualities could invite the attention of the law or quasi-legal bodies. These include service exclusion or inclusion, and determinations of risk and danger. Often these early appraisals are made in circumstances where limited time and stretched resources, cultural and language differences, conflicting expectations, and worker and potential client confusion, among other things, complicate clear decision-making. If civil law, in particular torts, is invoked as a result of the outcomes of the screening process it will not demand perfection but will look for evidence of reasonableness, lack of bias, efforts to inquire, and behaviour that is accepted generally by others working in the area as competent. If the decisions are made within a legislative framework, the wording and interpretation of the relevant Act will be critical in determining lawfulness or otherwise in processes and decisions. On occasions, human services actors may be solely responsible for initial decisions that are faulty in some way. At other times, human services actors and acts may constitute only part of the service response in these early stages of contact between people and services. However, the quality of the human services contribution can serve to either compound or minimise more widespread service deficiencies.

SERVICE INCLUSION AND EXCLUSION

Some people are inappropriately excluded from a service response which they do not want but need. For example, involuntary detention and treatment in mental health. Other people are inaccurately classified as eligible for a service or benefit which they desire. In both cases potential clients are likely to remain silent, despite the wrongfulness of the determinations. More commonly people suffer detriment from being found ineligible for a service for which they are in fact eligible and need, and also for being caught in a service response which is inappropriate for them or for which they are ineligible. These people are potential complainants, applicants for administrative review, and very occasionally civil litigants.

Many potential clients who are in need of services are refused them at initial contact, sometimes because they do not meet service criteria and sometimes because of a defect in the initial evaluation of their situation. Only some are referred to other services and thus many needy people go without service. There is no general legal right to a service and to establish a civil negligence suit a claimant would have to show duty, breach and damage. For all the reasons outlined in earlier chapters these elements are not easy to establish, especially in the face of an omission rather than a commission. In relation to duty in particular, the law has always been reluctant to find that duty is owed to an indeterminate class of people. An unknown person with only potential client status is easily placed in this class.

Potential service users legally entitled to a service through a legislative scheme can take administrative review action, examples of which will be seen later in this chapter. Others may approach internal or external complaints bodies. Some may claim discrimination and take action under state or federal discrimination or equal opportunity legislation as outlined in Chapter 3. For example, in *K v Domestic Violence Crisis Service Inc (ACT)* [1998] HREOCA 2 a man lodged a complaint with the Human Rights and Equal Opportunity Commission under the *Sex Discrimination Act 1984* (Cth) alleging that he had received minimal service by a domestic violence service during and after a crisis incident with his wife in the family home, because he was male. The Commission did not find that the service had been limited on the basis of his gender, but it was most uncomplimentary about the assumptions made by the domestic violence service and workers who attended the house and made assumptions about who was at risk and required assistance. The Commissioner said (at 16) 'The failure of the DVCS workers to establish with certainty . . . who had requested their presence and who was alleging that they were the victim of violence was a significant omission and an indicator of hopelessly ineffective, unprofessional and inadequate procedures being practised'. Coroners' courts may scrutinise service rejection that precedes a death. If service denial precedes a high-profile catastrophe, such as a killing, or provides yet another egregious example of an ongoing problem with a service area which comes to public attention, a formal enquiry may result.

A few cases are outlined in Chapter 6 where child abuse claimants have more recently argued successfully in civil cases that they were not removed from their abusive homes when they should have been. Similarly, the Iranian men in *S v Secretary, Department of Immigration and Multicultural and Indigenous Affairs* (2005) 216 ALR 252 who argued that their psychiatric conditions had gone untreated in immigration detention had some legal success in their civil claim for compelling a mental health assessment. However, in the main, potential clients who are wrongfully denied service do not activate a legal or quasi-legal process and their small private tragedies are seldom recognised in legal spheres. For example, there is evidence that screening for mental health problems in immigration detention has been both cursory and flawed (Coffey 2006) but few people have sued as did S, above. Kemshall (2002 p. 2), in discussing commonplace non-service or service exclusion in mental health, says that 'the exposure of a majority of mental health users to risk through social isolation, invisibility and neglect is contrasted to the intense regulation and surveillance of a high-risk minority deemed to pose a significant risk to public safety'. The same argument has been made for probation services (Fitzgibbon 2007). The minority group assessed as high risk is more likely to be unnecessarily gathered into service activity.

Members of this group, like others, may suffer harm if wrongfully caught in a service system, and there is a chance that their situations will come to the attention of complaints bodies, perhaps the law, or even found a formal inquiry as did those of Vivian Alvarez and Cornelia Rau. Vivian Alvarez was drawn into the DIMIA machine and incorrectly processed as an unlawful non-citizen as a result of which, as indicated in Chapter 5, she settled in a civil suit. Similarly, Cornelia Rau was detained for six months in immigration detention as a suspected unlawful non-citizen when she was an Australian citizen and her mental illness was not diagnosed, despite her strange behaviour (Palmer 2005). She too, as indicated, settled in a civil suit.

In these immigration examples, as in many human services situations, there is no question about the difficulties faced by workers charged with initial screening responsibilities. In both the Rau and Alvarez situations, mental health issues made communication difficult and both women were out of touch with immediate family members who might have assisted in the initial identification processes. Cornelia Rau claimed to be German and gave many false leads about her nationality, name and next of kin (Palmer

2005). Vivian Alvarez was 'combative' and 'argumentative' (McMillan 2005 p. 11) and had been using various name combinations during her transient life in Australia. However, bewildered, sick and angry clients and complex personal situations are the bread and butter, if not raison d'être, of human services activity and the difficulty defence is professionally self defeating. How the difficulty is negotiated by both agency procedures and worker behaviour is of greater importance.

The Palmer report concluded in relation to Cornelia Rau, but it is a widely applicable assertion, that the initial 'inquiries were assumption based, narrowly focused, unplanned and not subject to any review' (Palmer 2005 p. 27). Initial impressions, recorded comments and decisions in human services work can set in train a damaging chain of events, and once made they are hard to correct. A large service system that has gained momentum is not easily stopped, diverted or reversed. In fact, it is likely to strive to affirm its initial assumptions. In the Alvarez case, three senior officers were told by more junior officers on separate occasions that an Australian citizen had been deported but they took no action (McMillan 2005).

In a few recent landmark civil cases in the United Kingdom and Australia, courts have found a duty of care to children in situations of unwarranted removal from family into a state welfare system as a result of early flawed investigations. The Aboriginal claimant in *Trevorrow*, as detailed in Chapter 6, argued successfully in a civil suit that he had been taken quickly from his family without adequate reason and after insufficient initial inquiry. In that case Gray J detailed the assumptions and report made by the assessing social worker based on 'materially inaccurate' (at para 138) information about the child's family and concluded (at para 144) that the social worker 'may have been well intentioned but unwittingly prejudiced in her dealings with' the child's parents. Later Gray J said (at para 1077) that the social worker, who was new to the Aborigines Department, 'took "on board" adverse information from an unreferenced source about the plaintiff's parents and acted on that information without further adequate inquiry'.

CRISIS, EMERGENCY, SUICIDE AND THREAT TO OTHERS

Human services screening activities may take place in crisis circumstances, compound them, precipitate them or fail to detect them. In these situations a threat of physical harm in particular, to the potential client, third parties or staff, may lie. Client suicide and physical assault are two commonly feared occurrences in human services work. The latter may lead to criminal charges against the alleged perpetrator, but what happens when a client suicides or threatens to harm, or harms someone else subsequent to or contiguously with human services screening activity? Relevant civil actions have been few in Australia and to date they have not posed a significant civil legal risk to health or human services agencies or staff. Barker and Branson (2000 p. 89) reported a case from the United States in which a social worker evaluated a client and the ensuing report, which concluded that the client was not dangerous, was used as the basis of psychiatric opinion in court. A short time later the client shot several people and this resulted in civil suits against both the social worker and the psychiatrist.

If suicides in jail and immigration detention occur subsequent to a breach of internal procedures (eg concerning surveillance or medical intervention), disciplinary action against the staff involved may result. The agency may also be subject to internal or external review if it provides services under contract. Procedural failures may also help support a civil action by the family, although duty and causation will still have to be established. The child plaintiff's civil claim in *Batchelor v State of Tasmania* [2005] TASSC 11, after his father shot his mother and then himself, was based in part on an allegation that the police had not followed their own 'pro-charge, pro-arrest policy then in force' (at para 4). A civil claim that results from a suicide or suicide attempt will be determined largely on what is accepted by other professionals in the area as competent practice in the circumstances.

The mental health service in the case of *Walker v Sydney West Area Health Service* [2007] NSWSC 526, in which a man threatened suicide and then in the process of attempting it became a paraplegic, was protected in part in the civil claim against it because its service decisions and delivery were held by the court to be competent as determined by peer assessment. Another set of facts and statutory powers in *Kirkland-Veenstra v Stuart* [2008] VSCA 32 illustrate the potential for a civil challenge in relation to suicide, the responsibilities of state authorities and the incremental way in which law evolves. There a suicide's wife sued in torts, two police officers, and the state vicariously. The police had come across the man contemplating suicide in his car and decided not to detain him under the *Mental Health Act* 1986 (Vic). The man went home and later suicided. His wife, who discovered his body, suffered psychiatric injury. It was held by the majority that the police owed him a common law duty in the circumstances because he was clearly vulnerable and they

SERVICE DELIVERY – SCREENING, ASSESSMENT AND PLANNING

could reasonably have foreseen that failure to exercise their powers to detain him may result in him suiciding. The wife's appeal was upheld and a retrial ordered. The High Court subsequently unanimously upheld the appeal of the police in *Stuart v. Kirkland-Veenstra* [2009] HCA 15. The judges arrived at the same decision through different approaches to interpretation of the Mental Health Act, but there was general consensus that while the Act gave powers of apprehension to the police, these did not have to be exercised in circumstances such as these where the plaintiff's husband did not appear to be mentally ill when interacting with the police.

When third parties are threatened, warnings become significant. The United States case of *Tarasoff v Regents of the University of California* 526 P2d 553 (1974) and 551 P2d 334 (1976) resulted in a successful civil suit against the university and counsellor who did not directly warn the girlfriend who was murdered as threatened by their client. As explained in Chapter 6, it is not clear if the *Tarasoff* case is good law in Australia. Also in Chapter 6 were outlined an English case and the Canadian case of *Smith v Jones* [1999] 1SCR 455 in which psychiatrists, without consent, warned others of the danger posed by their clients, and survived breach of confidentiality actions by their clients. McMahon (1992 p. 16) offers a number of indicia for the defensibility in Australia of unauthorised releases of information in a warning to third parties. These have elsewhere (Kennedy and Richards 2007 p. 90) been extended from the majority ruling in the *Smith* case:

- The victim or the victim group is clearly identified.
- The plan to kill or do serious bodily harm is specific.
- The danger is imminent.
- The client has the means to act out the threat.
- Steps to protect the victim are practicable.

Human services workers may or may not hear of threats to harm or kill before such events occur. In the *Presland* case outlined in Chapter 5, the man voluntarily admitted overnight to a mental hospital did not say in hospital that he would murder his brother's fiancé. However, it is reported that the police who delivered him to the hospital testified that they had told the crisis assessment team social worker of his bizarre behaviour and threats to kill his friend's family, his screaming about devils, rats and ants, and that they had tried to ensure his involuntary admission (Scott 2006). Scott also claims that these comments were absent from the social worker's notes and she denied at trial that she had been informed of them. Either way, the accumulated data and combined activities of the staff in the hospital did not result in a decision by a psychiatrist to detain the man who subsequently killed.

Here is another case that confirms the critical place of information and accurate and comprehensive records in the earliest contact with a potential client. It also demonstrates the relative immunity of public authorities and the law's acceptance of less than ideal service delivery. In addition, it shows that a catastrophic outcome will not necessarily sustain a successful suit against an agency. However, the killing and its circumstances received a great deal of adverse publicity (see ABC 2005), and the case does not sanction complacency about legal liability in these circumstances. Its facts may indeed have resulted in formal complaints that are not in the public sphere. As far as is known, the fiancé's family did not make a civil claim. If they had, they would have faced the obstacle of showing a duty owed to a possibly indeterminate member of the public, but the question of the legal rights of people in their situation is not closed. The fact that the trial judge found against the health service on orthodox reasoning (Freckelton 2003) and that there was a strong dissenting judgment on appeal suggests that there is room for development in the law on these sorts of negligence cases against mental health services, civil liability Acts not withstanding. (Freckelton 2008b).

Emergency situations, especially where staff and clients are new to each other, raise special issues of physical and mental safety for everyone involved. Occupational health and safety legislative obligations in particular are relevant here for both employers and employees. Training, emergency procedures and post-emergency care services for employees are all critical. Clients, third parties and in some jurisdictions workers, can also take civil action against an agency in which they were harmed as a result of negligent management of a reasonably foreseeable risk. Freckelton (2008a) concludes that the position of employers in regard to civil liability for psychiatric harm to employees is uncertain in Australia. This is prompted by recent contradictory cases in which courts have attempted to deal with questions of proof of work-caused psychological injury, and to balance the operational needs of employers with employees' rights to a non-injurious workplace.

Two cases illustrate this uncertainty and suggest that much in future will hang on the wording of the civil liability legislation in the relevant jurisdiction and on the facts of the particular case. In the case of *New South Wales v Fahy* [2007] HCA 20, a police officer mounted a negligence action against the state claiming that she suffered post-traumatic stress disorder as a result of being left alone by her partner, contrary to police operating procedures, to help stop the extensive bleeding of a stabbing victim. She was awarded $469 893 at trial. The appeal was dismissed by the High Court. It agreed that she was owed a duty, which had been breached, as the risk to her was foreseeable and foreseen as evidenced by the operating procedures which set in place a buddy system of work. In contrast, the police officers in *Wicks v Railcorp* [2007] NSWSC 1346, who had attended the Waterfall railway crash scene in 2003, were not successful in their civil claims for mental harm caused by the nervous shock of seeing the carnage. This was largely because they had not witnessed the passengers being killed, injured or imperilled, as required by s 30 (20)(a) of the *Civil Liability Act 2002* (NSW).

LIABILITY CONSIDERATIONS

There is wisdom in agencies developing specific policies and procedures about suicide risk that are consistent with accepted professional practice. These agencies have an obligation to ensure that workers are trained in policies and procedures, are confident in applying them and are actively managed to ensure that they do apply them. These procedures would include protocols for assessing suicide risk in all new clients, requiring all new clients to sign consent forms about contact with next of kin and release of information in the event of an emergency, making contact with identified next of kin in an emergency, increasing contact with and monitoring of a client who is suicidal, and for eliciting psychiatric advice and other mental health service support. It is good practice for agencies to also have in place procedures to ensure accurate and detailed record keeping about client behaviour and staff actions.

Agencies are more likely to fail in their obligations to staff and clients and may be held to legal account for an organisational culture in which staff feel insecure about relying on their clinical judgments or hunches, and in asking for and receiving supervisory support and advice in the face of possible suicide risks. As Feldman (2005) points out, agency procedures, to be legally protective, cannot be mechanical, static and based on a single action such as a risk assessment tool or a no-harm contract with the client (the data on the effectiveness of the latter are mixed [Lewis 2007]). Worthwhile agency procedures are dynamic and involve ongoing assessment of motivation, plans, means, drugs and destabilising events in the client's life. They must provide for service coordination and ensure comprehensive, contemporaneous documentation of events and service actions.

Individual workers do well to follow their agency procedures carefully, assuming the procedures are sound. If the professional validity of the procedures is in doubt, workers face a decision about challenging them or non compliance. The latter response carries the risk of disciplinary action. For all workers, employed or self-employed:

> The best protection against liability for negligence resulting from a client's suicidality is to adhere to accepted standards of care of one's clinical profession in assessment, diagnosis, care planning and treatment; to familiarise oneself with jurisdictional guidelines addressing confidentiality and breach of confidentiality; to ensure that clinical interactions and clinical decisions are carefully documented in the client's permanent record; and to seek professional or peer consultation, particularly when inexperienced, uncomfortable or uncertain (Feldman et al. 2005 p. 102).

Agencies that function in crisis service areas where there are risks of physical harm and related dangers – for example, family law, substance abuse, mental health, and domestic violence – are obliged under occupational health and safety legislation to have in place procedures and mechanisms for the safety of staff, clients and third parties. These mechanisms and procedures will have little practical and legal protective value if they do no more than proscribe the most obvious risks of physical harm. If mechanisms and procedures are to have real substance, they will accommodate the complexities and the interactional components of the work and psychological, emotional and physical harm. Moreover, compliance with the procedures must be monitored and enforced and the procedures should be regularly reviewed. Individual staff members are wise to comply with agency procedures, for their own physical and legal safety.

ASSESSMENT

Assessment is a more comprehensive process of collecting and interpreting data about service users and their circumstances so that their needs may be better understood and service planning better informed. It follows initial screening. It is a process in which service users, carers and human service workers ideally come to a shared view about what is occurring, what is needed, what can and cannot be done, what will be done, how and when it will be done, and by whom. This may seem a relatively straightforward set of tasks, but such is not the case. Social theorists, as outlined earlier, have argued that the concept of risk pervades both the culture,

SERVICE DELIVERY – SCREENING, ASSESSMENT AND PLANNING

and assessment aims and technology in particular, of human services work (eg Kemshall 2002; Bessant 2003; Webb 2006). As indicated earlier in this chapter, there is contestation about how problems are identified and framed through worker interactions with clients. At the practice level, assessment is a sophisticated and complex negotiation task which at least recognises and at best accommodates variable understandings of the situation, and possibly conflicting goals. During assessment, data from diverse sources are gathered, sorted, agreed, evaluated, and knitted into a set of clinical judgments about the client's situation and the desirable, required and possible service responses. It is a 'highly skilled, multi-dimensional activity which has "intrinsic", "therapeutic" benefits beyond the goal of gathering information en route to the allocation of resources or to judgements of risk' (Dalrymple and Burke 2006 p. 202, referring to Millar and Corby 2005). All of the deficiencies in, and negative outcomes of, initial screening are present and often amplified in the assessment and planning process. For example, in relation to disability in the United Kingdom, assessments are commonly delayed, clients confused, decisions based on worker preferences and resource availability and service needs underestimated (Preston-Shoot 2000). The cases overviewed in the 'Crisis emergency' section are equally relevant to assessment as are the previous liability considerations.

Unsatisfactory assessment activity may be cursory and/or carried out contiguously and independently by multiple agencies, and/or proscribed by resource constraints. There are pressures for the process to be quick and impersonal (Jones 2001). The accuracy of information is often dubious and material, whatever its quality, is often not recorded satisfactorily (Brayne and Carr 2003). Assessment activity often gives insufficient attention to client and family member views or does not explore them. The measurements are imprecise and implications drawn are value-laden (Webb 2006). Assessment may be blunted by inappropriate or mechanically applied technical tools that do not provide for worker discretion (Lymbery 2000; Gillingham 2006) and actuarial inferences that lead to inflated assessments of risk (eg see Fitzgibbon 2007), as shown in Chapter 1. Assessment may focus on agency needs rather than those of the client (Milligan and Stevens 2006) and may be characterised by all or some of the other worker reasoning deficits detailed by Gambrill (2005, 2006). For example, correlations used to argue causation, facts and impressions magnified or minimised, inappropriate labels adopted, mental filters or 'mind sets' (Mellor et al. 1994) applied to information that challenge preconceived ideas, the rhetoric of caring relied on instead of specific details of service provision, and so on. First impressions often control all subsequent diagnostic activity (Glicken 2008). Client problems tend to be emphasised in this process and as commentators mentioned in Chapter 2 point out, assessment of positive risk is uncommon. On the other hand, recognition of problems with service options are seldom in evidence in the records of assessment activity.

As with the initial screening phase, assessment and planning can result in inappropriate service inclusion or exclusion, and failure to detect or manage risks to client, workers or third parties. Similarly, negative outcomes may result from faulty assessment and planning processes, or unexpectedly from competent processes. Human services intervention is a very inexact science that is sometimes attended by unfortunate events. Again, it must be said that the law will not require perfection. The assessment and planning process raises some particular issues that might activate legal or quasi-legal interest, in addition to those outlined around the screening process.

STATUS DETERMINATIONS

In circumstances where legislation imposes duties or creates eligibility, such as in immigration, social security, family breakdown and mental health, status determinations under law are critical in the conferral and loss of rights. For example, in the *Presland* case the admitting psychiatrists decided that he did not satisfy the criteria for compulsory care and control under s 9 and s 10 of the *Mental Health Act 1990* (NSW) and he claimed damage as a result of the killing that ensued. In another example, under s 189 of the *Migration Act 1958* (Cth), an authorised officer who 'knows or reasonably suspects' someone of being an unlawful non-citizen is obliged to detain that person. A number of High Court cases have resulted from claims about wrongful determinations under this section, and interpret what is meant by 'reasonable' and 'suspicion'. For present purposes it is enough to say that objectivity and efforts to search and investigate are required, while personal opinion that someone may be an unlawful non-citizen is not enough to satisfy the reasonable suspicion test. It has already been seen how some of these important determinations are founded (or founder) on flawed initial assessments, insufficient open-minded investigation and inattention to detail.

In the case of *Idris, Hayat Adam* [2004] MRTA 574, a most significant status determination went against the applicant because of inadequate attention to technical detail on the part of human services workers. In this case, the Migration Review Tribunal affirmed a decision to refuse a young Somalian woman permanent residence on spouse grounds. The woman review applicant had come to Australia on a spouse visa but had subsequently divorced her husband. She wished to remain in Australia and was seeking to show that she was not in a genuine and continuing relationship with her sponsor husband because of domestic violence. The regulations made under the *Migration Act 1958* (Cth) set out the type and form of evidence that is required to prove that domestic violence has in fact occurred. In brief, two independent statutory declarations are required. An acceptable one was supplied by a psychologist and another was needed to forestall deportation.

Two human services workers also provided statutory declarations, neither compliant with the provisions under the regulations. A cultural support and advocacy worker did not provide documentary evidence to show that she was a 'competent person' to give evidence under the Act, and her declaration was deficient in several other areas. Her amended declaration also failed to comply with the provisions. A social work manager, who showed that she was a 'competent person' through her membership of the Australian Association of Social Workers, had not personally met or observed the woman. Her conclusions were based on general assumptions about circumstances which precede admission to a domestic violence service, on second-hand information, and not on a first-hand judgment of the woman applicant and her state of mind. The tribunal concluded (at para 53): 'It is unfortunate that the review applicant must pay the price for the inadequate efforts of those who, despite their good intentions, have failed to meet the strict criteria imposed by the domestic violence provisions'. Notwithstanding its concerns about the technical rigidity of the regulations, the tribunal could not overturn the visa refusal. Here is a stark illustration of the impact of human service activity.

While proper investigation and attention to detail can benefit the person under scrutiny and minimise the risk of wrong or detrimental determinations, it is a two-edged sword as it may also preclude eligibility for a desired outcome. For example, Sleep et al. (2006) argue in relation to eligibility for social security benefits and the 'marriage-like relationship' test under the *Social Security Act 1991* (Cth) that the latter requires invasive surveillance of women in particular and the potential loss of benefits, reputation and financial viability. These surveillance processes and their outcomes are correct in law and illustrate the potential conflicts between legal, moral and personal value imperatives in many human service situations (see Kennedy and Richards 2007). Individual workers face decisions about whether or not they can work within such legislative requirements, whether they will work outside them as advocates for applicants or to bring about legislative change, and/or whether they will comply fully while working within them. Non-compliance by an internal worker with these surveillance processes so as to ensure a favourable outcome for a client or applicant is unlikely to result in complaint by the person so favoured. However, it is questionable in terms of professional ethics,[1] an invitation to disciplinary action by the employer, and or a possible action for breach of the Act in question or a public service Act.

Status determinations commonly will be challenged if at all through the associated review processes outlined in Chapter 4 and evidenced above in the *Idris* case. Seldom will they result in civil action as happened with *Presland*. Dalrymple and Burke (2006 p. 206) report an English case in which a person with a disability successfully pursued judicial review of an accommodation assessment conducted by his local authority, based on resource imperatives rather than his needs and preferences. Brammer (2003 p. 314) also reports a case in which a reassessment which resulted in reduced services on financial grounds was quashed because the resulting level of risk to the client would be too high. As far as can be determined such cases have not yet been seen in Australia.

LIABILITY CONSIDERATIONS

Service systems and agencies responsible for applying legislation that confers benefits or removes rights are particularly prone to quasi-legal and legal review of their procedures, guidelines, data systems, and training and management of staff. They will withstand this scrutiny more comfortably if their processes reflect substantive compliance with regulations, procedures manuals and current interpretations of the legislation in question.

Individual workers who have solid, up-to-date lay knowledge of the relevant piece of legislation and its interpretation are in a much more informed position from which to make decisions about rights of and risks to applicants or clients, and about their own employment circumstances.

DIAGNOSIS, PROTECTION AND REPORTING

All of the mistakes or failures in diagnosis, detection, reporting and protection that can occur during screening are just as relevant during assessment. Very occasionally a civil suit ensues. A mistaken assumption by a social

---

[1] Australian Association of Social Workers *Code of Ethics*, section 4.4; Australian Institute of Welfare and Community Workers *Code of Ethics*, s 5.

SERVICE DELIVERY – SCREENING, ASSESSMENT AND PLANNING

worker and psychiatrist founded the English civil case of *M v Newham London Borough Council* [1995] 2 AC 633. In this case, the two workers investigating an allegation of sexual abuse concluded that the child had identified the mother's partner as the perpetrator. In fact, the child had identified a cousin with the same name. The child was removed from her home for a year before the mistake was discovered and both she and the mother suffered psychiatric injury as a result of the separation. Both mother and child failed in their initial torts suits for policy reasons, but had some success under human rights legislation on the grounds that the mother had not been given an opportunity at the time of assessment to check the accuracy of the presumptions of the workers (*TP and KM v United Kingdom* (2001) 34 EHRR 42).

Assessment flaws were also argued in *W v Essex County Council* [2000] 2 ALL ER 237 and *L (A Child) v Reading Borough Council* [2001] 1 WLR 1575, outlined in Chapter 6, and in both cases the plaintiffs had some initial legal success. In the first case, a known sex abuser boy was placed with a foster family who had expressly asked that a child with that particular history not be sent to them. In the second, it was claimed that a social worker and police officer had misrepresented their improperly conducted interview with a child, such that the father was arrested as a suspected abuser. There have also been a small number of negligent adoption cases. For example, in the Australian extension of time case, *Radnedge v State of South Australia* (1997) 192 LSJS 131, a woman who had been fostered in and then adopted by a family in the 1960s and sexually abused by the adoptive father, 30 years later argued negligence on the part of the South Australian Department of Social Welfare which had approved the placement. No duty of care was found and it was affirmed that the actions of the officers who assessed the satisfactoriness of the family were to be judged by the standards of the 1960s when child sexual abuse was not commonly recognised, and not by the standards of the 1990s, when the case came to court. Similarly, in the New Zealand case of *AG v Prince and Gardner* [1998] 1 NZLR 262, an adult who had been adopted into an abusive family in the 1960s, and his birth mother, sued the crown under a number of actions including negligence on the part of the social workers who had recommended the adoption. Both of their negligence claims were struck out by the majority on policy grounds.

These civil actions in relation to flawed assessment and the screening ones, which they overlap, are exceptional. On the whole, claimants have had very limited success to date. Some complaints may result from contested assessment processes, few charges will flow from failures to comply with

180 | MISHAPS AND MISDEEDS THROUGH A HUMAN SERVICES LENS

mandatory notifications of suspected child abuse and neglect as explained in Chapter 4, and only occasionally will a formal inquiry be instigated.

REASSESSMENT

Ideally assessment is an ongoing process, even if the initial assessment and later service provision tasks carried out are by different actors (Gursansky et al. 2003). During reassessment initial hypotheses are tested and new ones developed as data emerges. Without regular reassessment, critical bits of information may be missed or not integrated into ongoing service and the chances of harm increased. In the case of *SB v New South Wales* (2004) 13 VR 527, which was detailed in Chapter 6, the service system failed to record, make sense of and act on emerging information about the abuse in both the foster placement and SB's later placement with her father. It appears that after initial decisions were made about placements, service inertia set in and reviews, if done at all, were cursory and not action orientated.

SERVICE PLANNING

Initial assessment merges into service planning which becomes the 'bridge' between assessment and intervention (Houston-Vega et al. 1997 p. 58). In this phase of human service activity, clients, family members, carers and workers in and across agencies ideally work in partnership (Braye and Preston-Shoot 1997) to develop a specific and goal-focussed plan designed to assist the client system with agreed difficulties, problems or needs. The plan provides direction for both the client and the service system and itemises who is to do what, by when, how, and towards what intended outcome. There are persuasive arguments for the plan being written and signed by all parties in the form of a quasi-contract (Barker and Branson 2000; Reamer 2003b), and for it to be constructed, as would a legal contract, with emphasis on consideration from all parties, offers, acceptances and clarification of intentions (Cordon and Preston-Shoot 1987). Planning, like assessment, is a sophisticated and complex task 'requiring practitioners to employ a range of communication, analytical and relational skills' (Dalrymple and Burke 2006 p. 225). During planning, a positive relationship is to be developed and managed while often very divergent expectations are explored, negotiated and prioritised into a genuinely joint agreement. In the words of Gursansky et al. (2003 p. 69), 'Planning involves troubleshooting, confrontation and a mixture of idealism and pragmatism in

SERVICE DELIVERY – SCREENING, ASSESSMENT AND PLANNING | 181

working with the client to create a plan of action that is accepted as an achievable challenge'.

The problems with planning in reality, as with assessment, are well documented in the human services literature. There is evidence from the aged care area that case managers are unclear what they are to do and why (Black 2007). Commonly, care plans, if they exist at all, are actually service plans or in the words of Smith in relation to child welfare (2008 p. 525) nothing more than 'lists of things' to be done by both workers and clients who both see them as a form of 'penalty' (p. 529) for parental conduct towards their children. Progress is commonly assessed against service activity and resource utilisation, rather than through outcomes for clients (Gursansky et al. 2003; Smith 2008). In addition, and not surprisingly in a risk-sensitive world, care plans are often more concerned with the technical administration of resources than with transformational engagement with clients (Dalrymple and Burke 2006). It is also common for plans to be vague in their conceptualisation and articulation of goals. They may be out of date, and roles and responsibilities insufficiently specified (Gilbertson and Barber 2004). They might be inattentive to cultural factors, time lines and contingency arrangements (Harwin and Owen 2003). Clients may have had limited or non-existent involvement in their development (Gilbertson and Barber 2004; Smith 2008). They may not demonstrate resolution of quite different expectations of clients and workers about goals and intervention. Workers who fear a hostile or otherwise challenging response (Brayne and Carr 2003), or feel discomforted by the intrusiveness of the planning process (Black 2007), will sometimes skirt around difficult conversations and obscure different perceptions. Moreover, clients may not have been told or fully understand the risks and benefits of the planned intervention (Houston-Vega et al. 1997). For all these inadequacies, the risks of legal or quasi-legal action are not high, although there are several issues around planning that can give rise to legal interest. Divergent expectations, mandated planning and planning review are considered here. The question of informed consent is also critical, but will be covered in Chapter 10.

SHARED OR DIVERGENT EXPECTATIONS

There is evidence that clients understand insufficiently what is happening or what is being agreed to during the planning process, and that workers wrongly assume that their explanations are synonymous with client understanding (Brayne and Carr 2003). This leads to confusion about what is intended in and from intervention. Unmet expectations or perceived failed promises are likely to result in client dissatisfaction, particularly if the service was sought voluntarily by the client and paid for. If this dissatisfaction is expressed, it is most likely to be heard by a manager, an internal or external complaints body or perhaps the media in the form of a complaint.

MANDATED PLANNING AND CLIENT INVOLVEMENT

There are a range of areas of human services practice in which legislation or attendant regulations mandate the development of care plans and the participation of clients in the process. Child protection and corrections are two such areas. So, for example, s 51C of the *Child Protection Act 1999* (Qld) specifies the children for whom a case plan is required. Section 51B outlines the characteristics of a case plan, including the fact that it will be in writing (s 51B(1)). In s 51D, the conduct of the planning process is spelled out, inclusive of the facilitation, involvement and understanding of the child, parents, other relevant family members and, in the case of Aboriginal and Torres Strait Islander children, relevant agencies. A copy of the plan must be given to the child, the child's parents and any other relevant person (s 51T). There are similar provisions under the *Crimes (Administration of Sentences) Regulation 2001* (NSW). Regulation 12 mandates that every inmate in a correctional centre will have a case plan, r 13, the content of the plan, r 14(2) reasonable steps to ensure inmate participation, and consideration of cultural factors is specified in r 21.

There is evidence of significant non-compliance with legislative provisions such as these on care planning. For example, the research of Gilbertson and Barber (2004) showed wide ranging non-compliance with South Australian child protection legislation. Liability for non-compliance is most likely to be carried by the system or agency, as the provisions require multiple actions within a service. Agencies are technically vulnerable to complaints, administrative and judicial review actions, or civil claims for negligence or breach of statutory duty. However, the forces that bear against a vulnerable or disadvantaged person taking action in such circumstances have been rehearsed. Major inquiries are more likely to result from endemic and long-standing failures in service systems such as child protection and corrections. Individual workers who do not comply with particular procedures and practice directions that make up part of the whole of a service planning process may be subject to disciplinary action by the employer or even charges under the relevant Act or a public service Act.

SERVICE DELIVERY – SCREENING, ASSESSMENT AND PLANNING | **183**

There has been less consideration by courts in Australia of care planning flaws than in the United Kingdom, since the enactment there of the *Human Rights Act 1998* (UK) (eg Brayne and Broadbent 2002; Harwin and Owen 2003). However, planning failures were both significant and scrutinised by the court in the Australian case of *SB*, referred to above. In that case, *SB* was returned to her father in contravention of the DOCS ward manual. There was no approved case plan or case conference as required (at para 357) and no satisfactory explanation for their absence (at para 358). The evidence outlined by Redlich J painted a picture of an organisation that was over-extended, disorganised, and only sporadically focussed or active in relation to care planning. It should be emphasised that a civil case of this kind is unusual, and yet it is most unlikely that the planning failures in *SB* were in any way unusual for other clients of DOCS.

PLANNING REVIEW

Good practice and sometimes legislation require that plans be reviewed regularly. For instance, s 51V of the *Child Protection Act 1999* (Qld) states that the care plan be reviewed at least every six months. Regulation 12(3) of the *Crimes (Administration of Sentences) Regulation 2001* (NSW) also requires that a plan be prepared and adopted not more than six months after the last one. Planning review merges into ongoing monitoring of intervention, and intervention is turned to in the next chapter.

LIABILITY CONSIDERATIONS

The points which follow are relevant throughout human service work, but have particular importance in the early stages of contact with potential clients when new data is being collected, first impressions consolidated and service options considered.

- Individual workers who think divergently and independently, consistently reflect on their own perceptual tendencies, are curious, seek and are open to new information, and show courage and persistence in bringing inconsistencies or inaccuracies in data to the attention of their managers, are less likely to be ambushed by unexpected events and resultant harm.
- Agencies and managers who create and nurture safe operating procedures, quality data recording and maintenance arrangements, regular client reviews, frequent operating system audits and an organisational

culture that values questioning by staff and clients, is in a stronger position to both deflect and defend a legal challenge.

- Service systems in which service interconnectivity, and protocols for information sharing are oversighted and genuinely sponsored by structural and financial incentives, are less likely to set the conditions for fragmented and individual agency driven assessments and plans.

Screening, assessment and planning in the human services are generally followed by some form of service implementation and, eventually, service closure. These phases of human services activity are considered in the next chapter.

10 | Service delivery – implementation and closure

In THE SERVICE DELIVERY phases of human services activity with clients, ideally plans are implemented, monitored, adjusted, and finally the service relationship is brought to closure at a mutually agreed or known point. However, all of the deficits that can increase legal liability during the screening and assessment stages are equally pertinent.

The intervention and closure phases have intrinsic characteristics that generate their own particular legal risks or accentuate some already canvassed. First, intervention indicates that something is to be done and this in turn requires decisions about the nature of that activity. There is nothing definitive about appropriate types and applications of intervention models, therapies and techniques in the human services, and this can give rise to a range of legal risks. Second, although all human services activities require informed consent, the intervention and data management decisions that accompany these activities are underpinned by consent questions. The law has definite positions on informed consent that demand attention in practice. Third, sensitivity to diversity is another matter that needs to be considered in circumstances of ongoing relationships and service delivery. Fourth, during intervention in particular, although not uniquely, workers and clients can be engaged in intimate and private activity which generates 'unrealistic and strong emotions and reactions' (Houston-Vega et al. 1997 p. 63) on both sides. In this environment, role conflicts and boundary violations with legal implications are not unexpected. Fifth, monitoring and review are ideally inherent in intervention, but in practice are often absent or perfunctory, and shortcomings of this kind also carry legal risk. Finally, case closure or termination may be performed such that damage results.

186 | MISHAPS AND MISDEEDS THROUGH A HUMAN SERVICES LENS

Each of these potential problems of intervention and closure are addressed in this chapter.

INTERVENTION APPROACHES, PRACTICE METHODS AND TECHNIQUES

On the face of it, human services intervention might seem low risk as it generally does not involve physically intrusive techniques, dangerous substances or equipment, or environmental damage (risk indicia from Health Workforce Australia 2008). However, intervention can cause damage and the prevalence of complaints about treatment in health and human services has been observed in Chapter 2. Sometimes intervention harms indirectly through masking the need for other essential intervention. Barker (2000) outlines a suit in the United States that arose when a man being treated by a social worker for anxiety symptoms in fact had a heart condition that required medical treatment. Mellor and colleagues (1994) describe an Australian example of an allied health team comprising a psychologist, social worker and dietician wrongly treating a child with an apparent eating disorder. The team pursued various hypotheses about family disturbance through a form of family therapy. The intervention was not successful and it was later found that the child had a pancreatic tumour. Human services intervention may also be damaging in its own right. An extreme example is provided by Reamer (2003b p. 96) of a social worker in the United States who was convicted of criminal offences and jailed when his use of a rebirthing technique resulted in the asphyxiation of the child client.

There are many reasons why intervention in the human services may be compromised. The quality of the relationship between worker and client is a major factor in positive outcomes from intervention, as will be shown in Chapter 12, yet relationships are not always ideal or planned and resourced in current funding models. Inadequately resourced and structurally fragmented and fractured service arrangements in the human services have been noted in earlier chapters. Limitations in program design, implementation, fidelity and evaluation are less recognised but common (Kennedy and Kennedy 2008). In the context of risk-adverse environments, funds may be spent disproportionately on assessment and resource allocation, at the cost of actual intervention (eg Lymbery 2000; Jordan 2001; Kemshall 2002; Weinberg et al. 2003; Lymbery 2004; Dalrymple and Burke 2006). Increasingly, assessment of client need is separated from service provision. Worker training and the skills necessary for the use of methods and techniques may be absent or lacking. Workers with insufficient knowledge about effective intervention often make multiple, costly, scattergun, ineffective referrals for clients (Steib and Blom 2004). In socially contested areas of work, such as child protection, it is not clear what intervention mandates services have and what goals are to be pursued (Whittaker and Maluccio 2002). Common problems with goal setting in service planning were summarised in Chapter 9. One consequence of ill-defined aims is rudderless intervention. Even if intervention is purposeful, it may have iatrogenic effects or doubtful efficacy (O'Brien-Malone and Diamond 2006).

In addition, for a variety of reasons related to tradition, workforce characteristics, resources, education and ideology, the human services lack a practice research culture in which activities, outcomes and effectiveness are routinely investigated, measured and reported. Thus, there is little consensus about which form of specific human services intervention activity works and under what conditions (eg Gibbons 2001; Whittaker and Maluccio 2002; Reamer 2003b). In the broad area of mental health, Stoesz (2002) demonstrated that the few interventions with solid evaluation data demonstrating effectiveness are the products of clinical psychology. More fundamentally, there is no agreement in human services academe about the value and place of positivist research evidence. Proponents of evidence-based practice contend that programs and practitioners rely unsatisfactorily on good intentions, 'emotional reasoning' (Gambrill 2006 p. 214), practice wisdom and organisational imperatives (Wilson and Chui 2006) in their choice and application of intervention strategies. Non-positivists critique an evidence-based approach to practice as mindlessly technocratic at worst and disregarding of professional discretion and values at best (eg Lymbery and Butler 2004; McDonald 2006; Webb 2006; Hall 2008). While the academic debate rages, policymakers, agencies and workers flail and grasp at decontextualised intervention approach and methodology straws, which float past them or which they bump into incidentally.

Unorthodox, 'irrational' (O'Brien-Malone and Diamond 2006 p. 165), 'loose screw' (Epstein 2005) or non-empirically based understandings of human distress and intervention techniques have thrived in the human services, particularly, but not exclusively, in private practice. Reamer's (2006 p. 191) overview of these approaches and their legal implications includes spiritual guide work, re-parenting therapy, rebirthing therapy and cradling techniques. Epstein (2005) includes boot camps, the 'cult of self esteem' (p. 57), tough love, rebirthing and catharsis in his list. Both Reamer and Epstein refer to the controversial matter of recovered memory syndrome; contentious both because of its disputed evidence base, and its use in convicting alleged perpetrators of sexual abuse (eg Madden and Parody 1998; Werren 2007).

Mainstream approaches and modes of service delivery, each with inherent legal risks, are always emerging. Case management, for example, has become ubiquitous as an approach to service delivery in the human services (Gursansky et al. 2003). Electronic forms of service delivery are expanding (McCarty and Clancy 2002); for example, telephone (Miller 2004) and online assessment and intervention (Banach and Bernat 2000; Finn and Banach 2002). Both method and application efficacy may be in doubt. As with all new developments, organisational infrastructure, management support, and training and competence of staff are fundamental in ensuring that approaches or methods, no matter how efficacious, are applied appropriately. There is evidence, for example, that the confidence and training of staff lags behind performance expectations in online environments (Humphries 2002; Humphries and Camilleri 2002). The problems of poor preparation within organisations and human service education for case management practice have been detailed (Kennedy et al. 2001, 2004).

How does this litany of potential problems reveal itself in legal or quasi-legal attention in Australia? Questions of standards and breach will be brought into sharp relief in a negligence case and it may be difficult for a plaintiff to show that the approaches or techniques used, or their applications, were beyond the scope of accepted practice by other professionals in the same field. This is due to the lack of research and consensus on modes of intervention. Moreover, the conduct under review will be judged on its acceptability at the time of its occurrence, rather than under current standards. This places an expectation on agencies and workers to use contemporaneously acceptable practices, as assessed by competent peer review processes, in contemporaneously acceptable ways. Thus, intervention activity that is not informed by current research and literature is potentially a legal time bomb. In the *Trevorrow* case detailed in Chapter 6, the government agency that did not act in accord with contemporary knowledge about maternal bonding was liable.

The chronicles of civil suits resulting from human services treatment harm in the United States (eg Houston-Vega et al. 1997; Barker and Branson 2000; Reamer 2003b; Reamer 2006) are not evident in Australia, in part because of the relatively limited role of clinical private practice in this country. Clinical private practitioners usually provide therapy of some sort and might be more adventurous, and certainly more active, than employees in their choice of models and techniques. In addition, their professional indemnity insurance, assuming they have it,

SERVICE DELIVERY – IMPLEMENTATION AND CLOSURE | 189

makes them attractive targets for legal action. There are few Australian civil cases involving problems with intervention. A case involving the giving of inappropriate advice was outlined in Chapter 6, but failures to act, more than harmful action, are more evident in Australia. For example, SB who sued successfully because of the abuse she suffered from her father had not received the protective and preventive intervention that she should have from the New South Wales Department of Community Services (DOCS).

It is relatively easy to think of human services interventions that could give rise to criminal charges, or civil actions based on trespass. For instance, during non-orthodox intervention, clients might be restrained, hit, locked up, massaged, held firmly or swaddled, either intentionally for non-traditional therapeutic reasons or the personal gratification of the worker, or by accident. Without proper consent, legislative protection, or the defence of necessity, these actions leave the actor open to state or private action. Again, the obstacles to both criminal and civil action apply and the case of *Wainwright and Anor v Home Office* [2003] UKHL 53, involving a prison search is unusual (see Chapter 7). Human services actors are much more likely to be the subject of an internal or external complaint; for example, to a complaints commissioner or professional body, if they offer or engage in distressing, harmful or unsuccessful treatment. In New South Wales, workers may also be investigated by the Health Care Complaints Commissioner under the code of conduct for unregistered practitioners, as explained in Chapters 4 and 8. Private practitioners who offer treatment or supply goods that are unproven or who mislead clients about their services could face state action under fair trading legislation or the *Trade Practices Act* (Cth) (Weir 2008; Wilson 2008).

LIABILITY CONSIDERATIONS

Despite the relative immunity of human service actors from a legal response to deficiencies in their intervention activities, complacency is unwise.

- Agencies and workers who are informed about the empirical bases of the models of service delivery and intervention methods that they use, and the currency and wide peer acceptability of the models and methods, are in a better position to function effectively and respond to legal scrutiny.
- Agencies and workers who ensure that the latter are properly trained, supported and competent with the models and techniques used are professionally more accountable and in a stronger position to withstand legal scrutiny.

190 | MISHAPS AND MISDEEDS THROUGH A HUMAN SERVICES LENS

- Agencies and workers who seek out and apply respectable guidelines, even from other related professional groups, on contested intervention methods (eg on recovered memories, Australian Psychological Society Ltd 2000), are better informed and better able to defend legal action.
- It is professionally (eg practice standard 1.2 Australian Association of Social Workers 2003) and legally advisable for workers to discuss fully with clients the nature and limitations of planned intervention activities. As O'Brien-Malone and Diamond (2006) observe, therein lies a paradox, as acknowledgement of the possible risks of intervention reduces the psychological power of that intervention and may increase the chance of an adverse outcome. However, a skilfully managed discussion that invites genuine airing of concerns, risks and expectations can to some extent offset this phenomenon.

CONSENT

The last point above re-introduces the matter of consent; in Reamer's (2003b p. 80) words, a 'centerpiece of professional practice'. Informed consent is fundamental to client autonomy and self-determination, and is enshrined in professional codes of ethics (eg Australian Association of Social Workers 2002, clause 4.2.3(1) and (2)). Failure to comply with a provision such as this can result in disciplinary action against members of the relevant profession. Consent must be obtained before service commences, and in relation to specific techniques and practices. However, consent is just as important in relation to disclosure of and access to information. What follows is a brief commentary on questionable consent and the place of consent in legal defences. A comprehensive overview of consent and capacity, and relevant procedures, context and forms, is beyond the scope of this book and is covered comprehensively elsewhere (eg MacFarlane 2000; Kerridge et al. 2005; McIlwraith and Madden 2006; Cavell 2007; Delany 2008).

Consent has a central place in law and is a defence to various legal actions. It is a defence to trespass to the person if the person understands what is being proposed and its effects. It will equally stand in the respondent's favour if they face a civil action and can show that the plaintiff was given enough information to be able to make an informed decision about the intended intervention and its risks in their circumstances. Consent is a major issue in health, where physical intervention is the norm. Although it is equally important in the various decisions made by, for and with people in human services activity, there are not many human services cases about

SERVICE DELIVERY – IMPLEMENTATION AND CLOSURE | **191**

alleged problems with consent. The few cases that do consider consent are the exceptions. Again, it is most likely that alleged failures to obtain proper consent will appear before complaints bodies if anywhere at all.

The first point about legal liability and consent is that the latter must exist. In the stolen generation *Trevorrow* case outlined in Chapter 6, the court found that there had been no family consent to remove and foster the child. This was a critical factor in the conclusion that the child had been taken by the state unlawfully in breach of the relevant child welfare legislation.

If there is consent it must be full and informed. Reamer (2003b pp. 83–8) presents six indicia for consent that are generally valid professionally and legally. Informed consent must be:

- Not given under circumstances of coercion and undue influence. This means that agencies and workers who pressure clients to agree to human services activity or use their unequal power base to ensure some sort of compliance are technically legally vulnerable. Placing direct or indirect pressure on clients to enter or leave programs, to agree to various sorts of conditions or undertakings, or to be a research subject, are some examples of coercion that might have legal implications. The central place of 'informed' in 'informed consent' is illustrated by the *Cubillo* stolen generation case covered in Chapter 6. It is not surprising that the question of consent arose and was contested, as vulnerable, non-English speaking and inexperienced Aboriginal women had to withstand and fully appreciate the demands, offers and promises of the Australian Inland Mission staff and possibly the Native Affairs Board of the Northern Territory in the case of Lorna Cubillo, and the director of welfare officers in Peter Gunner's case. The trial court thought consent to have been unlikely in the case of Lorna Cubillo (at para 107). Because of the lapse of time since the removals, and the unavailability of critical witnesses at trial, the court did not decide the matter. In Peter Gunner's case, his mother had placed her thumb print on a statement requesting his removal, among other things, for schooling to 'European standards' (at para 137). This was accepted by the trial judge as informed consent because of evidence from contemporaneous witnesses describing his mother's requests for the child to be taken, even though it was not known how much of the printed document was really understood by her. As O'Connor (2001) says, this is an inconclusive and unsettling case.

- Specific to specific acts or procedures. The important medical case of *Rogers v Whitaker* (1992) 175 CLR 479 [1992] HCA 58 established that people who are consenting to a procedure need enough information to make an informed decision, and information that is focused more on their concerns about risk than those of the practitioner's (McIlwraith and Madden 2006). Consent processes or forms that are general in character may not be protective in law. The fact that a person has signed a consent form is not conclusive evidence of informed consent, especially if the form is non-specific about what is intended (Cavell 2007). In the *Cubillo* case, the thumb print alone for Peter Gunner was not conclusive of consent. Reamer (2003b) discusses a number of examples of clients in the United States challenging in law, blanket forms that did not specify details of intervention occurring after a signature had been given. This point is relevant to the *Cubillo* case, where it is unlikely that either mother consented to future ill treatment of her child, but the question was not explored. Reamer also advises against the not unknown request for clients to sign blank consent forms on which the details will be added later.

- Premised on the right to withdraw.
- Based on comprehensive information about who will do what, when and why, risks, side effects and possible outcomes. A process for encouraging client questions strengthens evidence that consent is informed.
- In valid form – in general, this may be oral or in writing, but particular Acts may impose specific requirements. For instance, s 53B of the *Mental Health Act 1986* (Vic) details requirements for informed consent to treatment, including a prescribed printed information form in an appropriate language and an oral explanation of the treatment. Non-compliance with these legislative imperatives constitutes a breach of statute, which may carry a direct penalty and may sustain a civil case.
- Given by someone with the necessary mental capacity – thus minors, people with mental illness or intellectual disability, and many others whose mental functioning is impaired by drugs, alcohol or medical conditions, may not have full decision-making capacity. All such impairments are commonplace in the human services and invoke law that is relevant to substitute decision-making and/or emergencies. However, as Delany (2008) stresses, competence is specific, not general, and it may vary over time. In addition, disability or minority are not synonymous with incapacity to consent and the law will presume capacity, unless there is convincing evidence to rebut it (Jones and BasserMarks 2000; Kennedy and Richards 2007). Thus, human service actors need to be alert to factors that bear on capacity to consent, but wary of making judgments based on a generic descriptor of the person. The case of *K v Minister for Youth and Community Services* [1982] 1 NSWLR 311

illustrates this point in relation to age. A state ward, aged 15 and six months, was pregnant and intent on having an abortion, which the minister, her guardian, had refused to allow, probably on legal advice. The girl's mother took judicial review action on her behalf, seeking a ruling in favour of the abortion. Although the case turned largely on the scope of the minister's and the court's powers, the latter emphasised evidence showing the girl's clarity and persistence about her decision, her exposure to extensive information and her capacity to make the decision. The court ordered that the minister consent to the abortion and arrange it.

There are exceptions to the need for informed consent, most of which are relevant to human service actors because they involve legislative provisions for involuntary intervention and action without consent, and to court orders. Child protection, corrections, mental health and immigration are only some of the fields in which human services intervention can be imposed by law without consent. For example, the *Children, Youth and Families Act 2005* (Vic) provides for temporary assessment orders to be applied for in respect of children suspected of being in need of protection, with (s 228), or without (s 229), notice to parents. Also, all state and territory jurisdictions have legislative provision for involuntary detention and community treatment in mental health. However, this legislative authority is never a blanket exception to the need for consent that will continue to apply in all matters of intervention other than those specified in the relevant Acts.

LIABILITY CONSIDERATIONS

Four points about consent processes, procedures and forms are noted here.
- Ensuring that consent is both given and informed requires action and engagement on the part of workers. Informed consent is more than the relatively passive signing of a form. Information is to be given, along with disclosures about risk and limitations, questions encouraged and time allowed for consideration. Thus, agency policies, procedures and supervisory systems must view and support the consent process as an ongoing one.
- Involuntary clients have the right to be fully informed about which aspects of intervention are removed from their control, those which are within their capacity, and to consent or not to the aspects within their capacity.

- Consent is to be sought and given for all aspects of a planned service intervention. At the point of consent, clients will ideally agree to the actual intervention in detail, relevant and specific information releases, confidentiality limits, involvement of significant others in the planned activity, and conditions for cessation of intervention.
- In much human services work, even with involuntary clients, there is an ongoing tension between duress and persuasion. There is a fine line between therapeutic prompting and unconscionable coercion, and negotiation of this boundary is a sophisticated process. There is no formula for determining the boundary, which is defined by the facts and dynamics of each situation. However, agencies and workers who use solid case recording and review and audit procedures will be better placed to survive legal attention.
- Capacity is very commonly at issue in human services work. Agencies have a responsibility to ensure that workers are alert to signals of impaired capacity and confident about accessing substitute decision-making authorities. It is also wise practice to routinely check and record current guardianship arrangements for all clients.

DIVERSITY

Respect for and sensitivity to diversity is fundamental to respect for human dignity, a principle embedded in professional codes of ethics (eg Australian Institute of Welfare and Community Workers n.d., Principles 2.1, 2.2 and 3.3). It is also increasingly endorsed in legislation. It is of relevance at every stage of intervention, but addressed here because it can often be most tested during ongoing service relationships with clients of different gender, religion, race, age, culture, socioeconomic status, sexuality, parental status, political belief and capacity. Yet, for all these significant imperatives, human services activity can and does fall short of the ideal, is sometimes unlawful, and can result in legal or quasi-legal action. Institutional racism in the human services is well documented (eg Haebich 2000; Dutt 2001; Brammer 2003; Davis and Garrett 2004; Davis and Garrett 2004; Slatter et al. 2005; Dalrymple and Burke 2006). Some examples follow. As the court said of the resistance of the welfare worker to the child returning to his Aboriginal family in the *Trevorrow* case, it was 'well intentioned but unwittingly prejudiced' (at para 144). Cropley (2002) describes the negative sentiments held by German refugee support workers about their clients and their guilt about these feelings. Preston-Shoot (2000) details research showing negative stereotypes that prevail in social work assessments of clients with disabilities and belonging to other minority groups. Aarons and Powell (2003) report on the predominance and effects of negative stereotypes held by interviewers investigating sexual abuse in children with intellectual difficulties. At the worker level, discrimination can be intentional and malicious. More usually it is the product of ignorance or confusion about differences, sensibilities, appropriate responses, and about what constitutes direct and indirect discrimination (eg Fulcher 2002). It is possibly compounded in more recent times by the increased movement of practitioners between countries for human services work that is culturally context-specific (Welbourne et al. 2007).

Unsatisfactory responses to diversity also arise because of difficulties in balancing practical and resource demands with individuals' special needs, and perceptions that the latter are unreasonable or would cause undue hardship for the organisation. In most situations that involve the unaware and unfair management of difference, no formal action will be taken by those who are or believe themselves to be treated wrongly. The human services, like society in general, are replete with relationships and projects that founder on confusion and misunderstandings arising from diversity in backgrounds, expectations and approaches to problem solving. There is no general law, such as human rights legislation, which prospectively supports and enforces anti-discriminatory and anti-oppressive practice in all areas of life and service. The most common way in which human service actors attract legal or quasi-legal attention is through action that raises a specific complaint by an allegedly wronged person, under discrimination and related legislation, as outlined in Chapter 4.

Under this legislation, agencies may face claims by clients or, in some jurisdictions such as the Commonwealth, associates of these people. Claims of religious and disability discrimination against clients are illustrated in *State of Queensland v Mahommed* [2007] QSC 018 and *Moskalev and Anor v NSW Department of Housing* [2006] FMCA 876. Both are appeals against determinations of quasi-legal bodies; one based on state and one on Commonwealth discrimination legislation. In the former case, the Anti-Discrimination Tribunal Queensland found that Queensland Corrective Services discriminated against a Muslim prisoner under the *Anti-Discrimination Act 1991* (Qld) in failing to provide him with fresh halal meat on his request. He was discriminated against directly because he was given a diet (no fresh meat) that was different from other non-vegetarian prisoners, on the grounds of his religion. He was discriminated against indirectly because a higher proportion of Muslims than others in the general population would not have been able to eat the normal diet, and the imposition of the requirement that he eat it was unreasonable. The department was ordered to pay the prisoner $2000 compensation, and in the instant case appealed the tribunal's finding on the grounds of errors in its procedural fairness. The appeal was dismissed by the Supreme Court of Queensland, which noted that all Muslim prisoners who request halal meat while in prison in Queensland now receive it, largely due to the legal action of this claimant.

In the *Moskalev* case, a tenant of the New South Wales Department of Housing suffered anxiety, depression and persecutory delusions about neighbours such that he desired a freestanding house. He requested suitable housing near his wife's father, for whom she was the carer. He rejected the properties on offer and his wife, as his associate, lodged a complaint about discrimination on the grounds of his disability under the *Disability Discrimination Act 1992* (Cth). The Human Rights and Equal Opportunity Commission was unable to resolve the dispute by conciliation and in the instant case it was heard by the Federal Court, which found that neither direct nor indirect disability discrimination had occurred. However, it was reasoned that while the tenant was inflexible in his demands, the department had given insufficient consideration to his supporting medical evidence. The application was dismissed, but the department was ordered to reassess the tenant's eligibility for detached accommodation.

Recognition of cultural and other differences and related rights and needs is enshrined in many other areas of law relevant to human services activity. The use of interpreters is a common obligation in law. For instance, under s 87 of the *Mental Health and Related Services Act* (NT), a person who is admitted to a treatment facility or placed on a community management order must be given specified information, in a culturally appropriate manner, and through an interpreter (where necessary). Failure to comply with this sort of duty will constitute a breach of the Act in question, or can activate an administrative review process or an internal or external complaint. It might result in disciplinary action if the omission lies with workers. Sometimes diversity will be inherent, perhaps even causal, in a human situation that is being adjudicated under a more general area of law. Family, criminal and civil law are three obvious areas in which the response to, explanations of, and management of difference may expose human services insensitivity and cultural incompetence. The stolen generations cases are examples of cultural hegemony, damaging human services intervention and the later application of civil law. A micro-example is the *Lem* case, reviewed in Chapter 8, in which a criminal court castigated a worker who was inattentive to language differences and did not use an interpreter during a psychological assessment.

LIABILITY CONSIDERATIONS

Organisations and workers who have knowledge of discrimination and other relevant legislation of the Commonwealth and their own jurisdictions, of the grounds and areas in which particular acts are proscribed, and of the legislative definitions of direct and indirect discrimination, are in a better position to avoid actions under this legislation.

Ideally, organisations and workers should strive towards anti-discriminatory and anti-oppressive practice for philosophical and professional imperatives, which have a much wider scope and impact than current Australian discrimination law. If they succeed, they are also less likely to face substantiated complaints and civil actions for harm resulting from practices that are driven by ignorance of, intolerance to and unconcern for difference.

DUAL ROLES, BOUNDARIES AND CONFLICTS

During ongoing intervention, workers and clients often function in emotionally charged situations that produce complex responses in both worker and client. It is not uncommon for strong bonds or antipathies to form. The ensuing transactions can be both positive and negative, and the roles of transference and counter-transference in therapy are well documented (eg Pope and Bouhoutsos 1986; Bullis 1995; Abbott 2003; Hepworth et al. 2006; Corey et al. 2007). Professional and personal boundaries have to be managed, both in the interests of the client and to avoid adverse professional and legal implications. Workers, clients and community members may also come into contact, in a number of ways, beyond their professional relationship. Then dual or multiple roles will also need to be negotiated. Workers may serve multiple clients and face conflicting interests that are to be prioritised and balanced.

Not all scenarios that involve multiple relationships, conflicts or ambiguous boundaries are questionable, or avoidable. There is considerable professional controversy about the appropriateness of some role and boundary conduct (eg Kagle and Giebelhausen 1994; Reamer, 2001; DeJulio and Berkman 2003; Australian Psychological Society Ltd 2004a; Knowles 2006; Corey et al. 2007). For example, there is disagreement about whether a sexual relationship with a consenting adult ex-client or a trainee is defensible, although Freckelton (2008c) argues that in cases involving registered professionals (eg psychologists), courts are increasingly opting for broad constructions of inappropriately sexualised relationships, including those with ex-clients. There is debate about the extent to which a worker might be a positive part of a client's private life. There is also debate about use of humour, touching and self-disclosure (Raines 1996; Reamer 2003a; Dewane 2006). There are arguments about the extent to which a worker should be immersed or detached in community work (Ife 2008).

Some behaviour is clearly proscribed by professional codes of ethics, employer rules and sometimes the law. Sexual contact with clients is one example of unethical behaviour (Houston-Vega et al. 1997; Ellard 2001; Australian Association of Social Workers 2002 clause 4.1.4 9(h)). Knowles (2006 p. 91, referring to the work of Smith and Fitzpatrick 1995) differentiates between boundary crossings and violations. The former may be the subject of professional debate and generally cause no great harm to clients. That violations cause, or can cause, harm is generally accepted. North American research and evidence of widespread sexual improprieties by human service workers was outlined in Chapter 2.

There are many typologies of boundary and role issues in the human services, particularly relating to sexual conduct (eg Pope and Bouhoutsos 1986; Kagle and Giebelhausen 1994; Reamer 2001; Reamer 2003a; Reamer 2003b), and commentaries on sexual relationships with clients' partners (Demaine 2007), and non-sexual dual relationships (DeJulio and Berkman 2003). Hepworth and colleagues (2006 p. 544) offer a useful four-quadrant taxonomy of behaviours that result from the interaction of worker attitudes towards clients, and levels of worker involvement. The latter dimension is taken from Raine's (1996) suggested clues to transference. An under-involved worker with negative views may be inattentive and forgetful, and with positive views may, for example, set expectations for the client that are too high. On the other hand, an over-involved worker with negative views about a client might be argumentative, provocative, disapproving and inappropriately confrontational. Most conduct in each of these three quadrants will not give rise to legal or quasi-legal scrutiny, no matter how harmful or harmless its consequences, for all the reasons enumerated many times in previous chapters. The most likely outcome, if there is any at all, is a complaint about worker behaviour to an internal or external complaint body, or disciplinary action. The fourth quadrant, in which the worker has a positive reaction to the client and is over-involved, has more legal potential. Here the worker may seek out opportunities for intimacy or sex with clients, or give extra attention and sympathy.

The most extensive analyses of boundary matters in general and on conduct largely relevant to this fourth quadrant in particular are those of Reamer (2001; 2003a; 2003b). He proposes five themes in dual role and boundary issues in social work: intimacy, personal benefit, emotional and dependency needs, altruism and unanticipated events. 'Unanticipated events' covers unexpected collisions between workers and clients, and their respective families and friends, in social and other non-professional circumstances. These situations are not of the workers' making, should not lead to any form of legal liability unless poorly managed, and are not addressed further here. The other four themes, which are characterised by conduct consciously or unconsciously initiated by the worker, raise more obvious liability questions. Some examples of this conduct, which are or might become boundary violations, are presented in Table 10.1, which has been developed from Reamer's groupings.

The behaviours summarised in Table 10.1 often remain in the private sphere, even if they are egregious and harmful. All the general disincentives to complaints and legal action apply, along with others specific to boundary crossings and violations. Clients who are flattered or who have benefited by workers' attentions are less likely to complain. Often those who sense that a worker is troubled, vulnerable and needy are less likely to complain. These factors can suppress consequences that might otherwise flow from the emotional needs and altruism activities.

If the behaviours listed in Table 10.1 are serious or endemic, a formal inquiry may occur. A civil action is also possible if damage has resulted. The sexual assault negligence cases against state and religious institutions that were outlined in Chapter 3; for instance, *Moloney and Another v New Zealand and Another* (2006) 235 ALR 159 are examples of these exceptional civil law outcomes. Boundary violations may occasionally result in criminal charges. This is most likely to happen in relation to behaviours in the first two columns in Table 10.1; for example, where workers have engaged in financial dishonesty or other unconscionable dealing, or non-consensual sexual conduct. A criminal case against a worker for sexual boundary violations was outlined in Chapter 4 and more will appear in Chapter 12.

Some of the activities will stimulate complaints to internal or external bodies, and a number of them will result in disciplinary action, most

Table 10.1 *Dual relationships and conduct which may have legal implications (adapted from Reamer, 2001 pp. 8–17; Reamer, 2003a p. 124)*

Intimate relationships	Personal benefit	Emotional and dependency needs	Misplaced altruism
Sexual contact with client during professional relationship, or with clients' associates	Taking/accepting money beyond service fee	Sexual contact	Providing special accommodations
Non-erotic physical contact	Taking/accepting goods, services and gifts	Imposition of own values/beliefs	Extra activism on behalf of client or client group
Intimate gestures/gifts	Seeking/making use of information held by client	Intimate gestures, gifts and familiarity	Involvement in private life of client
Involvement in private intimate life of client	Seeking/accepting positive references and endorsements	Seeking/forming friendships with clients	Giving gifts or favours to clients
Interest in intimate life of client	Seeking/obtaining referrals/business	Seeking/accepting Involvement in private life of client	Self-disclosing to clients
Professional relationship with ex or current partner	Seeking/accepting business advantage, benefits and opportunities	Offering special assistance or not applying required sanctions	Being especially available
		Excessive self disclosure	Providing extra support and assistance
		Encouraging client dependence Role reversal – seeking assistance	

commonly by an employer. The behaviour may come to the attention of the employer through complaints by clients, peer reports or supervisor scrutiny. If the disciplinary action is contested, a legal case, generally industrial, might appear in the public domain and examples of these are found in previous and later chapters. In one outlined in Chapter 12, *The Salvation Army v Mejia-Rodriguez-Appeal* [2003] SAIRComm 65, the employer had dismissed the youth worker contending, among other things, that he had engaged in 'inappropriate behaviour with clients' (at para 3). In another, *Stuart Hill and the Department of Juvenile Justice* [2000] NSWIRComm 128, the worker had been dismissed for allegedly supplying cigarettes and marijuana to inmates of a juvenile justice centre. *Fiona Hall v Department of Justice Victoria (Correctional Services Division)* [1994] IRCA 136 provides another example of dismissal for a boundary violation. The prison officer therein had admitted having sexual contact with a prisoner and trafficking his letters. In *Squire v Intellectual Disability Services Council Inc – Appeal* [2006] SAIRComm 14, the program coordinator was dismissed on the grounds that he had sexual contact with a client in contravention of his employment conditions.

Another instance of conflict between employer and employee over boundary issues conducted under discrimination rather than industrial law appears in *Bock v Launceston Women's Shelter and Anti Discrimination Tribunal* [2005] TASSC 23. Here a lesbian support worker in a women's shelter had disclosed her sexual orientation during counselling with a client and suggested that the client could earn money, as she had done, as a prostitute. The client complained to the shelter committee that the worker, 'among other things... had crossed my personal boundaries completely' (at para 3). The shelter committee investigated the complaint and in general found it substantiated. Thereafter, the worker and the committee were in conflict about what constituted appropriate self disclosure. An interim policy on self-disclosure was introduced in the shelter, and the worker refused to comply with it. Her employment was terminated and she lodged a complaint with the Tasmanian Anti-Discrimination Commissioner arguing that the policy disadvantaged lesbians and her in particular, in her attempts to gain re-employment in the shelter. The Commissioner found that the policy indirectly discriminated on the grounds of sexual orientation in that a blanket prohibition on worker self-disclosure during assessment with clients might heighten a sense of oppression and enforced identity denial in lesbians. However, the discrimination was found to be reasonable in the circumstances. The complainant's appeal to the Supreme Court in the instant case failed.

LIABILITY CONSIDERATIONS

Many of the writers referred to in this section comprehensively detail mechanisms and procedures for managing dual relationships and minimising chances of boundary crossings in human services work. Several points are selected here for comment, because they are either critical or less commonly observed.

- It is said of the United States (Kagle and Giebelhausen 1994), but true also of Australia, that there is now less long-term clinical training in human services courses than previously. Thus, workers are not as well prepared as they might be for the emotional upheavals that often characterise human services work. There is a case for including more content on transference vulnerabilities in professional human services courses (Abbott 2003).
- Individual workers who care to monitor and maintain their professional competence and integrity may find it useful to undertake regular personal ethics self-examinations of the kind suggested by writers such as Reamer (2000) and Ellard (2001).
- The responsibility of agencies and managers to monitor, support and confront worker performance that is dubious, and to put in place plans for nurturing and restoring worker emotional and physical health when either is in doubt, cannot be overstated.
- Bullis (1995) offers four precepts for positively defensive social work which, if used by individual workers and embedded in organisational policy and procedure, can foster integrity and reduce legal risk. The first is worker disclosure of any potential role conflict or boundary issue. The second is a demand for fully informed client consent to all intervention activities. The third is careful divestiture by workers of clients wherever role conflicts are present. The fourth is documentation; recording of all and any events, words, or situations in which multiple roles or boundary crossings are implicated.
- Professional associations and agencies that acknowledge worker vulnerabilities resulting from impairment or other factors, and who have mechanisms for identifying and responding restoratively to them, are better placed to manage them before harm is done to clients.

MONITORING AND REVIEW

The importance, and sometimes legislated imperative, of monitoring and review, during both planning and planning implementation, was mentioned in the previous chapter. Client service plans are theoretically dynamic tools that provide for both monitoring of and response to fluid situations. Plans that are implemented mechanically, without attention to changing circumstances or inadequacies in service offerings, may actually be harmful to clients (Harwin and Owen 2003). Ongoing safe management, monitoring and review are very active processes and command all of the negotiation, influence, entrepreneurial, and confrontation skills demanded of human service workers in earlier phases of intervention. Nevertheless, there is evidence that plans are often not implemented and that they, and intervention in general, are commonly not monitored or reviewed satisfactorily. As Gambrill (2006) explains, vague outcome indicators are especially likely to be accompanied by errors in thinking about client progress and its causes. She includes wishful thinking, confirmation bias, reliance on observed rather than relative frequency, and hindsight bias in her list of problems with worker judgments about intervention. Lapses in safety management for clients and staff during intervention are also not uncommon.

Besharov (1985) summarises a range of cases in the United States in which failures to adequately monitor clients resulted in civil and occasionally criminal suits. Generally, these examples involve children being injured or killed while under the care of child protection authorities. Often the failures resulted from agency and worker inactivity, and their breaches were established either through non-fulfilment of their own case plans, non-compliance with a court order, or lack of response to a changing and dangerous situation. The few civil cases in the United Kingdom and Australia that involve deficiencies in monitoring have been outlined in Chapter 6. The English civil case of *Barrett v Enfield London Borough Council* [2001] 2 AC 550 is a good example of prolonged and harmful inactivity on the part of social service authorities. In this case, the plaintiff had been in state care from infancy to the age of 18 and when he left care as an adult after a lifetime of impermanent foster and residential placements he had no supports, no family connections and no social or emotional attachments. It appears that the *Human Rights Act 1998* (UK) might soon be interpreted to give courts the power to monitor case plans that they have decreed (Mole 2002). If this happens, the ongoing service delivery activities of social service actors will be exposed to considerably more court scrutiny in that jurisdiction.

There are few Australian civil cases where plans for clients in ongoing service arrangements have not been reviewed or adjusted as needed to prevent harm. The most relevant ones have been canvassed in earlier chapters.

MISHAPS AND MISDEEDS THROUGH A HUMAN SERVICES LENS

When such cases reach court, judges can be sharp and critical observers of service monitoring deficiencies. For example, in the *SB* case mentioned in this chapter, the court itemised planning and monitoring inertia. In the case of the removed Aboriginal child, *Johnson v DOCS* (No 2) [1999] NSWSC 1156, the court powerfully and starkly itemises service inaction. Master Harrison said (at para 29):

> In summary between the ages of 4 to 18 years, despite the Department recording the importance of the plaintiff maintaining contact with his natural family, the plaintiff met his sisters when he was 8, received a letter from his father when he was 10 years of age and wrote a reply. When he was 11 he met his natural father on one occasion. In 1983 when the plaintiff was 15 years he received two letters, one from his sisters and one from an aunt and some photographs of his natural family. In 1984 when the plaintiff was 16 years old his father and brother visited him in Sydney and he visited his family in Wilcannia.

In the *Trevorrow* case, the child was removed from his family illegally and then returned to it some years later, without any apparent planning for transitions or family relationship maintenance and rebuilding. The case of *New South Wales v Bujdoso* (2005) 222 ALR 663 provides a different example of damage caused during ongoing human services responsibility, which founded a civil action. In this case, the prisoner had been bashed by other prisoners when he could have expected security surveillance and action to prevent these assaults, especially in view of the prison staff's knowledge of the threats against him.

Intervention that is poorly monitored or badly managed may give rise to complaints to internal or external bodies. If endemic, it may also found a formal inquiry as happened with the Independent Commission Against Corruption (2006) investigation into corruption in the management of community service orders in New South Wales. The behaviour of human services staff with responsibility for the ongoing care of clients may result in criminal charges. This can happen, for instance, if clients are assaulted, defrauded or have their property stolen. Disciplinary action may attend these sorts of circumstances. Very occasionally, alleged mal-intervention will sustain a more innovative use of public law to test rights. For example, judicial review was sought in the case of *Fyfe v South Australia* [2007] SASC 272. In this case, the applicant was a prisoner who had been isolated from other prisoners since 1995 through an order of the prison's general manager exercising his discretion under the *Correctional Services Act 1982*

(SA). The prisoner sought review of the manager's most recent decision not to revoke that order. His application was dismissed after the court scrutinised the reasons and evidence founding the manager's decision. In another corrections case, *Rainsford v State of Victoria* (No 2) [2004] FMCA 707, a prisoner recovering from back surgery argued under the *Disability Discrimination Act 1992* (Cth) that he had been indirectly discriminated against in the way the prison was managed and controlled. He claimed in particular that transport in prison vehicles and lengthy incarceration in a cell without access to exercise facilities prevented him attaining satisfactory levels of comfort although the comfort levels of a higher proportion of people without his disability would have been satisfactorily accommodated under the regime. Much of the legal discussion in the case revolved around whether a service as defined in the Act was being provided to the prisoner. The court distinguished between a statutory duty to incarcerate and all that entailed, and a service that would benefit the prisoner, and decided that no service was being provided as defined by the Act. The proceedings were dismissed.

In the rough and tumble of ongoing intervention in the human services, clients, staff and others can be injured. Occupational health and safety actions by staff in particular, against employers, as outlined in Chapter 3, are common. Several more case examples illustrate the legal risk to employers. In *Inspector De Leon Stacey v the State on New South Wales (Department of Ageing, Disability and Home Care)* [2005] NSWIRComm 131, a nurse in a supported accommodation service for adults with intellectual disability was working in an office that did not have an emergency exit and she was there assaulted by a resident who was known to have aggressive outbursts. The state was successfully prosecuted, convicted and fined $227 500. New South Wales was similarly successfully prosecuted and fined in *Inspector Keniry v the Crown in Right of the State of New South Wales (Department of Community Services)* [2002] NSWIRComm 349, as a result of safety breaches in group homes for people with physical and intellectual disabilities. Employees had been assaulted and injured in one home that was too small and noisy for the client group; several of the clients had previously displayed aggressive behaviour.

TERMINATION OF SERVICE AND FOLLOW UP

It is accepted as good practice that case closure is a planned and orchestrated process that occurs when agreed outcomes have been accomplished, when a specified time or intervention process has ended or when referral to more appropriate services is indicated (Boyle et al. 2006; Hepworth et al. 2006; Sheafor and Horejsi 2007). It is less acknowledged that many endings are unplanned (Gambrill 2006; Kirst-Ashman and Hull 2006), sometimes because the client is not engaged, sees no value in continuing or is otherwise preoccupied. Reamer (2003b p. 234) introduces 'the concept of abandonment', which is pertinent when workers and agencies fail to adequately prepare clients for service ending, discontinue needed services, or are unavailable to the client. He discusses a range of civil cases in the United States that have resulted from premature termination and insufficient follow up and support.

These sorts of human services cases are not a common feature of the Australian legal scene, despite the fact that many service arrangements end precipitously, unsatisfactorily, or merely fade. Even if the causes lie with the agency or worker, legal or quasi-legal interest is unlikely. If a client is unhappy, they may take issue with the agency, or complain to another agency or a complaints authority. The obstacles to litigation are again applicable. Both the *Walker* and the *Presland* cases, detailed in Chapters 5 and 9 respectively, involved exceptional civil actions by mental health clients who claimed damage as a result of precipitous hospital discharge and inadequate follow up. Neither plaintiff succeeded; in each case they were defeated by issues of legislative provisions and wording and policy. However, a successful negligence claim cannot be precluded if a service is ceased or not followed up, contrary to widely accepted practice in that area, if damage caused by the 'abandonment' was likely and if reasonable steps could have been taken to limit the damage.

Legal implications may arise if the end of a professional relationship is not formally confirmed. In the case of *Howell v Psychologists Registration Board of Victoria* [2006] VCAT 1427, a private practice psychologist was suspended from practising, among other things, for transgressing professional boundaries with a client in a rural setting by forming a social relationship with the client, using confidential information gained in the professional relationship to make financial gain, inserting herself into the social and domestic world of the client, and engaging in an ongoing dispute with the client. A central issue in the appeal by the psychologist was whether the professional relationship had ended. The psychologist contended that it had ended, but her records were inconclusive. While registration actions are not relevant to most human service workers, questions of dual relationships and clarity about professional endings are. An unregistered human service practitioner in New South Wales who engaged in the sort of behaviour evidenced by the psychologist in *Howell* might find themselves in breach of the code of conduct for unregistered practitioners and of interest to the New South Wales Health Care Complaints Commission.

A few Australian civil cases exist where medical practitioners have been found liable for failing to follow up patients after consultations and diagnostic tests, in particular those that revealed a condition needing treatment. Ellis (2007 p. 421) offers a set of measures that may help doctors avoid litigation for flaws in follow up, and these have useful applicability to human services activity:

- Record and monitor non attendances.
- Ensure that test results are received and reviewed. In the human services context, this could be generalised to reports from other services or referral feedback.
- Ensure that patients are told of test results. In the human services context, this could be generalised to keeping clients informed about all referral activities carried out on their behalf.
- Ensure that patients understand the importance of investigative procedures. In the human services context, this could apply to assessment, referral and treatment options.
- Act quickly if test results indicate urgency. This is a more obvious concern in the medical area than in many human services fields of practice, but it is still relevant. Children may die in abusive situations, clients may suicide or harm others, young people may fall into the hands of predators, or patients without capacity to consent may die through lack of medical treatment, if human services actors do not respond swiftly to indicative evidence.
- Ensure that treatment once started is formally concluded. This is ideally done both orally and in writing.

This last point raises the matter of writing, which suggests records. In all the phases of human services activity canvassed thus far, information management and record keeping are essential components. Records and the information that sustains them are turned to in the next chapter.

11 | Information and records management

IN SCREENING, ASSESSING, implementing and monitoring planned interventions and in all other functions, human service workers manage information. They seek, acquire, sort, interpret, record and discard material. Electronic or paper records – case notes, files, reports, minutes, memos, emails, forms and letters, to name a few – are basic tools and core requirements of all human services practice. Workers repeatedly make conscious or unconscious decisions about what is important, about what is to be recorded, when, how and why, and about who will have access to information. The centrality of good-quality and purposeful information and information management practices in the human services is recognised in organisational codes (eg Department of Health 2006), promulgations of professional associations (eg Australian Association of Social Workers 2002, Code of Ethics 4.2.5 and 4.2.6; Australian Association of Social Workers 2003, Standards 1.6 and 1.7; Australian Psychological Society Ltd 2004b) and the professional literature, and emphasised in various inquiries into human services failures (eg Crime and Misconduct Commission 2004).

Multiple, sometimes conflicting, legislative requirements covered in previous chapters, to either divulge information or keep it secret are the tip of the information management iceberg and act in tension with a common preoccupation about confidentiality in the human services. Information and records management involves more than non-disclosure or confidentiality, and confidentiality, despite some human services beliefs to the contrary, is never absolute. It was argued in Chapter 7 that confidentiality about client matters is often 'deified' in the human services, despite the evidence of gaps between rhetoric and practice. There is also limited appreciation of the professional and legal nuances of confidentiality in contemporary professional relationships. For example, although confidentiality is not absolute, there is evidence that clients are inadequately warned of its limitations (McLaren 2007). Certainly, professional codes of ethics are neither specific enough to deal with many confidentiality situations that arise in practice (Kampf and MsSherry 2006), nor conceptualised in a way that accommodates competing legal and professional imperatives (Swain 2006; Clark 2006a). Confidentiality is also often confused with privacy in the human services (Collingridge et al. 2001; Clark 2006a; McMahon 2008). 'Privacy' has different meanings depending on the context in which the term is used, but is often taken to concern the sensitivity of the material and the method of its collection; 'confidentiality' is more about the communication of the material.

While confidentiality is based on critically important philosophical underpinnings, its sanctification can mask other equally important information issues and the legal implications of information mismanagement. Terry (2008 p. 29) makes the point in relation to health, but applicable to the human services, that the modern 'information domain' is complex, beset by conflicting needs and altered by new electronic technologies, all of which change the ways in which patient 'data are acquired, stored, aggregated, processed, accessed and distributed'. Each of these processes involves an array of legal imperatives and constraints. This chapter focuses on transgressions across this wider domain.

This chapter also attempts to bring together the various ways, many of which are canvassed in previous chapters, that information management lapses can come to the attention of the law. Civil legal actions specifically about information mismanagement – for example, in negligence, defamation or breach of contract – are possible but rare for all the reasons outlined earlier. As noted in Chapter 7, there have been no known civil cases for breach of confidence in the human services in Australia. However, in some of the other negligence cases outlined in Chapter 6, information mismanagement contributed to a string of human service failures that together resulted in damage and helped to sustain the claim. Those case names reappear in this chapter.

Charges for information mismanagement under various statutes of the kinds outlined in Chapters 3 and 4, or complaints by individuals to complaints and investigatory bodies, are more feasible than civil claims. As explained in Chapter 3, the widest relevant legislative net is cast in Australia by the *Privacy Act 1988* (Cth), under which complaints are made to the Privacy Commissioner, who investigates them if they are within jurisdiction. It is not always possible to identify human services cases dealt with by the commissioner, as the organisations involved are not named;

however, many seem to concern or could apply to human services activities. Health-related complaints are more identifiable, and some that are relevant to the human services are considered here. Privacy actions are usually most relevant to employers, as s 8 of the Privacy Act declares that information-related acts performed by individuals in the service of an agency are taken to have been done by that agency. Flaws in the accuracy, recording, use and interpretation of information, among other things, may also prompt or be exposed in administrative and judicial review processes corruption or other official inquiries. Cases of that type are covered in previous chapters. For example, in the Alvarez inquiry, which introduced Chapter 8, inaccurate information played a significant part is setting off a long chain of fault-ridden events. Individual workers whose actions in relation to records and information management are unsatisfactory may find themselves charged with breaches of the legislation under which they work, as outlined in Chapter 3. It is more likely that they will face disciplinary action by their employer and, very occasionally, by a professional association. Misuse of information by public officers can also provoke a corruption investigation.

Terry's (2008) model of the health information domain includes a number of properties, one of which is data protection. He argues that sensitive data in a system should be protected by both substantive and process controls. Substantive controls are confidentiality, which controls disclosure; privacy, which largely controls collection; and anonymity, which allows people whose personal information is collected to remove their identifiers, refuse to make the data available to others, or both. Of the process controls, security controls ensure that access is restricted to those with a right of access under the confidentiality arrangements in the workplace. Integrity process controls check the quality of the data and ensure that it cannot be amended without proper authority.

Three features of Terry's model are particularly useful for current purposes. First, it integrates confidentiality into a holistic approach to data management. Second, it recognises that confidentiality has both a relationship dimension and a process or organisational control dimension. In other words, workers must respect confidentiality in their interactions with their clients, but the organisation's records management processes must also ensure that the information collected and recorded is sound and secure. Third, the model assumes that information management systems are made up of both individual worker elements and organisational policy and procedural elements. It recognises that information management lapses can happen at many levels in service delivery.

INFORMATION AND RECORDS MANAGEMENT | 211

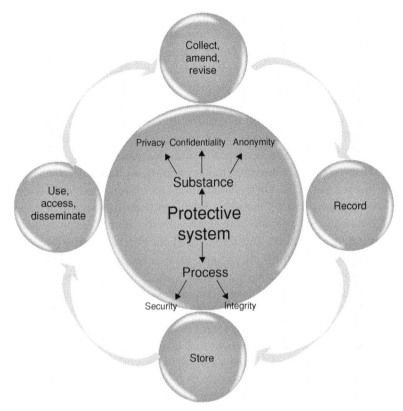

Figure 11.1 Information management in the human services (adapted from Kennedy, 2007 p. 82 and Terry, 2008)

This author (Kennedy and Richards 2007 p. 82) has previously proposed a diagrammatic cyclic schema for canvassing information activities in the human services, based on Australia's National Privacy Principles. The cycle begins with collection, and moves through recording, storing, accessing and amending. That schema and the Terry (2008) model can be combined to construct a more comprehensive representation of the information management functions and responsibilities of human services workers, organisations and systems, as shown in Figure 11.1. In that figure, the various stages of human services information activity are affected by data protection controls. The stages and the data controls are mandated or affected to greater or lesser degree by a range of current Australian laws and legal processes addressed in previous chapters, particularly

Chapters 3, 4 and 7. Figure 11.1 also provides a framework for sorting and analysing lapses in information management and legal responses.

This chapter follows each of the stages of data processing in its consideration of protective and other problems with data management in the human services, at the worker, organisation or system level.

The centrality of quality and purpose in quality recording in the human services is widely recognised in the literature (eg Kagle 1991; Barker and Branson 2000; Cumming et al. 2007; Healy and Mulholland 2007; Glicken 2008). It is understood that records must be valued as an integral part of human services endeavour, rather than as an administrative addendum (Cumming et al. 2007). Nonetheless, there is also extensive evidence of unsatisfactory record keeping and information management systems and processes. Records are commonly seen by human services workers 'as boring, of low status, and a routine chore that takes them away from the real work of helping people' and as 'an unnecessary burden or bugbear' (Cumming et al. 2007 p. 241, referring to work of various writers). Mechanical form completion and checklisting may be substituted for professionally discriminating judgments about what is important and what can be concluded from that information. Kagle (1991) argued that recording skills are not adequately taught in social work courses; her criticism is even more applicable in Australia now than when she made it, as subjects are rationalised and genericised.

Some agencies do not value record keeping, and in others recording is a source of dissension between supervisors and front-line workers (Kagle 1991). Human services records are commonly vague, incomplete, imprecise and inaccurate (Kagle 1991; Reamer 2005). Research studies show that recorded diagnoses are often based on biased first impressions (Glicken 2008). Australian writers have commented on human services workers' inadequate recording of what happens in intervention and how and why decisions are made (Swain 2002a; Lonne and Thomson 2005). Researchers have commented on some agencies' poor information management guidelines, especially guidelines that cover competing interests (Clark 2006a), and noted that bad practices are often learned on the job (Cousins and Toussaint 2004). Agency procedures and worker practices might not accommodate new tele and electronic intervention technologies (Banach and Bernat 2000; Finn and Banach 2002; McCarty and Clancy 2002), or meet the challenges posed by sharing, access and data integrity in electronic record keeping (eg Iacovino 2004). Lack of respect for the privacy of people and their personal information in group settings is noted (Kiraly 2002), as are problems with office spaces that do not allow for privacy to be respected. Reamer (1995) reports that claims for breaches of privacy and confidentiality made up about 9% of malpractice claims against social workers in the 1969–1990 period in the United States. Dickens (2004) observes a disjunction in the United Kingdom between the common practice of employing human services staff with limited earlier schooling, English as a second language and problems with formal writing, and legal expectations about competent written work and court processes that expose and dissect human services records. Some of these problems will be seen in the following sections.

INFORMATION COLLECTION AND AMENDMENT

The Privacy Principles (NPP 1; IPP 1, 2 and 3) state, among other things, that personal information must not be collected unless it is necessary for the functions of the organisation, must not be gained in an intrusive manner and must be collected directly from the individual concerned if that is reasonably and practicably possible. Collected personal information must be accurate, complete and up to date (NPP 3, IPP 3). These are matters of data integrity. With some exceptions, individuals about whom information is collected have access to that information, and the organisation is obliged to amend it if the individual can demonstrate its inaccuracy, incompleteness or lack of currency (NPP 6, IPP 6 and7). Individuals must also be made aware at the time of collection that the information is being collected and the purpose for which it is being collected (NPP 1.3). Sensitive personal information should be collected only with consent, unless particular exceptions apply (NPP 10).

Some difficulties with human services information management are specific to the process of collection. For example, human services clients often do not understand what information about them is being collected, why it is being collected and to whom it will be disclosed; often, their consent to collection is not sought (Clark 2006a). The seeking of sensitive information happens in many human services arenas, for example, in child abuse investigations, and requires a high level of competence. Connecting with clients and gaining their trust, while at the same time collecting intimate information that will satisfy a court, is a complex and highly skilled task. However, researchers have noted deficits in such areas. For example, interviewer preconceptions are common, as are structural problems in the ordering of interview questions and the use of hypothetical questions that distort the response and render it potentially inadmissible in court (Braye and Preston-Shoot 1997).

Inaccurate information (that is, data with compromised integrity) featured in the Alvarez inquiry, and in the *Trevorrow* case addressed in Chapter 6. In that case, some of the main obstacles to the return of the plaintiff to his mother were the original welfare worker's position that he should not return and her subsequent reports and letters to that effect. Conclusions that the welfare worker drew in a report about the family circumstances were said by Gray J to be based on 'materially inaccurate' information (at para 138). The welfare worker made assertions about the plaintiff's mothering skills in a letter about which the court said, 'again, this information was materially incorrect' (at para 141). This appears to be an example of poor-quality data underpinning even more dubious interpretations. Inaccurate information also featured in the English civil case of *M v Newham London Borough Council* [1995] 2 AC 633 outlined in Chapter 9, in which a child had been removed from her home after naming her abuser, whom the workers assumed to be someone else with the same name.

Klason v Australian Capital Territory [2003] ACTC 104 is another civil case concerning the accuracy and amendment of records. It demonstrates how a tenacious plaintiff can prevail and conscientious workers can find themselves at odds with the law. In this case, a divorced couple had made cross claims against each other about abuse of two of their children. A child protection investigator concluded that there was a high likelihood of sexual abuse of the daughter by the father, but that opinion was rejected by the Family Court. Several years later, the records of the ACT Department of Education and Community Services still indicated that the case against the father had been substantiated. Over the next decade, the father sought to have any mention of the allegation removed from the departmental records. A report from a project officer was commissioned, as a result of which the departmental record was changed to show that the allegations were 'revised – not substantiated' (at para 40). It appears that departmental staff members were concerned to keep a note of the allegation on file for some reason, perhaps connected with their view of the children's interests. Various further departmental communications, including a ministerial briefing note, addressed the ongoing problem with the records and the father's claims. The father eventually complained to the Privacy Commissioner about the inaccuracy of the information held by the department. He also sued for defamation by the project officer report and was awarded $2000 in damages. A subsequent investigation found that the project officer, other officers and the Executive Director of the department were in breach of the *Public Sector Management Act 1994* (ACT) and, as a consequence, they were obliged to undertake performance counselling. The Supreme Court in the instant case found that the amended statement about the plaintiff was defamatory and that there was hostility, although not malice, to him within the department. Later departmental written comments were not found to be defamatory, and the Court made a declaration that the father had not sexually abused his daughter. However, civil cases, claimants with the persistence of the father in *Klason*, and major inquiries of the *Alvarez* kind are exceptional.

Accuracy, comprehensiveness and necessity feature in cases that appear more routinely with the Privacy Commissioner. In *O v Tenancy Database Company* [2006] PrivCmrA 14, a person whose name was on a tenancy database objected to an annotation against it reading 'refer to lister'. The company then put 'absconded' against their name. The person complained to the Privacy Commissioner, who determined that general comments of the kind objected to were incomplete and could lead to incorrect interpretations, in contravention of NPP 3. Another annotation, 'rental arrears during tenancy', was found to be complete, accurate and up to date, and the commissioner refused the complainant's request to have that comment removed. The complainant in *L v Commonwealth Agency* [2003] PrivCmrA 10 objected, among other things, to his ex-wife having provided inaccurate information about him to a government agency. The agency was found to be in breach of IPP 8 for not checking the accuracy of the information about his address. Amendment of inaccurate personal records is required under privacy legislation if the subject of the record requests the change. However, altering records for other organisational or workers' purposes – such as hiding errors or portraying things later in a better light – is not appropriate and may invoke or be exposed in legal action (see, for psychologists, Hammond and Freckelton 2006). Later changes or additions should always be indicated as such (Cousins and Toussaint 2004; Reamer 2005; McIlwraith and Madden 2006).

The arena in which information is collected may be significant under privacy law. Public servants who collect, or at least solicit, information in social settings and use it in their professional capacity have caused their agencies to fall foul of IPP 1 and NPP 1, which cover unfair collection (Office of the Federal Privacy Commissioner 1996). In the reverse situation, collection in a work setting for use in a private one can also be unlawful. For example, an interpreter employed casually by a government welfare payment agency gained information about a person in their ethnic community through translating a letter alleging fraudulent receipt of benefits by that person (Office of the Federal Privacy Commissioner 1996). It seemed that the interpreter may have passed this information on to the community member. The letter writer complained to the Privacy

Commissioner, who found the agency that used the interpreter to be in breach of IPP 11, which concerns disclosure. The agency paid $5000 compensation to the complainant. While this was not technically a collection breach, it illustrates the importance of taking care that information collected for a particular purpose in one setting is not used in another setting or for a different purpose.

M v Health Service Provider [2007] PrivCmr 15 illustrates the issue of necessity. In that case, an individual visited a medical practitioner, who photographed them for their medical file. The person objected, but without effect, and then complained to the Privacy Commissioner. The photo was not necessary for the provision of health services, and the commissioner took the view that the medical practitioner had breached NPP 1. The photo was removed and the taking of photos in that medical practice was discontinued.

The requirement to make people aware of data collection and its purpose was tested in *T v Private Community Centre* [2008] PrivCmrA 20, in which a parent using a centre for access visits with their children claimed, among other things, that they had been unaware for six months that they were under video surveillance in the centre. The centre satisfied the Privacy Commissioner that the parent had been informed by producing a form that detailed the surveillance for security purposes, signed by the parent, and showing how the surveillance was explained to clients. The centre also supplied photos of large notices about surveillance around the premises.

A range of obligations in relation to information collection processes may be mandated by other law, particularly public law, and breaches of those obligations can come to light through administrative law cases. The case of *Idris, Hayat Adam* [2004] MRTA 574 outlined in Chapter 9, in which an African woman's case against deportation failed because of inadequately completed forms by two human services workers, is one such example. That case is a salutary and cautionary illustration both of the importance of proper information collection procedures and of precision in data recording in the human services.

RECORDS

Information in written form becomes a record, ideally purpose based, comprehensive, accurate and up-to-date. As Besharov (1985) observes, records are the agency's memory. Poor record-keeping can be fatal in human services situations. The inquiry report into the Alvarez deportation states, '[T]he biggest deficiency associated with the Alvarez files is the lack of adequate records. Vital information and crucial decisions were not recorded. There is evidence of irregularities in file dates. Original notes were "lost in the system", without copies having been made. Case details that were inaccurate and potentially misleading were forwarded to senior executive staff' (McMillan 2005 p. 32). Individual and system failures were involved, as the functions of the Department of Immigration and Multicultural and Indigenous Affairs (DIMIA) relied on at least five unconnected electronic databases and email retention procedures were flawed (McMillan 2005 pp. 37 and 72). A number of NPPs and IPPs are relevant to these deficiencies. Several concern the necessity for record holders to have records policies that allow people about whom records are kept to know what information is held and how they might access it (IPP5 and NPP 5).

Failure of a social worker to record critical information was alleged in the *Presland* case summarised in Chapters 5 and 10. Problems with precision in recording were evident in the *Klason* and *Idris* cases covered earlier in this chapter. In *Klason*, a word left in a client file created civil liability; in *Idris*, incomplete forms resulted in visa refusal for a client. A flawed form was also at issue in *Red Shield Housing Association v Calder* [2006] SARTT 6, which also shows that recording problems can have significant negative impacts on service providers, too. In that case, a welfare housing agency attempted to evict a tenant claimed to be dirty, damaging, disruptive, noisy and bothering neighbours. The agency served the tenant with the prescribed form for notice of termination under the relevant Act but attached conditions to the form and rendered it invalid in law. Legally, the tenant could thus stay on at least in the short term, and the agency probably had ongoing problems with damage to its property and community relations. In turn, that might well have eroded the resources and goodwill available to future welfare tenants.

The accuracy of a social work report was challenged in the judicial review case of *Trinh v New South Wales State Parole Authority* [2006] NSWCS 1352. The applicant was released from prison on parole, subject to a number of conditions including obeying the directions of a parole officer. The parole officer subsequently wrote one report recommending a warning about noncompliance with parole conditions, and two recommending revocation of parole, which then happened. The offender appealed unsuccessfully to the parole authority on the grounds that the reports were false and misleading. In the instant case, he appealed to the Supreme Court. In particular, he objected to statements in the reports about his failure to obey directions, to contact his parole officer and to cease his illicit drug use. In the event, the Supreme Court did not reach a conclusion about the reports because it had insufficient information on which to do so. The parole officer had not been cross-examined and the Parole Authority had not given reasons for its determinations. In its own deliberations, the court applied the principle that no opinion is better than an uniformed one, and the application was dismissed. This was also an example of a tenacious client willing to pursue a claim in the courts.

Some privacy cases in which data accuracy was at issue have been noted above in relation to information collection and amendment. Both data accuracy and security were at issue in *Q v Australian Government Agency* [2007] PrivCmrA 19, another privacy case illustrating potential risks with electronic databases that are not managed tightly enough. A person who used a post box number for mail in dealings with the government agency received letters from the agency at their home address, which had never been given to the agency. The person could not get an explanation from the agency and complained to the Privacy Commissioner, who investigated and discovered that the agency had a data-sharing arrangement with other government agencies. The residential address had been added to the agency file, from elsewhere, during handling of shared data. Data security had been compromised. The commissioner negotiated a settlement between the agency and the complainant.

Accuracy itself was not contested in *C v Australian Government Agency* [2007] PrivCmrA 3, but rather the retention of accurate information in a public record. There are some parallels here with the *Klason* case, but in the context of privacy law. The complainant had attended a hearing at a review agency and tendered a doctor's letter, which indicated that the complainant had a mental illness. The review agency subsequently published its decision online, omitting most of the complainant's personal details except a reference to a mental illness. The complainant tried unsuccessfully to persuade the agency to remove this reference. The agency argued that it was authorised by law to publish its decisions, relying on the exemption in IPP 11 (1) (d). The ensuing investigation by the Privacy Commissioner concluded that the review agency was in breach of its own policies, which provided for exclusion of personal medical details and allowed for decision-maker discretion when medical details were central to the case. The agency agreed to remove the reference to the medical condition in the transcript.

It has sometimes been argued in the human services that the best way to avoid legal problems with records, in particular reporting requirements that compromise confidentiality, is to not record, make very brief records, destroy records, or keep only private notes. These views are commonly discussed in the context of defensive social work (Harris 1987; Ames

INFORMATION AND RECORDS MANAGEMENT | 219

1999). It is generally agreed that none of these defensive actions complies with ethical or professional standards and that all would invite rather than protect against legal scrutiny (Ames 1999; Barsky and Gould 2002; Symons 2002) (Reamer 2003b; Reamer 2005; Armstrong 2006). That these sorts of actions might also defeat the purpose of human services activity is exemplified in the Canadian case of *R v Carosella* [1997] 1 S.C.R. 80. A woman had attended a sexual assault centre, been interviewed at length by a social worker and been told that whatever was said about the alleged assault could be subpoenaed. The woman accepted the stated constraints on confidentiality. She later went to the police about the assault, and a man was charged. At the beginning of the criminal trial of the accused, the assault centre was ordered to produce the woman's file. The agency could not do this because the notes had been shredded by a social worker in line with centre policy, which commanded vague, non-specific and abbreviated note taking, and file shredding to prevent the production of those records in court. The trial judge found that the trial of the accused would be prejudiced if he could not cross-examine the woman about her statements made at the clinic and that his rights under the Canadian Charter of Rights and Freedoms had been infringed. Thus, proceedings were stayed. The prosecution prevailed on appeal, but in the current case the majority in the Canadian Supreme Court found that the destruction of the relevant material and its nondisclosure to the court would not allow a full and fair defence, and the order to stay the proceedings was restored. Needless to say, the woman who had made the assault allegation was upset about the destroyed notes, the absence of which torpedoed her case.

LIABILITY CONSIDERATIONS

Several points are suggested by the preceding material:

- Familiarity with the Privacy Principles is warranted, because they are a legal imperative and also because they affirm good human services practice. They should be embedded in agency information management and general intervention polices and procedures. It is desirable both legally and professionally for information collection about clients to be done in partnership with them (Armstrong 2006) so that clients, workers and agencies have the same knowledge about what is being gathered, how and why.
- The purpose of information collection is critical under privacy law, making it imperative for agencies and workers to be clear about exactly what needs to be known for human services activities, and why.

The purpose of information collection and decisions about the importance and interpretation of information will be dictated by the agency's mandate, program parameters and intervention approaches. If these things are not clear, it is likely that information-related activities will be similarly imprecise and legally risky.

- Agencies face less legal risk if they have procedures in place for letting staff and clients know what information is being collected, and how and why. How they monitor compliance with those procedures is important in terms of their liability. Staff compliance with the procedures is important in terms of their individual risk of disciplinary action.
- Consent to collection should never be assumed and should always be sought.
- The importance of keeping records that are accurate, comprehensive, complete, free of gratuitous comments, contemporaneous, dated and signed is well rehearsed in human services literature and confirmed by the above case review.
- Records have a very long life, often longer than that of the worker who makes them, and should always be made with future scrutiny in mind.
- It is critical that individual workers attend to detail and precision in recording and responding to requests for information, particularly if the record or information is to have a legal audience.
- Agencies do well to have policies and procedures covering changes in records. Amendments to records and later inserts should always be clearly indicated as such and dated and signed by those who have made the changes.

INFORMATION STORAGE

NPP 4 and IPP 4 address the safe storage of information; the prevention of unauthorised access, use and amendment; and provisions for safe destruction. It is expected that more care will be taken with more sensitive information. Various legislative and policy regimes concerning government records, mentioned in Chapter 3, also cover some of this ground, along with other matters such as the length of time for which material must be held. All of these legislative provisions are particularly relevant to the security element of Terry's (2008) model of the health information domain.

However, records are sometimes organised and stored in ways that do not prevent leakage and loss. There are stories, apocryphal and true, of government and other records containing very sensitive personal information being lost in the post, found in waste dumps or accessed by computer hackers. Internal investigations follow in such cases, and disciplinary action and/or charges under a relevant Act may result. Information storage problems are often more prosaic; for example, when large numbers of staff without a legitimate interest have unrestricted access to sensitive personal information in agency records (Clark 2006a). If an individual pursues a complaint about the storage of personal information, the Privacy Commissioner is the most likely recipient of the complaint.

For example, in *D v Health Service Provider* [2008] PrivCmrA 4, a patient of a private medical clinic was asked to return for a consultation because their notes could not be found. The patient was told that they must have taken their notes or that the cleaners may have misplaced them. Taking those comments as evidence of lack of care, the patient complained to the Privacy Commissioner. On investigation, the commissioner found that the contested 'notes' were actually one sheet of paper, that there was no evidence that personal information had been written on it, and that the patient's privacy had not been compromised. However, the clinic presumably reconsidered its data-processing practices and its communications with patients.

Another medical example illustrates both loss and the law's tolerance of imperfections in its interpretations of the word 'reasonable'. *In V v Health Service Provider* [2006] PrivCmrA 21, a health service could not find the full medical records of a teenager, whose parent complained on their behalf. The Privacy Commissioner investigated the provider's information management system, which included 100 000 records, and found that it was reasonable. It was concluded that the record had been misfiled as result of human error, the provider had made serious efforts to find it, and all that could reasonably be done had been done.

Insecure storage was at issue in *B v Australian Government Agency* [2006] PrivCmr 2. An employee of the agency was concerned that sensitive personal information about their employment status was held in computer files which had allowed for unrestricted general access. The agency admitted to the Privacy Commissioner that it was in breach of IPP 4. The commissioner negotiated a series of outcomes, including an apology, payment for counselling for the complainant and changed data security practices in the agency.

Length of storage of records may be prescribed by legislation and challenged under privacy legislation. For example, in *P v Private Health Service Provider* [2008] PrivCmrA 16, a would-be patient made an appointment with a health service and filled out an initial information form. They then decided not to use the service and asked that the form containing their personal information be destroyed. The health service refused on the grounds of its obligations under the *Medical Practice Act 1992* (NSW). The Privacy Commissioner considered the effect of NPP 4.2, which states that reasonable steps must be taken to destroy personal information that is no longer needed, in relation to the Medical Practice Act. Because Regulation 7 under that Act required contemporaneous medical records to be made and kept for seven years, it was concluded that reasonable steps under NPP 4.2 would not include destruction.

ACCESS TO OR DISCLOSURE OF INFORMATION

Who has access to information and who should or should not are the main areas of disputation in information management, as explained at the start of this chapter, and some examples of cases in which access was one of the matters questioned have already been outlined. Balancing conflicting imperatives for privacy or confidentiality with those for disclosure involves sophisticated exercises of judgment. Access issues, in particular, invoke the substantive and the security controls in Terry's (2008) model. The substantive controls over confidentiality, privacy and anonymity in that model are not always easily conceptualised in complex human services situations, where there may be competing interests and needs. Differences arise between clients, between agencies, and between clients and third parties about access to material. For example, there is tension between the need for privacy and the need for transparency of decision making in the public records of tribunals. This can include tension between the rights of minors and those of their parents or guardians (Braye and Preston-Shoot 1997; Bartholomew and Carvalho 2005; McMahon 2008) and between the rights of agency clients and those of their carers (Clark and North 2007).

The most familiar of access matters is that of unauthorised access, in which people obtain particular information to which they have no right. This can happen when flawed data management processes disseminate or lose data, as in some of the stories mentioned above; when workers pass on information deliberately or unwittingly, perhaps breaching confidentially; and when unauthorised people obtain the information because of poor security in the agency. Less familiar are contests and complaints over refusals to release or provide access to information.

INFORMATION AND RECORDS MANAGEMENT | 223

UNAUTHORISED ACCESS OR DISCLOSURE

Unauthorised disclosure of sensitive personal information, or permitting access to it, may well be negligence or a breach of contract, confidentiality or a specific statute, or a breach of agency policy. Legislative requirements and agency policy were significant in the case of *Thomas Potter v Work-Cover Corporation* PR944320 [2004] AIRC 214, in which an employment support officer who assisted injured workers with employment allegedly disclosed information about a client, contrary to the confidentiality provision in s 112 of the *Workers Rehabilitation and Compensation Act 1986* (SA) and WorkCover's policies on confidentiality. The worker had allegedly disclosed information about one client to another client while discussing with the second client a possible employment opportunity. The first client had previously been placed in the position, but had been dismissed in unhappy circumstances. The first client complained to WorkCover, which conducted an investigation and found no impropriety. The first client then complained to his member of parliament, and a second investigation found the allegations against the employment support worker to be substantiated. The worker's employment was terminated on the grounds of serious and wilful misconduct, predicated on a breach of s 112. In the instant case, the employment officer challenged his termination. His arguments – that he did not identify the first client by name, and that he was attempting to inform the second client about the history and sensitivities in the potential workplace – did not prevail and his application failed. It was found that he had the experience to know better and that he had undergone confidentiality training in WorkCover. He also failed on appeal (*T Potter and WorkCover Corporation* re Appeal PR948009 [2004] AIRC 589). The Full Bench on appeal found that no errors had been made in the lower jurisdiction, even though it might have come to a different finding on the facts.

To digress here momentarily and pre-empt the lottery analogy offered in Chapter 13, the *Potter* case illustrates how a worker operating relatively routinely, in a relatively ordinary human services situation that called for balancing the rights of one client against those of another, might fall foul of the law through a constellation of factors. The case report notes that the first client was 'difficult' and that the worker was frustrated with him. The first client was tenacious and called upon a member of parliament. Perhaps claims makers were being marshalled, or that eventuality was feared. This contestation occurred at a time when the workers compensation system in South Australia was subject to considerable social and political attention and under review (Clayton 2005). A new enquiry was set up. Without

MISHAPS AND MISDEEDS THROUGH A HUMAN SERVICES LENS

endorsing or judging the worker's behaviour, it can be said that he was unlucky. He appeared to make a non-dramatic mistake in balancing competing interests, at a time of political sensitivity, and with a persistent client. He lost his job as a result.

Unauthorised disclosure or access is also in breach of the Privacy Act. NPP 2 and, to a lesser extent, IPP 11 allow for disclosure if the person consents, if the disclosure is for the primary purpose for which the information was collected or a directly related secondary purpose that would be within the reasonable expectations of the person, or where there is an imminent threat to life, health and safety. NPP 2 also allows for disclosure to a person, including a parent, responsible for another if that other person does not have the capacity to consent. As explained in Chapters 3, 4 and 7, there are exceptional circumstances in which public interest can prevail over confidentiality at common law or under privacy legislation, and a public interest defence or legislative immunity may prevent or defeat a breach of confidentiality claim.

Reamer (2003b) argues that most human services lapses involving the disclosure of information are relatively ordinary, albeit with potentially extraordinary consequences, and result from careless worker practices that may well represent the norm in the organisation. He catalogues phone calls made in public, unattended computer screens and papers on desks, conversations in public places, faxes sent astray, material left on photocopiers and files read on public transport, among other things (2003b pp. 67–9). A Canadian study found that hospital staff regularly discussed patients in public lifts (Vigod et al. 2003). Organisations may also have deficient security process controls, in Terry's terms (2008). For example, in a case outlined in Chapter 5, *S v Secretary, Department of Immigration and Multicultural and Indigenous Affairs* (2005) 216 ALR 252 (at para 16), the evidence given by the clinical psychology director about limited access to the electronic psychology and counselling files for detainees was inconsistent with that of DIMIA staff witnesses who explained how they accessed the files as part of their normal work practices.

Breaches of the more common kind may happen inadvertently. In *L v Contractor to Australian Government Agency* [2007] PrivCmrA 14, a health provider under contract to the complainant's employer had sent correspondence between it and the complainant to the employer without consent. While the reason for the sharing of correspondence is not clear in the case note, lack of thought at least can be assumed, as the contractor admitted the breach and could not justify it on legal grounds. A settlement involving an apology, a donation to a charity of the complainant's choice and changed confidentiality policies in the contractor agency were agreed.

Disclosure may also occur through deliberate action, which might or might not be well intentioned. For instance, in *M v Australian Government Agency* [2005] PrivCmrA 10, the complainant had, while working in a government agency, been investigated for alleged misconduct. They resigned before the investigation was finished and went to work for another employer. Another employee of the government agency had links with the complainant's new employers and gave them information about the incomplete misconduct investigation. A complaint to the Privacy Commissioner resulted in the government agency acknowledging that it had acted contrary to the Privacy Act, an apology and an explanation of the improper disclosure. If the government employee who passed on the investigation information did so contrary to agency policy and in the absence of management direction, it is fairly safe to assume that they were in breach of the *Public Service Act 1999* (Cth) or other Act covering the agency operations. They may in turn have faced a breach and/or disciplinary action.

Another conscious, and presumably considered, decision to disclose information of a particular kind was challenged in *C v Commonwealth Agency* [2003] PrivCmrA 1. In that case, an employee of a government agency applied for a job in another government agency, using their supervisor as a referee. The employee did not get the job and claimed that this was a consequence of their supervisor improperly revealing that they suffered from depression and epilepsy, did not cope well with stress, and took extensive sick leave. The Privacy Commissioner found that the employee would not have been reasonably likely to know that the supervisor would provide details of their health and sick leave in a reference and would not have impliedly consented to such disclosure. Thus, IPP 11 was breached and the complainant was paid $7000 compensation. However, there was no breach in relation to the comment about stress, as it was relevant to employment generally and to the position applied for and the applicant could have expected a referee to comment on this characteristic. A similar and no doubt considered decision to pass on unfavourable information was taken by a social worker in a case, noted in a Privacy Commissioner annual report (1994), in which the quasi-legal body involved was found to be at odds with the law. The social worker had given information, which was adverse to the interests of a person applying for refugee status, to the Immigration Review Tribunal and expected the information to be treated in confidence. Contrary to IPP 11, the tribunal passed on the information to the applicant, who later confronted the social worker at her home. As a result of the involvement of the Privacy Commissioner, the tribunal revised its guidelines on information disclosure and retrained its staff accordingly.

Unauthorised disclosure can occur even when people are not identified and a human service actor is engaging in useful public commentary. In *K v Health Service Provider* [2008] PrivCmrA 11, a health service worker gave information about the medical condition of an unnamed person in an interview with a newspaper reporter. The person lived in a remote community and complained that others in that community could identify them from the information that appeared in the newspaper article. The health service provider agreed that personal information had been divulged because the facts outlined could result in the complainant's situation being recognised. The Privacy Commissioner negotiated a financial settlement.

BROWSING

One of the more common and deliberate forms of unauthorised access in health (Kelly 1998) and, one can assume, in human services agencies is browsing among files by staff, for personal interest or use. Examples of this appear in the media from time to time. Often, disciplinary action will result from such behaviour. It was reported (Peters 2007) that 367 breaches of privacy regulations were made by Centrelink staff in the 2006–07 financial year and that two employees were sacked for privacy breaches. The same source states that browsing of one's own, or family members' or friends', records in Centrelink is also dealt with as a breach of the Australian Public Service Code of Conduct in the Public Service Act, overviewed in Chapter 3. Industrial and other consequences of browsing, as well as administrative review of decisions, are illustrated in the example of *Re Beer and Secretary, Department of Family and Community Services* [2004] AATA 598. The applicant had been accessing the files of relatives and other people while working for the Department of Social Security, and his employment had been terminated on the grounds that he had breached the code of conduct. He then applied for a Newstart allowance, and Centrelink imposed an activity test breach because his employment had been terminated due to misconduct. This meant that his allowance was reduced. He appealed the decision, which was affirmed by the Social Security Appeals Tribunal after internal review processes. He was now appealing to the Administrative Appeals Tribunal which found that he had engaged in misconduct, his termination was related to that misconduct and he was thus subject to the activity test breach rate reduction provisions of the *Social Security Act 1991* (Cth). The original decisions were affirmed.

Complaints about browsing will commonly go to the Privacy Commissioner. For example, in *F v Australian Government Agency* [2008] PrivCmrA 6, a person who had been employed in a government agency complained that a current employee in that agency had accessed the complainant's personal record to find out where they were living. The agency concerned had conducted an internal investigation and found that there had been unauthorised access to the complainant's record. It had also terminated the employment of the person who had accessed the record. The Privacy Commissioner found that the agency had not taken reasonable steps, as required by IPP 4 (a), to protect the information and that the information had been used for a purpose contrary to IPP 10. The commissioner's conciliation of the matter resulted in payment of costs. Similarly, in *H v Commonwealth Agency* [2005] PrivCmrA 5, an employee improperly browsed a client's personal information, for which his employment was terminated. He had also engaged in conversations about her with another agency staff member, off the worksite. The Privacy Commissioner did not pursue the complaint about the conversations, as they were not deemed to have been related to work functions and could not be attributable to the agency; nor did the commissioner pursue the browsing complaint, as the agency had dealt with it.

AUTHORISED ACCESS DENIED

While it is commonly understood in the human services that care should be taken with information disclosure, it is less well appreciated that some information must be disclosed or accessible. Legal requirements to pass on or report specific information are outlined in Chapter 3. People may have legal rights to access information held about them. These evolving rights (see, for example, McIlwraith and Madden 2006, pp. 293–5) are enshrined in one form, with some exceptions, in NPP 6 and IPP 6. Rights of access may be exercised many years after the information is recorded, for a variety of reasons, including therapeutic reasons (Horrocks and Goddard 2006). There may be rights to access information held by government agencies in freedom of information legislation (MacFarlane 2000; Devereux 2002). Refusal to comply with subpoenas that require information to be made available to a court could result in a charge of contempt of court (eg Davidson 2002; Gould and Barsky 2004).

K v Health Service Provider [2007] PrivCmrA 13 illustrates a common protective response to a request for information by a client. In that case, a patient wanted to access documents held by a health service but was denied access on the grounds that their health would suffer and the privacy of another would be invaded. One of the documents was from a member of the complainant's family who had specifically requested that the information not be given to the complainant. The ensuing Privacy Commissioner investigation rejected the arguments about threats to the complainant's health, and one document was released. The second one, from the family member, was not released because of the request for secrecy, because no consent to release had been given and because the information contained in it was said to be 'not of a commonplace nature' and likely to have negative consequences for that family member and other relatives. Similarly, in the case of *B v Surgeon* [2007] PrivCmrA 2, a patient of a surgeon requested a copy of their medical record and was refused on the grounds that they might not understand some of the medical terminology and because some of the forms in the file concerned the way in which the practice did business and were commercial in confidence. The patient was invited to view the file under staff supervision but was not satisfied with this response. As a result of the involvement of the Privacy Commissioner, the patient paid for the administrative costs to have some of the file copied and given to them. In *A v Private School* [2008] PrivCmrA 1, a school had conducted an investigation as a result of which a student was asked to leave the school. The student had sought access to their school records and, while the school had made some available, it had refused access to the rest on the grounds that the privacy and safety of other people might be compromised. The Privacy Commissioner reviewed some of the refused documents and agreed with the school's position. During the privacy investigation, yet other documents were discovered; these were passed on to the complainant.

In a complex human services system where multiple agencies are servicing one client, or one agency is servicing different members of a client family, protocols for consent to information release and information sharing between agencies and family members are essential. Given the various qualifications to confidentiality and the exceptions in the Privacy Principles, it is equally important that agencies have clear policies about limitations on confidentiality in their service agreements with clients and that staff apply the procedures that flow from them. However, there is evidence that these policies and procedures are underdeveloped in the human services and health sectors, leading to excessive information sharing, over-cautious approaches to sharing, and 'chaotic' information transfer (Richardson and Asthana 2006). A one-dimensional appreciation of both confidentiality and privacy can lead to either blanket refusals to release information for any purposes, inaction on information that should be passed on, or both (Kane et al. 2002; Marshall and Solomon 2004).

The absence of protocols for managing competing rights in relation to important information was explored in *Harvey v PD* [2004] NSWCA 97. A man and a woman planning marriage had jointly visited a doctor for tests for sexually transmitted diseases. The woman was known by the doctor to be particularly concerned about the risk of her partner having an HIV-positive status. The couple had one consultation, and there were no arrangements for joint follow-up. When the woman contacted the clinic about the test results, the receptionist refused her access to her fiancé's results on the grounds of confidentiality. The fiancé was in fact HIV-positive, although he lied to the woman about this, and after marriage the woman, too, became HIV-positive. She had continued to attend the medical clinic for other sexually related matters, and the matter of her safety had never been raised during the visits, although the doctor knew that her then husband was HIV-positive. She sued the doctor in negligence for failing to advise that, in the absence of consent by her fiancé, his information could not be legally disclosed to her, and for omitting to raise the question of joint consultations after the testing was done – in other words, for perfunctory pre and post-test counselling that resulted in damage to her health. Much is said in the judgment in this case about information management and record keeping; the need for cross-referencing in files; and the need to have systems, such as follow-up joint appointments, in place to ensure the safety of one client while respecting the confidentiality of another. The doctors had been found in breach of their duty in aspects of the first consultation, and their appeal failed.

Human services situations in which information release is neither planned for nor permitted, with resultant damage, are easily identified. The duty-to-warn cases mentioned in earlier chapters are one such example. In these cases, human service actors have confidential information that, if disclosed, might prevent injury to third parties. Less obvious but perhaps more common are situations in which deliberate or unplanned nondisclosure of information between agencies results in inefficient, duplicative and fragmented service. It is not hard to imagine a scenario in which a client does not receive adequate service because important human services actors do not have access to necessary information sequestered somewhere in the service system, and the client suicides, relapses, dies, deteriorates or is damaged in some other way. Such is the stuff of which civil claims, to say nothing of complaints, can be made.

LIABILITY CONSIDERATIONS

The points raised here are prompted by the preceding material and are not an exhaustive list of good information-management practices:

- Agencies can reduce their legal liability and enhance the quality of their practice by having comprehensive, up-to-date and legally compliant policies and procedures for the storage and destruction of records.
- All information that is collected should be accompanied by agency protocols for qualifications on confidentiality and consent to release. Discussion with clients about disclosure and release can be built into the treatment planning process (Clark and North 2007), with both therapeutic and legal advantages.
- Consent procedures and forms will not be legally protective if they are not specific about the details of information release – what can go where, under what circumstances, for what purpose and for how long?
- Agencies are wise to have policies on information sharing between themselves and other agencies and between other people in the client's family and social system. Those policies must be translated into guidelines or procedures that are fully discussed at the point of information collection.
- Agencies that have well-considered and well-articulated policies on how and under what conditions the subjects of records can access that material are in a stronger position to respond to requests when they occur and to marshal the necessary administrative and support resources.
- All records should be kept with an awareness that the person or body to which a record refers is likely to have a valid claim to access the record.
- Given the inevitability of human error, agencies are wise to have set in place an information breach policy in the organisation, consistent with guidelines promulgated by the Privacy Commissioner (Office of the Federal Privacy Commissioner 2008).

MISUSE OF INFORMATION

This section considers the misuse of information in terms of use for personal purposes, for purposes other than the primary purpose, non-use, or use in a way that damages another.

USE FOR PERSONAL PURPOSES

When information is used to benefit the user or to harm others, the corruption legislation covered in Chapter 8 may apply. For example, if agency records were sold or used to gain financial benefit or to damage other people or agencies, it is imaginable that crime and corruption investigations could result. Most misuse of information for personal purposes is on a smaller and more intimate scale; for example, an address or a relationship is sought. In these cases, some of which have been seen in this chapter, a privacy investigation and disciplinary action by the employer are the likely consequences if the behaviour is exposed.

There are also legal implications when information that is not work-related is relayed through work communication systems for personal purposes. In a case with echoes of the E team case outlined in Chapter 13 (or vice versa), a Centrelink worker in *Williams v Centrelink* [2004] PR942762 AIRC appealed termination of his employment. He had sent a number of pornographic and sexually explicit emails via the Centrelink system to other Centrelink staff and external recipients, and a Centrelink worker in another state had reported the behaviour. The current applicant was one of a number of staff who had been investigated. Two had resigned, several had been reprimanded or demoted, and he and another person had been terminated for breach of the Australian Public Service Code of Conduct. The commission commented, among other things, on the very poor management practices and culture in the relevant office in relation to email policies and code of conduct issues, but those shortcomings did not exonerate the applicant. It found that the applicant had sufficient maturity and seniority to understand that the material was offensive and should not have been circulated, and that he had failed to take advantage of the written and electronic material provided by the employer to warn of the risks of this sort of behaviour. The dismissal was held not to be harsh, unjust or unreasonable.

USE FOR OTHER THAN PRIMARY PURPOSE

Complaints that information has been used beyond its primary purpose can overlap complaints about its use for personal purposes. For example, the Privacy Commissioner notes a case that invoked IPP 10 (Office of the Federal Privacy Commissioner 1995). A client gave her personal details to a government agency in relation to employment. An employee of the agency used the information to contact her at home and ask her to go out with him. A consequence of her complaint was termination of his employment.

Complaints may also arise in more complex situations where the interests of various agencies and family systems are involved and perhaps in conflict. This is illustrated in *C v Health Service Provider* [2008] PrivCmrA 3.

A relative who had concerns about the health of a family member sent a letter marked 'confidential' to that family member's employer, enlisting the employer's assistance in getting treatment for the person. One might presume that there was a mental health issue here, although the case note does not state this. The relative alleged that the employer sent the letter on to the family member's health service, which discussed the details of the letter with the family member. The latter then allegedly harassed the relative who had sent the letter. The letter sender complained to the Privacy Commissioner. As the employer was a state government department, the Privacy Commissioner did not have jurisdiction over the complaint about the passing on of the letter to the health service. However, it did pursue the health service discussion of the letter with the family member under NPP 2.1, which prohibits the use of personal information for other than the primary purpose unless an exception applies. An apology was negotiated.

NO USE

Failure to use information is pertinent in many human services situations, although it will seldom come to the attention of the law. However, failure to use information may well sit behind some of the more tragic circumstances that arise in court or investigations. For example, in the *SB* case (which reappears throughout these chapters), there are many references by Redlich J to information in Department of Community Services files that the department did not review or apply in its decision making about SB's return to her father. He stated (at para 136) that she was returned to her father and insufficiently monitored despite all of the information in the records. In that case, information there was not misused as much as unused. In the Alvarez deportation case mentioned previously, the Filipino social worker who visited Ms Alvarez in the airport motel the day before her removal from Australia learned of Ms Alvarez's previous and married names. These were crucial bits of information that may have helped to accurately identify her as an Australian citizen, but they were not passed on to or sought by DIMIA officials (McMillan 2005, p. 27). Later, two junior DIMIA officers learned of the possibility of the deportation of an Australian citizen; each separately informed their supervisors, who took no remedial action about the new information.

USED IN A WAY THAT DAMAGES ANOTHER

Human services situations can occasionally give rise to defamation actions in which a plaintiff argues that untruthful and damaging information

INFORMATION AND RECORDS MANAGEMENT | 233

about them has been publicly promulgated. The case of *Cornwall and Ors v Rowan* [2004] SASC 383, in which a state government minister and another were found to have defamed a women's shelter administrator, is outlined in Chapter 7. The *Klason* case overviewed earlier in this chapter also demonstrated a claim about the retention of damaging information.

Defamation and privacy actions may be founded on the same set of facts, as demonstrated in the case of *N v Australian Government Agency* [2005] PrivCmrA 12. This case illustrates how the use to which information is put can have significant legal consequences for several actors in a situation, including those who are concerned to right a perceived improper practice. In this case, a person sent emails to several entities and a government agency, alleging misuse of funds by a third party affiliated with the government agency. Contrary to its own published policy that emails received by it would not be used for other purposes or disseminated without the sender's consent, the government agency sent the emails on to the accused third party. The third party then issued defamation proceedings against the person who had originally sent the emails, and that person complained to the Privacy Commissioner about the forwarding actions of the government agency. The agency agreed that it had breached its own policy but not IPP 11, arguing that the complainant would have reasonably known that the emails would be passed on or had impliedly consented to this action by sending one of them elsewhere as well. The Privacy Commissioner did not accept these arguments and conciliated a confidential settlement between the agency and the complainant. The complainant and the third party settled out of court on the defamation matter. Presumably, this complainant would think twice in future about reporting others' alleged misconduct – a negative outcome if the complaint was well founded and properly reported, and a positive outcome if it was weak and reported inappropriately. Also presumably, the government agency had internal work to do on compliance with its own policies, and individual employees may have faced scrutiny or disciplinary action.

Defamation actions invariably suggest unhappy relationships. Relationships, like records, are core components of human services activity. Relationships that go amiss are the focus of the next chapter.

12 Relationships, rifts and reactions

RELATIONSHIPS ARE THE bedrock of the human services. They are both the content of human services work and the vehicle through which most of it is conducted. Many human services relationships, particularly those with clients, come into existence because of distress, dislocation and disarray and involve high levels of emotion. As Camilleri (1996 p. 80) says in his elucidation of emotional labour, 'the *work* of social work is the managing, displaying and controlling of emotions and feelings . . . '. Many human services relationships are centred on sensitive personal matters and are realised in intimate environments, such as private offices, homes or residential facilities. Many of the relationships will, by virtue of the nature of human services work, occur in circumstances in which diversity, difference and vulnerability are significant. Many of them involve or invoke strong beliefs about rights, morality and justice. Many also expose or aggravate discord about intervention methods and practices, and program and organisational arrangements. Strong feelings, disparate expectations, capacities and passions, alone or in combination, can distort, fracture and stunt relationships. On the other hand, emotional intensity, intimacy and power imbalances can fertilise inappropriate relationships. Both relationships that sour, and those that flourish too vigorously, might attract the attention of the law.

Specht's (1985 p. 226) schema of social workers' interpersonal interactions is a useful starting place for thinking about the range of people involved in mainstream human services relationships. His list for individual workers covers clients and their intimates and associates, trainees and supervisees, consultants, colleagues, cognate colleagues (those more removed), community representatives, employers, policymakers and funders. He categorises the primary nature of interactions and power levels between workers and these 'others', which depending on their context are largely clinical, collateral, collegial or sociopolitical. Each of these types of interactions has its own rules of etiquette. Interactions with clients and their intimates are largely clinical. Interactions with those in the social network of clients are referred to as 'collateral'. Relationships with co-workers are collegial, while those with funders, for example, are largely sociopolitical. Some relationships, such as those with trainees under supervision and employers, involve more complex overlays of interactions: the former are largely collegial but with a clinical/coaching edge; the latter are a variable mix of collegial and sociopolitical. Specht's framework also proposes that professionals' levels of power and autonomy in relation to others increases or decreases according to the nature of the interaction. With clients in a clinical relationship those levels are high, and in sociopolitical relationships with employers or funders they are more commonly low. While questions of power and the nature of interactions invite hypotheses about motivations for legal action, their exploration in any depth is beyond the province of this book. Case reports do not provide enough evidence, or the right sort of evidence, to allow conclusions to be drawn about their roles.

This chapter addresses the legal implications of foundering or distorted relationships. It begins with the clinical and collateral relationships that workers have with clients and their associates, and then moves to collegial and sociopolitical relationships between workers, managers/employers, policymakers and funders. It closes with a section on relationships, which are also a mix of collegial and sociopolitical, between service providers. Given the fundamental role of relationships in human services life, this chapter might well be expected to be the longest in the book. If fact, it is one of the shortest, as it ties together threads from previous chapters and previously mentioned cases while introducing a few new case illustrations.

Troubled relationships may activate a legal response under public and/or private law. They may result in some sort of complaint or become the focus of an investigatory body. Dissatisfaction with screening, assessment and implementation of programs for clients and recording keeping may both cause and be caused by relationship difficulties. A relatively insignificant relationship problem may found a legal action, while a more dramatic one may remain between the parties for all the sorts of reasons presented in Chapter 12. And, yet again, the recurring disclaimer is made: most troubled relationships in the human services will not have a legal consequence, or at least not one that is heard in a court, and a complaint or industrial response is the most likely action if any action is taken.

RELATIONSHIPS BETWEEN WORKERS AND CLIENTS

It is trite but true that the most effective thing that workers can do to reduce the legal risks posed by their clients, their clients' intimates and their clients' associates is to stay on good terms with all of them. Hawkins (1985) reports in relation to medical care that two of the main underlying causes of complaints against doctors are the doctor's failure to communicate properly with the patient and patient resentment about the doctor's busy schedule, which precludes time to talk. He goes on to say that 'misunderstanding, not misdeeds, cause most problems' (1985 p. 158). Communication problems figured largely in the health and community services complaints figures outlined in Chapter 2. Webb (2006), in theorising risk in social work, is one of numerous writers to observe research which demonstrates that the power of a positive, caring relationship, rather than technical skill, cannot be overstated as a correlate of client satisfaction and trust. In the same vein, Besharov (1985) advises that sensing, acknowledging and attending to client dissatisfaction and anger is a useful tactic in reducing the risk of litigation in social work and, one could add, in generally maintaining effective professional relationships. It is well known that the quality of the relationship between client and worker is a better predictor of positive outcomes for clients than the intervention model utilised (see, for example, Hall 2008). The author of this book contends that a great deal of ineffective and technically unsophisticated human services activity goes unnoticed or is ignored by clients and others in their social systems largely because of the protective power of human service workers' goodwill, well-intentioned efforts and emotional engagement.

However, relationships do falter, sometimes despite the very best efforts of workers to keep them productive and positive, sometimes through deliberate action by workers, but mostly for reasons that lie between those extremes. Much has been said in previous chapters about pressures on human services actors to deliver more, to more people, with fewer resources. There are endless laments about how managerialism and new approaches to service delivery – for example, case management – have eroded the relationship component of client and worker interactions in favour of procedural and bureaucratic activities (see, for example, Dominelli 1997; Schorr 2000; Gursansky et al. 2003; Carey 2007). Much has been said about the impact of a negative risk preoccupation. In Green's words (2007 p. 402), 'Risk muscles its way into the professional relationship and demands priority'. There is evidence that workers, for many reasons, can be disrespectful, hostile, inflexible, threatening, intrusive, confusing and discouraging (Radey 2008). There is also evidence of what Sousa and Euseboi (2007 p. 235) refer to as 'disculpability', in which clients and workers feel that relationships and intervention outcomes are fully the responsibility of the other. When a relationship goes wrong or changes, the breakdown or shift may motivate some form of action, or it may underpin an action about decisions made within and allegedly tainted by that relationship.

Deliberate worker actions beyond the norms of a clinical relationship may invoke the criminal law, as has already been seen. In relationships in which a worker has been violent or abusive towards a client, criminal charges may result because either the client or another lays a complaint. The criminal law may also be activated if clients' finances or property are in some way misused by workers. As shown in Chapters 3 and 11, inappropriately intimate relationships between workers and clients can result in criminal charges, some for uninvited sexual activity and some arising from relationships that were not consensual in legal terms. The case of *South Australian Police v Moore* (Unreported, SA Magistrates Court, 24 September 2007) is one example of the latter situation. A youth support worker then employed by the Department of Family and Community Services was charged under s 80 (1a) of the *Criminal Law Consolidation Act 1935* (SA), an offence punishable by seven years imprisonment, and found guilty. He had gone interstate with his 15-year-old female client, who was under the guardianship of the minister, and both were found several days later in a motel room. As explained in earlier chapters, criminal actions against workers are likely to have industrial and, for a very few, professional association repercussions.

Depending on what is alleged to have happened, unsatisfactory worker–client relationships may lead to charges or complaints against workers and agencies under work-related statutes such as public service Acts or privacy or anti-discrimination law. The Centrelink social worker in the case of *Hensell v Centrelink* [2006] FCA 1844 (outlined in Chapter 3), who appeared to have troubled relationships with customers and colleagues, was charged with a breach of the Australian Public Service Code of Conduct in the *Public Service Act 1999* (Cth). Actions under human services related legislation may lie against the worker (as in the *Hensell* case) or the employer (as in the discrimination cases outlined in Chapter 10), depending on the operation of vicarious liability under the relevant Act. It is possible that administrative review actions are more likely to be taken by a client in the context of a troubled or mistrustful relationship with their human services workers. If a client takes action about the interactional conduct of their worker, that action is most likely to be directed to the worker's employer or a complaints authority. The resultant enquiries may well have industrial implications for the worker. No matter how troubled a worker–client relationship, the likelihood of a civil action is low. However, determined clients very occasionally pursue civil action; the *Klason* case mentioned in Chapter 11, which involved a successful defamation suit against workers in a government department, is one such example.

RELATIONSHIPS BETWEEN TRAINEES, WORKERS, EMPLOYERS AND POLICYMAKERS

Workers in conflict have not only information resources beyond those of many clients, but also careers, reputations, funding and programs at stake – all things appreciated by the law. Thus, in worker clashes, the building blocks of formal action are more readily available and accessible. Nevertheless, very few relationship breakdowns between trainees, workers, workers and their employers, and workers and policymakers attract the attention of the law and the civil law in particular. The examples of civil cases in the United States described by Lynch and Versen (2003) and Pollack (2004), in which social work supervisors were held directly liable for their own negligent supervision, are not a feature of Australian law. The law may of course be invoked for behaviour or events that are relatively independent of relational problems but are only noticed or reported because the relational problem provides the impetus. In most registered professions, relational problems between peers that could found a formal complaint go to registration boards, professional associations, or both. In the human services, where occupational registration is not widespread and there are low levels of association membership, these actions are less likely.

Some relationship tensions between staff, particularly if they concern inappropriate behaviour by one or a group of staff, may generate complaints to senior managers, members of parliament, corruption bodies, the police or even the media. Reports of these kinds are not unheard of, at least in the public service (Independent Commission Against Corruption 2007). Depending on how and to whom the complaints are made, the complainant may themselves be vulnerable to legal sanction; for example, for breaching the confidentiality provisions of applicable legislation or by falling outside the scope of limited protections offered by relevant whistleblower legislation. They may also be subject to harassment in the workplace. The difficulties of whistleblowers in the human services are legion and well documented (see, for example, De Maria 1996; Hunt 1998; Els and Dehn 2001).

Hierarchical relationship difficulties are most often formally tested in the industrial law arena. Contested disciplinary action or termination decisions appear in industrial court and commission reports, some of them suggesting serious ongoing breakdowns in staff relationships. Two cases illustrate how relationships between managers and staff appear to have been significant in leading to legal action. The two learning facilitation officers in *Australian Services Union of NSW v St Vincent De Paul Society* [2007] NSWIRComm 1044 participated with others in an authorised staff 'brainstorm' meeting in which comments on the manager's style were invited and given. After the session, there was internal organisational conflict about the source, content and style of the feedback. When the two staff involved in this case subsequently refused to submit written personal grievance reports about the issues discussed, they were dismissed on the grounds that they had not complied with agency policies on reporting obligations. The evidence reported in the case involved claims from both sides about bullying, disrespect, temper outbursts, control of equipment, and lack of acknowledgment of staff expertise, among other things. It seems that relationships between a manager and several staff had been tense for some time before the termination decisions and may have been the major determinant of them. Nonetheless, the Industrial Relations Commission believed that the relationships were not irretrievably damaged and that there was integrity and goodwill on both sides. It found that the dismissals were procedurally unfair and unsupported by valid reasons, and ordered the reinstatement of both workers. Similarly, in the case of *Cassidy v Department of Corrective Services* [2007] QIRComm 15 (outlined in Chapter 3), the commission also ordered reinstatement of the prison officer as a remedy for unfair dismissal, as it was not convinced that work relationships had broken down significantly prior to termination.

The employer in *The Salvation Army v Mejia-Rodriguez – Appeal* [2003] SAIRComm 65 seemed most concerned about a youth worker's client- and program-related behaviours, but the evidence also revealed entrenched animosities between that worker and his managers and between the worker and some colleagues. The worker in this case, employed in a youth accommodation service, was dismissed for alleged petty cash irregularities, disobeying reasonable directions, and inappropriate relationships with clients. The employer was evidently intent on parting company with the worker and successfully appealed the remedy of reinstatement from the worker's successful unfair dismissal case. The court here overturned the worker's reinstatement on the grounds that the employer–employee relationship was irretrievably damaged, and that there was a high likelihood of future disharmony in the agency should he return to work.

Relationship problems within staff groups may also prompt and be exposed through industrial action by an employer. *Mangiafico v Department of Human Services* [2005] AIRC PR963416 is one such example. The applicant was employed as a child, adolescent and family welfare officer at a juvenile justice custodial centre. While acting as a supervisor, he was stood down as a result of complaints by residents about his inappropriate behaviour. The subsequent investigation found that there was not enough evidence to proceed further with those complaints. However, during the enquiry, six new allegations of inappropriate conduct against staff came to light. It was alleged that the worker had made sexually offensive and suggestive comments to one female staff member and that he had sexually assaulted several female and male staff members by regularly touching, fondling, hugging and falling on them. Another investigation was held and the allegations found proved on the balance of probabilities. The worker was dismissed and in the instant case appealed, claiming that the allegations were fabricated, the behaviour normal in the work environment, and the dismissal harsh, unjust and unreasonable. The Industrial Relations Commission noted the inconsistency between the first two of these arguments. Evidence during the hearing suggested that at least two female workers were unhappy with his behaviour but had been too frightened to complain earlier, lest they be seen as informers. The commission found that the worker knew about sexual harassment, held a position of authority, had engaged in the misconduct alleged and had failed to satisfy his duties, and the dismissal was upheld. The commission also commented but did not find on evidence about an inappropriate culture of harassment and bullying in the custodial centre and reminded the department that it had a responsibility to eradicate that culture if it existed.

Some relationship difficulties between staff and employers will culminate legally in occupational health and safety cases. Emerging evidence about such things as the impact of leadership styles (eg see Mackie 2008), harassment, bullying, mismanaged change processes and team culture on worker wellbeing is increasingly being incorporated in 'safe work' legislative regimes (Cotton 2008). In jurisdictions, such as New South Wales, that continue to allow common law actions against employers, negligence claims may also result from damage caused by relational problems at work. If an employer has concerns about the unsafe behaviour of an employee, it has responsibilities to manage that behaviour, sometimes through industrial

RELATIONSHIPS, RIFTS AND REACTIONS | 241

action to ensure that the workplace is safe. However, employees commonly assert that they have been damaged through the failure of their managers to risk-manage the psychosocial and physical hazards in their workplaces. They may claim that they were harmed by events inherent in the work; for example, by being assaulted by aggressive clients or by experiencing psychological stress (examples of both sorts of case are outlined in previous chapters). While the High Court has in more recent times taken a fairly hard line against employees claiming psychological loss (Burns 2006), some state cases have found for the employee when the employer knew of the risk faced. Employees may also claim that they have been harmed directly by the behaviour of their leaders; for example, through intimidation, harassment or poor management practices.

The case of *O'Leary v Oolong Aboriginal Corporation Inc* [2004] NSWCA 7 is an illustration of a negligence claim arising from poor management practices. The claimant was a bookkeeper for a residential drug and rehabilitation centre. On return from leave, he found that the books and his computer had gone, his workspace had been moved to a veranda and he was not allowed to sign cheques. Other workers knew that he was suspected of taking money, but he was never confronted or given a chance to explain. He claimed that the isolation, suspicion and hostility at work caused his major depressive illness. At trial, it was found that the employer was in breach of its duty to take reasonable steps to prevent injury in employees but that the particular injury was too remote and not reasonably foreseeable by the employer. In the instant appeal, the employee claim was also rejected by the majority on slightly different legal grounds, but it was affirmed that the employer did not have knowledge of particular susceptibility in the worker; that psychiatric damage was not conceivably foreseeable, although normal work-related stress might have been; and that stress and psychiatric illness must be distinguished. Even so, all judgments acknowledged unsatisfactory management practices, described by Sheller JA in the majority as 'wrong if not disgraceful' (at para 57).

Relationship difficulties at several levels permeate and are central to the negligence case of *New South Wales v Mannall* [2005] NSWCA 367. The case was an appeal against a successful negligence claim by a team leader in the Department of Housing, for psychiatric injury caused by 'victimisation, harassment, humiliation, and abuse in the workplace' (at para 3). The team leader had been awarded $339 722 in damages. The set of circumstances that gave rise to this case are familiar in the human services. A popular leader was demoted, and the new team leader entered with limited experience and management training and a mandate to restructure service delivery.

MISHAPS AND MISDEEDS THROUGH A HUMAN SERVICES LENS

Some of the team were 'lazy and unmotivated and/or resented being called to account by their new team leader' (at para 10). They were hostile and uncooperative, and the area manager did not support the team leader in her reform efforts. He was also rude to her and failed to set in place any timely or effective mechanisms for conflict resolution once he knew of the staff tensions. Relationships between staff and the team leader became severely dysfunctional, and she left work after about 18 months with a depressive illness. She was not able to return to work and subsequently retired. At trial, it was found that the area manager had been on notice about the team leader's mental state and that a psychiatric illness was reasonably foreseeable. The trial judgment is 'replete with conclusory findings as to the [area manager's] negligence' (at para 97) largely concerning his failure to detect distress, and passivity in the face of a very significant and destructive work team dynamic. The area manager, and the state vicariously, were found to be negligent. The negligence of the manager was affirmed during this unsuccessful appeal by the state.

Discrimination claims either resulting from or causing relationship difficulties in the workplace are sometimes made by workers, managers and others, such as trainees, against each other and their employers. In *Crewdson v Director General of Community Services* [2008] NSWADT 279, conflict within a staff team seemed to underpin events that led to the action. A former residential care worker in a facility for disabled clients claimed that he had been discriminated against when refused re-employment in the same department on the grounds that he had a presumed mental condition. The Anti-Discrimination Tribunal found that the selection panel rated him highly for the job but did not give it to him on the basis of information from previous supervisors about his presumed mental illness. There was an expectation that he would have to prove his fitness – something not asked of other candidates. His discrimination claim was established and he was awarded $44 000 for lost wages. His assertion that he had been victimised by a supervisor who gave a negative reference because of his previous complaints about how other staff were treating clients was not substantiated. It was held that the supervisor's comments about the additional load he placed on other workers and his deficiency as a team player were genuine observations about his performance, separate from his complaints. In Chapter 10, continuing conflict between an employer and employee about self-disclosure with clients, played out in an anti-discrimination action, was revealed in *Bock v Launceston Womens Shelter and Anti Discrimination Tribunal* [2005] TASSC 23.

Ongoing tension between employer and employee also seem to shadow the evidence in *Power v Aboriginal Hostels Limited* [2004] FMCA 452, in which an assistant manager claimed he had been dismissed unfairly because of a depressive illness imputed to him by the employer. He had been unhappy with 'various aspects of his employment, particularly that he be on call at nights' (at para 8) and he had been away sick for several weeks. Before his dismissal, the worker had been the subject of various performance reviews and his probation period had been extended. He claimed that the dismissal was discriminatory, but failed in the first instance to convince the court of this. It found the dismissal lawful, as his disability rendered him unable to satisfy the inherent characteristics of the job. He appealed to the Federal Court, which set aside that decision and remitted the matter, thus giving rise to the instant case. The reasoning in the case is complicated by the difference between the illness imputed to him and the condition he actually had, which was a transient adjustment disorder. However, it was agreed that he had been dismissed on the basis of a disability, albeit imputed, and that he would not have been dismissed, at least at that point, if the employer had not had concerns about his perceptions of his disability and the implications for his work. The dismissal was held to be unlawful, and the worker was awarded damages of about $15 000 for injury to feelings and economic loss.

Information mismanagement matters may also found, expose or suggest relationship problems, and many illustrations of privacy law cases, in particular, are provided in the previous and other chapters. For example, in *C v Commonwealth Agency* [2003] PrivCmrA 1, a reference that revealed a supervisor's view of the reliability of a worker and the worker's use of sick leave was challenged successfully under privacy law. Workers faced censure for browsing other workers' records in *F v Australian Government Agency* [2008] PrivCmrA 6 and *H v Commonwealth Agency* [2005] PrivCmrA 5. In the latter case, conversations offsite between two workers about the complainant hint at ongoing tensions in collegial relationships. In *M v Australian Government Agency* [2005] PrivCmrA 10, a worker passed on information about another worker's incomplete misconduct investigation to the latter's new employer. Was this risky passing on of information motivated by colleagues' concerns about the behaviour of the complainant in the first workplace? The case report is silent on that question.

Organisational politics appear to sit behind *J v Two Individuals* [2003] PrivCmrA 8, a case not previously noted. An individual had been convicted on several counts of defrauding the Commonwealth, and all but one of the convictions were quashed on appeal. That individual then joined an association in which the state and national chapters were in conflict. In this context, press clippings about his convictions were allegedly sent anonymously to the national body and his employer and circulated within the association, and he lodged a privacy complaint. The Privacy Commissioner was of the view that the national chairman may have breached the *Crimes Act 1914* (Cth) in disclosing the information about the convictions without consent, but discontinued the investigation after the chairman had apologised.

Policymakers are not immune from legal actions by workers in their areas of responsibility, as attested to by *Cornwall and Ors v Rowan* [2004] SASC 383 (detailed in Chapter 7). In that case, the state minister was found guilty in a civil suit of misfeasance in public office and defamation, as was his review chairperson, in relation to a report containing negative information about a women's shelter administrator. The report and the legal action arose in a period in which there was a great deal of ill-feeling and disagreement about funding and restructuring in domestic violence services. However, this sort of case is unusual and unlikely unless the litigant is tenacious.

RELATIONSHIPS BETWEEN SERVICE PROVIDERS

The historical and ideological heterogeneity in the non-government sector of the human services and the tensions and challenges in contemporary human services provider networks more generally are well documented (see, for example, O'Connor et al. 2000b; McDonald 2006). In the context of rapid change and reduced state activity, there is competition between non-government agencies for limited funding and a 'share of the market'. Professional groups vie for territory and recognition. The reshaping of approaches to service delivery and the resultant shared responsibility for services to clients means that workers are increasingly expected to communicate and work in concert within and between agencies. This is a fraught environment in which, in Specht's (1985) terms, demands for shared clinical interactions have risen, as has the quantity of sociopolitical interaction. However, while many of the cases covered in this book point to failures to meet those demands, such that clients are ill serviced, damaged, or both, there is little evidence that conflict between providers or professionals results in much intra-service legal action. All obstacles to legal action enumerated in earlier chapters apply here, but there are additions. Professional and agency pride and reputations are on the line in legal action, and practices are opened up to scrutiny controlled by legal actors. The financial and professional risks of loss in an action are high. Future professional relationships, careers and funding possibilities may be

RELATIONSHIPS, RIFTS AND REACTIONS | **245**

jeopardised. The *Cornwall* case (above) is one type of exceptional case that might appear in times of change and contention. A defamation action is the sort of action that might be expected when workers and agencies believe that their reputations are at stake, but it, like any other, requires resources and persistence. Many individuals who believe themselves to be wronged are not in a position to or do not choose to commit to what can be an exposing and financially and emotionally draining legal exercise.

LIABILITY CONSIDERATIONS

It is impossible to reduce the vast canvass of relationships in the human services to a few points about legal liability that are in any way exhaustive. The most obvious and, on the face of it, trite point to make is that good relationships in which differences are aired and resolved are less likely to give rise to legal action. A few observations prompted by the cases discussed are as follows.

- Workers are wise to develop their sensitivity to clients and to client-related relationship issues that have complaint or legal action potential. Having the skill and confidence to confront client anger and disappointment is critical, as is clarity about expectations and limits in the service relationship. The keeping of detailed, accurate and contemporaneous records is always important, but especially so in these cases. Records will be critical in any subsequent investigation and may be instrumental in vindicating the worker and agency if nothing untoward has occurred.
- Agencies have a responsibility to ensure that they have in place procedures and management practices that educate, support and monitor workers in developing and using the knowledge and skills indicated above.
- Agencies have a responsibility to ensure that they have fair, accessible and responsive client and staff grievance procedures in place, that those procedures are used, and that those who implement them have sound investigatory and conflict management skills.
- Both workers and agency representatives are wise to recognise that once they take a relational conflict into the legal arena, they lose control of its conduct. Their case will not hang on the strength of their conviction about their own position but on a range of legal technicalities and on how they and other witnesses present. Any decision about taking legal action to solve a relationship problem must factor in the cost of loss as much as the benefit of a legal win. It should also consider carefully what the benefits of legal success might be, as the legal outcomes possible

under different sorts of actions might not include those practical things sought by the litigant.

- It is common to hear human services managers asserting that they cannot act, especially in relation to workers, because of legal constraints. Seldom are the risks of inaction mentioned. However, the cases, especially in the areas of occupational health and negligence, show that passivity and inertia are damaging and can quite easily found legal actions.
- In Chapter 8, the rather fraught matter of human service organisational responsibility for managing workers well was outlined. Some examples of rather blunt management practices are seen again in the cases mentioned in this chapter. Management is an active, knowledge-based and skilled function, and agencies are responsible for ensuring that their managers, supervisors and team leaders have the necessary training and capacity and knowledgeable human resources support.

In Parts 2 and 3 of this book, shortcomings have been canvassed from the perspective of law and from the perspective of human services activities that have provoked or might provoke that law. The next and final part brings those two perspectives together as it seeks an explanation for why only some mishaps and misdeeds invoke the interest of the law, and draws final observations about human services flaws and the law.

Part 4
Mishaps and misdeeds through a unified lens

13 | The consequences lottery

THROUGHOUT THIS BOOK, multiple reasons have been offered for the legal immunity of human service actors from legal action, from a practical and a legal standpoint. However, these overviews of legal cases and commentaries on complaints and investigation bodies provoke a nagging question – why did one situation or actor provoke a legal action or external complaint, while another that was similar or even worse did not? It is something of a mystery why law has a prominent place following only some adverse human services events. This question warrants attention because it accentuates the contextual factors that are so critical in determining the outcomes of unlawful or other suboptimal performance. It also challenges the simplistic notion (often held by human service actors) that legal risk derives only from law breaking. In fact, legal risk depends on the types of legal breaches or performance failures, when, how and under what circumstances they occur, and who is involved.

The discussion on barriers to legal action in earlier chapters introduced the idea that breaches of law are not synonymous with legal consequences. The material on complaints and investigation bodies exposed the flip side of this proposition, which is that scrutiny and legally based consequences can flow from behaviour that is not technically unlawful. This appositely numbered Chapter 13 thus briefly examines the conjunction of forces that bring some but not all unlawful or unsatisfactory human service activity to public attention (and perhaps to law courts) while other often more troubling events fail to germinate.

Only a minority of human service actors is ever confronted by a direct legal challenge. A few more will be exposed in criminal and civil actions against others when behaviour and practices within their field or organisation are examined. Many more will face the scrutiny of inquiries, and

249

MISHAPS AND MISDEEDS THROUGH A UNIFIED LENS

investigation and complaints bodies. Although all human service actors will at some time or other be confronted by grievances that are dealt with informally in the relationship or with varying degrees of formality within an organisation, these events are not the focus of attention in the present chapter.

In this chapter, a series of fictitious human services scenarios set the scene for an exploration of the forces that may attract and sustain legal attention.

ILLUSTRATING ADVERSE HUMAN SERVICE EVENTS AND CONSEQUENCES

The following scenarios describe human service events in the areas of aged care, disability support, private practice, and youth and mental health services.

SCENARIO – SERGE AND AGED CARE

Serge is one of four support workers in an ageing-in-place program, auspiced by a non-government organisation funded through a joint Commonwealth/state arrangement. He has a case load of approximately 20 elderly clients, mostly female, who live alone, and are socially isolated and frail – some have symptoms of early dementia. Serge is responsible for developing and implementing service case plans with each of these clients. He monitors and manages arrangements for clients' home cleaning, maintenance, gardening, health, meals and social connectivity. The program is innovative, has enhanced the profile of the host organisation and is smiled upon by the state and Commonwealth public servants who manage the funding contract. Early evaluation data indicate that clients in the program have lower hospital and nursing home admission rates than a comparative control group. The other support workers and supervisor are enthusiastic and committed, but younger and inexperienced. Serge, as the oldest member of the team and the only man, is a charismatic peer leader.

Serge spends a considerable amount of time in the homes of his clients. He is, in turns, affectionate, humorous, helpful, seductive and demanding with his clients, and they are both appreciative of and intimidated by him. He has initiated sexual activity with several clients and inappropriately touched others. None of the clients has suffered personal physical injury and there is no available evidence that any of them has developed a psychiatric illness as a result of his behaviour. He has also taken a number of small but valuable items from several of the clients' homes. His clients are privately confused, troubled, embarrassed and frightened. Several think that they either caused or misconstrued his sexual behaviour. Most believe that they misplaced the missing objects. All are terrified of losing their independence at home, and none could bear the indignity of public exposure of the sexual conduct. Nothing is said by any client to anyone about Serge's behaviour. Neither Serge's coworkers nor his supervisor are aware or suspicious of his improper behaviour.

SCENARIO – THE E TEAM IN DISABILITY SUPPORT

Ed, Elanta, Ely and Enver, are case workers in a government disability support service team. All are solid and respected workers with considerable experience. Ed has been engaging recently in sexually explicit chat with very young girls on the web, although he has never attempted to make direct contact with them. He sends annotated photos of the girls via his work email to his three colleagues. The group members email the photos back and forth to each other with humorous commentary. Another coworker accidentally stumbles on the email traffic and reports it to the team leader who takes no action. The coworker then reports it to the manager. When again nothing happens, the coworker approaches the director of the organisation. An internal investigation is instigated and the conduct of the E team, the team leader and the manager is held to be in breach of employer policies. Ed is charged by the police and suspended by his employer. His coworkers are disciplined. The team leader and manager undergo performance appraisal processes, during which time-limited performance goals arising from their inaction are negotiated.

SCENARIO – CHERRIE IN PRIVATE PRACTICE

Cherrie is a social worker running a counselling and psychotherapy practice specialising in women with relationship difficulties. Before setting up her sole practice, Cherrie worked in a variety of human service jobs in the public and non-government sectors. On the whole, she found her peers and managers, in particular, to be unsympathetic, judgemental and unethical. Most did not share her attitudes about human rights, advocacy, and the high priority necessarily accorded self-care in the workplace. She believed that social work values were not reflected in the uncaring, funding-driven cultures of the agencies. During this period, Cherrie had a number of relationship breakdowns, experienced considerable personal stress and had health problems.

Employers in Cherrie's view were unwilling to accommodate her needs. Cherrie believes that in private practice she is at last working ethically and advocating for clients. Some clients have required firm feedback and have since left her practice, others have resisted her efforts to help, but the small group of clients that remains is responsive, compliant and grateful. This group of women depends on her for emotional support, as she depends on them. Cherrie often makes contact with the partners of timid clients and demands changes necessary in the interests of their relationships. She is also willing to advocate with clients' employers on their behalf, if given permission by the client. Through her contacts with clients, her negative views of a number of other service providers have been confirmed, and she insures that prospective and future clients are informed about the shortcomings of these services.

SCENARIO – STREETCARE YOUTH SERVICE

StreetCare is a non-government, secular, state-funded youth service, which operates a shelter and outreach support services. At any one time there may be up to 10 young people between 12 and 18 years of age in the shelter and 20 more in supported independent accommodation. The service has been in operation for two years and is staffed mostly by recent graduates. There have been four managers since the service opened and the current acting manager has been in the job for three months. A committee of management has responsibility for corporate governance of the service. It is chaired by a medical practitioner and comprises a public health academic, two business people, an Indigenous person and a retired teacher. A state project officer is responsible for liaison with the service and oversight of the implementation of the funding contract. There have been three such officers since the service started and the current occupant of the position has been seconded, without replacement, to work in another department for some weeks.

The committee and all employed staff have been and continue to be enthusiastic about the work of the service, which is committed to assisting the most disadvantaged young people. Young men and women with extremely traumatic histories of abuse and neglect, many of them with mental health problems, are welcomed into the service. Life in the shelter is lively and exciting for both staff and residents. Drug use by clients is an ongoing problem and there have been many violent incidents, but serious injuries have not occurred. There have also been a number of sexual assaults by residents on other residents. One resident slashed his throat in the early days of the service and there was a bloody standoff between him and staff with other residents looking on. He survived. One girl in independent living overdosed and died, and a number of other young women in the service are subject to the attentions of a bikie gang, which has sent representatives to the shelter to threaten staff. The police are called to the shelter quite regularly. There are ongoing problems with neighbours of both the shelter and the independent living houses, who complain about noise, rubbish and intimidation. There have been several angry public interchanges between staff, residents and neighbours. There is no evaluative data available for the service, but the staff and management committee are united in their view that the service is essential and assisting the young people who have no other options.

SCENARIO – EAST WEST MENTAL HEALTH SERVICE AND JONAH

East West Mental Health is a state government body responsible for providing a full range of mental health services in a large region. Jonah has extensive experience as a mental health social worker. He, like many of the staff, was relocated four years ago from a psychiatric hospital into community offices, and his job designation changed to case manager. Jonah and most of his professional colleagues resent their loss of professional title and see case management as old work relabelled under a new name. He is also not alone in believing that community care poses safety risks for professional staff, or in resenting increased case loads of patients with very complex needs. He has a case load of 73 patients.

Jobb is a client of Jonah's. He is 26 and has been in and out of mental health services and jail for eight years. He has had multiple short hospital admissions, many case workers and involvement with several psychiatric services over the years. He self harms, resists medication, uses illegal drugs and is often confused and non-communicative, and can be explosive when others invade his space. His parents are very supportive and have constantly sought psychiatric assistance for him. He has been living with them since they found him in a squat one month ago. Jonah has been on stress leave for most of this period.

MISHAPS AND MISDEEDS THROUGH A UNIFIED LENS

Over the last month, a series of disturbances in Jobb's house make his parents fearful for their safety and that of a grandson who also lives with them. The East West crisis team responds to the last and serious incident, and decides against seeking involuntary admission for Jobb. In the absence of any other option for Jobb, the team places him temporarily in a boarding house. This is a noisy, crowded place where Jobb is harassed by other residents. Jonah returns from leave, but does not have time to visit Jobb although Jobb's parents phone several times to express concerns about their son's well being. Jobb is continually teased and bullied in the boarding house. He kills another resident in a violent outburst and is charged with murder. There is negative commentary in the press about the murder and mental health services. The family of the man who was killed is stridently outspoken about people like Jobb being allowed to live in the community. Jonah is more convinced than ever about the problems in his working environment. Jobb's parents are grief stricken and unhappy about the mental health services they and their son received.

LEGAL AND OTHER SIGNIFICANT CONSEQUENCES

The first question to ask about the workers, agencies and systems in these scenarios is whether or not their conduct or service is questionable, substandard or unlawful. Some tentative conclusions are possible on the limited information available. A follow-up question concerns the likelihood of legal responses.

In relation to the E team, the ages of the young girls or the damage that they might have suffered as a result of the email conversations are not known. Nonetheless, the conduct of the E team has been defined internally as unsatisfactory by the reporting coworker, the director and an investigation. This seems consistent with contemporary views about ethical and lawful professional practice in the human services. The state has taken criminal action against Ed, indicating that the law has been broken. The employer has taken disciplinary action against all members of the E team and set performance expectations for the team leader and manager. This all seems relatively straightforward.

In contrast, Serge appears to be engaged in criminal, unethical and substandard professional behaviour though his sexual activities and thefts. He has not been charged with any crime and charges are unlikely. On the face of it, disciplinary consequences also seem improbable. His clients are not going to bear witness against him. They are likely to die before revealing anything of his conduct, unlike victims of flawed child protection systems who may pursue legal action many years later in adulthood. It is also possible that the ageing-in-home program is in breach of its duty of care to its clients, and that trespass to the person has occurred, but there are no promising litigants.

What of the funding contract between the program and the state and Commonwealth governments? Does it contain express or implied terms about service standards, inclusive of supervision and staff performance indicia, and have these been breached? If they have, the contractual parties are not aware of it, but the data about the service on the public record is positive. If the clients are isolated, there are few family and friends who might be monitoring their wellbeing. Serge seems relatively safe from consequences, yet it can be argued that his conduct is more reprehensible than that of Ed and his coworkers.

It appears that well-meaning Cherrie fosters dependency in her clients and treads clumsily in their lives. Although her attitudes and behaviour may not be unusual in social work, they are inconsistent with ethical imperatives (DeJulio and Berkman 2003). Her conduct ignores all of Reamer's (2001; 2003b) warnings against dual relationships and inappropriate treatment, and also those of Barsky and Gould (2002) against blurring clinician and conflict resolution roles. Do her clients have a private cause of action? Possibly, but they have to overcome the obstacle of causation and prove psychiatric illness, or loss of employment or some other economic damage. The clients' partners may also argue that they have suffered damage as a result of her meddling, but they have to prove that she owed them a duty of care. It is possible that Cherrie defames other service providers, but they perhaps do not know this – even if they do, they may lack the resources or the inclination to pursue action. Clients or their partners may find their way to the office of a complaints commissioner who may or may not have jurisdiction over unregistered private practitioners. If the commission does have jurisdiction, Cherrie may be asked to participate in conciliation of a complaint, she may be named by the commission and have her practice rights limited if she lives in New South Wales. Cherrie's business will probably never really flourish and that is perhaps the most likely outcome for her.

What of StreetCare, where good intentions prevail? It provides an unsafe, unstable and violent living environment for its young clients. Care is being delivered by workers who probably do not have the necessary specialist program management and intervention expertise and skills. Depth in governance, youth program management and evaluation skills and expertise are also not obviously apparent in the management committee. However, the program is operated with enthusiasm and goodwill such that clients and the funding body may have little awareness of the potential for iatrogenic damage. The character and standard of the care is not unusual in alternative care practice today. Kiraly (2002) has detailed the blunt, discontinuous, disruptive, often humiliating and non-protective out-of-home care that is commonly currently experienced by children and particularly young people in Australia. She refers to this as the 'malpractice of our times' (p. 11). Unlike previous institutional regimes, where punishment, deprivation and other physical indignities were consciously inflicted upon residents, this newer type of 'malpractice' arises from a benign but fragmented, inexpert, careless and discriminatory approach to care. However common care of this kind may be, it is contrary to promulgated standards of quality care for children and young people in alternative care (eg Gilbertson and Barber 2004; Lonne and Thomson 2005).

It is likely that the young people in StreetCare are owed a duty of care by the service. A breach may be demonstrable, although the unsatisfactory conduct is more in the nature of omission than commission. Proving that the young people have injury caused by any breaches will be more difficult. Interesting questions are raised about the accountability and legal liability of the government department that continues to fund such a service without evaluative data, and to monitor it indifferently. In addition, there is also a question hanging over the contracting and contract management procedures – is the conduct of the service substandard in terms of the funding agreement with government?

All that said, the young people in StreetCare have experienced a disordered and risky life before entering the service and they can probably look forward to more of the same after they leave. They are not well placed to be initiating legal action of any kind, even if they become aware that they are experiencing a substandard service. The government department is unlikely to take legal action that would expose its poor contracting and client placement processes, and close an essential service. Some of the young people might consider their legal options later in life, but at that point, StreetCare will be one of the many agencies that litter their life histories – it may have disappeared by then, leaving no continuing corporate body to be sued. If the young people are state wards, the government will be the most likely legal target. StreetCare may become one of the subjects of an inquiry about youth homelessness or young people in care, but something will have to trigger this action. However, it is likely that neighbours will make complaints about noise and rubbish to whomever will listen, which could well be the media or a member of parliament. If either of these become involved, the service could expect uncomfortable exposure and its future might be in jeopardy for political rather than legal reasons.

Jonah and East West Mental Health Service, like StreetCare, may not have done anything out of the ordinary. Their story does not seem unusual and Jobb's tragedy is of a type that regularly and briefly flares in the media. However, the service provided to Jobb by a disaffected case manager and a fragmented service system falls far short of the integrated, proactive, holistic and tailored services detailed in case management text books (eg Moxley 1997; Gursansky et al. 2003). Jonah, or more likely the East West Mental Health Service, could possibly face action for negligence from Jobb or his family, or the family of the killed resident. If such an action is contemplated, much will hang on the interpretation of the relevant mental health legislation, on how the service to Jobb is evaluated by peers in that area of practice, and by the wording of the relevant civil liability legislation in relation to public authorities.

However, it is known from the appeal case of *Hunter Area Health Services v Presland* on somewhat similar facts, but perhaps different legislation, that a negligence claim by Jobb at least against the service might be unsustainable. In the *Walker v Sydney West Area Health Service* [2007] NSWSC 526 case, the standard of mental health care experienced by the suicidal young man was found to conform to widely accepted peer professional practice. Even though there was some expert evidence to the contrary, the client and his parents are reported in this case to have found it unresponsive and unhelpful.

Clever lawyers may be able to circumvent *Presland* in respect of the state. In fact, that case may have been decided differently in Victoria (Freckelton 2008b). It is unlikely, but possible, that the boarding house could be a legal target if it has pockets deep enough to make this worthwhile. Even if the substantive law obstacles could be overcome, other practical and personal barriers to legal action remain. As with StreetCare, wider inquiries, media interest and complaints bodies may be activated here, depending on the fortitude and tenacity of Jobb's family and that of the killed resident. Government mental health services such as East West and workers such as Jonah generally continue onwards in the same or similar form, regardless of scrutiny. All in all, most of the living 'victims' in the StreetCare and East West scenarios are probably preoccupied with their private griefs, tragedies and vulnerabilities, which may or may not have been compounded or caused by human service activity.

Thus, although the E team members face the most direct legal challenge for their inappropriate behaviour, it is arguably less harmful than some of the other conduct outlined in the scenarios, and probably less serious criminally than Serge's. The question thus becomes not why consequences are absent but why legal action, serious scrutiny and consequences do occur on occasions.

GENESIS OF INVESTIGATIONS AND LEGAL ACTIONS

Given the numerous obstacles, what circumstances or conditions might foster serious scrutiny or a legal action? Through anatomising social welfare scandals in the United Kingdom, Butler and Drakeford (2005) have theorised why some social welfare events become major scandals and others with similar characteristics remained concealed. Scandals and legal action are not synonymous, but their analytical framework can be applied and adapted here on a much smaller scale, to throw light on why some situations result in a legal or related action and others do not. The circumstances that produce a scandal have some parallels and are entwined with circumstances that activate a legal action. Scandals themselves commonly result in legal action against individuals and agencies. In some circumstances, legal action may trigger a scandal. In the Butler and Drakeford analysis, events only become scandals on exposure and when certain conditions give them meaning beyond the circumstances of the event itself. Similarly, events only have legal consequences when conditions prompt their scrutiny through a legal lens.

Butler and Drakeford (2005) contend that the raw materials of social welfare scandals are routine and often mundane events occurring in 'messy' (p. 222) environments where some level of risk and drama is the norm. These ordinary events are then converted into extraordinary phenomena through a process of social, political and professional construction. A scandal has three elements:

- it is unanticipated by the actors
- conduct that may have been accepted as unremarkable over time is exposed or 'discovered'
- disapproval follows exposure.

Disapproval is a contested process wherein the voices of the various actors compete for dominance in making sense of the gravity of wrongs, how they arose and who should take responsibility for them. Butler and Drakeford (2005) argue that many potential scandals lose momentum, if control of the story remains local and is constructed as one of individual aberration. 'Bad apples' have a place in these circumstances, but relatively blameless workers can also be targeted legally for behaviour that was either endemic or contributed to by others (Merry and McCall-Smith 2004). At this juncture, individual actors – 'bad apples' in fact or in designation – commonly face internal discipline or legal action, and a more generic public clamour may be contained or averted. For instance, when baby P was tortured to death in the United Kingdom in 2008 and his mother's boyfriend convicted for the killing, the director of the local social services is reported to have become the focus of media attention and to have been sacked because the council needed to be seen to be taking action (Campbell 2008). Whether or not this action prevents yet another incipient child protection scandal remains to be seen. Without commenting on the blameworthiness of the director, as the details of her conduct are unknown, it is impossible to imagine any complex child protection situation that does not involve many actors across various service levels, in combined multiple efforts to find the finest of balances between family integrity and child safety.

Beyond these three elements, three additional sets of factors operate for or against the emergence of a scandal – claims and counter claims-makers, timing and the policy context.

Claims-makers and counter claims-makers proclaim and resist discovery and disapproval, respectively. Butler and Drakeford (2005, using Best's [1990] classification) identify primary, secondary and tertiary claims-makers. Primary claims-makers are determined individuals, advocacy groups and others, generally outside of the suspect service system, who have not been colonised by its prevailing practices and explanations. Secondary claims makers are the mass media. Leaks to the press are not uncommon in the human services, particularly when there is organisational resistance to claims. Press attention is feared and fearful for most human service actors, as they commonly experience portrayals of human service activity as biased, unsympathetic and stereotypical (Brawley 1995; Mendes 2001) – in their view, it panders to the 'public's desire for omnicompetence on the part of central and local authorities' (Webb 2006 p. 1). Various commentators have shown how the media can set the agenda and influence, in the short term at least, polices and practices in relation to child protection (eg Franklin and Parton 1991; Mendes 2001). In the *SB* case, reference is made to SB's father's threats to go to the press about her abuse in foster care (at para 348) if contact with her was refused him. One can speculate how these threats might have undermined already strained and besieged departmental staff.

Tertiary claims-makers are the audience of the first two claims-makers. According to Butler and Drakeford (2005), this wide audience, inclusive of the 'public', other media and politicians (if they are not the current target of disapproval), is ambivalent about social welfare institutions, and receptive to stories that are emblematic of failures and that hint at even greater hidden horrors. This audience demands perfection of social welfare activity, while maintaining an underlying mistrust of it. Thus, any malfunction is immediately recognisable to the audience and perceived as a failure of human service actors alone. Counter-claims makers are those, often in positions of power (eg government ministers), who resist, deny and mystify the existence or explanation of scandal events, particularly during the discovery and disapproval processes.

Second, timing is important in the aetiology of a scandal. Embryonic scandals may thrive or wither, depending on the receptivity of an audience at any point in time. Events that can be portrayed or inflated as particularly disturbing or discordant attract attention, but audiences eventually suffer 'scandal fatigue' and saturation. Thus, if they have been exposed to too many terrible events in, say, child protection or mental health, they become jaded and lose interest. Similarly, if they are absorbed by the awfulness of events in one arena they may have little appetite for those in another area at that time.

Third, there are contextual policy factors that can nurture or stunt scandal development. These are the 'policy background, the political climate and the resources available to individuals and institutions' (Butler and Drakeford 2005 p. 233). The characteristics of these factors at any time will shape both the growth and explanation of a scandal.

At the risk of caricaturing Butler and Drakeford's (2005) elegant analysis, in brief, relatively commonplace events become extraordinary because they are discovered and cultivated by actors when there is fertile ground and a greedy market. A set of interests need to coincide in the making of a scandal. How might this explication of scandal making contribute to an understanding of which human service actors are sued, charged or investigated?

To begin with, it can be assumed that most human service actors go about their business doing what they normally do, not thinking of legal action or hoping that it will not happen. Then unexpectedly, some of their possibly commonplace actions are noticed and disapproval is voiced – discovery occurs. Once the condemning voice predominates, there is an impetus for some sort of response. If the exposure and disapproval are provoked by or occur in a receptive or sensitive policy and political context, if the negative claims-makers stand firm, and if those who would respond legally are sufficiently well resourced, the conditions for a legal challenge are established.

Depending on the policies and supervisory processes of the organisation, discovery may be a matter of serendipity or predictable. The exposed conduct or events may be so public or outrageous that exposure and disapproval is unavoidable. They may be relatively ordinary, but occurring at a time of particular sensitivity in the organisation or sector. They may be a substitute for other conduct that is more disapproved of, but elusive. They may be observed or come to the attention of vigilant claims-makers who prosecute vigorously. The last three of these factors are possibly implicated in the unfair dismissal appeal of *Re J Ashley* AIRC (unreported, Ross VP, O'Callaghan, SDP and Cribb, Commr 7 July 2005). In this case, the appellant, who in the instant case worked for Statewide Autistic Services Inc (SASI) in Victoria, had been the subject of unsubstantiated allegations of sexual activity with clients in previous employment. A member of the public saw the appellant in a park with autistic children and reported this to the Victorian Department for Human Services. Later, an anonymous telephone call about the appellant was made to SASI. Another telephone call from a different agency expressed concern about him, and set in train the dismissal that led to this case. It would appear that a number of claims-makers had an interest in the worker's human service employment history, and in curtailing his current and future prospects. His appearance in public with clients gave claims-makers the opportunity for voicing their concerns far beyond the walk in the park. The significance of whistleblowers more generally in exposing and influencing the disapproval negotiations is well known and detailed elsewhere (for the human services, see De Maria 1996; Hunt 1998; Els and Dehn 2001).

In Chapter 3, a number of criminal cases were outlined wherein human service workers were charged following relatively recent and inappropriate conduct. These workers were ostensibly 'bad apples' who were offered up to the criminal law, most likely through the activities of claims-makers within the organisations concerned. Possibly this occurred with impetus from or fear of an alert media. No major scandal ensued and it is assumed that the status quo of the organisations was not destabilised significantly.

There are now alert and active advocacy groups – for example, National Welfare Rights Network (NWRN), Care Leavers Australia Network (CLAN), Creating Opportunities for Children and Young People in Care (CREATE) – and committed individuals and community and specialist legal services, operating as claims-makers in many human service-related areas. For example, NWRN claims (AAP 2007c) that it had an influence on the Commonwealth Ombudsman's decision to set up an enquiry into Centrelink's implementation of welfare to work reforms (Commonwealth Ombudsman 2007). CLAN claims that its lobbying had a role in the establishment of the Australian Senate Inquiry into Children in Institutional Care (Penglase 2004).

These groups and individuals have resources to encourage and support those with grievances against human services actors. The media has attended to these claims and some have caught the public imagination (eg Daniel Valerio, Shelley Ward, Cornelia Rau) – the audience has had a momentary appetite for the details of the stories. Committees of inquiry have been established and have made recommendations. Sometimes full-blown scandals have developed. In this environment, legal actions against individuals and organisations are to be expected.

Targets of legal action will be chosen partly for reasons of legal strategy and partly because of the profile awarded them by exposure and disapproval. Daniel's (1998) examination of scapegoats in law and medicine may also have something to offer by way of explanation here. The professions she studied are more homogeneous than the human services and her analysis must be applied with caution, but it is possible that some individual human service actors 'stand for' the agency or for a wider group of workers. This can 'identify them with the troubles, lay the evils upon them, and publicly punish and expel them along with all the evils now become theirs to bear' (Daniel 1998 p. 163). This process serves to cleanse the professional group, or in the case of the human services, the organisation or field of practice of the 'infection'.

Contextual factors identified by Butler and Drakeford (2005) are likely to be influential in determining if individual workers become the subject of legal action, in the presence or absence of a scandal. Resources and staffing quality and quantity in an agency or service system, along with procedural and supervisory structures, will affect the discovery of and response to unsatisfactory performance. The culture and norms within the field of practice will colour the outcomes of disapproval negotiations. In addition, conduct or events that occur at times of particular political and or organisational policy sensitivity are likely to result in unanimous internal disapproval and a more attentive police response if criminality is alleged. The same conduct at a different time might remain undiscovered or contested if exposed. Beatings, if not the sexual abuse, that happened in some of the children's homes cases during the 1960s and earlier were the norm at the time. As a result of policy and practice changes, largely

THE CONSEQUENCES LOTTERY | **263**

brought about by scandals and kept alive by continuing tragedies, most organisations these days will react more actively to such behaviour when it occurs. It is unlikely that the walk in the park in the *Ashley* case would have attracted attention in 1960 or resulted in employer action. The definitions and responses to misdeeds and mishaps is largely a matter of the moment in history. Some human service actors time their unsatisfactory behaviour well in terms of the unlikelihood of detection and action; others evidence a poor sense of timing and are relatively unlucky.

THE SCENARIOS REVISITED

How might the Butler and Drakeford (2005) explication of scandal gestation help explain what happens to Serge, the E team, Cherrie, StreetCare and the East West Mental Health Service? The following hypotheses are offered.

In the Serge situation, discovery and disapproval are unlikely – there are no primary claims-makers to declaim his misdeeds. In terms of the policy and political context, ageing-in-place is currently the favoured approach in aged care. Serge's program will be viewed positively by policy makers and funders who would not anticipate or be susceptible to clues about his behaviour. Nursing homes are currently perceived by secondary and tertiary-claims makers as the risky face of aged care, and in-home care has a low profile. In relation to resources, the program lacks supervisory depth and staff experience. Thus, coworkers are perhaps not attuned to cues about Serge's activities – these no doubt exist and might be visible to more seasoned managers and peers. In contrast, Serge appears to be well endowed with interpersonal and experience resources. The clients have few resources that can threaten Serge. They are socially isolated and frail, and some have neurological deterioration. Ironically, their other positive personal resources serve Serge's ends; they are private, discreet, resilient and tenaciously protective of their independence.

The E team and Ed in particular are engaged in the type of conduct that primary and tertiary claims-makers are familiar with and anticipate. The conduct has occurred in a policy and political context in which child pornography and related internet activities are receiving considerable attention, and criminal law is being amended accordingly. They are discovered and disapproval prevails because the coworker whistleblower is a more forceful and active primary claims-maker than the team leader or manager. This is a public service agency, so it is likely to be relatively well resourced in terms of human resource and email policies and procedures, and codes of conduct for employees.

What is there to discover in relation to Cherrie's private practice? Her practices are no doubt acceptable in her own view and in the view of the remaining clients. If there is damage to clients, it is unseen and not easily quantifiable. Disaffected previous clients and clients' partners may act as primary claims-makers to contest the quality of the service if they have the necessary personal resources of energy, knowledge, money and time. Current clients may speak in her favour. The clients here are vulnerable, but they are voluntary and paying for a service that they can walk away from – many will do so. This small story of ineptitude, clumsiness and private angst lacks the elements of drama and spectacle that attract the attention of secondary and tertiary claims-makers. The current political context is one in which private psychotherapists and other unregistered practitioners are under scrutiny by governments and complaints commissions, so the latter may be responsive to any disapproval voiced by primary-claims makers about Cherrie. However, they have limited resources and she may be seen as a relatively small fish compared with those who sexually abuse clients and engage in high-risk physical interventions.

StreetCare's staff, management committee and funder do not give any indication that anything untoward or 'remarkable' is happening in the service. Drama and risk are the norm in this and similar services, and there is nothing unanticipated about the occurrences described. For the young clients, life in the service probably mirrors much of their previous experience, in and out of care. From the perspectives of each of these actors, there is nothing to discover and disapprove of. The service operates in a political and policy context where there is some sensitivity to child protection and youth homelessness issues. However, this is perhaps normally offset by limited resources (financial, staff and expertise) available to governments, by contract service policies, and by an acceptance of a culture of volatility and excitement in residential youth services. In addition, governments, departments and agencies have already weathered many previous adverse events and negative publicity in alternative care for children and young people. However, the service system in which StreetCare functions could found a major investigation in a later era with a different political and policy climate. Amateur and relatively uncontrolled youth services, which are de rigueur today, may well be judged harshly by future standards.

Were it not for the neighbours, StreetCare would probably proceed unhindered until a very major drama occurred (such as a death). However, the neighbours have the potential to become powerful primary claims-makers. If their lives are significantly impacted, they will have the motivation to dispute the appropriateness of StreetCare's operations and threaten its continued existence. Their claims are not likely to be driven by care quality arguments, but rather by issues of noise, rubbish, safety and perhaps immorality. The neighbours' claims will be countered by staff and the management committee with prevailing rhetoric about service accessibility, care in the community, self determination, and so on. There will be little common ground or language in the two sets of claims; however, those of the neighbours are likely to be more vociferous and attract the attention of secondary and tertiary claims-makers. Once this happens, a political response is likely. Even if the policy support for the StreetCare service remains, political imperatives may result in an interruption to current operations.

When the scandal schema is applied, StreetCare, and the East West Mental Health Service and Jonah have similarities. The service and Jonah are doing what they normally do – what is there to discover and disapprove of? Primary, secondary and tertiary claims-makers anticipate dangerous incidents in mental health work. There has been no glaringly faulty commission by the service or by Jonah – the accumulation of omissions may not be known about or their significance appreciated by secondary and tertiary claims-makers.

The story of Jobb and his victim is about marginal people. The audience is perhaps jaded by these mental health dramas. The policy and political context is similar to that of StreetCare, where the prevailing policy is one of community care and the problems with its implementation have been documented comprehensively. In this case, Jobb's parents and the family of the dead person have the potential to become primary claims-makers and to attract the attention of secondary and tertiary claims-makers. Their claims may resonate with advocacy groups and complaints bodies. However, whatever their successes, they are unlikely to threaten the constituent elements of the current East West Mental Health Service, including Jonah. There may be some reorganisation of the service and some embarrassment, but government mental health services and their staff will continue functioning.

The analysis provided in this chapter goes some way in explaining why particular actors and events detailed in the cases in this book became the focus of legal attention. All of these cases are products of their time, contextual situations and the persistence of claims-makers, as much as they are of the actors and acts involved. Any assessment of legal risk in a human services situation must take account of these external factors, as well as those inherent in the questionable actions. What else can be observed from cases that do stimulate legal interest? This is the subject of the next and final chapter.

Coda

IT WAS ARGUED in Chapter 1 that a heavy silence within attends the human service shadow world of mishaps and misdeeds. This book has attempted to displace the silence through compilation and analysis of a small body of behaviours and events in which a failure of a duty of care (or some other legal obligation) is alleged, and comes to the attention of the law and quasi-legal bodies.

The activities underpinning these legal actions or investigations have ranged from criminal, intentional and self-serving, through to inadvertent minor slips in everyday human services functioning. Some actors appear to have been unlucky, or from another perspective held to account, for behaviour that was either the norm in that arena or would not normally be detected or complained about. Some actors have engaged in activities where disaster was predictable. Some have found themselves subject to legal attention for a single event, others for involvement in a series of events. Individual workers have featured in the criminal law actions, as would be expected, in some statutory breach cases and in all industrial actions. Organisations and public authorities have figured largely in industrial, discrimination, occupational health and safety, information management, administrative and civil actions, and in numerous inquires into organisational failures. System representatives, most commonly state ministers, have appeared in administrative actions, occasionally in civil matters and also in public inquiries.

The quadrants in Figure 2.2 have been variously represented. In relation to acts, examples of misfeasance are more numerous than those of malfeasance. Quadrant A1 has been represented by individual workers who have committed criminal acts, often involving sexual impropriety and/or a civil wrong (eg trespass). Instances of employees alleging that their employer has wrongly disciplined them or terminated their employment have characterised quadrant B1, along with a wide array of administrative decisions and discrimination actions, most inadvertently unlawful and certainly without intention to harm. Several notable successful civil child protection cases have also been detailed; for example, the *Trevorrow* case in which the plaintiff alleged that child welfare authorities took actions that were unlawful, or breached a duty and injured them.

Not surprisingly, nonfeasance or malfeasance through inaction has been less in evidence. Absence of action is less visible and traditionally less significant in law. Quadrants D1 and C1 are most obviously represented by non-compliance with statutory obligations that compel action (eg reporting). However, few cases of this kind are in evidence. Quadrant C1 has been most notably represented by civil child protection cases, particularly that of *SB*, where a history of inaction or inadequate action by authorities resulted in serious injuries.

The anthology of cases and inquires outlined in this book has produced conspicuous 'noise' in the previously quiet space where shadows are considered – here a coda is offered. First, an earlier caution is repeated. Much legal activity concerning the human services goes on behind closed doors in conciliation and negotiation hearings, or never gets off the ground. In addition, apart from the few higher court cases, especially the recent Australian civil cases that have all been included (as far as can be determined), the cases itemised in this book are not statistically representative of all human service actions that arise. That said, the body of cases chosen in the most part does not represent human service activity that is particularly unusual. The evidence presented often makes clear that the actions under review are commonplace, longstanding, perhaps organisationally endorsed, and engaged in by other actors. Often the cases mirror concerns about quality of practice voiced in human service literature. These cases cannot be discounted as the product of aberrant human services situations or workers. So, what conclusions can be drawn about the law and human services failures?

The most remarkable point is that there is almost nothing in the cases or inquiries that contradicts fundamental human service rhetoric about desirable professional conduct and quality service delivery. This point is so obvious that it barely warrants comment, yet it is quite profound. The law in these cases does not expect anything of human service actors that human services ideals, training and literature does not already expect of them. Sexual contact with clients, unsafe work practices, incorrect interpretations of legislation, non-compliance with legislative requirements, lack of precision in record keeping, misuse of information, inadequate screening and assessment processes, poor service planning, implementation and monitoring, and disappointing relationships; these issues have been discussed in the cases in this book and all would be generally judged unsatisfactory or even unpardonable against human service ideals. In legal cases and inquiries, human service actors are judged and held to account against standards that are either congruent with their own, expressly their own or imputed to them through evidence from human services experts. In the cases in this book, actors may have felt exposed and isolated, savaged by the court processes, unfairly singled out or wrongly accused, but they would be hard pushed to argue that what they were accused of was right or defensible under human services ideals. There may be a few cases in which defendants have deliberately acted unlawfully because their conscience demanded it, but this situation does not emerge in the evidence and case reports compiled for this book. Thus, the legal destiny of human service actors is in their own hands, subject to the vagaries of the consequences lottery posited in Chapter 13, much more perhaps than they may appreciate or care to acknowledge.

The second point, equally plain and no less significant, is that human service actors can and do cause significant harm, most commonly mental harm, to each other, clients and third parties. Human services actions in the cases in this book have been instrumental in causing or failing to prevent physical and mental injury, death, deportation, discriminatory distress, damaged reputations and relationships, financial and property loss, loss of employment, loss of family, and loss of legislative entitlements. Harm may result from one actor and small actions (eg physical contact or an incorrectly completed form). However, it can also result from an accumulation of relatively minor events, involving multiple actors, over a long period. In the *SB* case, many workers over many years had seen her, her foster family and father, interviewed her and them, written case notes and reports and attended meetings about her. The moral and professional, rather than legal, responsibility for the harm caused to SB is dispersed across several system actors, managers and many individual workers. Harm may be a consequence of inattention, inaction and non-compliance with procedures as in the *SB* case. Harm can also result from individual workers acting firmly and with good intent, according to their own prejudices, but without reference to external requirements and frames of reference, as in the *Trevorrow* case. Thus, collectively and individually human service actors are more influential and have more of an impact than many would care to recognise.

Many areas of law have been covered in this book, broadly and relatively superficially from a legal perspective. Thus, it is not possible to draw generic conclusions about trends in legal thinking or in legal action. However, the cases reviewed do permit several observations. There has been a prevailing view in law, explicated throughout this book, that impediments to a successful civil suit against public authorities delivering welfare-type services have been almost insurmountable. The *SB* and the *Trevorrow* cases challenge that position. In both cases, on different facts and under different contextual legislation, child welfare authorities were found liable for the injury they caused the children. Legal risks in child protection may have increased as there are now precedents at the supreme court level for Aboriginal children removed from their homes and for children in care. Until governments successfully challenge such cases, change legislation, or organise satisfactory compensation schemes, subsequent cases are to be expected.

In *SB*, the department did not comply with its own policies and procedures about the management of children in care. Inexperience, staff shortages, staff turnover, lapses of time, placement crises and so on appear to have contributed, but these everyday pressures and the indemnity clause in the legislation did not allow the department to escape liability. Muddling along in difficult circumstances was not good enough in law, nor was it good enough in terms of human service ideals. This result has significant implications for human service actors at all levels, in child welfare in particular. In *Trevorrow*, the court assessed welfare decision making at the time of the child's removal against contemporary professional knowledge about maternal bonding, and found it wanting. Actions based on workers' personal conclusions about what was best for the child were not good enough. This has implications for the quality and extent of training and professional development for actors at all levels in the human services.

If, as contended, there are few surprises in the human services actions that have attracted legal attention and unfavourable judgement, it can also be said that legal risk arises less from the unknown than from failing to comply with known ideals and standards. Why standards are not met then becomes the fundamental question. This is a challenge for policy, organisational and individual actors.

Faced with successful civil claims, further tragedies and continued bad press, policy makers and organisations risk becoming even more risk adverse, more proscriptive and prescriptive, and more dependent on regulatory mechanisms. Workers may incline even more to inaction, rather than action. These responses will not improve human service practice; they may instead stunt quality intervention and ironically may lead to increased legal risk. As Preston-Shoot (2001 p. 14) says of the failure of increased and imposed regulation of social work practice, it 'represents a failure of thinking about complicated truths'.

At the service system and policy level, there are challenges for system controllers and policy makers in walking the fine line between over and under regulation, and in educating society about the complexities of social welfare aims and functions. Harris (1987) talks of the long slow task of lowering public expectations about what is possible in fraught and contested situations where there is no agreed or obviously desirable outcome. Schorr (2000 p. 133) advocates giving lay people 'candid information' and drawing them into hard and unpopular areas of human service practice, like child protection, such that the community becomes more a genuine partner in the work and less of an externalised judge absolved of responsibility for problems. This pedagogical task is essential, but it should aim to increase expectations about the quality of human service activity, while tempering expectations about simple solutions and definitive outcomes. This position also poses challenges for professions and professional education in the human services. Social work in particular is faced with deciding whether or not to rise to the challenge of working collaboratively with other occupational groups with whom it shares clients, with assuming practice leadership in the human services as suggested by commentators such as Healy (2004), and with deciding whether or not to aspire to a 'conspiracy of virtue' rather than a 'conspiracy of professionalism' (Sampford and Blencowe 2002 p. 267) in its goals, self awareness, contributions to public policy and public debate, and pronouncements about its contribution to society.

Two challenges in particular face human service educators. The first concerns the aims, content and standards of professional education. On this question, McDonald (2007) contends that the effectiveness of education in social work is compromised by the disparity between its value orientation and the realities of the human services workplace. Thus, graduates are not prepared for the experience of conflicting demands – the resultant dissonance can sabotage their efficacy. This position is endorsed in this book. An appreciation of the causes, forms and impact of mishaps and misdeeds, and hard-headed rather than defensive investigation of them, should be incorporated into all human service education courses. Educators also have a task to incorporate curriculum and develop cultures that encourage future work in unpopular and contested areas, such as child welfare where quality staff are essential, but hard to get or keep (eg Markiewicz

1996; Schorr 2000; Stoesz 2002). Difficulties in attracting high-achieving students, maintaining assessment standards, countering perceptions that human service courses are those of last resort, all contribute to what Stoesz (2002 p. 33) calls the degradation of 'social work education'. These issues need to be confronted and managed by educators.

The second challenge is for human service educators to reacquaint themselves with the role of the public intellectual (Karger and Hernandez 2004), participating in or leading Schorr's (2000) call to community education, forming alliances with dissidents and allies on matters of human service policy and practice, speaking out on professionally and socially unpopular issues and undertaking research that has direct service applications. All of these things will not be easy in an era of mass university education. There are financial imperatives on universities and academics to admit, teach and graduate ever greater numbers of students. There are also career pressures on academics to pursue more theoretical, prestigious and lucrative research agendas.

There are challenges for organisations to ensure that they have adequate external and internal controls and accountability in place (White and Terry 2008). There are challenges for them to develop depth in their management and human management resources, and to select and monitor staff with the requisite technical skills, ethical inclinations and 'moral character' (Clark 2006b). Organisations should expect strong performances from staff and should develop and support them. There is a challenge in creating an organisational culture in which poor performance is confronted and impaired workers are recognised and supported to recover, or to exit with dignity. There is a challenge in developing a culture in which positive risk is understood, valued and encouraged. Professional development and training in human service organisations is notoriously haphazard and relatively low level (eg Kennedy et al. 2004). There is a challenge to be met in ensuring that professional development is systematically organised, covers contemporary research, includes debates about alternative approaches to service delivery and intervention, is offered by competent personnel, and is integrated into service delivery practice in the organisation. Organisations face a challenge in developing policies, procedures, programs and approaches to intervention to a level that would be assessed by competent peers in that area of practice as appropriate, and in ensuring that they are complied with and reviewed regularly.

In relation to individual workers and the law's response to mishaps and misdeeds, external forces rather than the character of their own conduct may bring them to legal account. Some egregious individual behaviour will escape legal or any other form of attention. Some behaviour that is less serious, but unlucky in the consequences lottery, will attract fierce legal and other censure. In addition, for those who do come to legal attention, depending on the nature of the legal or quasi-legal action, the individual may escape individual liability or evident consequences.

On the one hand, individuals named as a party in an action can expect to be exposed, blamed and held culpable, despite the context that might have condoned or ignored their activities. This is particularly the case in criminal law actions, where 'bad apples' and unfortunate, sometimes impaired, individuals are brought to legal justice. Individuals may also find themselves the centre of attention in official inquires about events in which they have had a primary role or where their name has come to the fore.

On the other hand, individuals who are not a party to an action, but who have contributed to or been responsible for the events that caused harm and or legal action, commonly escape opprobrium. This is particularly the case in civil, discrimination and other actions where vicarious liability applies. Although such individuals' behaviour may be uncomfortably exposed in a court case, as they are not the legal target, the legal debate and the outcome do not attach to them. Some bad apples and many more very ordinary workers are not held accountable, unless disciplinary action accompanies a legal action. If behaviour reflects the norms of the organisation and if the organisation has been as lax in its human resource practices as it has with its client interventions, workers are likely to be immune from any form of external response to their role in harm doing. The oft-voiced concern about making individuals into scapegoats needs to be counterbalanced with an equally significant but less familiar concern about individuals avoiding legal and professional accountability.

These conclusions about individual responsibility and the law present a stark challenge for individual human service actors, whether they are front-line workers, policy makers, managers, educators or volunteers. Individual actors committed the crimes, made the mistakes, failed to see, failed to act, stood by, or colluded in the events in the cases in this book.

Most human service individuals are unlikely to face a legal action or be held legally accountable. Many work in service systems and organisations with structural impediments to quality performance; where quality performance is neither the norm nor supported and monitored. Thus, individual moral character (Clark 2006b) and its role in determining personal decision making becomes critical. Individual human service actors face a challenge to make decisions that are consistent with their own professional rhetoric and externally referenced against reputable, contemporary human services knowledge, despite contextual disinterest or obstacles. Individuals making conscious decisions may not change the course of human services history, but may influence the size and depth of its shadow world. The gauntlet has been thrown down, not to the minority who engage in self-serving and injurious behaviour, but to the majority (including the Cherries, those connected with StreetCare and East West Mental Heath Services and the like) who are mostly well intentioned, but internally and externally unanchored, unreferenced and undecided in the small and large actions of human services activity. Perhaps ordinary human services individuals who have faced the mirror in this book will be prompted to take up this challenge.

Appendix
Finding the law and cases

There are many introductory web-based and hard-copy resources that assist in finding, reading and making sense of the law. Some of these are referred to in Kennedy with Richards (2007, Appendix); more can be found in books on legal research; for example, Milne and Tucker (2008). The National Legal Aid website is also a useful starting place for help with legal material.[1] Legal dictionaries can be accessed through the publicly accessible Australian Legal Information Institute (Austlii) website, which is run by the Faculties of Law of the University of New South Wales and the University of Technology, Sydney.[2] These resources are neither duplicated nor listed exhaustively in this Appendix. However, a few introductory and explanatory points are made about the citations and location of legislation and cases in this book, which aim to make the reading and citations more accessible to non-law readers. As such, they do not always comply with strict legal citation protocols (eg for legal protocols, see Melbourne University Law Review Association Inc 2003; Rozenberg 2003).

LEGISLATION

Most of the legislation covered in this book is Australian and can be found on the Austlii website. Commonwealth legislation can also be found linked to from the Attorney-General's Department website.[3] Legislation of the states and territories is available through the parliamentary websites for each of the jurisdictions.

[1] http://www.nla.aust.net.au
[2] http://www.austlii.edu.au
[3] http://www.comlaw.gov.au

APPENDIX: FINDING THE LAW AND CASES

In general, in this book legislation is cited as follows: the name of the Act is followed by the year of its enactment and in brackets the jurisdiction responsible for it. So, for example, the *Corrections Management Act 2006* (Qld) refers to the Act of that name enacted by the Queensland Parliament in 2006 and the *Disability Discrimination Act 1992* (Cth) refers to the Act of that name enacted by the Commonwealth Parliament in 1992.

CASES

Most of the cases detailed in this book can be found on the Austlii website, or on the website of the relevant tribunal or body, and most of them are cited in what is known as a 'medium neutral form', which is based on the parties' names, date and number of the judgement of the relevant court or body (Milne and Tucker 2008):

- *Trevorrow v State of South Australia* (no 5) [2007] SASC 285, refers to the case mounted by Trevorrow against the State of South Australia, heard in 2007 by the South Australian Supreme Court with decision number 285.
- *New South Wales v Fahy* [2007] HCA 20, refers to the case between New South Wales and Fahy, heard in 2007 in the High Court of Australia with decision number 20.
- *Bock v Launceston Women's Shelter and Anti Discrimination Tribunal* [2005] TASSC 23, refers to the case between Brock and the Launceston Women's Shelter, heard in 2005 by the Tasmanian Supreme Court with decision number 23.

In cases cited this way, quotes from the judgments are referred to by paragraph. For example, when it is written that Harris J said (at para 23) 'all things are possible', this means that Judge Harris said these specific words in the judgement, which is reported in paragraph 23 of the medium neutral citation.

Some of the older and better-known cases are cited in this text in their more familiar 'law reports' form. These law reports are in hard copy (and not always online) and can be found in law and some other libraries. For example, *SB v New South Wales* (2004) 13 VR 527, refers to the case of SB against New South Wales, reported in the 13th volume of the *Victorian Reports* for the year 2004 starting at page 527. The medium neutral citation for that case is *SB v New South Wales* [2004] VSC 514. This means that it was the 514th decision of the Victorian Supreme Court in 2004.

Similarly, *Rogers v Whitaker* (1992) 175 CLR 479, refers to the case between those two parties, reported in volume 175 of the *Commonwealth*

Law Reports in 1992 at page 479. The medium neutral citation for this case is *Rogers v Whitaker* [1992] HCA 58. This means that it was the 58th decision of the High Court of Australia in 1992.

Quotes from cases cited in law report form are linked to the page numbers in the report where the words of the judge are cited. Thus, when it is said that 'the Department behaved badly' (at 14), it means that the judge said those words which are reported on page 14 of the report.

References

AAP (2007a). 'Child safely officers 'need more life skills': Minister'. *CCH News Headlines 27 September*, Retrieved 27 September 2007, from http://www.cch.com.au/fe_news.asp? document_id=94096&topic_code=7&category_code=34.

AAP (2007b). 'Compo for illegally detained man could be in six figures'. *CCH News Headlines 13 November*, Retrieved 4 December 2007, from http://www.cch.com.au/ fe_news.asp?document_id=95784&topic_code=8&category_code=0.

AAP (2007c). 'Investigation into welfare to work reforms'. *CCH News Headlines 29 October*, Retrieved 30 October 2007, from http://www.cch.com.au/fe_news.asp? document_id=95250&topic_code=7&category_code=0.

AAP (2007d). 'Juvenile justice workers sacked, fined over porn emails'. *CCH News Headlines 23 October*, Retrieved 29 October 2007, from http://www.cch.com.au/fe_ news.asp?document_id=95016&topic_code=9&category_code=0&news_appear_ date=23/10/2007.

AAP (2008a). 'Doctor claims suspension breaches human rights'. *CCH News Headlines 26 June*, Retrieved 27 June 2008, from http://www.cch.com.au/au/News/ShowNews. aspx?ID=26159&Type=F&TopicIDNews=9&CategoryIDNews=0&u_i=21901.

AAP (2008b). 'Law firm backs stolen claims in WA'. *CCH News Headlines 21 February*, Retrieved 21 February 2008, from http://www.cch.com.au/fe_news.asp? document_id=99170&topic_code=8&category_code=42&e_id=99763.

AAP (2008c). 'NSW: Director sacked as retirement village faces federal action'. *CCH News Headlines 31 October 2008*, Retrieved 31 October 2008, from http:// www.cch.com.au/au/News/ShowNews.aspx?ID=28212&Type=F&TopicIDNews= 9&CategoryIDNews=0&u_i=21901.

AAP (2008d). 'SA: Child sex abuse widespread in SA report says'. *CCH News Headlines 1 April 2008*, Retrieved 1 April 2008, from http://www.cch.com.au/au/News/ ShowNews.aspx?ID=24492&Type=F&TopicIDNews=8&CategoryIDNews=0& u_i=21901.

AAP (2008e). 'Youth workers have their pay cut by $200'. *CCH News Headlines 21 November 2008*, Retrieved 21 November 2008, from http://www.cch.com.au/au/ News/ShowNews.aspx?ID=28595&Type=F&TopicIDNews=9&CategoryIDNews =0&u_i=21901.

Aarons, N. and M. Powell (2003). 'Issues related to the interviewer's ability to elicit reports of abuse from children with an intellectual disability: a review' *Current Issues in Criminal Justice* **14**(3): 257–68.

Abadee, A. (1995). 'The medical duty of confidentiality and the duty to disclose: Can they co-exist?' *Journal of Law and Medicine* **3**: 75.

Abbott, A. (2003). 'Understanding transference and countertransference: risk management strategies for preventing sexual misconduct and other boundary violations in social work practice' *Psychoanalytic Social Work* **10**(2): 21–41.

Abbott, P. and L. Meerabeau, eds. (1998). *The Sociology of the Caring Professions*. London, UCL Press.

Abbott, P. and C. Wallace (1998). 'Health visiting, social work, nursing and midwifery: a history'. In: *The Sociology of the Caring Professions*. P. Abbott and L. Meerabeau, eds. London, UCL Press: 20–53.

ABC (2000). 'Parliament hears kerosene bath led to death'. *ABC net PM*, Retrieved 15 December 2008, from http://www.abc.net.au/pm/stories/s108761.htm.

ABC (2005). 'The case of Kevin Presland'. *Radio National Law Report 14 June*, Retrieved 2 November 2005, from http://www.abc.net.au/rn/talks/8.30/lawrpt/stories/s/1389098.htm.

ABC (2006a). 'Anglican Church cuts back spending to cover abuse compensation'. *ABC Online 17 May 2006*, Retrieved 28 November 2007, from http://www.abc.net.au/am/content/2006/s1640402.htm.

ABC (2006b). 'Victims of alleged paedophile priest offered $4m'. *ABC Online 26 February 2006*, Retrieved 28 November 2007, from http://www.abc.net.au/news/stories/2006/02/26/1578591.htm.

ABC (2007). 'Peddling dodgy medical cures'. *Radio National Law Report 15 May*, Retrieved 31 August 2008, from http://www.abc.net.au/rn/lawreport/stories/2007/1923022.htm.

ABC (2008a). 'Coronial inquests'. *Radio National Law Report 15 April 2008*, Retrieved 15 April, from http://www.abc.net.au/rn/lawreport/stories/2008/2214208.htm.

ABC (2008b). 'Qld disability centre under investigation'. *ABC net PM 8 February 2008*, Retrieved 15 December 2008, from http://www.abc.net.au/pm/content/2008/s2158378.htm.

Alexander, R. and C. Alexander (1995). 'Criminal prosecution of child protection workers' *Social Work* **40**(6): 809–14.

Allan, A. (2007). 'Apology in civil law: a psycho-legal perspective' *Psychiatry, Psychology and Law* **14**(1): 5–16.

Allsop, J. and L. Mulcahy (1996). *Regulating Medical Work: Formal and Informal Controls*. Buckingham and Philadelphia: Open University Press.

Allsop, J. and M. Saks (2002). *Regulating the Health Professions*. London: Sage.

Ames, N. (1999). 'Social work recording: a new look at an old issue' *Journal of Social Work Education* **35**(2): 227–37.

Armstrong, P. (2006). *Establishing an Allied Health Service*. Sydney: Thomson.

Aronson, M., B. Dyer, et al. (2004). *Judicial Review of Administrative Action*, 3rd edn. Sydney: Lawbook Co.

Arthur, R. (2006). 'Children's right to sue for social workers' negligence: the impact of the *Human Rights Act 1998* (UK)' *Tort Law Review* **14**: 135–47.

280 REFERENCES

Australian (2007). 'Rau offered $50,000 'interim' compo.' *Australian*, 23 January 2007, Retrieved 7 November 2007, from http://www.theaustralian.news.com.au/story/0,25197,16009429–2702,00.html.

Australian (2008). 'Test for stolen generations payout', *Australian* 29 February 2008, Retrieved 5 March 2008, from http://www.theaustralian.news.com.au/wireless/story/0,22282,601–23294261,00.html.

Australian Association of Social Workers (2002). *Code of Ethics*, 2nd edn. Canberra: Australian Association of Social Workers.

Australian Association of Social Workers (2003). *Practice Standards for Social Workers: Achieving Outcomes*. Canberra: Australian Association of Social Workers.

Australian Association of Social Workers (2004). *A Duty of Care: A Case for Statutory Regulation of Social Work*. Canberra: Australian Association of Social Workers.

Australian Association of Social Workers (2008). 'Media release: social workers at the heart of child protection', Retrieved 20 January 2009, from http://www.aasw.asn.au/advocacy/socialpolicydesk/MR110908_NCPW.pdf.

Australian Human Rights Commission (2008). *2008 Immigration Detention Report.*, Retrieved 14 January 2008, from http://hreoc.gov.au/human_rights/immigration/idc2008.html.

Australian Human Rights Commission (n.d.). 'Functions of the Australian Human Rights Commission', Retrieved 14 January 2008, from http://hreoc.gov.au/about/functions/index.html.

Australian Institute of Health and Welfare (2007). *Australia's Welfare No 8.*, Retrieved 26 October 2008, from http://www.aihw.gov.au/publications/index.cfm/title/10527.

Australian Institute of Welfare and Community Workers (n.d.). *Code of Ethics.*, Retrieved 20 March 2003, from http://www.aiwcw.org.au/codeOfEthics.html.

Australian Job Search (n.d.). 'Social workers: educational profile Australia', Retrieved 26 October 2008, from http://jobsearch.gov.au/Careers/jo_EduGraph.aspx?AscoCode=2511.

Australian Job Search (n.d.). 'Welfare and community workers: educational profile Australia', Retrieved 14 January 2008, from http://jobsearch.gov.au/Careers/jo_EduGraph.aspx?AscoCode=2512.

Australian Law Reform Commission (2008). *For Your Information: Australian Privacy Law and Practice, Report 108*. Canberra: Australian Law Reform Commission.

Australian National Audit Office (2006). Management of the Detention Centre Contracts – Part B, 2005/2006. Canberra: Australian National Audit Office.

Australian Psychological Society (2000). *Ethical Guidelines: Guidelines Relating to Recovered Memories*, Retrieved 14 April 2008, from http://www.psychology.org.au/Assets/Files/recovered_memories_ethical_guidelines.pdf.

Australian Psychological Society (2004a). *Ethical guidelines: Guidelines for Managing Professional Boundaries and Multiple Relationships*, Retrieved 14 April 2008, from http://www.psychology.org.au/Assets/Files/professional_boundaries_ethical_guidelines.pdf.

Australian Psychological Society (2004b). *Guidelines on Record Keeping*. Melbourne: Australian Psychological Society.

Baggott, R. (2002). 'Regulatory politics, health professionals and the public interest'. In: *Regulating the Health Professions*. J. Allsop and M. Saks, eds. London: Sage: 31–46.

REFERENCES | **281**

Bagot, K. (2002). 'Administrative accountability in prisons', *Australian Journal of Administrative Law* **9**: 143–58.

Banach, M. and F. Bernat (2000). 'Liability and the internet: risks and recommendations for social work practice' *Journal of Technology in Human Services* **17**(2–3): 153–71.

Bar-On, A. (1995). 'Social workers and case management' *Asia Pacific Journal of Social Work* **5**(1): 63–78.

Barker, R. and D. Branson (2000). *Forensic Social Work: Legal Aspects of Professional Practice*, 2nd edn. New York: Haworth Press.

Barsky, A. and J. Gould (2002). *Clinicians in Court*. New York and London: Guilford Press.

Bartholomew, T. and T. Carvalho (2005). 'General practitioners' competence and confidentiality determinations with a minor who requests the oral contraceptive pill', *Journal of Law and Medicine* **13**: 191–203.

Bates, F. (2002). 'Duty of care and the investigation of child sexual abuse: the ultimate Australian solution? *Sullivan v Moody; Thompson v Connon* (2001) 183 ALR 404', *Newcastle Law Review* **6**(1): 107–11.

Bell, L. and P. Tooman (1994). 'Mandatory reporting laws: a critical overview', *International Journal of Law and the Family* **8**: 337–56.

Bennett, B. and I. Freckelton (2006). 'Life after the Ipp reforms: medical negligence law'. In: *Disputes and Dilemmas in Health Law*. I. Freckelton and K. Petersen, eds. Sydney: Federation Press: 381–405.

Berliner, A. (1989). 'Misconduct in social work practice' *Social Work* **34**(1): 69–72.

Besharov, D. (1985). *The Vulnerable Social Worker*. Silver Spring: National Association of Social Workers.

Bessant, J. (2003). 'The science of risk and the epistemology of human service practice', *Just Policy* **31**(December): 31–8.

Bessant, J. (2004a). 'Procedural justice, conflict of interest and the stolen generations' case', *Australian Journal of Public Administration* **63**(1): 74–84.

Bessant, J. (2004b). 'Professional credibility and public trust in those working with young people' *Children Australia* **29**(2): 5–13.

Bessant, J., R. Hil, et al., eds. (2005). *Violations of Trust: How Social and Welfare Institutions Fail Children and Young People*. Aldershot and Burlington: Ashgate.

Black, K. (2007). 'Exploring case managers' advance care planning practices', *Journal of Social Service Research* **33**(3): 21–30.

Blaskett, B. and S. Taylor (2003). *Facilitators and Inhibitors of Mandatory Reporting of Suspected Child Abuse: A Research Study*. Canberra: Australian Institute of Criminology.

Boyle, S., G. Hull, et al. (2006). *Direct Practice in Social Work*. Boston: Pearson Education.

Brammer, A. (2003). *Social Work Law*. Edinburgh Gate: Pearson Education.

Brawley, E. A. (1995). *Human Services and the Media*. Luxembourg: Harwood Academic Publishers.

Braye, S. and M. Preston-Shoot (1997). *Practising Social Work Law*, 2nd edn. London: Macmillian.

Braye, S. and M. Preston-Shoot (2001). 'Social work practice and accountability'. In: *The Law and Social Work: Contemporary Issues for Practice*. L.-A. Cull and J. Roche, eds. Houndmills Basingstoke: Palgrave: 43–53.

Braye, S. and M. Preston-Shoot (2006). 'Broadening the vision: Law teaching, social work and civil society', *International Social Work* **49**(3): 376–89.

REFERENCES

Brayne, H. and G. Broadbent (2002). *Legal Materials for Social Workers.* Oxford: Oxford University Press.

Brayne, H. and H. Carr (2003). *Law for Social Workers,* 8th edn. Oxford: Oxford University Press.

Brennan, C. (2003). 'Third party liability for child abuse: unanswered questions', *Journal of Social Welfare and Family law* **25**(1): 23–37.

Bronitt, S. and B. McSherry (2005). *Principles of Criminal Law,* 2nd edn. Sydney: Lawbook Co.

Brown, T., M. Potoski, et al. (2006). 'Managing public service contracts: aligning values, institutions and markets', *Public Administration Review* **66**(3): 323–31.

Bullis, R. (1995). *Clinical Social Worker Misconduct: Law, Ethics and Interpersonal Dynamics.* Chicago: Nelson Hall.

Burdekin, B. (1989). *Our Homeless Children: Report of the National Inquiry into Homeless Children.* Canberra: Human Rights and Equal Opportunity Commission.

Burdekin, B. (1993). *Human Rights and Mental Illness: Report of the National Inquiry into Human Rights of People with Mental Illness.* Canberra: Human Rights and Equal Opportunity Commission.

Burns, K. (2006). 'Employers behaving badly? Negligence claims for work-related psychological stress', *Precedent* **77**(November/December): 10–14.

Butler, D. (2004). '*Gifford v Strang* and the new landscape for recovery for psychiatric injury in Australia', *Torts Law Journal* **12**(2): 108–27.

Butler, I. and M. Drakeford (2005). *Scandal, Social Policy and Social Welfare,* revised 2nd edn. Bristol: Policy Press.

Cambridge, P. (2001). 'Managing abuse inquiries: methodology, organisation, process and politics', *Journal of Adult Protection* **3**(3): 6–20.

Camilleri, P. (1996). *(Re)Constructing Social Work.* Aldershot and Brookfield: Avebury.

Campbell, D. (2008). 'Baby P case director is sacked without payout', *Guardian 9 December 2008,* Retrieved 12 December 2008, from http://www.guardian.co.uk/society/2008/dec/09/baby-p-sharon-shoesmith.

Cappa, C., C. Forrest, et al. (2003). 'Tort deform or tort reform? Winding back the clock on negligence', *Alternative Law Journal* **28**(5): 212–15.

Carey, M. (2007). 'White collar proletariat? Braverman, the deskilling/upskilling of social work and the paradoxical life of the agency manager', *Journal of Social Work* **7**(1): 93–114.

Carlton, A.-L. (2003). Regulation of the Health Professions in Victoria. Melbourne, Department of Human Services, Victoria.

Carlton, A.-L. (2006). 'National models for regulation of the health professions'. In: *Regulating Health Practitioners.* I. Freckelton, ed. Sydney: Federation Press: 21–51.

Carlton, A.-L. (2008). 'Occupational regulation of health practitioners in Australia'. In: *Allied Health Professionals and the Law.* R. Kennedy. Sydney: Federation Press: 56–78.

Carney, T. (2006). *Social Security Law and Policy.* Sydney: Federation Press.

Carroll, E. (2007). 'Wednesbury unreasonableness as a limit on the civil liability of public authorities', *Tort Law Review* **15**: 77–92.

Carson, D. (1996). 'Risking legal repercussions'. In: *Good Practice in Risk Assessment and Risk Management.* H. Kemshall and J. Pritchard, eds. London and Bristol: Jessica Kingsley Publishers: 3–12.

REFERENCES | **283**

Carson, D. (1997). 'Good enough risk taking', *International Review of Psychiatry* **9**(2–3): 303–8.

Carson, D. (2006). 'Arguing about risk decisions', paper presented at *Human Rights in a World of Fear and Diminishing Resources*, Australian and New Zealand Association of Psychiatry, Psychology and Law, 26th Annual Congress Lorne, Victoria, 9–12 November 2006.

Carson, D. (2007). 'Liability for system negligence', Paper presented at the *3rd International Congress of Psychology and Law*, Adelaide, 3–8 July 2007.

Carson, D. and A. Bain (2008). *Professional Risk and Working with People*. London and Philadelphia: Jessica Kingsley Publishers.

Carter, H. J. (2006). *Challenging Behaviour and Disability: A Targeted Response*. Report to the Honourable Warren Pitt MP, Minister for Communities, Disability Services and Seniors, Brisbane, Retrieved 19 June 2009 from http://www.disability. qld.gov.au/key-projects/positive-futures/documents/investing-in-positive-futures-full-report.pdf.

Cavell, R. (2007). 'Towards a better consent form', *Journal of Law and Medicine* **14**(3): 326–38.

CCH Australia (2007). *Torts Commentaries*, Retrieved 31 October and 19 November 2007, from http:/library2cch.com.audynaweb/torts/atorcomm@CCH_BooktextView.

Charles, M. and S. Butler (2004). 'Social workers' management of organisational change'. In: *Social Work Ideals and Practical Realities*. M. Lymbery and S. Butler, eds. Houndmills, Hampshire and New York: Palgrave Macmillan: 57–82.

Clark, C. (2006a). 'Against confidentiality? Privacy, safety and the public good in professional communications', *Journal of Social Work* **6**(2): 117–136.

Clark, C. (2006b). 'Moral character in social work', *British Journal of Social Work* **36**(1): 75–89.

Clark, D. (2007). *Principles of Australian Public Law*. Sydney: LexisNexis Butterworths.

Clark, K. and A. North (2007). 'Legality of disclosure by Victorian psychiatrists of patient information to carers', *Psychiatry, Psychology and Law* **14**(1): 147–67.

Clarke, J. (1998). 'Doing the right thing? Managerialism and social welfare'. In: *The Sociology of the Caring Professions*. P. Abbott and L. Meerabeau, eds. London: UCL Press: 234–54.

Clayton, A. (2005). *Review of the Framework for Rehabilitation in the South Australian WorkCover Scheme*. Adelaide: WorkCoverSA.

Cockburn, T. and B. Madden (2006). 'Intentional torts claims in medical cases', *Journal of Law and Medicine* **13**: 311–35.

Coffey, G. (2006). ''Locked up without guilt or sin': the ethics of mental health service delivery in immigration detention' *Psychiatry, Psychology and Law* **13**(1): 67–90.

Coffey, M., L. Dugdill, et al. (2004). 'Stress in social services: mental well-being, constraints and job satisfaction', *British Journal of Social Work* **34**(5): 735–46.

Collingridge, M. (1991). 'Legal risk, legal scrutiny, and social work', *Australian Social Work* **44**(1): 11–17.

Collingridge, M., S. Miller, et al. (2001). 'Privacy and confidentiality in social work', *Australian Social Work* **54**(2): 3–13.

Commonwealth Ombudsman (2007). *Annual Report 2006–2007*. Canberra: Commonwealth Ombudsman.

REFERENCES

Commonwealth Ombudsman (2007). 'Ombudsman recommends amendments to policy guidelines on marriage-like relationships', *Media Release 18 October 2007*, Retrieved 12 December 2007, from http://www.comb.gov.au/commonwealth/publish.nsf/Content/mediarelease_2007_09.

Commonwealth Treasury (Ipp Report) (2002). *Review of the Law of Negligence*, Retrieved 1 April 2003, from http://revofneg.treasury.gov.au/content/Report2/PDF/Law_Neg_Final.pdf.

Connolly, M. and T. Ward (2008). *Morals, Rights and Practice in the Human Services*. London and Philadelphia: Jessica Kingsley Publishers.

Consultation Committee for a Proposed Human Rights Act (2007). *A WA Human Rights Act*. Perth: Department of the Attorney General.

Cooper, L. (2007). 'Backing Australia's future: teaching and learning in social work', *Australian Social Work* **60**(1): 94–106.

Cordon, J. and M. Preston-Shoot (1987). *Contracts in Social Work*. Vermont: Gower Publishing Company.

Corey, G. (2009). *The Art of Integrative Counseling*, 2nd edn. Pacific Grove: Brooks/Cole.

Corey, G., M. Corey, et al. (2007). *Issues and Ethics in the Helping Professions*, 7th edn. Belmont: Thomson Brooks/Cole.

Cormier, S., P. Nurius, et al. (2009). *Interviewing and Change Strategies for Helpers: Fundamental Skills and Cognitive Behavioral Interventions*, 6th edn. Pacific Grove: Brooks Cole.

Cornes, M., J. Manthorpe, et al. (2007). 'Developing wider workforce regulation in England: lessons from education, social work and social care', *Journal of Interprofessional Care* **21**(3): 241–50.

Corruption and Crime Commission of Western Australia (2006). *Sexual Contact with Children by Persons in Authority in the Department of Education and Training of Western Australia*. Perth: Corruption and Crime Commission.

Corruption and Crime Commission of Western Australia (2007). *Misconduct Handling Procedures in the Western Australian Public Sector: Department for Community Development*. Perth: Corruption and Crime Commission.

Cotton, P. (2008). 'Psychological injury in the workplace', *In Psych Bulletin* April, Retrieved 14 February 2009, from http://www.psychology.org.au/inpsych/psych_injury.

Cousins, C. and S. Toussaint (2004). 'You wrote what?!... dangers and dilemmas in record keeping', *Developing Practice: The Child Youth and Family Work Journal* **10**(Winter): 38–45.

Crime and Misconduct Commission (2004). *Protecting Children: An Inquiry into Abuse of Children in Foster Care*. Brisbane: Crime and Misconduct Commission Queensland.

Crock, M. and E. Santow (2007). 'Privative clauses and the limits of the law'. In: *Australian Administrative Law; Fundamentals, Principles and Doctrines*. M. Groves and H. Lee, eds. Cambridge, New York, Melbourne: Cambridge University Press: 345–67.

Cropley, A. (2002). 'Problems and concerns of welfare paraprofessionals working with refugees', *British Journal of Social Work* **32**(2): 233–8.

Cull, L.-A. and J. Roche, eds. (2001). *The Law and Social Work: Contemporary Issues for Practice*. Houndmills Basingstoke: Palgrave.

Cumming, S., E. Fitzpatrick, et al. (2007). 'Raising the Titanic: Rescuing social work documentation from the sea of ethical risk', *Australian Social Work* **60**(2): 239–57.

REFERENCES | **285**

Daily Telegraph (2007). 'Delay in Cornelia Rau compo case', 3 July 2007, Retrieved 9 November 2007, from http://www.news.com.au/dailytelegraph/story/0,22049,22009932-5001028,00.html.

Dalrymple, J. and B. Burke (2006). *Anti-Oppressive Practice: Social Care and the Law*, 2nd edn. Maidenhead, New York: Open University Press.

Daly, K. and H. Hayes (2001). *Restorative Justice and Conferencing in Australia*. Canberra: Australian Institute of Criminology.

Daniel, A. (1998). *Scapegoats for a Profession*. Amsterdam: Harwood.

Davidson, G. (2002). 'Dealing with subpoenas: advice for APS members' *In Psych Bulletin* (October): 31–35.

Davis, A. and P. M. Garrett (2004). 'Progressive practice for tough times: social work, poverty and division in the twenty-first century'. In: *Social Work Ideals and Practice Realities*. M. Lymbery and S. Butler, eds. New York: Palgrave Macmillan: 13–33.

De Maria, W. (1996). 'The welfare whistleblower: in praise of troublesome people', *Australian Social Work* **49**(3): 15–24.

DeJulio, L. and C. Berkman (2003). 'Nonsexual multiple role relationships: attitudes and behaviours of social workers', *Ethics and Behavior* **13**(1): 61–78.

Delany, C. (2008). 'Decision-making and consent'. In: *Allied Health Professionals and the Law*. R. Kennedy, ed. Sydney: Federation Press: 81–107.

Demaine, L. (2007). "Playing doctor' with the patient's spouse', *Virginia Journal of Social Policy and the Law* **14**(3): 308–56.

Department of Health (2006). 'Code of Fair Information Practice', Retrieved 23 August 2008, from http://www.publications.health.sa.gov.au/ainfo/1.

Department of Human Services (2003). *Regulation of the Health Professions in Victoria*. Melbourne: Victorian Department of Human Services.

Department of Parliamentary Services (2005). *The Detention of Cornelia Rau: Legal Issues*. Canberra: Department of Parliamentary Services.

Devereux, J. (2002). *Australian Medical Law*, 2nd edn. Sydney: Cavendish Publishing.

Dewane, C. (2006). 'Use of self: a primer revisited', *Clinical Social Work Journal* **34**(4): 543–58.

Dickens, J. (2004). 'Teaching child care law: key principles, new priorities', *Social Work Education* **23**(2): 217–30.

Dietrich, J. (2005). 'Duty of care under the Civil Liability Acts', *Torts Law Journal* **13**(1): 17–40.

Dominelli, L. (1997). 'The institutional parameters of social work'. In: *Sociology for Social Work*. L. Dominelli, ed. Houndmills Basingstoke: Macmillan: 113–20.

Douglas, R. (2006). *Douglas and Jones's Administrative Law*, 5th edn. Sydney: Federation Press.

Doyle, C. and M. Bagaric (2005). *Privacy Law in Australia*. Sydney: Federation Press.

Dutt, R. (2001). 'Racism and social work practice'. In: *The Law and Social Work: Contemporary Issues for Practice*. L.-A. Cull and J. Roche, eds. Houndmills and New York: Palgrave: 20–30.

Eastwood, C. (2003). *The Experiences of Child Complainants of Sexual Abuse in the Criminal Justice System*. Canberra: Australian Institute of Criminology.

Ellard, J. (2001). 'Sex and the professions', *The Australian Law Journal* **75**(April): 248–56.

286 | REFERENCES

Elliot J. (Minister for Ageing) (2008). 'Release of Annual Report-Operation of Aged Care Act 2007–2008', *Media Release 25 November 2008*, Retrieved 15 December 2008, from http://www.health.gov.au/internet/ministers/publishing.nsf/Content/C7FA3E425938AF90CA25750C00170CB8/$File/je225.pdf.

Ellis, M. (2007). 'Patient follow-up: the scope of the duty, the impact of tort law reform and practical suggestions to comply with legal requirements', *Journal of Law and Medicine* **15**(3): 408–22.

Els, P. and G. Dehn (2001). 'Whistleblowing: public concern at work'. In: *The Law and Social Work*. L.-A. Cull and J. Roche, eds. Houndmills and New York: Palgrave: 105–19.

Epstein, R. (2005). 'The loose screw awards: psychology's top 10 misguided ideas', *Psychology Today* (January/February): 55–62.

Evans, T. and J. Harris (2004). 'Street-level bureaucracy, social work and the (exaggerated) death of discretion', *British Journal of Social Work* **43**(4): 871–95.

Exworthy, M. and S. Halford (1999). 'Professionals and managers in a changing public sector: conflict, compromise and collaboration?' In: *Professionals and the New Managerialism in the Public Sector*. M. Exworthy and S. Halford, eds. Buckingham: Open University Press: 1–17.

Feldman, S., S. Moritz, et al. (2005). 'Suicide and the law: a practical overview for mental health professionals', *Women and Therapy* **28**(1): 95–103.

Feldthusen, B. (1998). 'Vicarious liabiltiy for sexual torts'. In: *Torts Tomorrow: A Tribute to John Fleming*. N. Mullany and A. Linden, eds. Sydney: LBC Information Services.

Filippelli, J. and D. Goodman (2005). 'Child welfare and civil liability in the 21st century', *Canadian Social Work* **7**(1): 68–80.

Finn, J. and M. Banach (2002). 'Risk management in online human services practice' *Journal of Technology in Human Services* **20**(1–2): 133–53.

Fisse, B. and J. Braithwaite (1988). 'The allocation of responsibility for corporate crime: individualism, collectivism and accountability', *Sydney Law Review* **11**(March): 468–513.

Fitzgibbon, D. (2007). 'Risk analysis and the new practitioner: myth or reality?' *Punishment and Society* **9**(1): 87–97.

Forster, C. (2002). 'The failure of criminal injuries compensation schemes for victims of intra-familial abuse: the example of Queensland', *Torts Law Journal* **10**(2): 143–66.

Foucault, M. (1967). *Madness and Civilisation* London: Tavistock.

Franklin, B. and N. Parton (1991). 'Media reporting of social work: a framework for analysis'. In: *Social Work, the Media and Public Relations* B. Franklin and N. Parton, eds. London: Routledge: 7–52.

Franklin, B. and N. Parton, eds. (1991). *Social Work, the Media and Public Relations*. London: Routledge.

Freckelton, I. (2001a). *Criminal Injuries Compensation: Law, Practice and Policy*. Sydney: Lawbook Information Services.

Freckelton, I. (2001b). 'Editorial. Compensability for psychiatric injury: an opportunity for modernisation and reconceptualisation', *Journal of Law and Medicine* (November): 137–44.

Freckelton, I. (2002). 'New directions in compensability for psychiatric injuries', *Psychiatry, Psychology and Law* **9**(2): 271–83.

REFERENCES 287

Freckelton, I. (2003). 'Liability of psychiatrists for failure to certify', *Psychiatry, Psychology and Law* **10**(2): 397–404.

Freckelton, I. (2004). 'Regulation of health practitioners: grappling with temptations and transgressions', *Journal of Law and Medicine* **11**: 401–8.

Freckelton, I. (2005). 'Madness, migration and misfortune: the challenge of the bleak tale of Cornelia Rau', *Psychiatry, Psychology and Law* **12**(1): 1–14.

Freckelton, I. (2006a). 'Doctors and forensic expertise'. In: *Disputes and Dilemmas in Health Care*. I. Freckelton and K. Petersen, eds. Sydney: Federation Press: 406–35.

Freckelton, I. (2006b). 'Editorial. Human rights and health law', *Journal of Law and Medicine* **14**(1): 7–14.

Freckelton, I. (2006c). 'Ethics and the legal context'. In: *Ethics and Professional Practice for Psychologists*. S. Morrissey and P. Reddy, eds. Melbourne: Thomson Australia: 14–24.

Freckelton, I. (2006d). 'Limitation of actions for psychiatric injuries in intentional tort cases', *Psychiatry, Psychology and Law* **13**(2): 269–73.

Freckelton, I. (2006e). 'The margins of professional regulation: disjunctions, dilemmas and deterrence'. In: *Regulating Health Practitioners*. I. Freckelton, ed. Sydney: Federation Press: 148–70.

Freckelton, I., ed. (2006f). *Regulating Health Practitioners: Law in Context, Vol 23, No 2*. Sydney: Federation Press.

Freckelton, I. (2006g). 'Regulation of health practitioners'. In: *Disputes and Dilemmas in Health Law*. I. Freckelton and K. Petersen, eds. Sydney: Federation Press: 493–515.

Freckelton, I. (2007a). 'Editorial. 'Suing the welfare': The diminishing immunity for child protection authorities' *Journal of Law and Medicine* **14**: 443–448.

Freckelton, I. (2007b). Regulating psychology and psychiatry: developments and controversies, *3rd International Congress of Psychology and Law*, Adelaide, 3–8 July 2007.

Freckelton, I. (2007c). 'Regulation of health care practitioners: opportunities and developments for plaintiffs', *Precedent* **79**(March/April): 29–35.

Freckelton, I. (2008a). 'Employers' duties for reasonably forseeable psychiatric injuries', *Psychiatry, Psychology and Law* **15**(1): 17–24.

Freckelton, I. (2008b). 'Failure by police to detain', *Psychiatry, Psychology and Law* **15**(2): 175–87.

Freckelton, I. (2008c). 'Trends in regulation of mental health practitioners', *Psychiatry, Psychology and Law* **15**(3): 415–34.

Freckelton, I. (2009). 'Opening a new page', *Law Institute Journal* (June): 29–33.

Freckelton, I. and P. Molloy (2007). 'The health of health practitioners: remedial programs, regulation and the spectre of the law', *Journal of Law and Medicine* **15**(3): 366–82.

Freckelton, I. and D. Ranson (2006a). *Death Investigation and the Coroner's Inquest*. Melbourne: Oxford University Press.

Freckelton, I. and D. Ranson (2006b). 'The evolving institution of the coroner'. In: *Disputes and Dilemmas in Health Law*. I. Freckelton and K. Petersen, eds. Sydney: Federation Press: 296–323.

Freckelton, I. and H. Selby (2009). *Expert Evidence: Law, Practice, Procedure and Advocacy*. Sydney: Lawbook Co.

Freegard, H. (2006). 'What is law?' In: *Ethical Practice for Health Professionals*. H. Freegard, ed. Melbourne: Thomson Nelson Australia: 46–64.

Fulcher, L. (2002). 'Cultural safety and the duty of care', *Child Welfare* **LXXXI**(5): 689–708.

Furedi, F. (2004). *Therapy Culture: Cultivating Vulnerability in an Uncertain Age*. London and New York: Routledge.

Gaha, J. (1992). *Australian Social Work Index 1948–1991*. Canberra: Australian Association of Social Workers.

Galloway, G. (2005). 'Equivocating on reconciliation', *Australian Social Work* **58**(3): 257–74.

Gambrill, E. (1983). *Casework: A Competency-Based Approach*. Englewood Cliffs: Prentice Hall.

Gambrill, E. (2005). *Critial Thinking in Clinical Practice: Improving the Quality of Judgements and Decisions*, 2nd edn. Hoboken: John Wiley and Sons.

Gambrill, E. (2006). *Social Work Practice: A Critical Thinker's Guide*, 2nd edn. Oxford and New York: Oxford University Press.

General Social Care Council (2006). 'Social worker suspended from register after misconduct found', *Media Release 19 June 2006*, Retrieved 28 December 2007, from http://www.gscc.org.uk/News+and+events/Media+releases/2006+archive/Social+worker+suspended+from+register+after+misconduct+found.htm.

General Social Care Council (2007). 'Social worker admonished following conduct hearing in Blackpool', *Media release 18 December 2007*, Retrieved 28 December 2007, from http://www.gscc.org.uk/News+and+events/Media+releases/Social+worker+admonished+following+conduct+hearing+in+Blackpool.htm.

Germov, R. (2003). *Refugee Law in Australia*. Melbourne: Oxford University Press.

Gibbons, J. (2001). 'Effective practice: social work's long history of concern about outcomes', *Australian Social Work* **54**(3): 3–13.

Gibelman, M. and S. Gelman (2002). 'Should we have faith in faith-based social services?' *Nonprofit Management and Leadership* **13**(1): 49–65.

Gibelman, M. and S. Gelman (2004). 'A loss of credibility: patterns of wrongdoing among nongovernmental organisations', *Voluntas: International Journal of Voluntary and Nonprofit Organisations* **15**(4): 355–81.

Gilbertson, R. and J. Barber (2004). 'The systemic abrogation of practice standards in foster care', *Australian Social Work* **57**(1): 31–45.

Gillingham, P. (2006). 'Risk assessment in child protection: problem rather than solution?' *Australian Social Work* **59**(1): 86–98.

Gillingham, P. (2007). 'The Australian Association of Social Workers and social policy debates: a strategy for the future?' *Australian Social Work* **60**(2): 166–80.

Glenndenning, F. (1999). 'The abuse of older people in institutional settings'. In: *Institutional Abuse: Perspectives Across the Life Course*. N. Stanley, J. Manthorpe and B. Penhale, eds. London and New York: Routledge.

Glicken, M. (2008). *A Guide to Writing for Human Service Professionals*. Lanham: Rowman and Littlefield.

Goddard, C., B. Saunders, et al. (2002). *A Study in Confusion: Factors which affect the Decisions of Professionals when Reporting Child Abuse and Neglect*. Melbourne: Australian Childhood Foundation.

Goffman, I. (1961). *Asylums*. Harmondsworth: Penguin.

Golding, P. (1991). 'Do-gooders on display: social workers, public attitudes and the mass media'. In: *Social Work, the Media and Public Relations*. B. Franklin and N. Parton, eds. London: Taylor & Francis: 88–104.

REFERENCES | 289

Gould, J. and A. Barsky (2004). *Clinicians in Court: A Guide to Subpoenas, Depositions, Testifying, and Everything Else You Need to Know.* New York: Guilford Press.

Grabosky, P. (1989). *Wayward Governance: Illegality and its Control in the Public Sector. Australian Studies in Law, Crime and Justice.* Canberra: Australian Institute of Criminology.

Gray, M., K. Healy, et al. (2003). 'Social enterprise: is it the business of social work?' *Australian Social Work* **56**(2): 141–54.

Green, D. (2007). 'Risk and social work practice', *Australian Social Work* **60**(4): 395–409.

Groves, M. (2005). 'Outsourcing and non-delegable duties', *Public Law Review* **16**: 265–71.

Gumbel, E.-A., R. Scorer, et al. (2006). 'Recent developments in child abuse compensation claims', *Journal of Personal Injury Law* **2006**(1): 21–8.

Gursansky, D., J. Harvey, et al. (2003). *Case Management: Policy, Practice and Professional Business.* Sydney: Allen and Unwin; New York: Columbia University Press.

Haebich, A. (2000). *Broken Circles: Fragmenting Indigenous Families 1800–2000.* Perth: Freemantle Arts Centre Press.

Hall, A. and R. Johnstone (2005). 'Exploring the re-criminalising of OHS breaches in the context of industrial death', *Flinders Journal of Law Reform* **8**(1): 57–92.

Hall, J. (2008). 'A practitioner's application and deconstruction of evidence-based practice', *Families in Society: The Journal of Contemporary Human Services* **89**(3): 385–93.

Hall, M. (2000). 'After Waterhouse: vicarious liability and the tort of institutional abuse', *Journal of Social Welfare and Family Law* **22**(2): 159–73.

Hall, M. (2006). 'Institutional tortfeasors: systemic negligence and the class action', *Torts Law Journal* **13**(2): 135–57.

Hammond, S. W. and I. Freckelton (2006). 'Being the subject of a complaint to a regulatory board: complaints happen'. In: *Ethics and Professional Practice for Psychologists.* S. Morrissey and P. Reddy, eds. Melbourne: Thomson Australia: 150–62.

Handford, P. (2006). *Mullany and Handford's Tort Liability for Psychiatric Damage.* Sydney: Lawbook Co.

Haney, C., C. Banks, et al. (1973). 'Interpersonal dynamics in a simulated prison', *International Journal of Criminology and Penology* **1**: 69–97.

Harris, J. (1998). *We Wish We'd Done More: Ninety Years of CMS and Aboriginal Issues in North Australia*, revised. Adelaide: Openbook Publishers.

Harris, N. (1987). 'Defensive social work' *British Journal of Social Work* **17**(1): 61–9.

Harwin, J. and M. Owen (2003). 'The implementation of care plans and its relationship to children's welfare', *Child and Family Law Quarterly* **15**(1): 71–83.

Hasenfeld, Y. (1983). *Human Service Organisations.* Englewood Cliffs: Prentice Hall.

Hawkins, C. (1985). *Mishap or Malpractice?* Oxford: Medical Defence Union.

Hayne, K. (2002). 'Defining crime in the professions'. In: *Crime in the Professions.* R. Smith, ed. Aldershot: Ashgate: 27–32.

Head, M. (2008). *Administrative Law: Context and Critique*, 2nd edn. Sydney: Federation Press.

Health and Community Services Complaints Commissioner (2007). *Annual Report 2006–2007*, Retrieved 20 November 2008, from http://www.hcscc.sa.gov.au/cgi-bin/wf.pl?search=annual±report.

Health Care Complaints Commission (2007). *Annual Report 2006–2007*, Retrieved 22 November 2007, from http://www.hccc.nsw.gov.au/html/publications.htm.

REFERENCES

Health Care Complaints Commission (2008). 'Media release: public statement', 22 October 2008, Retrieved 18 November 2008, from http://www.hccc.nsw.gov.au.

Health Services Commissioner (2005). *Inquiry Into the Practice of Recovered Memory Therapy*. Melbourne: Health Services Commissioner.

Health Workforce Australia (2008). *National Registration and Accreditation Scheme, Intergovernmental Agreement*, Retrieved 2 May 2008, from http://www.nhwt.gov.au/natreg.asp.

Healy, K. (2004). 'Social workers in the new human services marketplace: trends, challenges and responses', *Australian Social Work* **57**(2): 103–14.

Healy, K. (2005). *Social Work Theories in Context: Creating Frameworks for Practice*. Houndmills and New York: Palgrave Macmillan.

Healy, K. and G. Meagher (2004). 'The reprofessionalisation of social work: collaborative approaches for achieving professional recognition', *British Journal of Social Work* **34**: 243–60.

Healy, K. and J. Mulholland (2007). *Writing Skills for Social Workers*. Los Angeles, London: Sage.

Henderson, L. and B. Franklin (2007). 'Sad not bad: images of social care professionals in popular UK television drama', *Journal of Social Work* **7**(2): 133–53.

Henderson, R., N. North, et al. (2005). 'Investigations of complaints and quality of health care', *Journal of Law and Medicine* **12**: 336–72.

Hepworth, D., R. Rooney, et al. (2006). *Direct Social Work Practice: Theory and Skills*, 7th edn. Pacific Grove: Brooks/Cole.

Hicks, H. and P. Swain (2007). 'Direct, facilitate, enable-the juxtaposition of the duty of care and the duty of disclosure in social work field education', *Social Work Education* **26**(1): 69–85.

Hill, D. (2007). *The Forgotten Children*. Sydney: Random House.

Hilson, C. J. and W. V. Rogers (1995). '*X v Bedfordshire County Council*: tort law and statutory functions-probably not the end of the story', *Torts Law Journal* **3**(1): 221–38.

Holt, B. (2000). *The Practice of Generalist Case Management*. Needham Heights: Allyn and Bacon.

Horrocks, C. and J. Goddard (2006). 'Adults who grew up in care: constructing the self and accessing care files', *Child and Family Social Work* **11**: 264–72.

Houston-Vega, M. K., E. Nuehring, et al. (1997). *Prudent Practice: A Guide for Managing Malpractice Risk*. Washington: NASW Press.

Howell, J. (1998). 'Public duties and resources: 'Wont pay-Wont do'', *Journal of Local Government Law* **3**: 49–56.

Hughes, L. (2008). 'Social care work in the recent past: revisiting the professional/amateur dichotomy', *Australian Social Work* **61**(3): 226–38.

Hugman, R. (2005). *New Approaches in Ethics for the Helping Professions*. Houndmills and New York: Palgrave Macmillan.

Human Rights and Equal Opportunity Commission (2004). *National Inquiry into Children in Immigration Detention – A Last Resort?* Sydney: Human Rights and Equal Opportunity Commission.

Human Rights Commission (2008). *Annual Report 2007–2008*, Retrieved 22 November 2008, from http://www.hrc.act.gov.au/index.cfm?MasterTypeID=1&SectionTypeID=7&MainTypeID=7.

REFERENCES | **291**

Humphries, P. and P. Camilleri (2002). 'Social work and technology: challenges for social workers in practice: a case study', *Australian Social Work* **55**(4): 251–9.

Hunt, G., ed. (1998). *Whistleblowing in the Social Sciences*. London: Edward Arnold.

Hunt, P. (2008). 'The health and human rights movement: progress and obstacles', *Journal of Law and Medicine* **15**(5): 714–24.

Iacovino, L. (2004). 'The patient-therapist relationship: reliable and authentic mental health records in a shared electronic environment', *Psychiatry, Psychology and Law* **11**(1): 63–72.

IBN News (2006). 'Hundreds of disability workers investigated for assault last year', *Agedcare crisis*, Retrieved 15 December 2008, from http://www.agedcarecrisis.com/news/1706-hundreds-of-disability-workers-investigated-for-assault-last-year.

Ife, J. (2008). *Human Rights and Social Work: Towards Rights-Based Practice*, revised. Cambridge: Cambridge University Press.

Independent Commission Against Corruption (2006). *Report on Investigation into the Case Management and Administration of Community Service Orders*. Sydney: Independent Commission Against Corruption.

Independent Commission Against Corruption (2007). 'New study shows public sector whistleblowing more widespread than previously believed', Public Sector Anti-Corruption Conference release 16 October 2007, Retrieved 21 December 2007, from http://www.icac.nsw.gov.au/index.cfm?objectID=A69022AA-C9D6–2367-FC8A47EA3EB29020.

Jones, A. and J. May (1992). *Working in Human Service Organisations*. Melbourne: Longman Cheshire.

Jones, C. (2001). 'Voices from the front line: state social workers and New Labour', *British Journal of Social Work* **31**(4): 547–62.

Jones, D. (1999). 'Regulating social work: key questions', *Practice* **11**(3): 55–63.

Jones, J. and A. Alcabes (1989). 'Clients don't sue: the invulnerable social worker', *Social Casework* **70**(7): 414–20.

Jones, K. and A. Fowles, eds. (1984). *Ideas on Institutions: Analysing the Literature on Long-Term Care and Custody*. London and Boston: Routledge and Kegan Paul.

Jones, M. and L. A. Basser Marks (2000). 'Valuing people through law – whatever happened to Marion?' In: *Explorations on Law and Disability in Australia*. M. Jones and L. A. Basser Marks, eds. Sydney: Federation Press: 147–80.

Jordan, B. (2001). 'Tough love: social work, social exclusion and the third way', *British Journal of Social Work* **31**(4): 527–46.

Kagle, J. (1991). *Social Work Records*, 2nd edn. Belmont: Wadsworth.

Kagle, J. and P. Giebelhausen (1994). 'Dual relationships and professional boundaries', *Social Work* **39**(2): 213–20.

Kampf, A., B. McSherry, et al. (2008). 'Psychologists' perceptions of legal and ethical requirements for breaching confidentiality', *Australian Psychologist* **43**(3): 194–204.

Kampf, A. and B. McSherry (2006). 'Confidentiality in therapeutic relationships: the need to develop comprehensive guidelines for mental health professionals', *Psychiatry, Psychology and Law* **13**(1): 124–31.

Kane, A. (1995). 'The effects of criminalization of sexual misconduct by therapists'. In: *Breach of Trust: Sexual Exploitation by Health Care Professionals and Clergy*. J. Gonsiorek, ed. Thousand Oaks: Sage: 317–37.

REFERENCES

Kane, M., M. K. Houston-Vega, et al. (2002). 'Documentation in managed care: challenges for social work education', *Journal of Teaching in Social Work* **22**(1/2): 199–212.

Karger, H. and M. T. Hernandez (2004). 'The decline of the public intellectual in social work', *Journal of Sociology and Social Welfare* **31**(3): 51–68.

Karger, H. and D. Stoesz (2003). 'The growth of social work education programs, 1985–1999: its impact on economic and educational factors related to the profession of social work', *Journal of Social Work Education* **39**(2): 279–95.

Kelly, G. (1998). 'Editorial: patient data, confidentiality and electronics', *British Medical Journal* **316**(7th March): 718–19.

Kelly, M. and R. Lewis (1994). 'Child abuse in residential homes', *New Law Journal* **March 11**: 367–68.

Kemshall, H. (2002). *Risk, Social Policy and Welfare*. Buckingham and Philadelphia: Open University Press.

Kemshall, H. (2008). 'Risks, rights and justice: understanding and responding to youth risk', *Youth Justice* **8**(21): 21–37.

Kennedy, R., D. Gursansky, et al. (2001). 'The response of Australian universities to case management', *Australian Social Work* **54**(4): 29–39.

Kennedy, R., D. Gursansky, et al. (2004). 'Work-based training for case management: assisting agencies to make better decisions', *Australian Journal of Case Management* **6**(1): 13–19.

Kennedy, R. and J. Harvey (2001). 'Advertised jobs in the human services: advice to prospective employees', *Australian Journal of Career Development* **10**(2): 28–31.

Kennedy, R. and B. Kennedy (2008). 'Case management in youth and family support programs: academic and Australian program manager reflections on things that matter', *Second International Forum of Social Workers from Siberia, Far East and Asia Pacific Regions, Union of Social Workers and Social Pedagogues of Russia*, Novosibirsk 22–24th July 2008.

Kennedy, R. with J. Richards (2007). *Integrating Human Service Law and Practice*, 2nd edn. Melbourne: Oxford University Press.

Kent, H. (2006). 'Protecting clients from harm: the role of continuing professional education', *Australian Social Work* **59**(4): 435–48.

Kerridge, I., M. Lowe, et al. (2005). *Ethics and Law for the Health Professions*, 2nd edn. Sydney: Federation Press.

Kerridge, I., M. Lowe, et al., eds. (2008). *Ethics and Law for the Health Professions*. Sydney: Federation Press.

Kiraly, M. (2002). 'What's wrong with child welfare? An examination of current practices that harm children', *Children Australia* **27**(3): 10–18.

Kirkham, R. (2004). 'Prevention is better than litigation: the importance of good administration', *Journal of Social Welfare and Family law* **26**(3): 301–11.

Kirst-Ashman, K. and G. Hull (2006). *Understanding Generalist Practice*. Belmont: Thomson Brooks/Cole.

Knowles, A. (2006). 'Boundaries, dual relationships and professional practice'. In: *Ethics and Professional Practice for Psychologists*. S. Morrissey and P. Reddy, eds. Melbourne: Thomson: 89–101.

Lane, W. and S. Young (2007). *Administrative Law in Australia*. Sydney: Thomson Lawbook Co.

Lanham, D., B. Bartal, et al. (2006). *Criminal Laws in Australia*. Sydney: Federation Press.

REFERENCES 293

Layton, R. (2003). *Our Best Investment: A State Plan to Protect and Advance the Interests of Children*. Adelaide: South Australian Department of Human Servicess.

Lewis, I. and N. Bolzan (2007). 'Social work with a twist: interweaving practice knowledge, student experience and academic theory', *Australian Social Work* **60**(2): 136–46.

Lewis, L. (2007). 'No-harm contracts: A review of what we know', *Suicide and Life Threatening Behavior* **37**(1): 50–57.

Lexisnexis (2007). 'Protection of reputation', *Australian Defamation Law and Practice*, Retrieved 24 January 2008, from http://www.lexisnexis.com/au/legal/results/docview/docview.do?risb=21_T2898998385&format=GNBFULL&sort=BOOLEAN&startDocNo=1&resultsUrlKey=29_T2898998388&cisb=22_T2898998387&treeMax=false&treeWidth=0&csi=267954&docNo=5.

Lipsky, M. (1980). *Street-Level Bureaucracy: Dilemmas of the Individual in Public Services*. New York: Russell Sage Foundation.

Lonne, B. and J. Thomson (2005). 'Critical review of Queensland's Crime and Misconduct Commission Inquiry into abuse of children in foster care: social work's contribution to reform', *Australian Social Work* **58**(1): 86–99.

Lonne, R. (2003). 'Social workers and human service practitioners'. In: *Occupational Stress in the Service Professions*. M. Dollard, T. Winefield and H. Winefield, eds. New York: Taylor and Francis: 281–309.

Luntz, H. (2005). 'A personal journey through the law of torts', *Sydney Law Review* **27**(3): 393–415.

Luntz, H. and D. Hambly (2006). *Torts: Cases and Commentary*, revised 5th edn. Sydney: LexisNexis Butterworths.

Lymbery, M. (2000). 'The retreat from professionalism: from social worker to care manager'. In: *Professionalism, Boundaries and the Workplace*. N. Malin, ed. London and New York: Routledge.

Lymbery, M. (2004). 'Responding to crisis: the changing nature of welfare organisations'. In: *Social Work Ideals and Practical Realities*. M. Lymbery and S. Butler, eds. Houndmills, Hampshire and New York: Palgrave Macmillan: 34–56.

Lymbery, M. and S. Butler (2004). 'Introduction'. In: *Social Work Ideals and Practical Realities*. M. Lymbery and S. Butler, eds. Houndmills, Hampshire and New York: Palgrave Macmillan: 1–10.

Lymbery, M. and S. Butler, eds. (2004). *Social Work Ideals and Practical Realities*. Houndmills, Hampshire and New York: Palgrave Macmillan.

Lynch, J. and G. Versen (2003). 'Social work supervisor liabiltiy: risk factors and strategies for risk reduction', *Administration in Social Work* **27**(2): 57–72.

Lynch, P. (2008). 'Commonwealth Attorney-General to consult on federal charter of human rights', *Alternative Law Journal* **33**(1): 53.

Lyons, M. (2001). *Third Sector: The Contribution of Non Profit and Cooperative Enterprises in Australia*. Sydney: Allen and Unwin.

MacFarlane, P. (2000). *Health Law: Commentary and Materials*, 3rd edn. Sydney: Federation Press.

Mackay, A. (2006). 'Harm suffered by children in immigration detention: can tort law provide redress?' *Tort Law Review* **14**(1): 16–32.

Mackie, D. (2008). 'Leadership derailment and psychological harm', *In Psych Bulletin*, April 2008, Retrieved 14 February 2009, from http://www.psychology.org.au/inpsych/derailment/.

REFERENCES

Macleod, A. and B. McSherry (2007). 'Regulating mental healthcare practitioners: towards a standardised and workable framework', *Psychiatry, Psychology and Law* **14**(1): 45–55.

Madden, B. and T. Cockburn (2007). 'Bundaberg and beyond: duty to disclose adverse events to patients', *Journal of Law and Medicine* **14**: 501–27.

Madden, R. and M. Parody (1998). 'Helping without harming: a reply to Feld and Fetkewicz', *Clinical Social Work Journal* **26**(2): 227–32.

Magnusson, R. (2007). 'Legal issues in teamwork: liabiltiy within medical teams and hierarchies in NSW', *Precedent* **79**(March/April): 10–16.

Malin, N., ed. (2000). *Professionalism, Boundaries and the Workplace*. London and New York: Routledge.

Manela, R. and D. Moxley (2002). 'Best practices as agency-based knowledge in social welfare', *Administration in Social Work* **26**(4): 1–23.

Mann, S. (2003). 'Tort law reform', *Alternative Law Journal* **28**(5): 216–24.

Manthorpe, J. and N. Stanley (1999). 'Conclusion: shifting the focus, from "bad apples" to users' rights'. In: *Institutional Abuse: Perspectives Across the Life Course*. N. Stanley, J. Manthorpe and B. Penhale, eds. London and New York: Routledge: 223–40.

Markiewicz, A. (1996). 'Panacea or scapegoat: the social work profession and its history and background in relation to the state welfare department in Victoria', *Australian Social Work* **49**(3): 25–32.

Marshall, T. and P. Solomon (2004). 'Confidentiality intervention: effects on provider-consumer-family collaboration', *Research on Social Work Practice* **14**(1): 3–13.

McBride, N. and M. Tunnecliffe (2001). *Risky Practices: a Counsellor's Guide to Risk Management in Private Practice*. Palmyra: Bayside Books.

McCarthy, M. (2008). 'Mandatory domestic violence reporting to become territory law', *Northern Territory Government Media Release 25 November 2008*, Retrieved 13 December 2008, from http://newsroom.nt.gov.au/index.cfm?fuseaction=viewRelease&id=4805&d=5.

McCarty, D. and C. Clancy (2002). 'Telehealth: implications for social work practice', *Social Work* **47**(2): 153–61.

McDonald, C. (1999). 'Human service professionals in the community services industry', *Australian Social Work* **52**(1): 17–25.

McDonald, C. (2000). 'The third sector in the human services: rethinking its role'. In: *Contemporary Perspectives on Social Work and the Human Services: Challenges and Change*. I. O'Connor, P. Smyth and J. Warburton, eds. Sydney: Longman: 84–99.

McDonald, C. (2006). *Challenging Social Work: The Context of Practice*. Houndmills and New York: Palgrave Macmillan.

McDonald, C. (2007). '"This is who we are and this is what we do": social work education and self efficacy', *Australian Social Work* **60**(1): 83–93.

McDonald, C. and L. Chenoweth (2009). '(Re)Shaping social work: an Australian case study', *British Journal of Social Work* **39**(1): 144–60.

McDonald, C., J. Harris, et al. (2003). 'Contingent on context? Social work and the state in Australia, Britain, and the USA', *British Journal of Social Work* **33**(2): 191–208.

McDonald, C. and A. Jones (2000). 'Reconstructing and re-conceptualising social work in the emerging milieu', *Australian Social Work* **53**(3): 3–20.

McDonald, C. and D. Zetlin (2004). 'The promotion and disruption of community service delivery systems', *Australian Journal of Social Issues* **39**(3): 267–82.

McDougall, B. (2008). 'Teachers ignoring child abuse', *Herald Sun*, 2 June 2008, Retrieved 14 June 2008, from http://www.news.com.au/heraldsun/story/0,21985,23795022–662,00.html.

McGlone, F. and A. Stickley (2009). *Australian Torts Law*, 2nd edn. Sydney: LexisNexis Butterworths.

McIlwraith, J. and B. Madden (2006). *Health Care and the Law*, 4th edn. Sydney: Lawbook Co.

McInnes, A. and V. Lawson-Brown (2007). '"God" and other "Do-Gooders": A comparison of the regulation of services provided by general practitioners and social workers in England', *Journal of Social Work* 7(12): 341–54.

McIvor, C. (2006). 'The negligence liability of child welfare professionals and policy-based immunities: A critique of recent English developments', *Torts Law Journal* 14(2): 205–18.

McLaren, H. (2007). 'Exploring the ethics of forewarning: social workers, confidentiality and potential child abuse disclosures', *Ethics and Social Welfare* 1(1): 22–40.

McLaughlin, K. (2007). 'Regulation and risk in social work: the General Social Care Council and the Social Care Register in context', *British Journal of Social Work* 37(7): 1263–77.

McLay, G. (2004). 'Antipodean perspectives on child welfare tort claims against public authorities'. In: *Child Abuse Tort Claims against Public Authorities*. D. Fairgrieve and S. Green, eds. Aldershot and Burlington: Ashgate: 117–59.

McMahon, M. (1992). 'Dangerousness, confidentiality and the duty to report', *Australian Psychologist* 27(1): 12–16.

McMahon, M. (1997). 'Criminalising professional misconduct: legislative regulation of psychotherapist-patient sex', *Psychiatry, Psychology and Law* 4(2): 177–93.

McMahon, M. (1998). 'Confidentiality and disclosure of crime related information', *Psych Bulletin* (February): 12–13.

McMahon, M. (2006a). 'Confidentiality, privacy and privilege: protecting and disclosing information about clients'. In: *Ethics and Professional Practice for Psychologists*. S. Morrissey and P. Reddy, eds. Melbourne: Thomson: 74–88.

McMahon, M. (2006b). 'Re-thinking confidentiality'. In: *Disputes and Dilemmas in Health Care*. I. Freckelton and K. Petersen, eds. Sydney: Federation Press: 563–603.

McMahon, M. (2008). 'Confidentiality, privacy and health information management'. In: *Allied Health Professionals and the Law*. R. Kennedy, ed. Sydney: Federation Press: 108–30.

McMillan, J. (2005). *Inquiry into the Circumstances of the Vivian Alvarez Matter*. Canberra: Commonwealth Ombudsman.

McSherry, B. (2001). 'Confidentiality of psychiatric and psychological communications: the public interest exception', *Psychiatry, Psychology and Law* 8(1): 12–22.

McSherry, B. (2006). 'The government's duty of care to provide adequate health care to immigraton detainees', *Journal of Law and Medicine* 13: 281–4.

McSherry, B. (2008). 'Mental health and human rights: The role of the law in developing a right to enjoy the highest attainable standard of mental health in Australia', *Journal of Law and Medicine* 15(5): 773–81.

McSherry, B. and L. Darvall (2008). 'Public Health and Human Rights', *Journal of Law and Medicine* 55(5): 6565–668.

REFERENCES

McSherry, B. and A. Dastyari (2007). 'Providing mental health services and psychiatric care to immigration detainees: what tort law requires', *Psychiatry, Psychology and Law* **14**(2): 260–71.

Meagher, G. and K. Healy (2005). *Who Cares? Volume 1: A Profile of Care Workers in Australia's Community Service Industries*. Sydney: Australian Council of Social Service.

Meagher, G. and K. Healy (2006). *Who Cares? Volume 2: Employment Structure and Incomes in the Australian Care Workforce*. Sydney: Australian Council of Social Service.

Mehr, J. and R. Kanwischer (2008). *Human Services: Concepts and Intervention Strategies*, 10th edn. Boston: Allyn and Bacon.

Melbourne University Law Review Association (2003). *Australian Guide to Legal Citation*, 2nd edn. Melbourne: Melbourne University Law Review Association.

Mellor, D., M. Manias, et al. (1994). 'Doing a good job badly: mind sets in family therapy', *Australian and New Zealand Journal of Family Therapy* **15**(1): 39–44.

Mendelson, D. (1993). '"Mr Cruel" and the medical duty of confidentiality', *Journal of Law and Medicine* **1**(2): 120–9.

Mendelson, D. (2004). 'Australian tort law reform: statutory principles of causation and the common law', *Journal of Law and Medicine* **11**: 492–509.

Mendelson, D. (2007). *The New Law of Torts*. Melbourne: Oxford University Press.

Mendes, P. (2001). 'Blaming the messenger: the media, social workers and child abuse', *Australian Social Work* **54**(2): 27–36.

Mendes, P. (2008). 'Public criticisms of social work', *AASW National Bulletin* **18**(2): 15–16.

Merritt, C. (2008). 'Canberra to pay Rau $2.6m compensation'. *Weekend Australian 8–9 March*: 12.

Merry, A. and A. McCall-Smith (2004). *Errors, Medicine and the Law*. Cambridge: Cambridge University Press.

Miley, K., M. O'Melia, et al. (2007). *Generalist Social Work Practice*, 5th edn. Needham Heights: Allyn and Bacon.

Milgram, S. (1965). 'Some conditions of obedience and disobedience to authority', *Human Relations* **18**(1): 57–76.

Miller, K. (2004). 'Working with clients on the telephone'. In: *Practice Skills in Social Work and Welfare: More than just common sense*. J. Maidment and R. Egan, eds. Sydney: Allen and Unwin: 257–72.

Milligan, I. and I. Stevens (2006). 'Balancing rights and risk: the impact of health and safety regulations on the lives of children in residential care', *Journal of Social Work* **6**(3): 239–54.

Milne, S. and K. Tucker (2008). *A Practical Guide to Legal Research*. Sydney: Lawbook Co.

Mole, N. (2002). 'A note on the judgement from the perspective of the European Convention for the Protection of Human Rights and Fundamental Freedoms 1950 – Re B; Re W (Care Plan) and Re S (Minors) (Care Order: Implementation of Care Plan)', *Child and Family Law Quarterly* **14**(4): 447–63.

Moulden, H., P. Firestone, et al. (2007). 'Child care providers who commit sexual offences', *International Journal of Offender Therapy and Comparative Criminology* **51**(4): 384–406.

Moxley, D. (1997). *Case Management by Design: Reflections on Principles and Practices*. Chicago: Nelson-Hall Publishers.

Mudaly, N. and C. Goddard (2006). *The Truth is Longer than a Lie*. London and Philadelphia: Jessica Kingsley Publishers.

REFERENCES 297

Mullighan, T. (2008). *Children in State Care Commission of Inquiry Report: Allegations of Sexual Abuse and Death from Criminal Conduct.* Adelaide: Government of South Australia.

Murray, H. and P. Swain (1999). 'Queries and complaints: the maintenance of ethically justifiable standards of conduct', *Australian Social Work* **52**(1): 9–16.

Murray, S., J. Malone, et al. (2008). 'Building a life story: providing records and support to former residents of children's homes', *Australian Social Work* **61**(3): 239–55.

Nagle, J. (1979). *Royal Commission into New South Wales Prisons.* Sydney: NSW Government Publishing Office.

Neukrug, E. (2007). *Theory, Practice and Trends in Human Services*, 4th edn. Pacific Grove: Thomson Brooks/Cole.

NSW Health (2008). *Unregistered Health Practitioners Code of Conduct: Impact Assessement Statement.* New South Wales Department of Health, *3 January 2008*, Retrieved 15 August 2008, from http://www.health.nsw.gov.au/pubs/2008/unreg_practise_impct.html.

NSW Ombudsman (2006). *DADHC: Monitoring Standards in Boarding Houses.* Sydney, NSW Ombudsman, Retrieved 12 December 2007, from http://www.ombo.nsw.gov.au/show.asp?id=426.

O'Brien-Malone, A. and M. Diamond (2006). 'Tell your clients you might hurt them: negligence, consent and contemporary psychological practice', *Australian Psychologist* **41**(3): 160–7.

O'Connor, I., P. Smyth, et al., eds. (2000a). *Contemporary Perspectives on Social Work and the Human Services: Challenges and Change.* Sydney: Longman.

O'Connor, I., P. Smyth, et al. (2000b). 'Introduction: the challenges of change'. In: *Contemporary Perspectives on Social Work and the Human Services: Challenges and Change.* I. O'Connor, P. Smyth and J. Warburton, eds. Sydney: Longman: 1–10.

O'Connor, P. (2001). 'History on trial: *Cubillo and Gunner v The Commonwealth of Australia*', *Alternative Law Journal* **26**(1): 27–31.

Office of Health Review (2000). 'Sterilisation of persons not competent to consent', Retrieved 26 February 2009, from http://www.healthreview.wa.gov.au/publications/docs/Formal%20report%20on%20sterilisation%20of%20persons%20not%20able%20to%20consent_42.doc.

Office of Health Review (2007). *Annual Report 2006–07.* Perth: Office of Health Review, Retrieved 20 November 2008, from http://www.healthreview.wa.gov.au/publications/index.cfm#1.

Office of the Federal Privacy Commissioner (1994). *Complaint Case Notes and Complaint Determinations: 1993–1994 Annual Report of the Privacy Commissioner.* Canberra: Office of the Federal Privacy Commissioner, Retrieved 6 December 2003, from http://www.privacy.gov.au/act/casenotes.

Office of the Federal Privacy Commissioner (1995). *Complaint Summaries 1994–1995: 1994–1995 Annual Report of the Privacy Commissioner.* Canberra: Office of the Federal Privacy Commissioner, Retrieved 24 August 2008, from http://www.privacy.gov.au/act/casenotes/cs1994.html.

Office of the Federal Privacy Commissioner (1996). *Complaint Summaries 1995–1996: 1995–1996 Annual Report of the Privacy Commissioner.* Canberra: Office of the Federal Privacy Commissioner, Retrieved 24 August 2008, from http://www.privacy.gov.au/act/casenotes/95–96_pcs.pdf.

Office of the Federal Privacy Commissioner (2008). *Guide to Handling Personal Information Security Breaches*. Canberra: Office of the Federal Privacy Commissioner, Retrieved 14 September 2008, from http://www.privacy.gov.au/news/media/2008_16.html.

Office of the Health Complaints Commissioner (2005). *Report of an Investigation into Ward 1E and Mental Health Services in Northern Tasmania*. Hobart: Office of the Health Complaints Commissioner.

Office of the Health Complaints Commissioner (2007). *700–0410028 – Disabiltiy Services – Allegations of Assautlt of Client by Residential Support Worker – Whether Actions Reasonable*. Hobart: Office of the Health Complaints Commissioner, Retrieved 15 December 2008, from http://www.healthcomplaints.tas.gov.au/_data/assets/pdf_file/0003/84234/March_2007_-_Disability_Services_-_allegations_of_assault_of_133.pdf#March%202007%20-%20Disability%20Services%20-%20allegations%20of%20assault%20of%20client%20by%20residential%20support%20worker.

Olsson, T. and D. Chung (2004). *Report of the Board of Inquiry into the Handling of Claims of Sexual Abuse and Misconduct Within the Anglican Diocese of Adelaide*. Adelaide, Diocese of Adelaide.

Ombudsman Tasmania (2007). *Investigation of a Complaint Against Corrective Services: Final Investigation Report: Complaint 700–0511023*. Hobart: Ombudsman Tasmania, Retrieved 12 December 2007, from http://www.ombudsman.tas.gov.au/investigations.

Ombudsman Victoria (2007). *Investigation into the Use of Excessive Force at the Melbourne Custody Centre*. Melbourne: Ombudsman Victoria.

O'Neill, N., S. Rice, et al. (2004). *Retreat From Injustice: Human Rights Law in Australia*, 2nd edn. Sydney: Federation Press.

Orme, J. and G. Rennie (2006). 'The role of registration in ensuing ethical practice', *International Social Work* **49**(3): 334–44.

Overington, C. (2008). 'Child welfare is "not working": staff shortage', *Australian 12 November 2008*, Retrieved 13 November 2008, from http://www.theaustralian.news.com.au/story/0,25197,24639376–2702,00.html.

Palmer, M. (2005). *Inquiry into the Circumstances of the Immigration Detention of Cornelia Rau*. Canberra, Attorney General's Department.

Parton, N. (2001). 'Risk and professional judgement'. In: *The Law and Social Work: Contemporary Issues for Practice*. L.-A. Cull and J. Roche, eds. Houndmills and New York: Palgrave: 61–70.

Patti, R. (2003). 'Reflections on the state of management in social work', *Administration in Social Work* **27**(2): 1–11.

Pelling, N. and B. Sullivan (2006). 'The credentialing of counselling in Australia', *International Journal of Psychology* **41**(3): 194–203.

Pemberton, J., S. Mavin, et al. (2007). 'Scratching beneath the surface of communities of (mal)practice', *The Learning Organisation: The International Journal of Knowledge and Organisational Learning Management* **14**(1): 62–73.

Penglase, J. (2004). 'Forgotten Australians: the report of the Senate Inquiry into Children in Institutional Care', *Developing Practice: The Child Youth and Family Work Journal* **11**(Summer): 32–7.

Penovic, T. and A. Sifris (2006). 'Children's rights through the lens of immigration detention', *Australian Journal of Family Law* **20**(1): 12–44.

Peters, D. (2007). 'Centrelink staff snooped 367 times', *News.com.au 25 September 2007*, Retrieved 13 September 2008, from http://www.news.com.au/story/0,23599,22479436–2,00.html.

Phillips, J. (2007). *Care*. Cambridge: Polity Press.

Pithouse, A. (1998). *Social Work: The Social Organisation of an Invisible Trade*, 2nd edn, Aldershot: Ashgate.

Pollack, D. (2003). *Social Work and the Courts: A Casebook*, 2nd edn. New York and Hove: Routledge.

Pollack, D. and J. Marsh (2004). 'Social work misconduct may lead to liability', *Social Work* **49**(4): 609–12.

Pope, K. and J. Bouhoutsos (1986). *Sexual Intimacy Between Therapists and Patients*. New York, Wesport and London: Praeger.

Preston-Shoot, M. (2000). Clear voices for change: Messages from disability research for law, policy and practice. In: *Disability and the Law*. J. Cooper and S. Vernon, eds. London and Philadelphia: Jessica Kingsley Publishers: 267–95.

Preston-Shoot, M. (2001). 'Regulating the road of good intentions: observations on the relationship between policy, regulations and practice in social work', *Practice* **13**(4): 5–20.

Preston-Shoot, M., G. Roberts, et al. (2001). 'Values in social work law: strained relations or sustaining relationships?' *Journal of Social Welfare and Family law* **23**(1): 1–22.

Public Interest Advocacy Centre Limited (2008). 'Religious group's refusal of gay foster parents was unlawful', *CCH News Headlines 3 April 2008*, Retrieved 3 April 2008, from http://www.cch.com.au/au/News/ShowNews.aspx?ID=24543&Type=F&TopicIDNews=8&CategoryIDNews=0&u_i=21901.

Radey, M. (2008). 'Frontline welfare work: understanding social work's role', *Families in Society: The Journal of Contemporary Human Services* **89**(2): 184–92.

Raines, J. (1996). 'Self-disclosure in clinical social work', *Clinical Social Work Journal* **24**(4): 357–75.

Ranson, D. (2006). 'Ethical, professional and legal regulation of medical practice', *Journal of Law and Medicine* **14**(1): 20–23.

Raper, M. (2006). *Independent Social Security Handbook Online*. Sydney: National Welfare Rights Network.

Raynor, M. (2005). 'The lost children: child refugees'. In: *Violations of Trust: How Social and Welfare Institutions Fail Children and Young People*. J. Bessant, R. Hil and R. Watts, eds. Aldershot and Burlington, Ashgate: 117–32.

Reamer, F. (1992). 'The impaired social worker', *Social Work* **37**(2): 165–70.

Reamer, F. (1995). 'Malpractice claims against social workers: first facts', *Social Work* **40**(5): 595–601.

Reamer, F. (2000). 'The social work ethics audit: A risk management strategy', *Social Work* **45**(4).

Reamer, F. (2001). *Tangled Relationships: Managing Boundary Issues in the Human Services*. New York: Columbia University Press.

Reamer, F. (2003a). 'Boundary issues in social work: managing dual relationships', *Social Work* **48**(1): 121–33.

Reamer, F. (2003b). *Social Work Malpractice and Liability*, 2nd edn. New York: Columbia University Press.

REFERENCES

Reamer, F. (2005). 'Documentation in social work: evolving ethical and risk-managment standards', *Social Work* **50**(4): 325–34.

Reamer, F. (2006). 'Nontraditional and unorthodox intervention in social work: ethical and legal implications', *Families in Society: The Journal of Contemporary Human Services* **87**(2): 191–7.

Regehr, C., B. Marvin, et al. (2001). 'Liability for child welfare social workers', *Canadian Social Work* **3**(2): 57–67.

Richardson, S. and S. Asthana (2006). 'Inter-agency information sharing in health and social care services: the role of professional culture', *British Journal of Social Work* **36**(4): 657–69.

Ringstad, R. (2005). 'Conflict in the workplace: social workers as victims and perpetrators', *Social Work* **50**(4): 305–13.

Roberts, J. (2008). 'Judge lifts payout to $775,000', *The Weekend Australian 2–3 February*: 6.

Rogers, W. V. (1994). 'Tort law and child abuse: an interim view from England', *Tort Law Review* **3**: 257–74.

Rotheram-Borus, M. J. and N. Duan (2003). 'Next generation of preventive interventions', *Journal of American Academy of Child and Adolescent Psychiatry* **42**(5): 518–30.

Rothman, J. and J. S. Sager (1998). *Case Management: Integrating Individual and Community Practice*, 2nd edn. Boston: Allyn and Bacon.

Rozenberg, P. (2003). *Australian Guide to Uniform Legal Citation*, 2nd edn. Sydney: Lawbook Co.

Saltzman, A. and D. Furman (1999). *Law in Social Work Practice*, 2nd edn. Belmont: Wadsworth.

Sampford, C. and S. C. Blencowe (2002). 'Raising the standards: an integrated approach to promoting professional values and avoiding professional criminality'. In: *Crime in the Professions*. R. Smith, ed. Aldershot: Ashgate: 251–67.

Sarre, R. and J. Richards (2005). 'Responding to culpable corporate behaviour: current developments in the industrial manslaughter debate', *Flinders Journal of Law Reform* **8**(1): 93–111.

Schön, D. (1991). (First published 1983) *The Reflective Practitioner; How Professionals Think in Action*. Aldershot: Avebury.

Schorr, A. (2000). 'Comment on policy: the bleak prospect for public child welfare', *Social Service Review* **74**(1): 124–36.

Schwehr, B. (2001). 'Human rights and social services'. In: *The Law and Social Work: Contemporary Issues for Practice*. L.-A. Cull and J. Roche, eds. Houndmills and New York: Palgrave: 73–80.

Scott, R. (2006). '*Hunter Area Health Service v Presland*: liability of mental health services for failing to admit or detain a patient with mental illness', *Psychiatry, Psychology and Law* **13**(1): 49–59.

Scull, A. (1984). *Decarceration: Community Treatment and the Deviant*, 2nd edn. Cambridge: Polity Press.

Senate Standing Committee on Community Affairs (2004). *Forgotten Australians: A Report on Australians who Experienced Institutional or Out-of-Home Care as Children*. Canberra: Parliament of Australia.

Senate Standing Committee on Community Affairs (2005). *Protecting Vulnerable Children*. Canberra, Parliament of Australia.

Seymour, C. and R. Seymour (2007). *Courtroom Skills for Social Workers*. Exeter: Learning-Matters.

Sharpe, R. (1989). *The Law of Habeas Corpus*, 2nd edn. Oxford: Clarendon Press.

Sheafor, B. and C. Horejsi (2007). *Techniques and Guidelines for Social Work Practice*, 8th edn. Boston and New York: Pearson Education.

Slatter, M., J. Adkins, et al. (2005). 'A glimpse of the invisible: sex discrimination in housing', *Alternative Law Review* **30**(1): 15–18, 46.

Sleep, L., K. Tranter, et al. (2006). 'Cohabitation rule in social security law: the more things change the more they stay the same', *Australian Journal of Administrative Law* **13**: 135–46.

Sloan, L., T. Edmond, et al. (1998). 'Social workers' knowledge of and experience with sexual exploitation by psychotherapists', *Social Work* **43**(1): 43–53.

Smith, B. (2008). 'Child welfare service plan compliance: perceptions of parents and case workers', *Families in Society: The Journal of Contemporary Human Services* **89**(4): 521–32.

Smith, R., ed. (2002). *Crime in the Professions*. Aldershot: Ashgate.

Sousa, L. and C. Eusebio (2007). 'When multi-problem poor individuals' myths meet social service myths', *Journal of Social Work* **7**(2): 217–37.

South Australian Coroner (2009). *Finding of Inquest: Ricky Glen Cox. 18 March 2009*, Retrieved 7 April 2009, from http://www.courts.sa.gov.au/courts/coroner/index.html.

South Australian Office of the Director of Public Prosecutions (n.d.). *Prosecution Policy*, Retrieved 24 December 2008, from http://www.dpp.sa.gov.au/03/prosecution_policy_guidelines.pdf.

Spall, P. and D. Zetland (2004). 'Third sector in transition – a question of sustainability for community service organisations and the sector?' *Australian Journal of Social Issues* **39**(3): 283–98.

Specht, H. (1985). 'Managing professional interpersonal interactions', *Social Work* **30**(3): 225–30.

Spigelman, J. (2006). 'Tort law reform: an overview', *Tort Law Review* **14**(1): 5–15.

Staller, K. and S. Kirk (1998). 'Knowledge utilization in social work and legal practice', *Journal of Sociology and Social Welfare* **XXV**(3): 91–113.

Stanley, N. (1999). 'The institutional abuse of children'. In: *Institutional Abuse: Perspectives Across the Life Course*. N. Stanley, J. Manthorpe and B. Penhale, eds. London and New York: Routledge: 16–43.

Stanley, N., J. Manthorpe, et al., eds. (1999). *Institutional Abuse: Perspectives Across the Life Course*. London and New York: Routledge.

Steib, S. and W. W. Blom (2004). 'Fatal error: the missing ingredient in child welfare reform: Part 2', *Child Welfare* **83**(1): 101–4.

Stein, M. (2006). 'Missing years of abuse in children's homes', *Child and Family Social Work* **11**: 11–21.

Stevens, B. (2007). *Crossfire: How to Survive Giving Evidence as a Psychologist*. Brisbane: Australian Academic Press.

Stewart, C. (2008). 'Allied health professions, professionalism, ethics and law'. In: *Allied Health Professionals and the Law*. R. Kennedy, ed. Sydney: Federation Press.

Stoesz, D. (2002). 'From social work to human services', *Journal of Sociology and Social Welfare* **XX1X**(4): 19–37.

Strang, H. (2001). *Restorative Justice Programs in Australia: A Report to the Criminology Research Council*. Canberra: Australian Institute of Criminology.

Strom-Gottfried, K. (2003). 'Understanding adjudication: origins, targets, and outcomes of ethics complaints', *Social Work* **48**(1): 85–90.

Stuhmcke, A. (2005). *Essential Tort Law*, 3rd edn. Sydney and London: Cavendish Australia.

Stuhmcke, A. and A. Tran (2007). 'The Commonwealth Ombudsman: an integrity branch of government', *Alternative Law Journal* **32**(4): 233–6.

Summers, N. (2009). *Fundamentals of Case Management Practice: Skills for the Human Services*, 3rd edn. Pacific Grove: Brooks/Cole.

Swain, P. (1996). 'Social workers and professional competence – a last goodbye to the Clapham omnibus?' *Torts Law Journal* **4**(1): 42–59.

Swain, P. (1998). 'What is "belief on reasonable grounds"?' *Alternative Law Journal* **23**(5): 230–3.

Swain, P. (2001). 'Business under new management: lessons from Canada on regulation of the social work profession', *Australian Social Work* **54**(2): 55–67.

Swain, P. (2002a). 'Confidentiality, record keeping and social work practice'. In: *In the Shadow of the Law: the Legal Context of Social Work Practice*. P. Swain, ed. Sydney: Federation Press: 28–49.

Swain, P., ed. (2002b). *In the Shadow of the Law: The Legal Context of Social Work Practice*. Sydney: Federation Press.

Swain, P. (2005). '"No expert should cavil at any questioning": reports and assessments for courts and tribunals', *Australian Social Work* **58**(1): 44–57.

Swain, P. (2006). 'A camel's nose under the tent? Some Australian perspectives on confidentiality and social work practice', *British Journal of Social Work* **36**(1): 91–107.

Swain, P. and M. Roberts (2003). 'Care, responsibility and cumulative error – coronial review of deaths of children under State care in Victoria', *Australian Journal of Family Law* **17**: 62–75.

Swain, S. (2008). 'Writing social work history', *Australian Social Work* **61**(3): 193–6.

Sydney Morning Herald (2008). 'Tasmania pays $5m to stolen generations', *Sydney Morning Herald*, 23 January 2008, Retrieved 9 March 2008, from http://www.smh.com.au/news/national/tasmania-pays-5m-to-stolen-generations/2008/01/22/1200764264522.html.

Symons, M. (2002). 'Privacy Act legislation: I've read the theory, now what about the practice?' *InPsych* (February): 10–11.

Tasmania Law Reform Institute (2007). *A Charter of Rights for Tasmania*. Hobart: Tasmania Law Reform Institute.

Terry, K. and A. Ackerman (2008). 'Child sexual abuse in the Catholic Church: how situational crime prevention strategies can help create safe environments', *Criminal Justice and Behavior* **35**(5): 643–57.

Terry, N. (2008). 'Electronic health records: international, structural and legal perspectives', *Journal of Law and Medicine* **12**(1): 26–39.

Thackrah, A. (2008). 'From neutral to drive: Australian anti-discrimination law and identity', *Alternative Law Journal* **33**(1): 31–35.

Tilbury, C. (2006). 'Accountabiltiy via performance management: the case of child protection services', *Australian Journal of Public Administration* **65**(3): 48–61.

Titterton, M. (1999). 'Training professionals in risk assessment and risk management: What does the research tell us?' In: *Risk Assessment in Social Care and Social Work*. P. Parsloe, ed. London and Philadelphia: Jessica Kingsley Publishers: 217–47.

Titterton, M. (2005). *Risk and Risk Taking in Health and Social Care*. London and Philadelphia: Jessica Kingsley Publishers.

Tobin, R. (1999). 'Public authorities and negligent investigations into child abuse: the New Zealand and the English approaches', *Tort Law Review* **7**(3): 232–43.

Todd, S. (1992). 'Tort actions by prisoners against their custodians', *New Zealand Recent Law Review*: 93–109.

Todd, S. (2004). 'Tort actions by victims of sexual abuse', *Tort Law Review* **12**: 40–50.

Tranter, K., L. Sleep, et al. (2007). 'After *Pelka*: marriage-like relationships under social security law', *Alternative Law Journal* **32**(4): 208–12.

Trindade, F., P. Cane, et al. (2007). *The Law of Torts in Australia*, 4th edn. Melbourne: Oxford University Press.

VanSlyke, D. (2003). 'The mythology of privatization in contracting for social services', *Public Administration Review* **63**(3): 277–96.

VanSlyke, D. (2007). 'Agents or stewards; using theory to understand the government-nonprofit social service contracting relationship', *Journal of Public Administration Research and Theory* **17**(2): 157–87.

Vaughan, G. (2006). *Information Relating to the Community Services Workforce: Working Paper*. Canberra: Australian Institute of Health and Welfare.

Vigod, S., C. Bell, et al. (2003). 'Privacy of patients' information in hospital lifts: an observational study', *British Medical Journal* **327**(1st November): 1024–5.

Vogelsang, J. (2001). *The Witness Stand – A Guide for Clinical Social Workers in the Courtroom*. New York: Haworth Social Work Practice Press.

Vrachnas, J., K. Boyd, et al., Eds. (2005). *Migration and Refugee Law: Principles and Practice in Australia*. Melbourne: Cambridge University Press.

Walker, J. (2008). 'Trial and error' *Australian, 11 September 2008*, Retrieved 2 October 2008, from http://www.theaustralian.news.com.au/story/0,25197,24325582–28737,00.html.

Walmsley, S., A. Abadee, et al., Eds. (2007). *Professional Liability in Australia*. Sydney: Thomson Lawbook Co.

Wangmann, J. (2004). 'Liability for institutional child sexual assault: where does *Lepore* leave Australia?' *Melbourne University Law Review* **5**: 1–35.

Wearing, M. (1998). *Working in Community Services: Management and Practice*. St Leonards: Allen & Unwin.

Webb, S. (2006). *Social Work in a Risk Society: Social and Political Perspectives*. Houndmills and New York: Palgrave Macmillan.

Weinberg, K., K. Stewart, et al. (2003). 'What do case managers do? A study of working practice in older people's services', *British Journal of Social Work* **33**(7): 901–19.

Weir, M. (2008). 'Intervention methods and processes'. In: *Allied Health Professionals and the Law*. R. Kennedy, ed. Sydney: Federation Press: 131–53.

Welbourne, P., G. Harrison, et al. (2007). 'Social work in the UK and the global labour market: recruitment, practice and ethical considerations', *International Social Work* **50**(1): 27–41.

Werren, J. (2007). 'Civil litigation and repressed memory syndrome: how does forgetting impact on child sexual abuse?' *Tort Law Review* **15**: 43–62.

White, J., A. Day, et al. (2007). *Writing Reports for Court*. Brisbane: Australian Academic Press.

White, M. and K. Terry (2008). 'Child sexual abuse in the Catholic Church', *Criminal Justice and Behavior* **35**(5): 658–78.

REFERENCES

Whittaker, J. and A. Maluccio (2002). 'Rethinking "child placement": a reflective essay', *Social Service Review* **76**(1): 108–34.

Wild, R. and P. Anderson (2007). *Ampe Akelyernemane Meke Mekarle/Little Children are Sacred: Report of the Northern Territory Board of Inquiry into the Protection of Aboriginal Children from Sexual Abuse.* Darwin: Northern Territory Government.

Williams, J. (2004). 'Social work, liberty and law', *British Journal of Social Work* **34**(1): 37–52.

Williams, J. and F. Keating (1999). 'The abuse of adults in mental health settings'. In: *Institutional Abuse: Perspectives Across the Life Course.* N. Stanley, J. Manthorpe and B. Penhale, eds. London and New York: Routledge: 130–51.

Williams, J. and J. Nash (2001). 'Meeting the advocacy needs of people who have been abused by health and social care practitoners', *Journal of Community and Applied Social Psychology* **11**: 361–70.

Williams, K. (2004). 'Revising liability for child abuse in Britain', *Tort Law Review* **12**: 63–70.

Wilson, B. (2002). 'Health providers, complaints and unprofessional behaviour in a changing environment'. In: *Crime in the Professions.* R. Smith, ed. Aldershot: Ashgate: 123–38.

Wilson, B. (2008). 'Legal risks of unprofessional behaviour'. In: *Allied Health Professionals and the Law.* R. Kennedy, ed. Sydney: Federation Press: 157–75.

Wilson, J. and W. H. Chui (2006). 'Looking for the "best" in practice: An introduction'. In: *Social Work and Human Services Best Practice.* Sydney: Federation Press: 1–12.

Wilson, R. (1997). *Bringing them Home-National Enquiry into the Separation of Aboriginal and Torres Strait Islander Children from their Families.* Sydney: Human Rights and Equal Opportunity Commission.

Wood, J. (2008). *Report of the Special Commission of Inquiry into Child Protection Services in NSW.* Sydney: NSW Government.

Woodside, M. and T. McClam (2006). *An Introduction to Human Services*, 5th edn. Belmont: Thomson Brooks/Cole.

Zins, C. (2001). 'Defining human services', *Journal of Sociology and Social Welfare* **XXV111**(1): 3–21.

Index

A Practitioner v The Medical Board of Western Australia [2005] WASC 198 82
A v Private School [2008] PrivCmrA 1 228
AASW *see* Australian Association of Social Workers
abandonment concept 206
ABC Developmental Learning Centres Pty Ltd v Wallace [2006] VSC 171 52
Aboriginal people
  Australian Inquiry into the Separation of Aboriginal and Torres Strait Islander Children from Their Families 38
  Power v Aboriginal Hostels Limited [2004] FMCA 452 60
Aboriginal reconciliation 11
absolute privilege 132
abuse
  child abuse 70–1, 102–3
  high-profile cases 87–8, 168–9
  sanctioned abuse and re-abuse 53
  sexual abuse 38, 101, 109
  of vulnerable groups 3–4
access (information) 222–9
  authorised access denied 227–9
  browsing 226–7
  private rights and access to law 12–13
  unauthorised disclosure or access 222–6
accountability
  accountability systems in the human services 36
  human service accountability 15–16
accreditation
  of human service workers 83
  standards for 70
Administrative Appeals Tribunal 77
administrative law 75–81
  decision-making principles 76

administrative review 77
  barriers 80–1
  disputed decisions 80
  existence and causes of administrative error 80
  mechanisms 77–8
  tribunals 77–8
advocacy groups 261–2
AG v Prince and Gardner [1998] 1 NZLR 262 179
Aged Care Accreditation and Standards Agency 70
Aged Care Act 1997 (Cth) 40, 56, 70
aged-care facilities
  aged care scenario 250–1
  formal reports of failures 4
  and negligent advice or information 122
AHRC *see* Australian Human Rights Commission
allegations 76
alternative care systems 6
Alvarez inquiry 87, 165, 168–9, 214, 216–17, 232
anonymity 210
Anti-Discrimination Act 1977 (NSW) 62
Anti-Discrimination Act 1991 (Qld) 61, 62–3, 195
appraisal 165–6
  see also screening
Archbishop of Perth v 'AA' to 'JC' inclusive; 'DJ' and others v Trustees of the Christian Brothers and others (1995) 18 ACSR 333 102
assault 127, 169–73
assessment
  diagnosis, protection and reporting 178–80
  flaws 179–80
  liability considerations 178–80
  and negative stereotypes 194–5

305

INDEX

assessment (*cont.*)
  reassessment 180
  risk assessment tools 13–14
  service delivery assessment 174–8
  status determination 176–8
  unsatisfactory assessment activity 175–6
Attorney-General 153
Australian Association of Social Workers
  (AASW) 10, 24, 157, 177
  accreditation of human service workers 83
  mechanisms for managing code of ethics
    violations 157–8
  membership 158
  regulation of social work title 81
*Australian Competition and Consumer
  Commission v Rana* [2008] FCA 63
Australian Department of Immigration and
  Citizenship 77
Australian Government Department of
  Veterans' Affairs 77
Australian Human Rights Commission
  (AHRC) 144–5, 196
Australian Inquiry into the Separation of
  Aboriginal and Torres Strait Islander
  Children from Their Families 38
Australian Institute of Welfare and Community
  Workers (AIWCW) 24, 157
Australian Law Reform Commission 65, 126
Australian Public Service Code of Conduct 66,
  226, 231
Australian Services Union (ASU) 698
*Australian Services Union of NSW v St Vincent
  De Paul Society* [2007] NSWIRComm
  1044 239
Australian Social Work [journal] 6–7

B v Australian Government Agency [2006]
  PrivCmr 2 221
B v Surgeon [2007] PrivCmrA 2 228
'bad apple' imagery 28–9, 160, 259, 261
Barrett v Enfield London Borough Council [2001]
  2 AC 550 106, 203
Batchelor v State of Tasmania [2005]
  TASCC 11 93–4, 170–1
battery 127
*Behrooz v Secretary, Department of Immigration
  and Multicultural and Indigenous Affairs*
  (2004) 208 ALR 271 111
Bennet v Minister of Community Welfare (1993)
  176 CLR 408 121, 134
*Bhagwanini v Registrar of the Occupational
  Therapist Registration Board of South
  Australia* [2003] SASC 34 82
*Bock v Launceston Women's Shelter and Anti
  Discrimination Tribunal* [2005] TASSC
  23 201, 242
boundaries (interventions) 197–202

boundary violations 199
controversy regarding role and boundary
  conduct 197–8
dismissal for boundary violations 201
four-quadrant taxonomy of
  behaviours 198–9, 202
liability considerations 202
themes in dual role and boundary issues 199
breach
  breach of duty 115–19
  of confidence 42, 123, 135, 137, 171
  of fiduciary duty 134–5
  privacy breaches and browsing 226
  and public authorities 115–16
  relationship between the act, the intention
    and the breach 42–6
  statutory breaches 73–5
  of statutory duty 92, 106, 132–3
  unintended breaches 29
Bringing Them Home report 151
browsing 226–7
'but for' test (of causation) 119

C v Australian Government Agency [2007]
  PrivCmrA 3 218
C v Commonwealth Agency [2003] PrivCmrA 1
  225–6, 243
C v Health Service Provider [2008] PrivCmrA
  3 231–2
Care Leavers Australia Network (CLAN) 261
care plans 181, 203
  mandated planning 182–3
case management 24, 188
Cassidy v Department of Corrective Services
  [2007] QIRComm 15 66, 239
causation and damage 119–24
  'but for' test of causation 119
  as civil suit hurdles 120–1
CCC *see* Corruption and Crime Commission
Centrelink 146
certiorari writs 78
*Chan v Minister for Immigration and Ethnic
  Affairs* (1989) 169 CLR 379 133
*Chan Yee Kin and the Minister for Immigration,
  Local Government and Ethnic Affairs and the
  Commonwealth of Australia* (1991) 103
  ALR 499 130–1, 133
*Charter of Human Rights and Responsibilities Act
  2006* (Vic) 19, 146–7
child abuse 70–1
  child abuse claimants' lack of faith in the legal
    system 102–3
  CMC inquiries into child abuse 154–5
  and statutes of limitations 102
child care failures 4
Child Protection Act 1999 (QLD) 51, 71, 182,
  183

Child Protection (Offender Reporting) Act 2004
 (Qld) 54
Child Protection (Offenders Registration) Act 2000
 (NSW) 54
child protection systems 10, 36, 98
 British child migrant cases and statutes of
  limitations 101
 child protection as source of private law
  cases 88
 child protection legislation 68–9
 child protection registers 54–5
 coronial reports on child protection
  deaths 153
 criminal charges against social workers 50–1
 duty of care and child protection 105–10
 formal reports of failures 4
 and legal action 35
 statistics of predatory behaviour 37–8
Child Support Agency 146
Child Welfare Act 1939 (NSW) 107
Children and Community Services Act 2004
 (WA) 74
Children and Young People Act 1999 (ACT) 70
Children and Young People Commissioner 148
Children and Young Persons Act 1989 (Vic) 74
Children and Young Persons (Care and Protection)
 Act 1996 (Vic) 52
Children and Young Persons (Care and Protection)
 Act 1998 (NSW) 70, 72
Children, Youth and Families Act 2005 (Vic) 70,
 71, 193–4
Children's Protection Act 1993 (SA) 75
Children's Services Act 1996 (Vic) 52
citizenship 77
civil law
 civil liability legislation 90–1, 92–3, 116–17
 civil suits 34, 45, 87–90, 170–1
 individual or advocacy civil cases 98
 as mechanism for dealing with human
  traumas 97–8
 plaintiff obstacles 100–1
 private negotiations in civil law 87–8
 reasons for not undertaking civil legal
  action 98–9
 and the screening process 166
 types of civil law action 89
civil liability 45, 173–4
Civil Liability Act 2002 (NSW) 94–5, 116–17,
 173
claims-makers and counter
 claims-makers 259–60
CLAN *see* Care Leavers Australia Network
clients 172, 182–3
 client actions under discrimination,
  vilification and harassment
  legislation 61–2
 client suicide 169–73

collateral interactions 235
disinclination to report crime 56–7
experiences of failure 26
involuntary clients 193, 194
monitoring 202–5
as potential litigants 99
relationships between workers and
 clients 236–8
service inclusion and exclusion 166–9
and sexual impropriety claims 38–9
clinical private practice 188–9
CMC *see* Crime and Misconduct Commission
codes of conduct 27, 83–4
codes of ethics 190, 194, 208, 209
 ethics self-examinations 202
 unethical behaviour 198
coercion 191
cohabitation rule 72–3
collateral exposure 140–1
collateral interactions 235
collegial relationships 235
Commission for Children and Young People Act
 1998 (NSW) 55
Commission for Children and Young People and
 Child Guardian Act 2000 (Qld) 55
commissions 150–6
Commonwealth Privacy Act 65
community services 23
 Australian Institute of Welfare and
  Community Workers 24
 complaints 40–6
 complaints regarding communication
  problems 236
 Department of Youth and Community
  Services (DOCS) 107, 108
compensation schemes 103
complaints 40–6
 complaints regarding communication
  problems 236
 interventions giving rise to
  complaints 204–5
 regarding browsing 226–7
 standing complaints 143–50
 treatment complaints 40
complaints commissions 147–50
confidence (breach of) 135–7
 defences to 135
confidentiality 39, 40, 42, 123, 135, 171,
 208–9, 210
 and data management 210
 duties concerning security, confidentiality and
  rights 69–70
 privacy compliance 64–5
 prohibitions against information
  disclosure 71
 see also confidence (breach of); privacy
conflict 197–202, 238

308 | INDEX

consent 190–4, 220, 230
  central place of consent in law 190–1
  coercion and undue influence 191
  comprehensive information regarding 192
  exceptions to the need for informed consent 193
  indicia for consent 191–3
  informed consent 150, 190–4
  liability considerations 193–4
  and mental capacity 192–3
  specificity of 191–2
  valid form 192
consumer protection legislation 63
contract law 137–9
  providing consideration 138, 139
Convention on the Elimination of All Forms of Discrimination against Women 18
Convention on the Protection and Promotion of the Rights and Dignity of Persons with Disabilities 18
Convention on the Rights of the Child (CRC) 18
Cornwall and Ors v Rowan [2004] SASC 383 129–30, 131, 132, 141–2, 233, 244, 245
Coroners Act 2008 666
coroners' courts 151–4
  coronial reports 152–4
  powers 152
  reporting to the Attorney-General 153
  and scrutiny of service rejection 167–8
Corporations Act 2001 (Cth) 51
correctional services 69
  brutalising of prisoners 4
  corrections as source of private law cases 88
  duties concerning security, confidentiality and rights of prisoners 69–70
  duty of care 110–11
  grants and exercise of powers 72
  Perera v Commissioner of Corrective Services [2007] NSWADT 115 62
  prisoner safety standards 118
  prohibited conduct 71–2
  and secondary victims 110
  suicides in jail and immigration detention 170
  unlawful detention 128–9
Correctional Services Act 1982 (SA) 204
Corrections Management Act 2006 (Qld) 69
Corrections Management Act 2007 (ACT) 73, 74
Corrective Services Act 2000 (Qld) 66
Corrective Services Act 2006 (ACT) 72, 74
Corruption and Crime Commission (CCC) 155, 156

courts 150–6
  coroners' courts 151–4
  court work 141–3
Cowell v Corrective Services Commission of New South Wales (1998) 13 NSWLR 714 128
CRC *see* Convention on the Rights of the Child
Creating Opportunities for Children and Young People in Care (CREATE) 261
Crewdson v Director General of Community Services [2008] NSW ADT 279 242
Crime and Misconduct Commission (CMC) 154–5
crime commissions 154–6
Crimes (Administration of Sentences) Regulation 2001 (NSW) 73, 182, 183
Crimes Act 1900 (NSW) 50
Crimes Act 1958 (Vic) 50
Crimes Act 1961 (NZ) 54
Criminal Code Act (1995) (Cth) 51, 52–3, 61
Criminal Code (WA) 51–4
criminal law 45, 49–59
  activities of investigating bodies 56, 57–8
  avoiding publicity 58–9
  'beyond reasonable doubt' 56
  boundary violations 199
  credible witnesses 57
  'culture of silence and fraternity' 59
  impact of criminal cases on workers 54–6
  mounting a defence 54
  prosecution guidelines 58
  provisions for human service workers 49
  risks of criminal charges 56–9
  sexual offences 49–50
  unprofessional conduct 52
  workplace death 60
Criminal Law Consolidation Act 1935 (SA) 49, 51, 237
criminal negligence 49
crisis circumstances 169–73
Cubillo v Commonwealth (2000) 103 FCR 1, [2001] FCA 1213 113, 134, 191–2
culpability 53–4, 56–7
  disculpability 237
  under occupational health and safety legislation 60

D v East Berkshire Community NHS Trust [2004] 2 WLR; [2005] 2 AC 373 106, 107, 108, 109
D v Health Service Provider [2008] PrivCmrA 4 221
Dalton v Department for Families and Communities [2006] SAWCT 31 51
damages 100
data protection 210

Davidson v Queensland (2006) 226 CLR 234 102
DDP v Barnes [2007] VSCA 51 50
DDP v Scott [2004] VSC 129 50
decision making
  administrative law decision-making principles 76
  challenges to administrative decisions 77
  considerations 72–3
  decision-making bodies 31–2
defamation 131–2, 214, 245
  defences to 132
  information used in a way that damages another 232–3
  slander versus libel 131
defendants 100, 101
Department of Immigration and Citizenship 146
Department of Immigration and Multicultural and Indigenous Affairs (DIMIA) 217, 224
Department of Youth and Community Services (DOCS) 107, 108
  Johnson v DOCS (No 2) [1999] NSWSC 1156 113–14
  SB v New South Wales (2004) 13 VR 527 107–8, 117–18, 120–1, 141, 142, 183, 189
detention
  high-profile cases of abuse 87–8, 168–9
  immigration detention 89, 97–8, 100, 111–12, 118–19, 170
  unlawful detention 128–9
DIMIA *see* Department of Immigration and Multicultural and Indigenous Affairs
directness 125
Disability and Community Services Commissioner 148
disability care 36
  Convention on the Protection and Promotion of the Rights and Dignity of Persons with Disabilities 18
  disability complaints 42
  disability support scenario 251–2
  inhumane treatment of 4
Disability Discrimination Act 1992 (the DDA) (Cth) 60–1, 196, 205
disapproval 258–9
disciplinary actions and sanctions 156–61
  contested disciplinary actions 239
  employers and employees 158–61
  industrial action 160–1
  professional associations 156–8
  range of disciplinary actions 158–9
  unfair dismissal 159
disclosure (information) 222–9
  unauthorised disclosure or access 222–6

discrimination
  Anti-Discrimination Act 1991 (Qld) 61
  Convention on the Elimination of All Forms of Discrimination against Women 18
  Disability Discrimination Act 1992 (the DDA) (Cth) 60–1
  discrimination claims regarding relationship difficulties 242
  and diversity 195–6
  liability considerations 197
  Sex Discrimination Act 1984 (Cth) 18, 62
discrimination, vilification and harassment legislation 60–3, 144
  client discrimination complaints 61–2
  employees and volunteers discrimination complaints 62
  would-be service providers discrimination complaints 62–3
disculpability 237
dismissal
  for boundary violations 201
  dismissal triggers 159–60
  legal ramifications of dismissal 160–1
diversity 194–7
  and discrimination 195–6
  liability considerations 197
DOCS *see* Department of Youth and Community Services
Domestic and Family Violence Act 2007 70
domestic violence 177
dual roles (intervention) 197–202
  controversy regarding role and boundary conduct 197–8
  four-quadrant taxonomy of behaviours 198–9, 202
  liability considerations 202
  themes in dual role and boundary issues 199
due diligence 52
duties (declared under human service-specific Acts) 69–71
duty of care 92, 104–19
  breach of duty 115–19
  and child protection 105–10
  and corrections 110–11
  decision-making factors 105
  and immigration detention 111–12
  and Indigenous stolen children 112–15
  and public authority liability arguments 108
  scope 108–9
duty to warn or inform 122–4

education 30
EM v St Barbara's Parish School [2006] SAIRComm 1 75
emergency situations 172–3
Employees' Liability Act 1991 (NSW) 96

INDEX

employment
  impact of criminal cases on worker
    employment 54–6
  police checks 55
equitable declarations 78
ethics (codes) 190, 194, 198, 202
European Court of Human Rights 106
evidence 152
Evidence Act 1929 (SA) 136
exercise of powers 72
expert witnesses 142–3

F v Australian Government Agency [2008]
    PrivCmrA 6 227, 243
failure (human services)
  abuse, neglect and maltreatment 4
  clients' experiences 12–13, 26
  control of the mishaps and misdeeds
    agenda 12
  effect of law cases on 15
  failure to adequately monitor clients
    203
  formal reports of failures 4
  improving service quality 12–13, 26–7
  international literature – social work
    malpractice and legal liability 7–8
  law's response to mishaps and
    misdeeds 14–16
  levels of responsibility for mishaps and
    misdeeds 28–37
  limited human services commentary of
    failure 7
  mechanisms dealing with failure within 8–9
  responsibility for shortcomings within the
    human services 9–10, 12
false imprisonment 127–9
Family Court Act 1975 (Cth) 71
family law 89
Family Law Act 1975 (Cth) 70, 73, 83
Federal Privacy Commissioner 64
fiduciary duty 134–5
*Fiona Hall v Department of Justice Victoria
    (Correctional Services Division)* [1994]
    IRCA 136 201
follow up (of service) 205–7
foreseeability of harm 105, 120
four-quadrant taxonomy of behaviours 198–9,
    202
fraud 138
Fyfe v South Australia [2007] SASC 272 204–5

Gay v Department of Corrective Services [2005]
    NSWIRComm 1212 73–4
Goldie v Commonwealth of Australia (No 2)
    [2004] FCA 156 128
Graham Barclay Oysters Pty Ltd v Ryan [2002]
    HCA 54 92, 105

grants 72
Guardianship and Administration Act 1990
    (WA) 150

H v Commonwealth Agency [2005] PrivCmrA
    5 227, 243
habeas corpus writ 78, 79
Harvey v PD [2004] NSWCA 97 229
Health and Community Services Complaints
    Commission (NT) 148
Health and Community Services Complaints
    (SA) 148
Health Care Complaints Act 1993 (NSW) 84,
    149
Health Care Complaints Commission 148,
    189
Health Care Complaints Commission v Moore
    [2008] NSWPST 2 82
Health Complaints Commissioner 148, 149
Health Quality and Complaints
    Commission 148
Health Records and Information Privacy Act 2002
    (NSW) 64
health services
  complaints 40–6, 82
  complaints regarding communication
    problems 236
  *Health Records and Information Privacy Act
    2002* (NSW) 64
  M v Health Service Provider [2006] PrivCmA
    12 65
  meaning of health services under the Privacy
    Act s 6 64
  overlap with human services 23
Health Services Act 1988 (Vic) 71
Health Services Commissioner (ACT) 148
Health Services Commissioner (Vic) 148, 150
Hensell v Centrelink [2006] FCA 1844 66–7,
    237
Herald and Weekly Times LTD v Hassard
    (unreported, VSC, Beach J 8 December 20
    January 1998) 74–5
High Court 121
  Davidson v Queensland (2006) 226 CLR
    234 102
  Graham Barclay Oysters Pty Ltd v Ryan [2002]
    HCA 54 92
  and the *Migration Act 1958* (Cth) 176
  *New South Wales v Lepore; Samin v
    Queensland: Rich v Queensland* (2003)
    77ALJR 558 96, 97
  Sullivan v Moody [2001] HCA 59 105
Howard v Jarvis (1958) 98 CLR 177 110
*Howell v Psychologists Registration Board of
    Victoria* [2006] VCAT 1427 206–7
Human Rights Act 1998 (UK) 106, 183, 203
Human Rights Act 2004 (ACT) 19, 64

Human Rights and Discrimination
Commissioner 148
Human Rights and Equal Opportunity
Commission *see* Australian Human Rights
Commission (AHRC)
Human Rights Commission 148
human rights law 18–19
state and territory human rights
legislation 18–19
*Victorian Council for Civil Liberties and
Vadarlis v Minister for Immigration and
Multicultural Affairs* [2001] FCA
1297 79–80
human services
accountability systems in the human
services 36
accreditation of human service workers 83
and *Australian Social Work* [journal] 6–7
breach and level of worker experience 116
clinical training 202
conduct and legislative developments in New
South Wales 83–4
the consequences lottery 247–65
court work for human service workers 141–3
definitions 22–3
duties declared under human service-specific
Acts 69–71
function 5
generic human service workers 142
guides to action 27
heterogeneity of 10
human rights law and the human
services 18–19
human services behaviours giving rise to
private law action 88
and ideals 22–8
images of 3, 5, 12, 25, 28–9
international literature – social work
malpractice and legal liability 7–8
lack of research funds 8–9
limited human services commentary 7
major failures 4, 6
mechanisms dealing with failure within 8–9
mishaps and misdeeds in 37–46, 165–84,
185–207, 208–33, 234–46, 247–65
paradox of the human services 5
physical damage resulting from human service
activity 121
public image 5
reasons for apparent silence regarding
failure 8, 11
reasons for compromised human services
interventions 186–7
reasons for consideration of shadows 12–14
relationships 234–46
residential facilities 69
responsibility for shortcomings 9–10, 12

risk of private law suits in the human
services 97–103
scenarios – adverse human service events and
consequences 250–8
service delivery 165–84, 185–207
and society's ambivalence regarding function,
rights and status of the vulnerable and
marginalised 4–5
technical conversation deficit within 9
views of 9
workforce of 23, 25
see also social work; health services
Hunter Area Health Services v Presland (2005) 63
NSWLR 22 94, 257

ICAC *see* Independent Commission against
Corruption
ICCPR *see* International Covenant on Civil and
Political Rights
Idris, Hayat Adam [2004] MRTA 574 176–7,
216, 217
immigration
British child migrant cases and statutes of
limitations 101
care by/in immigration systems 4, 6
high-profile cases and detention 87–8, 89,
168–9
immigration as source of private law
cases 88, 97–8
immigration detention 100, 111–12,
118–19, 170
*Minister for Immigration and Multicultural
and Indigenous Affairs v B* (2004) 219 CLR
365 89
and negligent advice or information 122
suicides in jail and immigration
detention 170
immunity 50–1, 70, 93, 172
good faith statutory immunities 95
immunity clauses 93
police immunity 93
public law and immunity provisions 73
indemnity 90
Independent Commission against Corruption
(ICAC) 155, 156, 204
Indigenous people
Bringing Them Home report 151
compensation schemes following the
Apology 103
Indigenous families and human services
failure 6
Indigenous stolen children and duty of
care 112–15
*Minister for Immigration and Multicultural
and Indigenous Affairs v B* (2004) 219 CLR
365 89
treatment of Indigenous children 4

312 INDEX

individual responsibility (for
  mishaps/misdeeds) 28–37
industrial action 160–1
information and records management 208–33
  access to or disclosure of information 222–9
  accuracy of information 213–15, 220
  authorised access denied 227–9
  centrality of quality and purpose in
    recording 212
  critical purpose of 219–20
  data protection 210
  detail and precision 220
  difficulties specific to information
    collection 213
  electronic or paper records 208, 212
  information collection and
    amendment 213–16
  information mismanagement 209–10, 243
  information protocols 228–9, 230
  information storage 220–2
  liability considerations 219–20, 230
  misuse of information 230–3
  policies on information sharing 230
  records 216–19
  research regarding recording 212–13
information privacy and records management
    legislation 63–5
  prohibitions against information
    disclosure 71
  statutory duties of confidentiality 64–5
information privacy principles (IPP) 64, 215,
    217, 225–6
  and information collection 215–16
  and information storage 220–2
informed consent 150, 190–4
injunctions 78
injury 205
innominate actions 125–6
inquests 151–2, 154
inquiries 150–1, 156
*Inspector De Leon Stacey v the State of New South
    Wales (Department of Ageing, Disability and
    Home Care)* [2005] NSWIRComm
    131 205
*Inspector Keniry v the Crown in Right of the State
    of New South Wales (Department of
    Community Services)* [2002]
    NSWIRComm 349 205
*Inspector Lewis v The Crown in the Right of the
    State of New South Wales (Department of
    Juvenile Justice)* [2006] NSWIRComm
    8 60
institutional racism 194
insurance
  community concerns regarding increased
    costs 90
  insurance claims 38

intent 54
  mental intention (*mens rea*) 49
  relationship between the act, the intention
    and the breach 42–6
International Convention on the Rights of the
    Child 145
International Covenant on Civil and Political
    Rights (ICCPR) 18, 145
International Covenant on Economic, Social
    and Cultural Rights (ICESCR) 145
interpreters 196–7, 215–16
interventions
  accepted practice 188
  approaches, methods and techniques
    186–90
  consensus regarding intervention form 187
  giving rise to complaints 204–5
  and injuries 205
  liability considerations 189–90
  potential problems 185–207
  regulation of 81–6
  and risk 186
  shared or divergent expectations 181–2
  unorthodox techniques 187–8
investigatory bodies 143–50
  genesis of investigations and legal
    actions 258–63
  risk of complaints to 150
IPP *see* information privacy principles

J v Two Individuals [2003] PrivCmrA 8
    244
job titles 24–5, 81–6
Johnson v DOCS (No 2) [1999] NSWSC
    1156 113–14, 204
judicial review 77, 78–9, 93, 204–5, 217–18
juvenile justice 69

K v Domestic Violence Crisis Service Inc (ACT)
    [1998] HREOCA 2 167
K v Health Service Provider [2007] PrivCmrA
    13 227–8
K v Health Service Provider [2008] PrivCmrA
    11 226
K v Minister for Youth and Community Services
    [1982] 1 NSWLR 311 192–3
Kirkland-Veenstra v Stuart [2008] VSCA
    32 170–1
Klason v Australian Capital Territory [2003]
    ACTC 104 214–15, 217, 218, 233, 238

L (A Child) v Reading Borough Council [2001] 1
    WLR 1575 109, 110, 179
L v Commonwealth Agency [2003] PrivCmrA
    10 215
L v Commonwealth of Australia 1976 10 ALR
    269 110

INDEX **313**

L v Contractor to Australian Government Agency [2007] PrivCmrA 14 224–5
L v State of SA [2004] SADC 110 111
law
  administrative law 75–81
  central place of consent in law 190–1
  centrality of individual responsibility 30–1
  child abuse claimants' lack of faith in the legal system 102–3
  child protection legislation 50–1, 54, 55, 68–9
  civil law 97–9, 100–1, 166
  civil liability legislation 90–1, 92–3, 116–17
  consumer protection legislation 63
  contract law 137–9
  criminal law 45, 49–59
  discrimination, vilification and harassment legislation 60–3
  effect of law cases on human services shortcomings 15
  family law 89
  fear of legal action 15
  genesis of investigations and legal actions 258–63
  harm through inaction and harm through action 29
  human rights law and Australian law 18–19
  human rights law and the human services 18–19
  human service accountability 15–16
  and human service ideals and guides 27–8
  immunity 50–1, 70
  information privacy and records management legislation 63–5
  law of equity 134–7
  law of torts 126–33
  law's response to mishaps and misdeeds 14–16
  legal immunity for public authorities 34–5
  legal ramifications of dismissal 160–1
  legal scrutiny 140–1
  legislation limiting the role of judicial review 78–9
  legislative developments in New South Wales 83–4
  non-compliance with legislation 182
  'normal fortitude' rule 120
  occupational health and safety legislation 59–60
  private law 87–103, 104–24, 125–39
  private rights and access to law 35–6
  public law 49–67, 68–86
  public service legislation 65–7
  relationship between the act, the intention and the breach 42–6
  and a risk culture 14
  social security legislation 69

state and territory human rights legislation 18–19
  Tasmania Law Reform Institute 19
  torts law 90
law of equity 134–7
  breach of confidence 135–7
  breach of fiduciary duty 134–5
law of torts 126–33
  breach of statutory duty 132–3
  defamation 131–2
  misfeasance in a public office 129–31
  trespass to the person 126–9
Law Reform (Vicarious Liability) Act 1983 (NSW) 96
Layton Report 151
legislation *see* law
liability
  and assessment 178–80
  and boundaries 202
  civil liability 45, 92–3, 173–4, 247–65
  Civil Liability Act 2002 (NSW) 94–5, 116–17
  civil liability legislation 90–1, 116–17
  and consent 191–4
  criminal liability of human services organisations 51–4
  of decision-making bodies 31–2
  and discrimination 197
  Employees' Liability Act 1991 (NSW) 96
  and human services relationship 245–6
  and information management 219–20, 230
  international literature – social work malpractice and legal liability 7–8
  and intervention 189–90
  liability of public authorities 92–5, 110–11
  for non-compliance with legislation 182
  and service planning 183–4
  strict liability 45, 53, 127–9
  and suicide 173–4
  vicarious liability 31, 52, 53, 61, 95, 96–7, 129–30
Limitations of Actions Act 1974 (Qld) 102
litigation
  clients as potential litigants 99
  compensation schemes 103
  costs of litigation 99–100
  identification of defendants 100
  measures to avoid 207
Littler [2001] A Crim R 512 57–8

M v Australian Government Agency [2005] PrivCmrA 10 225, 243
M v Health Service Provider [2006] PrivCmA 12; [2007] PrivCmr 15 65, 216
M v Newham London Borough Council [1995] 2 AC 633 178–9, 214
malpractice 7–8, 11

INDEX

mandated planning (service) 182–3
Mangiafico v Department of Human Services
[2005] AIRC PR963416 240
marriage-like relationship test (social
security) 146, 177–8
McAlister v SEQ Aboriginal Corporation [2002]
FMCA 109 61–2
*Medical Board of South Australia v Christopoulos
(No 1)* [2000] SADC 47 75
Medical Practice Act 1992 (NSW) 222
Medical Practitioners Board of Victoria 85
mens rea 49
mental capacity (consent) 192–3, 194
mental harm
limited claims for 119–20
pure mental harm 119
Mental Health Act 1986 (Vic) 71, 170–1, 192
Mental Health Act 1990 (NSW) 94, 176
Mental Health and Related Services Act
(NT) 196
mental health systems 23, 36
and human services failure 4, 6
investigation into mental health services 149
mental health as source of private law
cases 88
mental health service scenario 253–4
and negligence 94
and suicide 170–1
migrants 4
Migration Act 1958 (Cth) 72, 73, 79–80, 83,
128, 133, 176
and domestic violence 177
*Minister for Immigration and Multicultural and
Indigenous Affairs v B* (2004) 219 CLR
365 89
misconduct commissions 154–6
misfeasance 44–5, 88, 114, 129–31
misuse of information 230–3
no use 232
use for other than primary purpose 231–2
use for personal purposes 230–1
used in a way that damages another 232–3
Moloney and Another v New Zealand and Another
(2006) 235 ALR 159 54, 57, 199
monitoring (clients) 202–3, 205
*Moskalev and Anor v NSW Department of
Housing* [2006]FMCA 876 195, 196
multi disciplinary team work 24

N v Australian Government Agency [2005]
PrivCmrA 12 233
Nada v Knight [1990] Aust Tort Reports
81–032 118
NASW *see* National Association of Social
Workers
National Association of Social Workers
(NASW) 38–9

National Privacy Principles (NPP) 64, 123–4,
137, 211–12, 213, 215
familiarity with 219
and information storage 220–2
and record deficiencies 217
unauthorised disclosure 224
National Welfare Rights Network
(NWRN) 261
negative licensing 83–4, 85
negative risk 13–14, 27
negative stereotypes 194–5
neglect 3–4
negligence
advantages of trespass claims over
negligence 126–7
causation and damage 119–24
criminal negligence 49
duty of care 104–19
duty to warn or inform 122–4
elements 104–24
and inappropriate relationship advice 122
negligent advice or information 122
New South Wales v Mannall [2005] NSWCA
367 241–2
Presland v Hunter Area Health Service [2003]
NSWSC 754 94
negotiations
management of 5
private negotiations in civil law 87–8
New South Wales Court of Appeal 113
New South Wales Crimes (Administration of
Sentences) Regulation 2001 71–2
New South Wales Health Care Complaints
Commission 84, 149
New South Wales v Bujdoso (2005) 222 ALR
663 110, 204
New South Wales v Fahy [2007] HCA 20 172–3
New South Wales v Godfrey [2004] NSWCA
113 110
*New South Wales v Lepore; Samin v Queensland:
Rich v Queensland* (2003) 77ALJR 558 96,
97
New South Wales v Mannall [2005] NSWCA
367 241–2
NGO human service organisations 25
non-compliance (with legislation) 182
nonfeasance 88
'normal fortitude' rule 120
Northern Territory Director of Native
Affairs 113
NPP *see* National Privacy Principles
NWRN *see* National Welfare Rights Network

O v Tenancy Database Company [2006]
PrivCmrA 14 215
Occupational Health and Safety Act 2000
(NSW) 60

INDEX

occupational health and safety
legislation 59–60, 82, 172–3
agency culpability 60
occupational health and safety cases 240–1
Occupational Therapists Act 1974 (SA) 82
Office of Health Review 148
Office of the Privacy Commissioner 65
O'Leary v Oolong Aboriginal Corporation Inc
[2004] NSWCA 7 241
ombudsmen 145–7
power of 145
and report on monitoring and licensing of
NSW boarding houses 147
reporting function 145–6
operating procedures 27
organisations 32–6
and civil suits 34
criminal acts of employers 53–4
criminal liability of human services
organisations 51–4
legal immunity for public authorities 34–5
organisational politics 244
policies, procedures and practices 36
position of workers relative to employing
organisation 54
unprofessional conduct 52
vicarious liability criminal suits against
organisations 35
O'Sullivan v the Queen [2002] NSWCCA
98 95–6

P v Private Health Service Provider [2008]
PrivCmrA 16 221–2
*PEH v Department of Justice (Occupational and
Business Regulation)* [2007] VCAT 470 55
Perera v Commissioner of Corrective Services
[2007] NSWADT 115 62
physical assault 169–73
Pickering v McArthur [2005] QCA 294 122
planning (service) 180–3
*Plymouth City Council v Her Majesty's Coroner
for the Count of Devon* [2005] EWCH
1014 (Admin) 154
police checks 55
positive risk 14
positivist research evidence 187
Power v Aboriginal Hostels Limited [2004]
FMCA 452 60, 242–3
predatory behaviour 34, 37–8
Presland v Hunter Area Health Service [2003]
NSWSC 754 94, 171–2, 176, 206, 217
Prisons Act 1981 (WA) 69, 73
privacy 39, 209, 210, 222
*Health Records and Information Privacy Act
2002* (NSW) 64
information privacy and records management
legislation 63–5

privacy breaches and browsing 226
privacy law 126
see also confidentiality; National Privacy
Principles (NPP)
Privacy Act 1988 (Cth) (the Privacy Act) 63–5,
209
Australian Law Reform Commission (2008)
review of 65
and information collection 215
unauthorised disclosure 224
private law 87–103
civil law 87–90
human services behaviours giving rise to
private law action 88
negligence 104–24
public authorities 92–5
risk of private law suits in the human
services 97–103
targets of private legal action 95–7
torts and civil actions 125–39
torts law 89, 90
private rights 35–6
private settlement 87–8
privilege (absolute) 132
professional associations 156–61
likelihood of professional sanctions
156–7
private practice scenario 251–2
professional codes of ethics *see* codes of ethics
prohibition writs 78
prohibitions 71–2
Psychologists Board of Qld v Robinson [2004]
QCA 405 82
psychology
psychologists as expert witnesses 143
qualifications 24
reports on psychologists 42
public authorities 92–5, 172
and breach 115–16
challenges to resource allocation 93
civil action against 88–9
High Court arguments regarding 92
liability of 110–11
Redlich J – duty of care and public authority
liability arguments 108
public enquiry 8–9
Public Health Act 1991 (NSW) 84
public interest 135–6
public law
administrative law 75–81
appeals and creative legal actions 85–6
decision-making considerations 72–3
duties 69–71
general application 49–67
grants and exercise of powers 72
immunity provisions 73
prohibitions 71–2

INDEX

public law (*cont.*)
  regulation of occupational/professional title or interventions 81–6
  of relevance to human services 68–86
  statutory breaches 73–5
Public Sector Employment and Management Act (NT) 66, 67
Public Sector Management Act 1994 (WA) 65–6, 214
Public Sector Management Act 1995 (SA) 65
Public Service Act 1996 (Qld) 66
Public Service Act 1999 (Cth) 28, 65, 66, 225, 226, 237
public service legislation 65–7
pure mental harm 119

Q v Australian Government Agency [2007] PrivCmrA 19 218
qualifications 23–4
quasi-contracts (service) 180
quasi-legal and legal review 178–80
Queensland Department of Child Safety 141

R v Carosella [1997] 1 S.C.R. 80 219
R v Lem (no 1) [2004] SASC 416 143, 196
R v Lowe (1997) 2 VR 465 135–6, 137
R v Tognini and Maguire [2000] WASCA 51
Racial and Religious Tolerance Act 2001 61
Racial Discrimination Act 1975 61
racism (institutional) 194
Radnedge v State of South Australia (1997) 192 LSJS 131 179
Rainsford v State of Victoria (no 2) [2004] FMCA 707 205
Re Beer and Secretary, Department of Family and Community Services [2004] AATA 598 226
Re J Ashley AIRC (Unreported, Ross VP, O'Callaghan, SDP and Cribb, Commr 7 July 2005) 261
reassessment (service provision) 180
recklessness 49
reconciliation (Aboriginal) 11
records 216–19, 220
  amendments to 220
  length of storage 221–2
  records storage problems 220
records and information management 208–33
  accurate and comprehensive records and client contact 172
  information privacy and records management legislation 63–5
Red Shield Housing Association v Calder [2006] SARTT 6 217
registration
  absence of 23–4
  case for social worker registration 10–11

  information collected by registration boards 40
  legal cases regarding registration 82
  negative licensing approach of NSW 83–4
  regulation and registration models 84
regulation
  a cautious approach to occupational regulation 84–5
  regulation and registration models 84
  regulation of occupational/professional title or interventions 81–6
Reidy v Trustees of the Christian Brothers and Ors (1994) 12 WAR 583 102
relationships 234–46
  observations 245–6
  between service providers 244–6
  between service trainees, workers, employers and policymakers 238–44
  between workers and clients 236–8
reporting
  of child abuse 70–1, 74–5
  coronial reports 152–4
  diagnosis, protection and reporting during assessment 178–80
  human services reporting, and defamation 131–2
  legal reporting requirements 71
  legislative requirements for 70
  mandatory reporting under the *Children's Protection Act 1993* (SA) 75
  reporting function of ombudsmen 145–6
  see also courts
responsibility
  of agencies and managers regarding dubious worker performance 202
  individual responsibility 28–37
  organisational responsibility 32–6
  service systems 36–7
Review of the Law of Negligence (Ipp Report) (Commonwealth Treasury 2002) 90
review process (service delivery) 202–5
  deficiencies in the review process 203–4
  measures to avoid litigation 207
rights
  Australian Human Rights Commission (AHRC) 144–5
  Charter of Human Rights and Responsibilities Act 2006 (Vic) 19
  Convention on the Protection and Promotion of the Rights and Dignity of Persons with Disabilities 18
  Convention on the Rights of the Child (CRC) 18
  duties concerning security, confidentiality and rights 69–70
  Human Rights Act 2004 (ACT) 19

International Covenant on Civil and Political Rights (ICCPR) 18
private rights 35–6
the right to withdraw 192
status determinations and conferral or loss of rights 176–8
see also confidentiality; privacy
risk 13–14
anxiety about 13, 14
and assessment 174
high-risk minority groups and service activity 168
and information collection 220
and intervention 186
law as mechanism to regulate and control activity 14
liability considerations – suicide 173–4
negative risk 13–14, 27
positive risk 14
within professional relationships 236
risk and need 13
risk control 13, 27
risk of private law suits in the human services 97–103
risks of criminal charges 56–9
and service delivery 33–4
Tarasoff v Regents of the University of California 526 P2d 553 (1974) 551 P2d 334 (1976) 123
Robinson v Australian Association of Social Workers Ltd (2000) 206 LSLS 209 158
Rogers v Whitaker (1992) 175 CLR 479 116, 122, 191–2
Ruddock v Taylor (2003) 58 NSWLR 269; [2005] HCA 48; 79 ALJR 1534; 221 ALR 32 128
Ruddock v Vadarlis [2001] FCA 1329 79
Rundle v Salvation Army NSWSC [2007] 443 101, 102

S v Secretary, Department of Immigration and Multicultural and Indigenous Affairs (2005) 216 ALR 252 224
S v Secretary, Department of Immigration and Multicultural and Indigenous Affairs (2005) 216 ALR 252; FCA 459 112, 118–19, 168
safety
occupational health and safety legislation 59–60, 82, 172–3
prisoner safety standards 118
sanctioned abuse 53
sanctions and disciplinary actions 156–61
employers and employees 158–61
industrial action 160–1
professional associations 156–8

range of disciplinary actions 158–9
unfair dismissal 159
SASI *see* Statewide Autistic Services Inc
SB v New South Wales (2004) 13 VR 527; VSC 514 107–8, 117–18, 120–1, 134, 141, 142, 183, 189, 204, 232, 259
and reassessment 180
scandals 258–60
screening 166–73
crisis, emergency, suicide and threat to others 169–73
service inclusion and exclusion 166–9
security 69–70
self disclosure 201
sensitive information 213
service delivery
clinical private practice 188–9
consent 190–4
diversity 194–7
dual roles, boundaries and conflicts 197–202
electronic forms 188
implementation and closure 185–207
monitoring and review 202–5
screening, assessment and planning 165–84
termination of service and follow up 205–7
service planning 180–3
care plans 203
liability considerations 183–4
mandated planning and client involvement 182–3
planning problems 181
planning review 183
shared or divergent expectations 181–2
service systems 36–7
criticisms of models of service delivery 33–4
relationships between service providers 244–6
service inclusion and exclusion 166–9
would-be service providers discrimination complaints 62–3
Sex Discrimination Act 1984 (Cth) 18, 62, 167
sexual abuse 109
Rundle v Salvation Army NSWSC [2007] 443 101
statistics of predatory behaviour 37–8
Sexual Contact with Children by Persons in Authority in the Department of Education and Training of Western Australia report 156
sexual exploitation 50
sexual impropriety 38–9, 40, 198
sexual misconduct 96
and 'close connection' 96–7
sexual offences 49–50
Shayan Badraie by his tutor Mohammad Saeed Badraie v Commonwealth [2005] NSWSC 112

INDEX

Sleiman v Commissioner for Corrective Services; Hamzy v Commissioner for Corrective Services [2009] NSWSC 304 128

Smith v Jones [1999] 1SCR 455 123, 171

Social Security Act 1991 (Cth) 226
  benefits eligibility 72, 177–8
  decision-making considerations 72–3
  marriage-like relationship test (social security) 59–60, 146

social security system
  and negligent advice or information 122
  social security decisions 77
  social security legislation 69, 177–8

social work
  Australian Association of Social Workers (AASW) 10, 24, 39–40, 157
  case for social worker registration 10–11
  criminal charges against social workers 50–1
  defensive social work and records 218–19
  and human rights law 18
  mechanisms investigating social worker misconduct 82–3
  National Association of Social Workers (NASW) 38–9
  qualifications 24
  sexual impropriety claims 38–9
  Specht's schema of social workers' interpersonal interactions 234–5
  unreliability of data relevant to social work 38
  see also human services

society
  ambivalence regarding function, rights and status of the vulnerable and marginalised 4–5
  vulnerable groups 3–4

sociopolitical relationships 235, 244

South Australian Police v Moore (Unreported, SA Magistrates Court 24 September 2007) 237

Specht's schema of social workers' interpersonal interactions 234–5

spent convictions 51

Sprod BNF v Public Relations Oriented Security Pty Ltd [2005] NSWSC 1074 96

Squire v Intellectual Disability Services Council Inc – Appeal [2006] SAIRComm 14 160, 201

standards 27, 208
  accreditation standards 70
  actions assessed against 117–18
  'beyond reasonable doubt' standard 56
  immigration detention standards 118–19
  'on the balance of probabilities' standard 87

professional standards and civil liability legislation 116–17

'the exercise of reasonable care to avoid foreseeable risks' standard 115

standing complaints 143–50

State of NSW v Wayne Eade [2006] NSWSC 84 96

State of Queensland v Mahommed [2007] QSC 018 195–6

Statewide Autistic Services Inc (SASI) 261

statutes of limitations 101–2
  British child migrant cases 101
  and child abuse claimants 102

statutory authority 30

statutory breaches 73–5, 92, 106, 132–3

statutory declarations 177

Staunton-Smith v Secretary Department of Social Security (1991) 32 FCR 164 73

stolen generation, the 89, 98, 112–15
  see also Cubillo case; *Trevorrow* case

storage (information) 220–2

strict liability 45, 53, 127–9

Stuart Hill and the Department of Juvenile Justice [2000] NSWIRComm 128 159–60, 201

Stuart v Kirkland-Veenstra [2009] HCA 15 171

subcontractors 25

suicide 169–70, 173–4

Sullivan v Moody [2001] HCA 59 (2001) 207 CLR 562 105, 108–9

surveillance 177–8, 216

T v Private Community Centre [2008] PrivCmrA 20 216

Tarasoff v Regents of the University of California 526 P2d 553 (1974); 551 P2d 334 (1976) 123, 171

Taylor v Trustees of the Christian Brothers and Ors; Reidy v Trustees of the Christian Brothers and Ors. VSC 9753/4 102

TC by his tutor Sabatino v New South Wales [2001] NSWCA 380 107

termination (of service) 205–7
  contested termination decisions 239

The Salvation Army v Mejia-Rodriguez-Appeal [2003] SAIRComm 65 142, 201, 239–40

Thomas Potter v WorkCover Corporation PR944320 [2004] AIRC 214; Appeal PR948009 [2004] 223–4

Thomson v Intellectual Disability Services Council [2006] SAIRComm 21 160

threats (of harm) 171–2

timing (of scandals) 260

torts law
  'actions on the case' 125–6

'close connection' between work and the
tort 96–7
community concerns regarding increased
costs 90
fluidity of 90
law of torts 126–33
negligence 104–24
overlapping nature 89
statutes of limitations 101–2
TP and KM v United Kingdom (2001) 34 EHRR
42 179
Trade Practices Act 1974 (Cth) 63, 189
transference and counter-transference 197,
198–9, 202
treatment complaints 40
trespass to the person 126–9
advantages of trespass claims over
negligence 126–7
battery 127
defences to 129
false imprisonment 127–9
Trevorrow v State of South Australia (no 5)
[2007] SASC 285 89, 102, 114–15, 118,
121, 128, 129, 134–5, 141, 191, 194, 204,
214
damages 100
and service assessment 169
Trinh v New South Wales State Parole Authority
[2006] NSWCS 1352 217–18

UK Court of Appeal 106
unfair dismissal 159
unified privacy principles (UPP) 65
United Kingdom General Social Care
Council 83
United Nations
Australia as signatory to UN treaties and
conventions 18
Convention on the Elimination of All Forms
of Discrimination against Women 18
Convention on the Protection and Promotion
of the Rights and Dignity of Persons with
Disabilities 18
Convention on the Rights of the Child
(CRC) 18
International Covenant on Civil and Political
Rights (ICCPR) 18
unprofessional conduct 52
UPP *see* unified privacy principles
Uzsoki v Macarthur [2007] QDC 110
122

V v Health Service Provider [2006] PrivCmrA
21 221
vicarious liability 31, 52, 53, 95
of employers for worker action 61
and misfeance 129–30

sexual misconduct and 'close
connection' 96–7
*Victorian Council for Civil Liberties and Vadarlis
v Minister for Immigration and Multicultural
Affairs* [2001] FCA 1297 79–80
Victorian Crimes Act 50
*VMT v The Corporation of the Synod of the
Diocese of Brisbane* [2007] QSC 219
58–9
vulnerable groups (in society)
abuse and neglect of 3–4
society's ambivalence regarding function,
rights and status 4–5

W and W (2001) 28 Fam LR 45 143
W v Egdell and others [1990] 1 ALL ER
835 123, 135
W v Essex County Council [2000] 2 ALL ER
237 109, 179
W v W (2005) 34 Fam LR 129 142
Wainwright and Anor v Home Office [2003]
UKHL 53 127, 189
Walker v Sydney West Area Health Service [2007]
NSWSC 526 94–5, 116–17, 170, 206,
257
Walsh v St Vincent de Paul Society Queensland
(No. 2) [2008] QADT 32 62
Welfare to Work reforms 146
whistleblowers 238–9, 261
Wicks v Railcorp [2007] NSWSC 1346 173
Williams v Centrelink [2004] PR942762
AIRC 231
*Williams v Minister, Aboriginal Land Rights Act
1983* (2000) Aust Torts Rep 81 578 113
witnesses (expert) 142–3
women's shelters 129–30, 201
Wood Commission 151
WorkCover 223–4
*Workers Rehabilitation and Compensation Act
1986* (SA) 223
workforce
careless worker practices and disclosure
224
generic human service workers 142
human service workers 25
inexperience of 30, 32
job titles designation 24–5
qualifications 23–4
relationships between service trainees,
workers, employers and
policymakers 238–44
subcontractors 25
tests determining employee status 96
worker vulnerabilities 202
workers in conflict 238
workforce and position diversity 85
Working with Children Act 2005 (Vic) 195

Working with Children (Criminal Record Checking) Act 2004 55
workplaces, effect of the work environment on worker behaviour 32–4
potentially dangerous workplaces 33

X (Minors) v Bedfordshire County Council [1995] 2 AC 633 106
X v State of South Australia (No3) (2007) 97 SASC 125 110–11

XD v Department of Justice (Occupational and Business Regulation) [2008] VCAT 118 55

youth support 36
formal reports of failures 4
youth service scenario 252–3

Z v United Kingdom (2001) 34 EHRR 97, [2001] 2 FCR 246 106

For EU product safety concerns, contact us at Calle de José Abascal, 56–1°,
28003 Madrid, Spain or eugpsr@cambridge.org.

www.ingramcontent.com/pod-product-compliance
Ingram Content Group UK Ltd.
Pitfield, Milton Keynes, MK11 3LW, UK
UKHW020202060825
461487UK00017B/1505